Neglected Classics of Philosophy

Neglected Classics of Philosophy

Volume 2

Edited by

ERIC SCHLIESSER

OXFORD
UNIVERSITY PRESS

OXFORD
UNIVERSITY PRESS

Oxford University Press is a department of the University of Oxford. It furthers
the University's objective of excellence in research, scholarship, and education
by publishing worldwide. Oxford is a registered trade mark of Oxford University
Press in the UK and certain other countries.

Published in the United States of America by Oxford University Press
198 Madison Avenue, New York, NY 10016, United States of America.

Library of Congress Cataloging-in-Publication Data
Names: Schliesser, Eric, 1971– author.
Title: Neglected classics of philosophy / Eric Schliesser.
Description: New York, NY, United States of America :
Oxford University Press, [2022] |
Includes bibliographical references and index.
Identifiers: LCCN 2022002578 (print) | LCCN 2022002579 (ebook) |
ISBN 9780190097196 (hb) | ISBN 9780190097202 (pb) |
ISBN 9780190097226 (epub)
Subjects: LCSH: Russell, Bertrand, 1872–1970.
History of western philosophy. | Philosophy—History.
Classification: LCC B72.R83 S35 2022 (print) | LCC B72.R83 (ebook) |
DDC 190—dc23/eng/20220218
LC record available at https://lccn.loc.gov/2022002578
LC ebook record available at https://lccn.loc.gov/2022002579

DOI: 10.1093/oso/9780190097196.001.0001

1 3 5 7 9 8 6 4 2

Paperback printed by Marquis, Canada
Hardback printed by Bridgeport National Bindery, Inc., United States of America

Dedicated to Anneke Luger-Veenstra, Rob Brouwer, and Jan Stronk

Contents

Acknowledgments   ix

Author Biographies   xi

Introduction   1
Eric Schliesser

1. The *Theogony* and the *Works and Days*: The Beginnings of
   Philosophical Questioning in Hesiod   18
   Barbara M. Sattler

2. *Zhuangzi*   40
   Amy Olberding

3. Vasubandhu's *Viṃśatikākārikā*   57
   Bryce Huebner

4. Hōnen's *Senchaku-Shū*   78
   Yumiko Inukai

5. Sor Juana's "Let us pretend I am happy"   97
   Lisa Shapiro

6. Anton Wilhelm Amo: *Treatise on the Art of Soberly and
   Accurately Philosophizing* (1738)   118
   Justin E. H. Smith

7. On Mary Shepherd's *Essay upon the Relation of
   Cause and Effect*   141
   Jessica Wilson

8. Ida B. Wells-Barnett's *The Red Record*   172
   Liam Kofi Bright

9. The de Lagunas' *Dogmatism and Evolution*:
   Overcoming Modern Philosophy and Making
   Post-Quinean Analytic Philosophy   192
   Joel Katzav

10. B. R. Ambedkar on "Castes in India: Their Mechanism,
    Genesis and Development"   215
    Meena Krishnamurthy

11. Civility, Silence, and Epistemic Labor in Audre Lorde's
    Sister Outsider   239
    Serene J. Khader

12. Ethics in Place and Time: Introducing Wub-e-ke-niew's
    We Have the Right to Exist: A Translation of Aboriginal
    Indigenous Thought   261
    Alexander Guerrero

Index   287

Acknowledgments

Peter Ohlin is a wonderful editor at Oxford University Press. During the past decade we have collaborated on many different kinds of projects, each intellectually ambitious in their own way. Unlike many other edited volumes, this series, which is Peter's brain-child, on "neglected classics" is pure joy. The authors of these chapters are eager to share their passion about works they want you, dear reader, to take seriously and be enchanted by. And I have the distinct privilege to read their chapters first. Thank you, Peter, for your support and trust.

I thank my home institution, "Challenges to Democratic Representation," housed in the Amsterdam Institute for Social Science Research and the Political Science Department of the University of Amsterdam. I am also very grateful to the Smith Institute for Political Economy and Philosophy at Chapman University for providing me a home away from home. I am grateful to John Ruig for his help in preparing the index, and Dorothy Bauhoff for her superb copy-editing.

I am very lucky to have a supportive family, my late father, Micha; my mom, Marleen; and my sister, Malka. My wife, Sarit, and our son, Avi, are always supportive of my research.

This book is dedicated to Anneke Luger-Veenstra, Jan Stronk, and Rob Brouwer, my learned high school teachers, who encouraged a love of the classics.

Eric Schliesser, November 20, 2020

Author Biographies

Liam Kofi Bright is Associate Professor in the Department of Philosophy, Logic, and Scientific Method at London School of Economics.

Alexander Guerrero is Professor of Philosophy at Rutgers University, New Brunswick.

Bryce Huebner is an Associate Professor in the Department of Philosophy at Georgetown University.

Yumiko Inukai is Associate Professor of Philosophy at the University of Massachusetts, Boston.

Joel Katzav is Senior Lecturer in Philosophy at the University of Queensland.

Serene J. Khader is Jay Newman Chair in the Philosophy of Culture at Brooklyn College and Professor of Philosophy at the CUNY Graduate Center.

Meena Krishnamurthy is an Assistant Professor of Philosophy at Queen's University in Canada.

Amy Olberding is Presidential Professor of Philosophy at University of Oklahoma.

Barbara M. Sattler taught at Yale, UIUC and St. Andrews and is now Professor for Ancient and Medieval Philosophy at the Ruhr-Universität Bochum. She is author of the book *The Concept of Motion in Ancient Greek Thought* (Cambridge University Press 2020).

Eric Schliesser is Professor of Political Science, University of Amsterdam and visiting scholar in the Smith Institute for Political Economy and Philosophy, Chapman University.

Lisa Shapiro is Professor of Philosophy at Simon Fraser University.

Justin E. H. Smith is Professor of Philosophy in the Department of History and Philosophy of Science at the University of Paris.

Jessica Wilson is Professor of Philosophy at University of Toronto.

Introduction

Eric Schliesser

In this introduction I use Bertrand Russell's (1945) *The History of Western Philosophy* (hereafter: *History*) to introduce the metaphilosophical themes that recur throughout the chapters of this book. In particular, I focus on the way the distinction or opposition between *rustic* thought, which is supposed to characterize *barbarous* societies, and the *urbane* thought that is purported to characterize *civilized* society can help explain some entrenched patterns of exclusion visible in contemporary philosophy. I embed these remarks in a larger, speculative historiography of the very idea of "Western philosophy." Along the way, I provide an overview of the chapters of this volume.

In the twelfth century Ibn Tufayl, writing in what we would call Spain, presented himself as a "Western" philosopher in order to remind his readers that he was at the periphery in the vast world of learning within the interconnected Islamic empires. He did so not without pride, but also to call attention to the fact that he lacked access to manuscripts of some of the books he knew existed, penned by ancient authors like Plato and Aristotle and more recent luminaries writing in the "East," like Al-Farabi, Ibn Sinna (Avicenna), and Al-Ghazali.[1]

Ibn Tufayl's book, *Ḥayy ibn Yaqẓān*, is a philosophical allegory that in addition to Islamic themes draws on Platonic, Sufi, and revealed sources. It offers the theoretical and spiritual journey of a man (Hayy ibn Yaqzan, or "Alive, Son of Awake") who grows up and develops intellectually outside civilization. It connects metaphysical speculation with subtle hints about the political context of philosophizing.

---

[1] *Ibn Tufayl's Hayy Ibn Yaqzan: A Philosophical Tale*, translated by Lenn Goodman (Chicago: The University of Chicago Press, [1972] 2009). See especially p. 99.

Eric Schliesser, *Introduction* In: *Neglected Classics of Philosophy*. Edited by: Eric Schliesser, Oxford University Press. © Oxford University Press 2022. DOI: 10.1093/oso/9780190097196.003.0001

A 1671 Latin translation gave it the subtitle *Philosophus autodidactus*, or "The Self-Taught Philosopher"; this made it available to learned Europeans, who in turn translated it into various vernaculars. For example, Simon Ockley, who plays a nontrivial role in Edward Said's account of the origins of orientalism,[2] translated it into English in 1708 as *The Improvement of Human Reason Exhibited in the Life of Hai Ebn Yokdhan By Ibn Tufail*.[3] In 1672 it was translated into Dutch in the circle of Spinoza's friends. It then remained familiar to intellectuals for another century. For example, at the height of the German Enlightenment, Lessing enthused about the book, sending it to Mendelsohn, urging him to read it.[4]

Did Ibn Tufayl originate the very idea of Western philosophy? I would not bet on it. Perhaps the phrase was already used in late antiquity, contrasting philosophical or clerical work being done in the Western Roman Empire with that being done in the Eastern Roman Empire. Of course, somebody may object that what Ibn Tufayl meant by "Western philosophy" is not quite how more contemporary thinkers use it. After all, in the present context, Ibn Tufayl's work would, despite its many debts to Plato and Aristotle, be often treated as "non-Western" in virtue of the fact that is the product, in part, of the Islamic world.

The first use of "Western philosophy" that I am familiar with to mark an implied contrast between the speculative thought of Europe with that of a distinct, contrasting civilization occurs in volume 4 of the *Letters Writ by a Turkish Spy* (originally in French: *L'Espion Turc*).[5] This once hugely popular, eight-volume work was published around the time when translations of Ibn Tufayl's *Ḥayy ibn Yaqẓān* first circulated

---

[2] See, for example, Edward W. Said, *Orientalism* (London: Routledge, [1978] 2003), 75–76.

[3] See here: https://www.gutenberg.org/files/16831/16831-h/16831-h.htm.

[4] Samar Attar, *The Vital Roots of European Enlightenment: Ibn Tufayl's Influence on Modern Western Thought* (Lanham MD, Lexington Books, 2007).. For a more cautious treatment, see Jan Assmann, Religio Duplex. Die Ringparabel und die Idee der 'doppelten Religion,' in Ortrud Gutjahr (Hrsg.), *Nathan der Weise von Gotthold Ephraim Lessing* (Würzburg: Koningshausen and Neumann:, 2010), 73–85.

[5] *Letters Writ by a Turkish spy, who lived five and forty years undiscovered at Paris: giving an impartial account to the Divan at Constantinople, of the most remarkable transactions of Europe: and discovering several intrigues and secrets of the Christian courts (especially of that of France). Continued from the year 1637, to the year 1682*, 26th ed., volume 4 (London: Wilde, 1770), 286–287.

in European circles. The book is surrounded by mystery and mystifica-
tion, and the author of volume 4 is unknown. The conceit of the book is
a series of missives from Paris sent to Constantinople, commenting on
European mores, politics, and philosophy (among many other topics).
The work is clearly a model for Montesquieu's (1721) *Lettres Persanes*,
one of the foundational texts of the Enlightenment.[6]

The context of that first use of "Western philosophy" in the more familiar sense is a bit complicated to convey succinctly, in part because it
occurs in the midst of a ridiculing digression by the "spy" on the misguided faith in the divine origin of holy texts by various peoples. That was
an explosive topic, then much debated in the wake of Spinoza's suggestion that the Hebrew Bible as we have it was pretty much the work of Ezra
at the refounding of Israel as a political entity. He (the "spy") goes on to
offer a heterodox argument to the effect that whatever else is true, something, be it God or a vacuum, must exist eternally. And at that very point
the "spy" introduces a scholastic distinction, in part for comic effect, with
terminology used by "Western philosophers." Part of the comedy is that
the scholastic terminology of the Western philosophers must have felt already dated to the learned audiences of the *Letters Writ by a Turkish Spy*
because a new, modernizing anti-scholastic philosophy (familiar to us
through names like Bacon, Descartes, Hobbes) was sweeping away the
Scholastic kind in that very "West."[7]

With such suspect origins, it is no surprise that "Western philosophy" rarely gets used in subsequent centuries.[8] In fact, as a scholarly
term it starts to receive modest traction only as late as the start of the
twentieth century, alongside growing interest in the very idea of a
"Western civilization."[9] In the context of an imperial and globalizing

[6] Virginia H. Aksan, Is There a Turk in the Turkish Spy? *Eighteenth-Century Fiction* 6(3) (1994): 201.

[7] However, for the enduring vitality of Scholastic thought throughout the early modern period, see Daniel Novotny, *Ens rationis from Suárez to Caramuel: A Study in Scholasticism of the Baroque Era* (New York: Fordham University Press, 2013). See also Justin Smith's Chapter 6 in this volume and my brief summary of it below.

[8] For some rough, approximate data supporting the claims in this and subsequent paragraphs, see the NGRAMS discussed here: https://digressionsnimpressions.typepad.com/digressionsnimpressions/2020/01/whats-western-in-russells-history-of-western-philosophy-ii.html.

[9] I do not mean to deny the existence of dismissive and outright racist attitudes toward non-Europeans and their philosophy by European philosophers during

world economy, the phrase "Western philosophy" is *then* used regularly in scholarly discussions of what we would now call "comparative philosophy," comparing the philosophies of different "great" civilizations, primarily those found in Europe, India, and China.

The phrase "Western philosophy" gains wider currency in the wake of Albert Schweitzer's (1923) *Civilization and Ethics*. Schweitzer, a great humanitarian, was an admirer of classical Indian and Chinese philosophy especially, and so for him "Western philosophy" was not the standard by which he judged others. But he treats "Western" philosophy as the contrast to Indian and Chinese philosophy.

Bertrand Russell admired Schweitzer and his writings,[10] but he wrote a critical review of *Civilization and Ethics* which included some reservations about Schweitzer's tendency to disparage Western philosophy at the expense of the philosophies found at the other "great" civilizations.[11] When Russell published his *History* he focused, as the title suggests, nearly exclusively on "Western philosophy."

Russell was one of the outstanding philosophers of the first half of the twentieth century who made major contributions to logic, epistemology, philosophy of mathematics, and philosophy of language. Together with Frege, he is naturally thought of as one of the founders of analytic philosophy. When he wrote his *History*, Russell had already become a public intellectual, well known for his pacifism and atheism, among other causes. In fact, the book is an enduring bestseller. As it turns out Russell's *History* did not just popularize the phrase "Western philosophy"; it has shaped how philosophers think of their own past to this day.

The grand theme of Russell's *History* is the very survival of Western civilization—then in doubt amidst world war (pp. 400, 556, 640, 790).

---

this period. See Louis Sala-Molins, *Dark Side of the Light: Slavery and the French Enlightenment* (Minneapolis: University of Minnesota Press, 2006); Pauline Kleingeld, Kant's Second Thoughts on Race, *The Philosophical Quarterly* 57(229) (2007): 573–592; Silvia Sebastiani, *The Scottish Enlightenment: Race, Gender, and the Limits of Progress* (Dordrecht: Springer, 2013).

[10] Herbert Spiegelberg, The Correspondence between Bertrand Russell and Albert Schweitzer, *International Studies in Philosophy* 12(1) (1980): 1–45.

[11] Bertrand Russell, "Does Ethics Influence Life?" (1924), in John. G. Slater (ed.), *Volumes of the Collected Papers of Bertrand Russell, Volume 9: Essays on Language, Mind and Matter, 1919–26* (London: Unwin Hyman, 1988), 351.

For Russell it would not be the first time that civilization could collapse. This is connected to the history of philosophy because Russell argues that ages and nations are shaped by philosophy and, in turn, shape it (pp. xiii–xiv). And so Russell gives special attention not just to academic philosophy, but to thinkers whose ideas had a big impact on the intellectual development of "the West."

Russell was, in turn, reflecting a wider discussion in English intellectual circles in which proposals for Anglo-Atlantic or Western federation (sometimes including their colonies) were a matter of great public interest. It was thought only such a federation could help save Western civilization against the twin evils of fascism and communism.[12]

For Russell, philosophy is an intrinsic part of civilization. When it disappears, philosophy also vanishes. This is for Russell an urgent question, and this, alongside his opinionated and often insightful treatment of other thinkers, gives his book much of its poignancy. Because Russell and his early readers assumed there were multiple civilizations, the focus on Western philosophy in *History* can be a matter of intellectual humility; it does not entail superiority toward the philosophies of other (great) civilizations.

For example, Russell admits, in passing, his "undue concentration on Western Europe," noting for example how "the brilliant civilization of Islam flourished" from India to Spain during Europe's "dark ages" (*History*, 399). And he predicts that "if we are to feel at home in the world after the present [world] war, we shall have to admit Asia to equality in our thoughts, not only politically, but culturally" (*History*, p. 400).

However, embedded in this generous and capacious vision, Russell adopts a contrast between civilization and barbarism which,[13] together with his definition of philosophy, involves a number of intellectual exclusions, some of which were new with Russell and some

---

[12] See, for example, Or Rosenboim, *The Emergence of Globalism: Visions of World Order in Britain and the United States, 1939–1950* (Princeton, NJ: Princeton University Press, 2017).

[13] Russell uses "barbarian" and its cognates and "civilization" and its cognates about a hundred times each in the *History* (although sometimes in quoted passages from others). For the long history of this contrast, see John Greville Agard Pocock, *Barbarism and Religion*, Volume 1: *The Enlightenments of Edward Gibbon, 1737–1764* (Cambridge: Cambridge University Press, 1999).

very entrenched in philosophy since Plato to this day. And I suspect that one unfortunate, and possibly unintended, effect of the manner in which the contrast is deployed shifts the use of "Western philosophy" from a comparative perspective where Western philosophy is one of several great intellectual traditions to a use of "Western philosophy" to be opposed to a more homogeneous category, non-Western philosophy, which in practice risks becoming no philosophy at all.[14]

For Russell treats philosophy as standing halfway between science and theology. While echoing some Enlightenment philosophers, Russell treats religion as resting on the illicit authority of faith and tradition; science, by contrast, is the application of reason and rational methods of inquiry to generate secure knowledge. Philosophy is intrinsically speculative, but is based on autonomous reason (*History*, pp. xiii–xiv, 835–836). Because of this attitude, the ninth-century monk John Scotus of Erigena, who maintained the "authority of a philosophy independent of revelation" (p. 403), is one of the unlikely and memorable heroes of the *History*. By contrast, works primarily influenced by theology and revelation, or that present themselves as so influenced, are de facto treated as unphilosophical. Here Russell echoes the contrast between Athens and Jerusalem in which Jerusalem is disparaged.

While the previous paragraphs are a bit speculative, they help to account not just for the tendency to treat philosophy as Western, and to treat non-Western writings as religious and non-rational, but also for some of the curious patterns of exclusion in his work.[15] So, for example, in Russell's *History*, Hesiod is mentioned a few times when Russell is conveying the views of other thinkers on Hesiod (pp. 40–41), including the views of Xenophanes, Heraclitus, Socrates (as reported by Plato in the *Apology*), and Plato (in the *Republic* as summarized by Russell). With the exception, perhaps, of Socrates's desire to converse with Hesiod in the afterlife (p. 89, quoting *Apology* 41a), none of these passages suggests there is any philosophical merit in Hesiod, and he is treated as belonging to Greek religion rather than philosophy.

[14] See the controversy surrounding, and reported in, Bryan W. Van Norden, *Taking Back Philosophy: A Multicultural Manifesto* (New York: Columbia University Press, 2017).
[15] I owe the idea to Bryce Huebner. It's possible that Russell reflects the tendency rather than causes it.

By contrast, in the first chapter of the present volume, Barbara
Sattler makes the case that Hesiod's "poems can be seen as the starting
point for central philosophical discussion, which has made him an important point of reference for philosophers in the past and that as such
he should also be taken into account by philosophers today." And while
she does not insist on the claim that Hesiod should be taken to be a
philosopher, she argues for the claim that he is a systematic thinker.

Another consequence of Russell's distinction is that the Hebrew
Bible is treated as lacking in philosophical content and quality. This
helps explain why Russell spends quite a bit of time on The Fourth
Book of Maccabees, which self-consciously shows that Judaism is
in accord with Stoic philosophy. Yet, Philo of Alexandria, in whose
writings one can find, say, a criticism of slavery and an early argument
for gender equality, is only treated "as the best illustration of Greek influence on the Jews in the sphere of thought" (p. 322). The influence of
Judaism on Christianity is treated as "simple" (p. 326).

Now, another view of the possibility of Jewish philosophy, and the
significance of at least one rustic perspective, could emerge if we take
Machiavelli's, Thomas More's, and Spinoza's conception of Moses as an
exemplary rustic statesman seriously. In the Hebrew Bible, a key moment in Moses's education as a legislator occurs when, while dwelling
in the desert, he accepts the advice of his (pagan) father-in-law, Jethro,
who suggests to create a hierarchical judiciary, which will be guided
by "statues and theory" [אֶת-הַחֻקִּים וְאֶת-הַתּוֹרֹת]. Moses is advised to
create norms or mores and articulate their works. That is to say, Jethro
encourages Moses not just to embrace the judicial division of labor,
but also to become a genuine lawgiver and an encompassing political theorist. Jethro is a nomadic shepherd. And it is a familiar trope
of the Torah—derived from the root ירה, which means "to guide" or
"to teach"—to treat rustic wisdom favorably, in contrast to the corrupt
cosmopolitan and urbane civilizations of the great empires of the day
(Egypt, Babylon, etc.).[16]

By contrast, in Plato's *Phaedrus* (e.g., 230D), Socrates is critical
of rustic wisdom, which he thinks cannot ground the path toward

---

[16] For a different but more developed argument along these lines, see Yoram Hazony,
The Philosophy of Hebrew Scripture (Cambridge: Cambridge University Press, 2012).

self-knowledge. In particular, as the Stoics developed the point, rusticity stands for lawlessness and lack of self-control, that is, if we take the platonic inspired analogy between city and soul seriously, a tyrannical soul.[17] Throughout the *History*, Russell echoes the Socratic polemic against rusticity, which is homogenized as non-philosophical. One thing I am suggesting here is that undifferentiated, rusticity is itself a very broad category involving many different kinds of intellectual productions of different kinds of societies and examples.

A further problem is that the rustic perspective on this polemic tends to be underexplored. In Alexander Guerrero's Chapter 12 in this volume, "Ethics in Place and Time: Introducing Wub-e-ke-niew's *We Have the Right to Exist: A Translation of Aboriginal Indigenous Thought*," the question of who counts as "civilized," or who should become civilized, is never lurking far from the argument. The target of Wub-e-ke-niew is "an abstract entity, Western Civilization." And, as Guerrero shows, the picture that is presented is far from flattering.

One may suspect that the reason the rustic perspective is less familiar is that it tends not to be written down. However, traditional Islam is also treated as rustic by Russell in the *History*. Whatever philosophical sophistication it contains is, according to Russell, derived from Persian and Hellenic sources. Even so, according to Russell's definitions, Ibn Tufayl's allegory ought to be classified as a work of philosophy. Oddly, when Russell mentions how Ibn Tufayl's famous student, Ibn Rushd (also known as Averroes), was introduced to the "Caliph" Abu Yaqub Yusuf "as a man capable of making an analysis of the works of Aristotle," Russell does not mention Ibn Tufayl, the very man who introduces Ibn Rushd! This is no surprise because Russell treats the Islamic philosophers in brief, and as uninteresting and derivative.

In principle, Russell could have been more favorably disposed to intellectual history of India and China,[18] which are not treated as rustic. Russell acknowledges that these traditions have a long

---

[17] René Brouwer, *The Stoic Sage: The Early Stoics on Wisdom, Sagehood and Socrates* (Cambridge: Cambridge University Press, 2014), especially, 150–151.

[18] Since a lot of Chinese philosophy is Buddhist, this distinction may well confuse. I thank Bryce Huebner for alerting me to this.

history of sophisticated metaphysical, epistemological, and ethical theorizing. In his *History*, Russell primarily associates engagement with Buddhist philosophy with the thought of Schopenhauer, who was genuinely interested in Buddhism (p. 754). Unfortunately, Schopenhauer is treated as one of the key dangerous "romantic" thinkers to devalue knowledge. Even so, that Russell could appreciate Buddhism (which he associates with urbane philosophy (p. 772)) is clear from the following curiosity: when he turns to Nietzsche, Russell uses a fictional dialogue between Buddha and Nietzsche to try to refute Nietzsche (*History*, p. 771ff.)! Russell admits it will not fully persuade everybody.

By contrast, the present volume includes two chapters on two very different Buddhist thinkers. In Chapter 3, Bryce Huebner discusses Vasubandhu's *The Treatise in Twenty Verses* (*Viṃśatikākārika*). He seems to have been a Buddhist monk from Gandhāra (the northernmost part of the Indian subcontinent), who wrote during the fourth and fifth centuries CE. In discussing Vasubandhu's fascinating epistemology and metaphysics, Huebner argues that these, in the encounter with our own commitments, "can help us to change how we experience the world, by disclosing possibilities that have been obscured by the historical situation where we find ourselves." Yumiko Inukai, in Chapter 4, discusses Hōnen's *Senchaku Hongan Nembutsu Shū*. Hōnen is a Japanese Buddhist monk who founded the Pure Land ("Jōdo" in Japanese) School as an independent sect of Buddhism in Japan in the twelfth century CE. *Senchaku Hongan Nembutsu Shū* defends and explains the uses of the recitation of the name of Amida Buddha, "Namu Amida Butsu." In Inukai's presentation, this is a book about the transformative journey of the self.

Russell name-checks Confucius a few times in the *History*, but there is no mention of Mencius, Master Mo, Master Zhuang (369–298 BCE), or the (purported) authors of any of the other Chinese philosophical classis. This is no surprise, given his focus on "Western philosophy." In Chapter 2, Amy Olberding takes on the challenge of "commending the *Zhuangzi* to others"; it is a challenge because it is by no means obvious "how to accurately represent a text that not only declines to stay put, but that effectively mocks you for trying to hold it still." It would be misleading to suggest that the main interest in *Zhuangzi* is its therapeutic pretensions of curing us from certain philosophical maladies (of the sort now often associated with Russell's colleague, Wittgenstein); but that's because, as Olberding argues, part of the point is to dwell on living, not philosophy.

Given Russell's embrace of progressive commitments (including women's suffrage, contraconception, and more liberal divorce laws), the most surprising, perhaps,[19] pattern of exclusion in Russell's *History* is the near-complete absence of women philosophers in the philosophical West, while a number of queens, royal princesses, mothers, and wives of philosophers are mentioned! Even when women of considerable philosophical ability are noted—e.g., Princess Elizabeth of the Palatine, who corresponded astutely with Descartes—Russell rarely mentions their philosophical ability or views. The exception to the rule, Hypatia, is primarily mentioned in order to illustrate the dangers of religious bigotry.[20]

This pattern of exclusion is also illustrated by the major works penned by women that Russell praises. These are Jane Harrison's *Prolegomena to the Study of Greek Religion*, Mary Shelley's *Frankenstein*, and the novels of Jane Austen. The latter two are discussed because they fit his criticism of romanticism. Shelly's mother, Mary Wollstonecraft, who helped shape the feminist thought of subsequent ages, goes unmentioned altogether.

In his *History*, Russell offers an unwavering polemic against John Stuart Mill without ever once mentioning Harriet Taylor or their feminism. Feminism is mentioned only in the context of the cult of Bacchus and its impact on Plato's views. Russell's stance in all of this is really shocking because he was familiar with excellent female philosophers, including his then famous contemporary, Susan Stebbing, and he had

[19] It is ought not be surprising; see Eileen O'Neill, Disappearing Ink: Early Modern Women Philosophers and Their Fate in History, *Philosophy in a Feminist Voice: Critiques and Reconstructions* Princeton: Princeton University Press (1998): 17–62. This work makes clear that the early development of mass democracy coincides with a gendering of philosophy, especially academic philosophy worth having, as male.

[20] This use of Hypatia goes back to John Toland's *Hypatia: Or, The History of a Most Beautiful, Most Vertuous, Most Learned, and Every Way Accomplish'd Lady; who was Torn to Pieces by the Clergy of Alexandria, to Gratify the Pride, Emulation, and Cruelty of Their Archbishop, Commonly But Undeservedly Styled St. Cyril* (London: M. Cooper, W. Reeve, and C. Sympson, 1753) (first published in 1720).

reviewed May Sinclair, a philosopher of the previous generation, with whom he had corresponded.[21]

In the present volume, several chapters show how much is lost by Russell's stance. In Chapter 7, Jessica Wilson treats Mary Shepherd (1777–1847) not just as an astute critic of Hume's account of causation, but as herself a formidable and original metaphysician whose arguments are very interesting and whose positions anticipate views taken to be more recent inventions. While the neglect of Mary Shepherd raises important historiographic issues, to which I return below, that she should be treated as a philosopher does not require any interrogation of contemporary ideas or re-examination of contemporary categories about the nature of philosophy.

Liam Kofi Bright, in Chapter 8, also takes advantage of the idea that argument is constitutive of philosophy in order to show that a famous work of journalism, Ida B. Wells-Barnett's *The Red Record* (1895), is philosophical. In particular, Bright shows that in her critical survey of lynching, Wells-Barnett pioneers a form of argument that we now call "severe testing." Bright explains how this form of argument is especially suitable to a form of activism by those whose standing may be questioned.

By contrast, Lisa Shapiro's exploration of Sor Juana Inés de la Cruz's poem "Let us pretend I am happy" (circa 1680–1690), in Chapter 5, self-consciously explores the nature of such categorization. On the surface, this is a poem about, in part, the futility of arguments to refute skepticism about the possibility of knowledge. But there is more to thought than argument. And Shapiro suggests that "in the poem Sor Juana presents a conception of thought as essentially affective." And this opens the door to a kind of therapy that tempers our epistemic desires and so opens the possibility to "move beyond skepticism."

Audre Lorde was a poet, activist, and essayist. While she never worked in academic philosophy, her work has become a lodestone for recent feminist scholarship. In Chapter 11, Serene Khader focuses on *Sister Outsider* (1984), a collection of essays and speeches that is already "a classic source on what is now called 'epistemic oppression.'" In

---

[21] Emily Thomas, The Idealism and Pantheism of May Sinclair, *Journal of the American Philosophical Association* 5(2) (2019): 137–157.

particular, Khader shows that Lorde provides a useful guide to a form of epistemology often ignored by professional philosophers: how "oppression impedes the attainment of knowledge about social reality."

One chapter that confronts the risk of intellectual effacement in nuanced yet polemical fashion is Joel Katzav's Chapter 9, "The de Lagunas' *Dogmatism and Evolution*, Overcoming Modern Philosophy and Making Post-Quinean Analytic Philosophy." *Dogmatism and Evolution* (1910) was written by Theodore de Laguna and Grace de Laguna. And Katzav takes full theatrical and argumentative advantage of the fact—highly significant from the perspective of such internal dialectics—that Grace de Laguna was part of the same symposium where Quine first presented "Two Dogmas of Empiricism." Katzav offers the post facto judgment that the de Lagunas represent an epistemically and metaphysically more adventurous form of holism than the one Quine settled on.

I do not mean to suggest that this volume was conceived primarily as a corrective or in polemical opposition to Russell, or even to recent analytic philosophy. Russell's *History* is, despite its limitations, a gripping read that seduces people toward an intellectual voyage. In addition, we know that Russell was admired, not without qualification, by B. R. Ambedkar, just after he first wrote "Castes in India: Their Mechanism, Genesis and Development" (1916).[22] In Chapter 10, Meena Krishnamurthy shows how Ambedkar argues that "the oppression of women—through the practices of sati, widowhood, and girl marriage—played an essential role in the establishment and maintenance of the caste system by ensuring the rigid boundaries of caste." Krishnamurthy uses Ambedkar's essay to show how analysis of concrete reality in political philosophy can lead "to new ideas about how to resolve social and economic inequality."

---

[22] Bhimrao R. Ambedkar, Mr. Russell and the Reconstruction of Society, first published in 1918, republished in *Writings and Speeches*, vol. 1 (Bombay: Government of Maharashtra, 1989), 483–492. I thank Shruti Rajagopalan for helping me locate a copy. For how this review fits in the intellectual development of Ambedkar, see Scott R. Stroud, Pragmatism, Persuasion, and Force in Bhimrao Ambedkar's Reconstruction of Buddhism, *The Journal of Religion* 97(2) (2017): 214–243. See also Scott R. Stroud and Landon C. Elkind, Exploring the Influence of Russell on Ambedkar, *Forward Press* (August 1, 2017), https://www.forwardpress.in/2017/08/exploring-the-influence-of-russell-on-ambedkar/.

In addition, the intent of this volume is not to offer a programmatic statement of a new unified way of doing an inclusive history of philosophy. Even if the editor's heavy invisible hand were to try to nudge his authors in that direction, the underlying material would be recalcitrant. This resistance to our classificatory desiderata, and intellectual fashion, is, perhaps, best illustrated and thematized by Justin Smith's Chapter 6 on Anton Wilhelm Amo's *Treatise on the Art of Soberly and Accurately Philosophizing* (1738). Amo was born and died in Ghana, but "from 1707 to 1747, he lived in Germany, and from 1729 made a series of contributions to German jurisprudence and philosophy at the Universities of Halle, then Wittenberg, then Jena." Smith does not deny that "Amo's work is interesting and revelatory, both because it tells us quite a bit about the intellectual world he inhabited in early eighteenth-century Germany, and because it is a testament to the life and existence of a remarkable individual." But Smith also explains why one might feel unease with the idea that this is a work of "African philosophy." If Amo's *Treatise* has to be categorized at all, Smith prefers to call it an "academic Latinate German philosophy in the modern Lutheran university tradition, closely reflecting the curricula in place at the universities of Halle, Wittenberg, and Jena, and with a curious admixture of French Catholic late Scholasticism."

Rather, the main conceit behind this volume and its predecessor, *Ten Neglected Classics of Philosophy* (hereafter: TNCP), is to ask leading professional philosophers to share their passionate commitment to works in the history of philosophy they think their peers unfairly ignore.[23] Behind the conceit lies the idea that this will not just tell us something about the commitments and aspirations of these thinkers, but also provide us with an oblique glimpse into the state of philosophy today and, perhaps, open spaces for reflection on its renovation where needed.

One other reason why the aims of the volume are less revisionary than they might seem at first is that unlike, say, in social theory or English literature, the dominant strain of contemporary anglophone philosophy, analytic philosophy, does not treat a canon as constitutive

---

[23] Strictly speaking, the work need not be thought "historical." But I do not permit them to write about active philosophers.

of the field. Perhaps because analytic philosophy's self-identity is constantly reinvented over time, it has no felt requirement for a fixed canon of texts to give it identity. So, for example, Feigl and Sellars's (1949) *Readings in Philosophical Analysis* was welcomed as a "book" which "contains a good number of the classics of analysis and should therefore provide useful source material for courses in Contemporary Philosophy, Problems, and Methods." Most of the authors of these classics are still familiar names: "Feigl (4 essays), Kneale, Quine (2), Tarski, Carnap (3), Frege, Russell, [C. I.] Lewis (3), Schlick (4), Aldrich (2), Adjukiewicz, [Ernest] Nagel, Waismann, Hempel (4), Reichenbach (2)."[24] But it is to be doubted that most of the articles themselves, or even what they argue for, play much of an explicit role in contemporary undergraduate or graduate education (outside those that cater to specialists in the history of analytic philosophy). I also bet a few names are completely unfamiliar even to seasoned scholars. One can play a similar game with Rorty's (1967) more recent (and larger) *Linguistic Turn*.[25] To be a classic *within* analytic philosophy is to risk oblivion quickly from the perspective of eternity.

The claims in the previous paragraph are compatible with the further thought that contemporary philosophy, despite re-enacting a gesture familiar from Descartes—to start totally anew without any reference to what has gone before—is shaped by commitments derived from preexisting canons and intellectual traditions that have generated relatively enduring classics (Plato, Aristotle, Descartes, Hume, Kant, etc.). In the introduction to TNCP, I aimed to capture how there are many ways to be a classic within philosophy, and how many classics are capable of serving multiple functions.

---

[24] Russell L. Ackoff, Book Review: Readings in Philosophical Analysis, Herbert Feigl, Wilfrid Sellars, *Philosophy of Science* 16(3) (1949): 266. The author of the review just quoted, Russell L. Ackoff, became one of the founders of operations research and systems thinking in management science. Even the limited biography of Wikipedia suggests wonderful avenues of research for sociologists of analytic philosophy. For some scholarly directions, see Alan Richardson, What Good Is a (Indeed, This) History of Pragmatism? *Transactions of the Charles S. Peirce Society: A Quarterly Journal in American Philosophy* 49(3) (2013): 405–412.

[25] As an undergraduate three decades ago, I encountered both collections. I doubt they are used today.

Drawing on, and appropriating, J. M. Coetzee's "What Is a Classic"[26] to my own ends, I argued in the introduction to TNCP that classics sustain and survive ongoing scrutiny in the long run from a variety of perspectives, which may include their creative rewriting. Such ongoing scrutiny comes close to being a necessary condition on being a philosophical classic; one may suspect it is a kind of performative requirement for a classic.

With Coetzee, I identify five features that enable a work to become a classic: (1) the work needs to be studied and discussed in small circles, relatively untouched by the general public's fashion; (2) one can become an advanced student in a discipline based on some kind of competent engagement with such works; (3) there needs to be ongoing learned commentary or criticism; and (4) the existence of a form of advanced emulation through creative imitation or reworking. In addition, (5) a work counts as a classic only if it can eventually catch the interest of a wider audience beyond the most advanced professionals.

In editing the volume in your hands, my dear adventurous reader, I see no reason to revise my earlier appropriation of Coetzee's analysis. I hope the twelve chapters collected here give you pleasure and food for thought. All of these chapters contribute to ongoing discussions in more general meta-philosophy, as well as ongoing discussions about particular philosophers and more specialist topics. I hope they invite you to explore and study some excellent philosophy and, perhaps, reconsider what you thought you already knew about its nature.

Bibliography

Ackoff, Russell L. (1949). Book Review: Readings in Philosophical Analysis, Herbert Feigl, Wilfrid Sellars. *Philosophy of Science* 16(3): 266–267.

Aksan, Virginia H. (1994). Is there a Turk in the Turkish Spy? *Eighteenth-Century Fiction* 6(3): 201–214.

Ambedkar, Bhimrao R. (1918). Mr. Russell and the Reconstruction of Society. Republished in *Writings and Speeches*, vol. 1. Bombay: Government of Maharashtra, 1989, 483–492.

---

[26] John Maxwell Coetzee, What Is a Classic? *Current Writing: Text and Reception in Southern Africa* 5(2) (1993): 7–24.

Anonymous (1710). *Letters Writ by a Turkish spy, who lived five and forty years undiscovered at Paris: giving an impartial account to the Divan at Constantinople, of the most remarkable transactions of Europe: and discovering several intrigues and secrets of the Christian courts (especially of that of France). Continued from the year 1637, to the year 1682*, 26th ed., vol. 4. London: Wilde.

Assmann, Jan (2010). Religio Duplex: Die Ringparabel und die Idee der 'doppelten Religion.' In Ortrud Gutjahr (Hrsg.), *Nathan der Weise von Gotthold Ephraim Lessing* Würzburg: Koningshausen and Neumann, 73–85.

Attar, Samar (2007). *The Vital Roots of European Enlightenment: Ibn Tufayl's Influence on Modern Western Thought*. Lanham, MD: Lexington Books.

Brouwer, René (2014). *The Stoic Sage: The Early Stoics on Wisdom, Sagehood and Socrates*. Cambridge: Cambridge University Press.

Coetzee, John Maxwell (1993). What Is a Classic? *Current Writing: Text and Reception in Southern Africa* 5(2): 7–24.

Feigl, Herbert, and Wilfrid Sellars (1949). *Readings in Philosophical Analysis*. New York: Appleton-Century-Crofts.

Hazony, Yoram (2012). *The Philosophy of Hebrew Scripture*. Cambridge: Cambridge University Press.

Kleingeld, Pauline (2007). Kant's Second Thoughts on Race. *The Philosophical Quarterly* 57(229): 573–592.

Norden, Bryan W. Van (2017). *Taking Back Philosophy: A Multicultural Manifesto*. New York: Columbia University Press.

Novotny, Daniel (2013). *Ens rationis from Suárez to Caramuel: A Study in Scholasticism of the Baroque Era*. New York: Fordham University Press.

O'Neill, Eileen (1988). Disappearing Ink: Early Modern Women Philosophers and Their Fate in History. In Janet A. Kourany (ed.), *Philosophy in a Feminist Voice: Critiques and Reconstructions*. Princeton, NJ: Princeton University Press, 17–62.

Pocock, John Greville Agard (1999). *Barbarism and Religion*, Volume 1: *The Enlightenments of Edward Gibbon, 1737-1764*. Cambridge: Cambridge University Press.

Richardson, Alan (2013). What Good Is a (Indeed, This) History of Pragmatism? *Transactions of the Charles S. Peirce Society: A Quarterly Journal in American Philosophy* 49(3): 405–412.

Rorty, Richard, ed. (1967). *The Linguistic Turn: Essays in Philosophical Method*. Chicago: University of Chicago Press.

Rosenboim, Or (2017). *The Emergence of Globalism: Visions of World Order in Britain and the United States, 1939-1950*. Princeton, NJ: Princeton University Press.

Russell, Bertrand (1924). Does Ethics Influence Life? In John. G. Slater (ed.), *Volumes of the Collected Papers of Bertrand Russell*, Volume 9: *Essays on Language, Mind and Matter, 1919-26*. London: Unwin: Hyman, 1988, 350–353.

Russell, Bertrand ([1945] 1972). *The History of Western Philosophy*. New York: Simon & Schuster.

Sala-Molins, Louis (2006). *Dark Side of the Light: Slavery and the French Enlightenment*. Minneapolis: University of Minnesota Press.

Schweitzer, Albert (1923). *Civilisation and Ethics: The Philosophy of Civilization, Part II*. Translated by John Nash. London: A. C. Black.

Sebastiani, Silvia (2013). *The Scottish Enlightenment: Race, Gender, and the Limits of Progress*. Dordrecht: Springer.

Spiegelberg, Herbert (1980). The Correspondence between Bertrand Russell and Albert Schweitzer. *International Studies in Philosophy* 12(1): 1–45.

Stroud, Scott R. (2017). Pragmatism, Persuasion, and Force in Bhimrao Ambedkar's Reconstruction of Buddhism. *The Journal of Religion* 97(2): 214–243.

Stroud, Scott R., and Landon C. Elkind (2017). Exploring the Influence of Russell on Ambedkar. *Forward Press* (August 1, 2017). https://www.forwardpress.in/2017/08/exploring-the-influence-of-russell-on-ambedkar/.

Thomas, Emily (2019). The Idealism and Pantheism of May Sinclair. *Journal of the American Philosophical Association* 5(2): 137–157.

Toland, John ([1720] 1753). *Hypatia: Or, The History of a Most Beautiful, Most Vertuous, Most Learned, and Every Way Accomplish'd Lady; who was Torn to Pieces by the Clergy of Alexandria, to Gratify the Pride, Emulation, and Cruelty of Their Archbishop, Commonly But Undeservedly Styled St. Cyril*. London: M. Cooper, W. Reeve, and C. Sympson.

Tufayl, Ibn [1972]. *Ibn Tufayl's Hayy Ibn Yaqzan: A Philosophical Tale*. Translated by Lenn Goodman. Chicago: University of Chicago Press.

1

The *Theogony* and the *Works and Days*

The Beginnings of Philosophical Questioning in Hesiod

Barbara M. Sattler

1.1. Introduction

You may think I got mixed up with the field that this volume is focusing on—sure, Hesiod is a classic in ancient Greek literature, and as such perhaps now less neglected than he used to be,[1] but this volume is meant to deal with neglected classics in *philosophy*. Let me assure you—I did read the title of the volume carefully, and I want to show you that if we think of the beginning of philosophy, we should think of Hesiod's two works, the *Theogony* and the *Works and Days*, as two works that are neglected in philosophy today but that should be part of a tradition that would be helpful for philosophers to be aware of. For a long time in the history of philosophy, philosophers have seen Hesiod as a crucial starting point for natural philosophy, as well as for philosophy of history, ethics, and political philosophy.[2] Hesiod can

---

[1] But also in Classics departments in the Anglophone world, Hesiod is usually still in Homer's shadow to the degree that many Classicists still speak as if Homer stood alone as the earliest Greek poet (*pace* Martin West's important work on Hesiod). Part of the reason for this may still be his devaluation in the nineteenth century for lack of the "poetic"; see Schadewaldt 1978, 93.

[2] Hesiod is usually seen to have lived sometime around 700 BCE in Boeotia, and to be the first writer whose works have been handed down to us after Homer. Some scholars have argued, however, that his poems are pre-Homeric (prominently West 1966, 46–47, who assumes Hesiod's works to be composed between 730 and 690). And Herodotus II.53 understands Homer and Hesiod to be contemporaries who lived roughly 400 years before him. In any case, Hesiod probably lived roughly a century before Thales and three centuries before Plato.

Barbara M. Sattler, *The* Theogony *and the* Works and Days In: *Neglected Classics of Philosophy.*
Edited by: Eric Schliesser, Oxford University Press. © Oxford University Press 2022.
DOI: 10.1093/oso/9780190097196.003.0002

be understood as the beginning of what we would call "nonfiction writing,"[3] and as such, as we will see, also as the ground for philosophy. We are used to philosophy originally including almost all of the sciences, which then gradually developed out of it, such as physics, biology, psychology, and so forth. But before we can find anything we are used to calling "philosophy," there is literature that we can divide into fiction and nonfiction writing; the latter, as we will see, also includes philosophical sections.[4]

Hesiod has sometimes been seen as the first Presocratic;[5] but he is hardly ever mentioned in a philosophy department in the Anglophone world today. If Hesiod is mentioned at all by philosophers nowadays, it is usually in order to exemplify the time when there wasn't yet any philosophy and to show what mythological thinking looked like before philosophy attempted to give a *logos* about the world. Thus, Hesiod is at best *contrasted* with the first philosophers and seen as standing on the other side of philosophy,[6] even if clear criteria for why Thales counts as philosopher and Hesiod does not are usually missing. If we look at past philosophers, however, things look quite different: Heraclitus

---

[3] If we look for the genre under which Hesiod's work is usually grouped, we find somewhat of a mess. Often his poems are labeled "didactic poetry" or "didactic epic," but sometimes these terms are restricted to the *Works and Days*, while the *Theogony* is simply labeled "theogonic poetry." Scholars who treat "epic" as a matter of meter and language classify the Hesiodic poems as "epic" but not "heroic epic." Similarly, in French scholarship Hesiod is variously classed under *poésie didactique*, *genre épique*, or simply by the meter as belonging to the literature using *hexamètre dactylique*. In German scholarship, Hesiod has been seen as the beginning of the "Sachepos" (see Latacz 1991). West (1978) understands the *Works and Days* as "wisdom poetry," partly to mark the connection with Near Eastern tradition. The last two labels, "Sachepos" and "wisdom literature," already stress those features of Hesiod's poems that will be of interest for us.

[4] This is not to say that Hesiod's poems would not also include fictitious elements (and Homer may think of his work as quasi historic). Fiction can of course also raise philosophical questions, but the nonfiction writing of Hesiod seems to do so more directly without needing a "translation" of the circumstances of a specific person or story into general rules or the environment of the audience.

[5] For example, Schadewaldt (1978, 82), claims that in Hesiod we meet thinking itself, even if not yet in the form of pure *logos*, and on p. 83 that Hesiod should be part of an edition of the Presocratics. Interestingly, however, Hesiod is not seen as one of the seven sages—there are different groups handed down to us under this heading, but Hesiod does not belong to any of the standard groups—presumably because he and Homer were seen to play in a different league: they were *the* two teachers of the ancient Greek world.

[6] For example, Kirk, Raven, and Schofield (1983, 73) contrast him with Anaximander, claiming that "there is an enormous gulf" between both.

mentions Hesiod in one breath with Xenophanes and Pythagoras (when attacking his predecessors by claiming that much learning does not teach men to think, fr. B40).[7] And in a further attack on him, he tells us that Hesiod is seen as a teacher for most people even though Hesiod does not know that night and day are one (fr. B57). Hesiod is also an important reference point for Plato and Aristotle in a variety of fields, as well as for reflections on the history of mankind and the philosophy of history by nineteenth-century thinkers, such as Nietzsche and Dilthey. I will not argue here that Hesiod should be regarded as a full-blooded philosopher, but that in several fields, his poems can be seen as the starting point for central philosophical discussions, which made him an important point of reference for philosophers in the past, and that as such he should also be taken into account by philosophers today.

In this short chapter, I can look at only a few of the philosophically interesting topics that can be found in Hesiod. We will concentrate on the temporal and spatial structures he presents, on his account of human and moral history, and on his discussion of normativity.[8] For the temporal and spatial structures, this chapter will start with a look at his *Theogony*—Hesiod's cosmogony and genealogy of the gods. Along with his story of the creation of the different deities of the ancient Greek world, their family relationships, and their fights with each other that led to the current age of Zeus, it includes interesting ideas about time and space and presents a kind of systematization of the different realms of the world in general. And for a discussion of human history and normativity, we will look at his *Works and Days*, a work that presents what may be understood as a farmer's calendar that tightly connects natural observations with guidelines for moral actions.

But before we start with these topics, I will give a brief general sketch of why Hesiod should be of interest to philosophers.

---

[7] By contrast, Homer is paired with the poet Archilochos in B42. Cf. also Clay 1992, 138, for Hesiod's influence on later philosophers.

[8] The second topic can be seen as connecting the first and the third.

1.2. Systematicity, Truth, and the Big Questions: Why Hesiod Should Be Read by Philosophers

If by philosophy we want to include only thinking that follows a rigid scheme of presenting us first with all the necessary premises and subsequently with the conclusion we can derive from them, then obviously Hesiod could not play a part in the philosophical tradition (but neither could, on this account, several of the thinkers we have come to call philosophers—Anaximander, Plato, Hume, or Wittgenstein may be excluded, to name just a few). Furthermore, you may point out that there seem to be certain inconsistencies in Hesiod's claims that make it hard to see how he can be important for philosophers.[9] But if we were to exclude all philosophers from the tradition in whose work we find something that seems like an inconsistency, then, once again, I am not sure how many there would be left.[10]

Finally, you may claim that Hesiod's style is rather unphilosophical—it seems to be full of mere associations and metaphors, and it is in verse, which seems to put him clearly in the poet's rather than the philosopher's camp. However, Parmenides and Empedocles, two champions of Prescocratic philosophy, also wrote in verse form. All three of them seem to be much more concerned with the content they express than with poetic qualities. And Lucretius, Cavendish, and Emerson use the verse form as well.

By contrast, there are the following four points that suggest that we should take Hesiod seriously as a sparring partner for philosophy:

---

[9] For example, if, as Hesiod says, in the silver race childhood extends for 100 years during which children stay with their mothers, while they are adults for only a very short time, it seems difficult to see how mothers will have time for the prolonged adolescence of their children, when they themselves do not have much time for adulthood. Or will they miraculously not need 100 years to grow up themselves?

[10] This is not to say that consistency, obeying the principle of non-contradiction, is not a very important criterion for philosophy; it is just to say that human beings tend to be not terribly good at obeying it thoroughly.

1.2.1. Systematic Thinking

Hesiod presents the first attempt in Western literature to account systematically for different natural and divine aspects in the universe. It is the beginning of nonfiction writing.[11] We do find a representation of different aspects of life and a display of some forms of knowledge in Homer's epics[12] (for example, treatment of technical matters with the technique of chariot races by Nestor, in *Iliad* XXIII, 306–348, and the technique of building rafts in *Odyssey* V, 234–261). In Hesiod the treatment of nonfiction topics is, however, made explicit, much more far-reaching, and, most importantly for our purpose, far more systematic. The most obvious area Hesiod starts to treat in a systematic way concerns the different deities, but we will see that this includes ample systematization of the natural world as well.[13] Hesiod shows how all the different divine and natural powers depend on and interact with each other—a dependency that is spelled out in genealogical terms.[14] His poems also concern discussions of human actions in general, the good life, and human norms, which brings us to the second point.

1.2.2. Hesiod Asks Some of the "Big Philosophical Questions"

While Hesiod's poems show, without doubt, narrative features, they also, for the first time in Western thought, raise some of the most

---

[11] This is not to claim that the ancient Greek writers of this time would have consciously made a distinction between fiction and nonfiction writing.

[12] What Havelock 1982 sees as the encyclopedic elements of Homer.

[13] The systematicity of Hesiod's thinking is also granted by some more contemporary philosophers; for example, Kirk, Raven, and Schofield acknowledge that Hesiod's *Theogony* is a systematic achievement and talk of "the classificatory craft of Hesiod" (74). Schadewaldt (1978, 93), talks of a gigantic family tree of what is ("ein riesiger Stammbaum des Seienden"). While West (1966) claims on p. 14 that we should not see Hesiod as the first person to systematize the Greek beliefs about the gods, he gives no evidence for this claim (and in conclusion of his overview of theogonic writing in other cultures, 1–14, he claims that it is unlikely that Hesiod was influenced by them).

[14] Miller (2018, 219) has pointed out that Hesiod omits tales of Zeus's abusive sexual aggression that would have been inconsistent with his depiction of Zeus as representing cosmological and ethical justice.

fundamental problems that philosophy has been dealing with for the past 2,600 years. Hesiod may not deal with them in the same explicit way that philosophers do, but his poems clearly raise them as questions. They are questions such as: How should we lead our lives, and what is the good life? What is the basis for how we should act? What does the whole of the world look like? Was there a beginning of the world, and if so, what came first? How do we human beings relate to the divine? Is human history a story of progress or decline?

You may object that these "big questions" are also raised by religion, so they are not specific to philosophy.[15] And while Hesiod's poems are not sacred texts and do not represent a religious revelation in the way we are used to from the Abrahamic tradition, in both his works he seems to rely on the Muses, and thus on divine inspiration to some degree. We should, however, also bear in mind that it is rather anachronistic to try to distinguish neatly between religious and philosophical thought in early Greek thinking. Furthermore, we see that Hesiod's poems cover a wide range of human and natural affairs. And ethics and religion are often close, to say the obvious. Hesiod's work may also connect us to older wisdom literature that existed in oral form and shows parallels to Near Eastern Wisdom literature;[16] for example, a catalogue of the days telling people which work to do on which day of the calendar given the cosmic and divine constellations can also be found in Babylonian literature.[17]

1.2.3. The Question of Truth Is Central

In the prologue to both of Hesiod's poems, we see him pointing out the centrality of truth: In the *Theogony* we are told that when the Muses first got in touch with Hesiod, they taught him that

---

[15] Cf. also Aristotle, who in his *Metaphysics* claims that these questions were raised by the mythologists.

[16] See West 1978, 3–15, for possible parallels.

[17] We should, however, not expect arguments in Hesiod in the way we are used to from later thinkers.

[w]e know to say many false things (*pseudeas*), similar to true
(*etumoisin*) ones,
But when we want, we also know to proclaim true things (*alêthea*).
(*Theogony*, lines 27–28)[18]

The Muses then go on to breathe a divine voice into him so that he can
proclaim what will be, what was, and the everlasting kind. It is a very
interesting question what Hesiod understands by true things here,
what the relationship is between ἀληθής and ἔτυμος, and in which respect false things can be similar to true ones,[19] but for reasons of space
we will not be able to deal with these questions here.

In his *Theogony* it is made clear that what is true and false is the
realm of the Muses, while in his *Works and Days*, Hesiod addresses
the Muses at the beginning, and then claims that he himself will announce the truth: "I will proclaim what is true (ἐτήτυμα) to Perseus"
(*Works and Days*, line 10). He will show his deceitful brother Perseus,
who cheated on him when dividing their inheritance and against
whom he is leading a case at court, what the truth is—which, as we
will see, includes what justice is and what a good farmer should do.
And then Hesiod goes on to what seems to be a correction of his own
account of strife in the *Theogony*: in the earlier work there was just one
goddess of strife mentioned, Eris, but now he makes it clear that there
are in fact two, one which is productive and makes us work, as we are
motivated in productive competition with our equals, and the other
which is awful and leads to enmity (line 11 ff.). It seems to be clear for
Hesiod that if there are two different phenomena or a phenomenon
with genuinely two different aspects we capture as strife, then there
needs to be two different goddesses as personification or origin. And

---

[18]   While later authors, like Xenophanes fr. 11, and Plato, *Republic* 378d ff., will accuse
Hesiod and others of making up false stories about the gods—claiming them to possess
all kinds of negative moral traits, like being adulterous and violent—this is a criticism
uttered from their particular point of view of gods or a god as being supremely good.

[19]   Think about the intricate discussion this question raises in Plato's *Sophist*.
Schadewaldt (1978, 85–86) thinks that what is similar to true things is a characterization of poetry, as we find it in the idea of the beautiful-seeming from the sophists to up
to the eighteenth century, while he understands the clear delineation between seeming
and being true as one beginning of philosophy. The same phrase is, however, also used by
Homer to describe Odysseus's ability to craft lies (*Odyssey* XIX, 203).

the two sides of strife also seem to be what structures the *Works and Days* as a whole—the negative Eris is at play in his juridical fight with his brother, while the positive Eris is at work when we look at what is necessary for the farming year.[20]

While we cannot deal with the question here of what Hesiod understands by what is true in his works,[21] it seems clear that talking about what is true is somehow related to our understanding of the world; and for Hesiod this understanding should have immediate repercussions for our actions.

1.2.4. Reference Point for Philosophers

Philosophers such as Plato, Aristotle, Dilthey, and Nietzsche took Hesiod as an important reference point for their own thinking.[22] We may assume that Plato understood Hesiod mainly as a sophist and exponent of eristic, for example, in his *Protagoras* and *Theaetetus*.[23] But Plato also takes up Hesiod for important philosophical points, as we will see below;[24] and it has been claimed that Hesiod "comes across as epistemologically self-aware [. . .] in a way which is characteristic of philosophy as Plato will come to understand it."[25] Aristotle refers to Hesiod in discussions of natural philosophy,[26] metaphysics,[27] politics, and ethics. Nietzsche takes up Hesiod for the connection between temporal and moral structures; while Dilthey sees in him one stream of thought leading away from the mythical world.[28]

---

[20] See Schadewaldt 1978, 83.

[21] And whether it is related to what is sometimes called "ontological truth."

[22] To name just those who discuss him more extensively, and not just in passing, like Schopenhauer, Hume, or Montaigne.

[23] In this, Plato may also reflect his cultural background.

[24] On the relationship between Plato and Hesiod, see in general the volume edited by Boys-Stones and Haubold 2010. I can only touch upon some of the many allusions to Hesiod in Plato.

[25] Boys-Stones in: Boys-Stones and Haubold 2010, 32.

[26] When discussing space or zoological questions.

[27] When discussing whether the principles of perishable things are the same as those of non-perishable things in the 10th aporia of his *Metaphysics*; and Hesiod is named as the first to look for efficient causation, as we will see below.

[28] In his *Einleitung in die Geschichtswissenschaft*, Dilthey claims that two developments led to the destruction of the mythical world picture, one of them being that all processes in the world start being captured in terms of procreation, as we find it in the *Theogony*.

Hesiod's two poems are important to show that philosophical ideas in the area of natural philosophy, ethics, and political philosophy do not come out of the blue, but that earlier thinkers whom we tend not to call philosophers, like Hesiod, were already thinking systematically about the foundation of human norms, as well as about time and space.

1.3. Time and Space

Hesiod's two poems are the first texts in Western literature that offer a general account of time and space. And Hesiod is the first thinker in the Greek world to present the idea of a beginning of the world:

> In truth, first of all Chasm came to be, and then broad-breasted Earth, the ever immovable seat of all the immortals who possess snowy Olympus's peak and murky Tartarus in the depth of the broad-pathed Earth, and Eros, who is the most beautiful of all gods, the limb-melter—he overpowers the mind and the thoughtful counsel of all the gods and all human beings in their breasts.
>
> From Chasm, Erebos [Darkness] and black Night came to be; and then Aether and Day came forth from Night, who conceived and bore them after mingling in love with Erebos. Earth first of all bore starry Sky, equal to herself, to cover her on every side, so that she would be the ever immovable seat for the blessed-gods. (*Theogony*, lines 116–127, Most's translation)

This beginning is interesting not only for an investigation of time, as we will see below, but also for the very beginning of thinking about space.[29] Hesiod claims that first of all, Chasm (χάος) came to be—the Greek word χάος usually indicates some gap within a (or between two) spatially extended thing.[30] We do not find any further characterisation

---

[29] A related attempt to give an account of the ultimate beginning is found in Plato's *Timaeus*, where the idea that we need something for sensible things to come into being leads to the assumption of what Plato calls the receptacle and wet-nurse of becoming, his account of space.

[30] The Greek term χάος is often translated as "chaos." However, Most in his translation of the *Theogony* rightly points out that this misleadingly suggests a jumble of disordered

of Chasm, but it seems to be something spatial—a reading that is also supported by Aristotle's *Physics*, 208b29-33. There Aristotle understands Chasm as a proto-notion of space, since it shows that we first need something *where* all other things can come into being; the possible existence of things is tied to them being somewhere. This fits also with the fact that of the next thing that comes into being, Gaia, the spatial dimension is stressed—"broad-breasted Earth." In addition, Earth also possesses the summit of Mount Olympus, which makes her "the ever immovable seat of all the immortals"—she provides *location* for the gods. Thus also the gods are given a space, snowy Olympus, before they come into being.[31]

After Chasm and Earth have come into being, Eros (Love) appears. It is the reason for gods to start procreating with each other and thus a connecting force. Ever since Aristotle, Hesiod's Eros has been understood as a first kind of an efficient cause, and we find Eros as the first cosmological efficient cause in Parmenides's cosmology.[32] With Chasm and Earth, their strong spatial connotation suggests that we need a place first for something to come into being, while with Eros we get the idea that subsequently we need some kind of a force starting a generation or process. It is true that not all forms of generation enumerated by Hesiod require two partners and thus Eros as a driving force[33]—for example, Chaos brings forth Darkness and Night without a partner—but it is the most common way. In introducing Eros as the force to explain the generation of other divinities, Hesiod gives prominence to the idea that there needs to be a cause or reason for something to come into being—a first inkling of what later has been called the principle of sufficient reason, which will play a major role in Greek philosophical tradition and beyond. Also the background assumption

matter. By contrast, Hesiod's term indicates a gap or opening; it is connected with an open jaw; cf. also Kirk, Raven, and Schofield 1983, 37.

[31] And in lines 720ff., Hesiod depicts the spatial extension of the whole world in symmetrical terms. I investigate Hesiod's account of space in more detail in my book manuscript *Conceptions of Space in Greek thought*, chapter 1.

[32] Parmenides B13. The idea of Eros as the oldest god is also taken up by Plato in his *Symposium* 178b, where it is pointed out that Parmenides agrees with him in this respect, and by Kierkegaard in his *Either-Or*.

[33] See also West 1966, 195-196.

of the spatial beginning, that it is impossible for something to originate nowhere, seems to follow this kind of reasoning.

Hesiod gives us the first recorded genealogy of primordial and Olympic gods, natural deities, nymphs and nereids, monsters and heroes, and thus a systematization of divinities and natural phenomena.[34] His account also includes the coming into being of rivers, such as the Nile and the Ister, and continents, like Asia and Europa, of stars and winds; and with certain gods, like the goddess of the morning, we get different temporal phenomena.[35] Also in this genealogy we find the principle that if one name captures two different phenomena, Hesiod makes sure it is connected with two different divinities. For example, Typhoeus, the offspring of Gaia and Tartarus, is given as a source for the evil winds at sea, as these winds are explicitly distinguished from the ones on Earth and the good ones at sea, which have as their origin other wind gods, such as Zephyrus, Boreas, and Notus.[36] While prima facie we may see this simply as an unnecessary multiplication of entities, it is in fact following an idea that we find also in more scientific thinking: that different physical phenomena need to have different reasons or origins to explain their difference. You may object, however, that it is also a sign of philosophical and scientific thinking to have one cause explain different phenomena. But in order not to be simply mysterious, the multiplicity of effects then needs some multiplicity in the cause, for example, in the form of internal complexity.[37]

The different phenomena and deities are systematized with the help of a set of different relationships, for example, founded on contrasting opposites, or on common pairs, like Earth and Sky (when Earth, Gaia, is claimed to bring forth Sky, Uranus).[38] Let us look at Night and its kin as a particularly fruitful example for these different

[34] West (1966), who gives a different taxonomy of the different divinities introduced in the *Theogony*, adds "abstractions" like death and sleep to this list (33).

[35] Hesiod's *Theogony* also explains things like why ash trees do not burn in fire (line 560) and the coming into being of certain rituals.

[36] Lines 378–380.

[37] See also Plato's insistence in the *Phaedo* that one kind of cause needs to bring about only one kind of effect (otherwise we have not yet found the proper cause); cf. Sattler 2018.

[38] Hesiod can obviously draw on a large quantity of earlier stories received as part of an oral tradition. But we know from the beginning of the *Works and Days*, where Hesiod introduces a second Eris, that he is willing to modify this tradition.

kinds of relationships, since Night is a natural phenomenon and temporal notion as well as a phenomenon that carries strong evaluative
connotations. We find relationships of opposition (Night gives raise to
Day), but also of similarity (Chasm, which presumably lacks daylight,
gives rise to Night and Darkness). Night also gives rise to what we may
think of as happening usually at night—like sleep, and dreams; and
perhaps this is also the reason why Night gives birth to *philotês* (fond-
ness or love). It also seems to be seen as the privation of what is usually
there, and thus brings forth death and old age,[39] as well as generally
things that have a negative connotation,[40] like blame and distress.[41]
Similarly, Eris, the goddess of strife, one of the children of Night, gives
rise to everything that is a possible consequence of strife: among other
things, hunger, tearful pains, battle, and war.[42] Hesiod thus captures
what we would think of as relationships between natural phenomena,
necessary conditions, and value associations, all into family relations,
and thus presents a unified way of connecting everything. Everything
visible and concrete seems to derive from Earth, while abstractions
and everything intangible seem to descend from Chasm.[43]

Many points of cosmological significance in this systematization are
taken up by Presocratic philosophers. For example, in Parmenides's
cosmology we find Night and Light as the basic cosmological principles.[44] And Hesiod's image of the house of Night as the meeting
place of Night and Day such that one is always going out while the
other is coming back (lines 746–55) is taken up by the opening frag-
ment of Parmenides's poem, B1, lines 11ff. These lines describe how

[39] We also talk about the eve of one's life.

[40] This may still be seen in our talk about "children of the night."

[41] It may also be the reason why the three Moirai are said to be borne by Night, even
though in the end we are also told that Themis, the goddess of divine order and law, gives
birth to them. While their descent from Night presumably accounts for them being experienced as terrible, their kinship with Themis stresses another aspect, namely that they
are seen as acting justly.

[42] For a different account of the progeny of Night that I find less illuminating, see West
1966, 35–36.

[43] See West 1966 and Schadewaldt 1978; by contrast, Arrighetti (2006) claims that the
beings of the first generation have a double physiognomy, physical and divine, while the
later generations personify intellectual properties or ethical principles.

[44] See Parmenides fr. B8, 53–59 and A37, *Theogony*, lines 123ff., and Kirk, Raven,
and Schofield 1983, 257, who take Hesiod's *Theogony* also as the model for Parmenides's
treatment of the origin of Love, and War and Discord.

Parmenides (or some youth) is driven by the daughters of the Sun from the house of Night toward the gate between the paths of Night and Day, a gate that must be passed to achieve enlightenment.[45]

With the help of a systematization of the different generations of the divinities, Hesiod also provides a clear temporal structure that runs linearly from the beginning of the world to the presumed current time, the age of the reign of Zeus. There are three general kinds of divinities: first, we find the primordial gods, Chasm, Gaia, Tartarus, Eros, and their immediate offspring, like Erebos, Night, and Uranus. Second, we get the generation of the children of Gaia and Uranus—the Titans, Cyclopes, and giants and monsters. Most prominently among them is the Titan Kronos. And third, there are the Olympic gods, the children of Kronos and Rheia.[46] The change of generation of gods is marked in both cases by the castration of the father: first Kronos castrates his father Uranus, and then Zeus castrates Kronos, thus bringing to an end in each case the possibility of reproducing this generation of divinities.[47] In the case of the reign of the Olympian gods, a long fight with a previous generation is necessary: the Olympian gods fight the Titans,[48] the children of Gaia and Uranus, and only succeed when employing the help of the giants.[49]

In the *Theogony* we thus get a model in which the current condition is seen as a high point, a completion of a linear development: after the reign of Uranus, first Kronos takes over, and then Zeus, who is all wise and bestows order. This model of temporal development—linear toward a climax—contrasts clearly with the cyclical model which we find in the human and natural world in his *Works and Days*. In both cases, these temporal structures are used for the purpose of legitimization: the linear order of the creation of the different divine kinds

[45]   See also Miller 2018, 220.

[46]   Aphrodite does not fit this general pattern, since she is worshipped in connection with the other Olympian gods, but she came into being from the severed genitals of Uranus and the foam they produce in the sea.

[47]   However, Gaia still mingles with Tartarus at the end, thus two primordial gods still produce an offspring, Typhoeus, whom Zeus has to fight, line 820. But Uranus can no longer be active in this sense.

[48]   Lines 624–721.

[49]   These changes in the generations of divinities presumably also reflect cultural changes in the rites and cults of the Greeks from worshipping general primordial powers to more specific and abstract gods.

legitimizes the last one, Zeus, and his power as the best so that the linear development can be seen as a process toward goodness. By giving an account of the cyclical structure of the year in his *Works and Days*, Hesiod legitimizes himself as the genuine farmer, who does not deserve being robbed of his share of the paternal farm by his brother; and we see that human beings are good if they follow the natural circle.

But Hesiod is not only the first to offer two different models of understanding time in different realms, a linear and a cyclical one, so that we could say divine time is linear for him, and human time is cyclical. Rather, we also find a linear temporal structure with human beings; but in the human case, a linear order shows a decline, as we will see in the next section.[50]

1.4. The History of Human Beings

The linear temporal structure in the human world is found in the Myth of Ages in Hesiod's *Works and Days*.[51] This myth has been taken up centrally by later philosophers as a starting point for political thought and philosophical reflections on history. Let me first give a rough reminder of the myth before we touch upon some of its treatment by philosophers: according to the *Works and Days*, human beings first came into being as a "golden race" under the reign of Kronos. Their lives resemble those of the divinities—they are friends of the gods, without illness and problems of old age. When, in contrast to the gods, they eventually die, they have a peaceful death, "as if overpowered by sleep." These are the times when human and divine lives are as similar as possible[52]—according to the *Theogony*, what was a less good time

---

[50] Loney (2018) interestingly divides what I call linear time into "omnipresent," "etiological," and "teleological" *synchronic* temporalities, and what I call "cyclical time" into seasonal and cyclical *diachronic* temporalities, but it seems to me that both cyclical and linear times can be diachronic. And on p. 112 he calls human lives "cyclical" because they end, while having an end (and a beginning) for me does not yet constitute cyclical time.

[51] For possible Eastern forerunners of individual aspects of this myth, see West 1978, 174–177.

[52] We also find a close connection between the gods and human beings, and the realm of the gods even being pervious for human beings, in the *Theogony*: line 535 claims that now men and gods were finally separated from each other, which suggests that before, this was not the case. In lines 950ff. we are told that Heracles, after his extraordinary

for the gods (who reach their best time in the age of Zeus) is the best time for human beings. From there on, we see a rise of the gods and a decline of human beings, which ensures that the gap between both groups keeps widening until we end up with a vast divide between gods and human beings in current times.

The next race of human beings is the silver race. Though this race is still called blessed, these human beings are worse in body and mind. Their inferiority in body shows in that they need a hundred years for puberty and growing up, while their mental lack is displayed in their suffering due to their folly—they cannot keep away from reckless violence against each other and do not offer sacrifices to the gods.[53] This last point is the reason why the gods move on to bring forth another race;[54] but no explicit reason is given why the gods moved from the golden to the silver race in the first instance.[55] The next race after the silver one is the "wild and violent brazen race." With the first three races, we find a clear decline—in the behavior of people toward the gods, toward each other, and in the amount of pain they suffer. Before Hesiod then moves on to the current and worst race, however, we are told that Zeus creates a wiser and better race, the race of the demigods, who now live on the isle of the blessed.[56] But Hesiod (and his readers) are part of

deeds, is married to the goddess Hebe and lives with the gods, separate from human suffering and aging. Finally, the very fact that there are offspring of the union of gods and human beings—a group with which the *Theogony* ends—indicates that the divine realm is accessible to human beings.

[53] Lines 134–137.

[54] In line 138 we are told that Zeus concealed them in anger because they did not honor the gods—here for the first time Zeus comes into the myth of the ages. He will also be responsible for the origin of the bronze and heroic races (lines 143 and 156) and, eventually, for the end of the iron race (line 180).

[55] We were, however, given the story of Prometheus beforehand (line 47ff.), which could be seen as a general explanation for why humankind must suffer—because Zeus had been cheated by Prometheus, who gave human beings fire and thus what is not their due, Zeus sent as a revenge Pandora and her jar which contains sorrow, mischief, illness, and so forth. Accordingly, moving from the golden to the silver race may be part of poetic justice. Strauss Clay (2003, 87) thinks the golden race became extinct because it consisted solely of males and thus could not procreate. But this is not a claim we find in Hesiod's text.

[56] Hesiod's introduction of the race of the demigods seems to be an interruption of his general decline-story. Nietzsche, in *his Genealogy of Morals*, understands this as Hesiod's attempt to deal with the terrific world of Homer by including it into the story of the development of human beings. Alternatively, it has been suggested that the race of the heroes, together with the previous three races, forms something like a ring-composition: after

the fifth, the iron race, which is morally and physically corrupt, "worn out by suffering,"[57] and which will be destroyed by Zeus when their moral wrongs are so great that "babies are born with gray hair."

This last point of the story of moral decline of mankind shows that at some point the perversion of morality reaches a point when it even leads to a perversion of the temporal structure—babies, the starting points of human beings, are born gray-haired, and thus as old persons. Temporal structures are not indifferent to our actions, but are affected by moral mistakes. Time is not experienced as a neutral framework in which different actions, events, or processes can be situated, but rather as an expression of moral decline or rise.[58]

In Hesiod's account of human decline, the gods are responsible at least for the move from the golden race to the silver one. And someone born into the iron age, like Hesiod and ourselves, cannot get back to a golden age. But, according to Hesiod, we can still follow Dike, Justice[59]—how so we will discuss in the next section—and thus can cease to pervert moral structures any further.

With this myth, we have the first attempt to sketch the big structures of human history—it does not focus only on one event, like a war (whether fictive or real), but looks at the development of human beings as such. It is done in a rather abstract way, by concentrating on the development of the moral behavior and sufferings of human beings. This first account of the whole of human history is a story of decline. And the account of an increase in suffering and decrease in morality is paired with different metals, whose value decreases with the decline in morality and thus ascribes different values to the different ages. It is the origin of all talk about a "golden age," here specifically, a morally

the good race of the golden age and the two bad ages of silver and bronze, we return to the good heroic age. In this case it would be the iron race that was awkwardly added; see, for example, Querbach 1985, who follows ideas by Vernant and Walcot. In this case, Hesiod would have used a previous cyclical myth and formed it into a linear decline by adding his own, iron age.

[57] In line 174, Hesiod wishes he had died earlier or been born later; the latter may suggest that history may thus not be at its ultimate end, but could become better again.
[58] For a more detailed discussion of the relationship between temporality and morality, see my book manuscript *Ancient Notions of Time from Homer to Plato*.
[59] See, for example, *Theogony* Line 212, where we are told that Perseus should listen to Dike and not go with *hybris*.

golden age, that was once possible for human beings under Kronos, but to which we cannot return.[60]

Using different metals which are of different monetary value is an easy and clear way to indicate differences in moral or human value. You may think that this way of capturing Hesiod's account depicts things the wrong way around—after all, it is because we human beings are the kind of beings that bestow value onto things or actions that at some point we also bestowed it on metals. I am not denying this, but it seems clear that at the time of Hesiod the difference in value between different metals was clearly established,[61] and he uses this difference prominently in order to explicate the less tangible, less clear differences in moral behavior, in a way that has been taken up prominently all through the history of thought.

Hesiod's account of human decline does not fit the common picture of progress in human history which the Enlightenment seems to have rather strongly instilled in us,[62] prominently expressed, for example, in D'Alembert's introduction to the *Encyclopédie*.[63] Even if today many may feel a moral decline in political discourse, this still seems to go together with the idea of intellectual progress or moral progress of a part of society—about which Hesiod is silent. In this, Hesiod's account of a decline of the morality of human beings is an interesting alternative to the prevailing story of progress.

The myth's clear understanding of human history as a story of decline was taken up in a strongly affirmative way by Nietzsche, who in his *Vom Nutzen und Nachteil der Historie* claimed that we can find in his, Nietzsche's, time what Hesiod has predicted as the end time of human history so far, gray-haired children, since the current historic education is a kind of "inborn grayness."[64] In Plato, we find at least two

[60] Empedocles, in his fr. 128, spells out the idea of the golden age further by claiming that it had no god of war yet, only Kypris, the queen of love.

[61] As difference of currency, for example, even if at that time not yet as coins, which only seems to have started in Greece in the sixth or fifth century BCE.

[62] In spite of the criticism of belief in human progress, most prominently perhaps in Horkheimer and Adorno.

[63] Where he gives a genealogy of human understanding and a historical account of the progress of knowledge since the sixteenth century. Cf. also the very optimistic outlook of progress of all of humanity by Marquis de Condorcet, *Esquisse d'un tableau historique des progrès de l'esprit humain*, and Voltaire's *La philosophie de l'histoire*.

[64] Here it seems to be the education system, rather than the temporal structure, that has come to be perverted.

different ways in which the myth is taken up: first, the originally diachronic myth is transformed into a synchronic account in his famous
noble lie in the *Republic*, according to which belonging to different
classes is tied to the metal inside us with which we are born. In the
Republic, this noble lie is used as a way to keep the different classes in
the *kallipolis* in check, which is helped by the fact that gold is immediately understood as more valuable than silver and bronze. Second,
the connection between temporal and moral structures that Hesiod
establishes is also in the background of the myth in the *Statesman*
which claims that an earlier innocent age of Kronos, when human
beings are supervised by god, has been replaced now by the age of Zeus
in which we are instead supervised by other human beings.

1.5. Normativity

Hesiod's understanding of the current human condition as a result of
continued decline shows that he is worried about the current moral
state, which results in a discussion of the basis for normativity. Human
decline is expressed by an increase in suffering and a decrease of moral
reliability. Hesiod's reflections on normativity are presented as starting
from personal experience and thus as an individual case—his being
exposed to the injustice committed by his brother Perseus. But his
reflections soon become more general in audience and topic—they
start being addressed not only to his brother, but also to people in
power in general (*WD*, line 248), and they extend to principal concerns
about human behavior and norms, which are expressed as concerns
about adhering to Dike.

In these reflections, ideas about what we would call utility, the
moral and the legal realm, are closely intertwined. And the normative
ideas discussed seem to be valid for divine as well as human beings.[65]
Thus, gods are not beyond the normative realm—here we find a clear

---

[65] As we can see, for example, from the fact that Zeus is also asked to preserve the laws
with justice (*dikêi d'isthune themistas*) in *Works and Days*. Given that the relationship of
human beings to Dike seems to be something they share with the gods, it is not derived
from human nature.

positioning in the later so-called Euthyphro problem.[66] Hesiod's gods have, however, a more complex relationship to normativity—not only are they also meant to obey rules (*themis*), they also found these rules in part.

In the *Theogony*, Dike is introduced as the daughter of Themis, of law and custom: together with Zeus, Themis brings forth Eunomia, Dike, and Eirene, that is, Good Order, Justice, and Peace (lines 901–902). In the *Works and Days*, Dike is characterized as the opposite to *hybris*; it includes everything that is morally right. Hesiod is constantly moving between Dike as a person and a concept; a semi-personification in the nebulousness between abstraction and godliness.[67]

Furthermore, we seem to deal with two different understandings of Dike: in *Works and Days*, lines 37–40, we read that when dividing their inheritance, Perseus took more than his share and then bribed the "gift-eating" kings at court, who were happy to lay down the law (*dikên dikazô*) in the sense Perseus wanted. Hesiod characterizes what is spoken at court as the outcome of bribery.[68] Accordingly, what we can understand as the human legal realm, and thus human Dike, seems to be separable from true or divine Dike.[69] And human Dike seems to

[66] The problem whether something is good or pious because the gods or god have declared it to be such or whether the gods declared something to be good or pious because this is the way it is, named after its prominent occurrence in Plato's *Euthyphro*.

[67] See also West 1978 ad line 224, who takes Dike as a good example for Hesiod's free combination of personifying and non-personifying language. Accordingly, it is difficult to decide in each case whether to use a small or a capital letter for this word; I have decided simply to use a capital letter in all instances. Miller (2018, 218–219) is right to emphasize that we see a lot of de-anthropomorphizing in Hesiod as he "shifts focus from the familiar personifications of the structures of nature to these structures themselves." However, there are also passages like line 255 in his *Works and Days*, where Hesiod calls Dike a virgin and thus clearly treats her as a person.

[68] By contrast, in the *Theogony*, lines 85–86, we are presented with kings who are influenced by the Muses and thus unerring when they speak justice.

[69] Graf and Thür (2006) take Dike to be the personification of human law "made concrete in legal pronouncements," as opposed to Themis, the divine order. However, this strict division does not fit with Hesiod's depiction of Dike in *WD* 220ff. And the natural philosophers to come emphasize Dike as preserver of cosmic laws: we find the idea of a just cosmos already explicitly in Anaximander, who claims in fr. 1 that the basic elements pay retribution to each other for their *injustice*. And Heraclitus thinks that it is Dike and the Erinyes who keep the sun in its path (B94). In Parmenides's cosmology, Dike and Necessity are the beginning and origin of all generation and motion (A37). By contrast, according to his ontology, Dike not only holds the key to the gates of the path of Day and Night (B1, line 14), but she also keeps Being fast and does not allow it to come to be or to perish.

be such that even Hesiod does not want to be just in this sense at the moment (lines 269ff.), since the more unjust person (*adikôteros*) will receive greater "justice" at the moment.[70] But Hesiod is hopeful that Zeus will not allow this for much longer, so presumably divine Dike will be the dominant force again.

In Hesiod it seems still to be left open whether this distinction reflects a right and a wrong understanding of Dike, so that whenever the human Dike does not fit the divine, this is an indication of a wrong understanding, or whether we find here a first inkling of a division that will become prominent in the fifth century, between (human) *nomos* and (divine or natural) *physis*, between humanly assigned and super-humanly given norms.[71]

In Hesiod, normativity seems to be based on the internal structure of the world, which is closely tied to the cycle of the year. Acting in accordance with this cycle—what is right to do at which time—is not only useful in order to make sure that your harvest is substantial, but also what is required of you in order to ensure you will not be a burden for others. And so Hesiod urges his contemporaries to stick to the natural or divine Dike by working in accordance with the yearly cycle laid out by him in the poem, and to keep traditional social conventions.[72]

Dike, who observes whether these norms are kept and reports to Zeus if somebody goes against them, is also named as the best thing given to human beings by the gods. As such, it gives us a share in something of the divine and distinguishes us from animals, which do not possess Dike.[73]

While human beings may try to sculpt what they call Dike to their needs, Hesiod makes it clear that some form of universal justice will balance this out: to those who chase out natural Dike (for example, by claiming something else to be Dike), evil will be brought (such as illness or starvation), while those who act justly will ultimately flourish.[74]

---

[70] In line 219ff. we hear that Horkos, the custodian of oaths, follows the crooked judgments (*dikesin*) when greedy men drag Dike around.

[71] In *Theogony* line 66, the Muses sing about the *nomos* of all things.

[72] From line 212 onward we get an explanation of how to relate to Dike and avoid *hybris*.

[73] Even if following the yearly cycle also implies adapting to the weather, seasons, and other natural phenomena, which to some degree animals can do.

[74] Zeus will prevent them from being confronted with a war, and the Earth will carry plenty of fruit; lines 222ff.

Accordingly, whoever misbehaves morally prepares bad things for herself.[75]

The general claim of Hesiod—which in the very form Hesiod gave it has become a commonplace—is that the road to vice is smooth, while the immortal gods have put sweat before achieving excellence.[76] The further idea that the path to *becoming* good is hard, but once one has set out on this path, *being* good is easy, has been taken up and varied in the poet Simonides. And both Hesiod's and Simonides's versions are examined in Plato's *Protagoras* (339aff.), which discusses in detail whether it is at all possible for human beings to *be* good, or whether *becoming* good for a short time is all that is achievable.[77] Hesiod seems confident that human beings can become and be good. It is, however, hard to achieve, and so he presents his *Works and Days* as a guide to moral progress in the midst of moral decline.

Philosophy displays some proudness about its "children," i.e., about fields that originally belonged to philosophy, but at some point became independent sciences. It should, however, also not forget about its "parents" in wisdom literature and nonfiction writing that we find for the first time in Western thought in Hesiod's two poems.[78]

Bibliography

Arrighetti, Graziano (2006). Theogony. In Hubert C. and Helmuth S. (eds.), *Brill's New Pauly*, English Edition by Christine F. Salazar. Leiden: Brill. (http://dx.doi.org/10.1163/1574-9347_bnp_e1208970).

Boys-Stones, George, and Haubold, Johannes (2010). *Plato and Hesiod*. Oxford: Oxford University Press.

Diels, Hermann, and Kranz, Walter (1954). *Die Fragmente der Vorsokratiker*, 5th ed. Berlin: Weidmann.

Clay, Diskin (1992). The World of Hesiod. *Ramus* 21: 131–155.

---

[75] Line 264. Accordingly, Perseus is asked to make sure he listens to Dike, he renounces violence (lines 274) and works hard to feed himself, rather than come begging to Hesiod (395).

[76] Lines 289–292.

[77] *Republic* 364c–d also quotes the first part of these lines, and *Laws* IV, 718e–719a the second part.

[78] I want to thank Sarah Broadie, Michael Della Rocca, Arnaud Macé, and Eric Schliesser for useful comments on this chapter.

Graf, Fritz, and Thür, Gerhard (2006). Dike. In Hubert C. and Helmuth S. (eds.), *Brill's New Pauly*, English Edition by Christine F. Salazar. Leiden: Brill. (http://dx.doi.org/10.1163/1574-9347_bnp_e317890).

Havelock, Eric A. (1982). *Preface to Plato*. Cambridge, MA: Harvard University Press.

Kirk, G. S., Raven, J. E., and Schofield, M. (eds.). (1983). *The Presocratic Philosophers*, 2nd ed. Cambridge: Cambridge University Press.

Latacz, Joachim (ed.) (1991). *Die griechische Literatur in Text und Darstellung*, Bd. I: *Archaische Periode*. Stuttgart: Reclam.

Loney, Alexander (2018). Hesiod's Temporalities. In Loney, A. C., and Scully, S. (eds.), *The Oxford Handbook of Hesiod*. Oxford: Oxford University Press, 109–124.

Miller, Mitchell (2018). The Reception of Hesiod by the Early Pre-Socratics. In Loney, A. C., and Scully, S. (eds.), *The Oxford Handbook of Hesiod*. Oxford: Oxford University Press, 207–224.

Querbach, Carl W. (1985). Hesiod's Myth of the Four Races. *The Classical Journal* 81: 1–12.

Sattler, Barbara M. (2018). Sufficient Reason in the *Phaedo* and Its Presocratic Antecedents. In Cornelli, G., Bravo, F., and Robinson, T. (eds.), *Plato's Phaedo: Selected Papers from the Eleventh Symposium Platonicum*. International Plato Studies. St. Augustin: Academia Verlag, 239–248.

Sattler, Barbara M. *Conceptions of Space in Ancient Greek Thought*, monograph manuscript in preparation for Cambridge University Press for the series *Key Themes in Ancient Philosophy*.

Sattler, Barbara M. *Ancient Notions of Time from Homer to Plato*, monograph manuscript.

Schadewaldt, Wolfgang. (1978). *Anfänge der Philosophie bei den Griechen*. Frankfurt am Main: Suhrkamp.

Strauss Clay, Jenny. (2003). *Hesiod's Cosmos*. Cambridge: Cambridge University Press.

West, Martin L. (1966). *Hesiod Theogony*, ed. with Prolegomena and Commentary. Oxford: Oxford University Press.

West, Martin L. (1978). *Hesiod Works and Days*, ed. with Prolegomena and Commentary. Oxford: Oxford University Press.

2

Zhuangzi

Amy Olberding

Like many early Chinese texts, the *Zhuangzi* is titled with the name of its purported author, Master Zhuang, even as the authorship of parts of the texts is unknown.[1] Following the organizational structure outlined by Jin Dynasty scholar Guo Xiang, the text of the *Zhuangzi* is standardly divided into three sections: The "Inner Chapters" (chapters 1–7), the "Outer Chapters" (chapters 8–22), and the "Miscellaneous Chapters" (chapters 23–33). Of these, the Inner Chapters are widely considered those most likely to have been authored by Zhuangzi himself, or at least to have been authored during or near his lifetime (traditional dates, 369–298 BCE). The remaining sections blend work issuing from a Zhuangist school and largely elaborating on themes in the Inner Chapters, with work more evocative of other strains of early Chinese thinking (e.g., Primitivist, Yangist, and Syncretist elements). Classified as a "Daoist" text in the Han Dynasty (206 BCE–220 CE), the work nonetheless defies easy characterization. As A. C. Graham observes, the text is "obscure, fragmented, but pervaded by the sensation, rare in ancient literatures, of a man jotting the living thought at the moment of its inception" (Graham 1989, 48).

Little can be known with certainty about Zhuangzi, the eponymous author and the striking narrative protagonist featuring in the work. He would have lived during the Warring States period (403–221 BCE), a time of unrivaled internecine conflict in which warlords of competing

---

[1] Strictly speaking, the authorship of the text entire must be counted unknown. While long-standing convention has been to treat the Inner Chapters as authored by Zhuangzi, independently verifiable historical detail about Zhuangzi himself, detail that would vouchsafe the historical existence of the author and the persona ascribed him throughout the text, is unavailable.

Amy Olberding, Zhuangzi In: *Neglected Classics of Philosophy*. Edited by: Eric Schliesser, Oxford University Press. © Oxford University Press 2022. DOI: 10.1093/oso/9780190097196.003.0003

feudal states vied for dominance and during which philosophical activity blossomed. Unlike most of his contemporaries, Zhuangzi was comparably uninterested in discussions of political and social order, and apparently even unwilling to act as philosophers during this time most typically did. While contemporaries such as Mengzi sought to counsel rulers toward humane governance, Zhuangzi features as an iconoclast without high ambitions for political service, declining to seek position even when it is offered. The persona ascribed to Zhuangzi throughout the text foreshadows descriptions of sages that would become commonplace in Zen (Chan) Buddhism: he is unconventional in his presentation, oblique and often comedic in his comments, and, most basically, distinctively free and happy—the sort of person for whom wisdom includes much ribald joy, some hearty wisecracking, and no shortage of laughter.

At the outset, it is important to note emphatically that on any global conception of philosophy the *Zhuangzi* cannot possibly count as a *neglected* text. Moreover, to count a text neglected is already to adopt a frame for understanding it. To be sure, some philosophical texts may be generally neglected—works that simply go unread and unengaged, their insights inert upon a shelf. But the *Zhuangzi* is a text read, engaged, and indeed loved by many and for millennia. It has enjoyed generations of readers, has influenced millions, and has inspired countless philosophers. The "neglect" I seek to remediate, then, is quite specific. The *Zhuangzi* needs a Western audience— more particularly, it needs the attention of Western-trained academic philosophers.

One compelling case for such attention can be made with reference to the many and millennia for whom the *Zhuangzi* is familiar. Philosophers should, on principle, worry about the costs of ignorance when they are wholly unacquainted with material that stands as classic in philosophical traditions outside their own. But this is not the case I plan to make. Rather, I think philosophers who do not know the *Zhuangzi* are simply missing out—missing out on much that can nurture philosophical thinking of the sort we already avidly pursue, but more pointedly, missing out on an alternative exemplar of what a philosopher is and can be. As a philosopher, Zhuangzi is different in kind, both from the West's canonical exempla and, most emphatically, from the model of professional philosopher we are presently encouraged to adopt. Put plainly, what most commends the *Zhuangzi* to me is Zhuangzi himself, the narrative persona who emerges—comically, uncertainly, and playfully—from the text.[2] Here is a philosopher who declines to lodge in self-seriousness, who skewers the unrecognized vanities on which much philosophy regrettably relies, and who, above all, practices a form of philosophy that declines earnest truth-seeking in favor of playful and exultant uncertainty. Joyful philosophy is perhaps always and everywhere in short supply, but under Zhuangzi's humor and play, I think, is serious business. The serious undercurrent I find in his work is a commitment to understanding that our uncertainties and confusions are *gifts*. However, in describing Zhuangzi's philosophical orientation in an essay of this sort—an essay meant to explain what Zhuangzi is up to—I feel quite unequal to the task.

2.1. Views and Flit

One struggle in commending the *Zhuangzi* to others concerns how to accurately represent a text that not only declines to stay put, but that effectively mocks you for trying to hold it still. More fundamentally, I doubt whether it is possible to write about the *Zhuangzi* without ruining it. I sometimes fancifully think the text is akin to a butterfly. It certainly is possible to pin a butterfly inert upon a board and thereby gain a closer look at its features, but doing so not only kills the creature, it sacrifices appreciating the creature's movement and flight. Such is to say that Zhuangzi *flits*, but to write about Zhuangzi is to pin him down. One must assign him views that, once wrought in academic language and committed to paper, take on the staid and stable quality we expect of "views." To be sure, Zhuangzi does *have* views—perhaps even many. I'm just not sure that they are what he is *about*, much less that any of them count as stable. I can't convince myself that any of his views

---

[2] In describing the text as I do here, I largely look to the Inner Chapters and to those parts outside them that offer a vivid depiction of Zhuangzi, qua philosopher and narrative persona. All citations of the *Zhuangzi* given here are from A. C. Graham's translation: *Chuang Tzu: The Inner Chapters* (Indianapolis, IN: Hackett, 1989).

amounts to more than a branch upon which a butterfly might alight for a restful moment before again flitting off.

Zhuangzi himself, it must be noted, was once not entirely sure he was a man, not butterfly:

> Once, Zhuang Zhou dreamt he was a butterfly, a fluttering butterfly, doing as he pleased, unaware of Zhou. He suddenly awakened, solidly, evidently Zhou. But he didn't know: was it that Zhou dreamt he was a butterfly, or that the butterfly was dreaming he was Zhou? Thus, between Zhou and the butterfly a differentiation had surely come about: this is what is called the transformation of things. (Graham 1989, 61)

This passage has invited multiple scholarly interpretations, interpretations that target its epistemological implications, but given that the passage, offered in its entirety here, is so brief, my temptation is to see it as Zhuangzi alighting on a thought and then flitting away. At the very least, Zhuangzi does not evince the all-too-common philosophical impulse to greet ambiguity with a resolve to *sort things out*, to establish a boundary between real and dreamt, or to articulate the conditions for separating knowledge from fancy. Here and throughout the text, Zhuangzi appears content to rest and even to revel in uncertainty. But how exactly ought a philosopher interpret such a posture? This is my trouble.

Between myself and the writer of this essay, a differentiation has surely come about. To be sure, I am neither asleep nor a butterfly, but I here write as an academic philosopher about a text I most appreciate as a person. This differentiation between philosopher and person does not register as happy flit but heavy affliction. The philosopher ought to commend this text with sense. She should show you its ideas and its method, for these are what you will first find novel. There are claims to make that likely ought to here be made: Zhuangzi offers epistemological insight that would likely profit those interested in the nature and limits of skepticism, relativism, and even anti-rationalism.[3] He

---

[3] A helpful overview of several interpretations is given in Steven Coutinho, Conceptual Analyses of the *Zhuangzi*, in Liu Xiaogan (ed.), *Dao Companion to Daoist*

also incisively observes how pushing for good and worthy outcomes—
be they moral, intellectual, or personal—can be so self-defeating.[4] In
this, he seems to draw a bead on targets we too often miss, our failures
to notice how efforts conspicuous and deliberate so often undermine
our getting what we want. I should likely note as well that Zhuangzi
is uncommonly insightful about death—like Lucretius but without
the haunting sadness, Seneca without a Roman's bizarre fascination
for the martial and austere, Montaigne but much funnier, a Socrates
content to lose an argument, even one against a human skull. I should
also likely write of emulation and imagination, of what it means when
one with intellect seeks to be like one without.[5] Zhuangzi would have
us look to birds and beasts, to trees and wind, for leads on what well-
being may just mean. There are also things to say about both the prosaic and sublime, about, say, what friendship is or what reality itself
may be—though which should count as prosaic and which as sublime
is an issue not well sorted out. Best to talk that over with some friends,
I expect Zhuangzi himself might say.[6] A philosopher should detail all
of this, and surely more besides. Yet the text itself, and Zhuangzi as
the figure cut all through it, seems to ask both more and less than this.
These are things for philosophers, but Zhuangzi rather openly defies
our special arts, even as he will at times employ them. The academic
philosopher in me could find in this frustration, but the person in me
likes it and finds in Zhuangzi welcome respite. For here at last is a philosopher who doesn't really want to be one. I think that there are not
enough of those around.

Philosophy (New York: Springer, 2015), 159–191. See also the rich discussion of interpretive possibilities in Paul Kjellberg and Philip J. Ivanhoe, eds., *Essays on Skepticism,
Relativism, and Ethics in the Zhuangzi* (Albany: State University of New York Press,
1996); and Scott Cook, ed., *Hiding the World in the World: Uneven Discourses on the
Zhuangzi* (Albany: State University of New York Press, 2003).

[4] For an accessible, focused presentation of this aspect of Zhuangzi, see Edward
Slingerland, *Trying Not to Try: The Art and Science of Spontaneity* (New York: Crown,
2014), especially chapters 1, 2, and 6.

[5] See, e.g., Ian Kidd, Following the Way of Heaven: Exemplarism, Emulation, and
Daoism, *Journal of the American Philosophical Association* (2019) 6(1): 1–15.

[6] Albert Galvany, Distorting the Rule of Seriousness: Laughter, Death and Friendship
in the *Zhuangzi, Dao* 8 (2009): 49–59.

2.2. Uselessness Has Its Uses

As philosophers we are pitched for finding truth and for disputation as a way to get us there. Zhuangzi appears not just skeptical but dismayed by both. He comprehends them as a trap in which we may get caught: "You and I having been made to argue over alternatives, if it is you not I that wins, is it really you who are on to it, I who am not? If it is I not you that wins, is it really I who am on to it, you who are not? Is one of us on to it and the other of us not? Or are both of us on to it and both of us not?" (Graham 1989, 60). He notes that we might find a third party to help us sort ourselves into resolution and shared conclusion. But this too is prey to how we align ourselves on sides—if we find one who agrees with me, I will "win" our disputation, but will I know I'm right? I may be inclined to think I am, but this is an error or at least an artifact of selection, one most plainly seen where the third party to whom we appeal agrees with you. Zhuangzi seems here to say plainly something we may often notice but rarely mention, the way that our disputations turn on us and against any truth we hope to find. We seek out and heed those who answer us with approval, avoid and distrust those who do not. This can foul our efforts to think better by thinking together, as we will not hear or heed those not inclined to favor us and what we already think. Win or lose, disputation can seem to leave almost all intact, as was and unimproved. But over and above this obvious style of human failing is a kind of deeper fog that settles heavy over disputation as a method.

Sometimes when I am with philosophers, the person under my professional persona ruptures my complacency and upsets my contentment with a life of argument hashed out endlessly and ever inconclusively across our interactions. The person in me recalls a bit of Zhuangzi then: "Is it not sad how we and other things go on stroking or jostling each other, in a race ahead like a gallop which nothing can stop? How can we fail to regret that we labor all our lives without seeing success, wear ourselves out with toil in ignorance of where we shall end?" (Graham 1989, 51). At my worst, I hear him whisper, "Is [human] life really as stupid as this? Or is it that I am the only stupid one, and there are others not so stupid?" The practice of our disputations has a bathetic effect. It is too often all vigor and energy, competition and intellectual agon, but productive of little more than itself as spectacle. This is a defeated thought, of course, and if it were all that Zhuangzi offered, he could simply join the skeptics or those who would have us better take up more useful trades, like welding. But it is leavened everywhere with lightness.

In a dispute with his friend and the philosopher Huizi over whether some fish they see are happy, Zhuangzi gamely engages, each poking the other with quick wit and riposte, until Zhuangzi ends their conversation with a joke (Graham 1989, 123). If you will stand with a good friend, gazing at a river where fish cavort, there may come a time but to enjoy it. The company of neither friends nor fish should be wasted, so sorting out the experience of fish can likely wait. Indeed, Zhuangzi's original assertion that the fish are happy may have been but a remark on the entirety of the scene, on what it's like to stand atop a bridge, astride a flowing river with a friend, and on a day that's fine—as this is happy, perhaps we may as well, in an infection of a pleasant mood, call the fish below us happy too. Zhuangzi's and Huizi's argument over the happiness of fish has no real conclusion, but neither might we want decisive endings when talking with our friends. Talk and experience are instead the thing, and if our talk becomes a little whimsical, we may enjoy it even more. Huizi is sometimes wont to lament that Zhuangzi's talk, fanciful and full of ambiguity, is useless. It is talk that doesn't lead to knowledge, and we might even call it stupid. But Zhuangzi would be well with that, content with the description. For Zhuangzi offers no route to lead us out of stupid. Instead, he seems to seek to sacralize the stupid. The stupid, to be sure, is far less useful than the smart, but perhaps the really clever thing is to see that uselessness has its uses.

One of the finer stories in the *Zhuangzi* concerns a tree that is of no use for timbering (Graham 1989, 72–73).[7] The tree is derided as knotty where it is not gnarly, its wood resistant to any plane or plumb line. But because of this the carpenters will scorn it and it is left to reach

---

[7] Two other discussions of "useless" trees are found in the *Zhuangzi*. In the "Inner Chapters," Huizi compares Zhuangzi's talk to a useless tree (Graham 1989, 47) and in chapter 20 (Graham 1989, 121), Zhuangzi remarks on the longevity of a "useless" tree and is queried about his own apparent inconsistency in lauding the useless.

maturity, growing unmolested and unbothered by its "failure" to be useful. The power of this story spins in several "useful" directions. It is most basically a remark on Zhuangzi's time, an age of war in which those who sought to be of use could end up mercilessly cut down, a case for some retraction from a violent, chaotic world one cannot change. Zhuangzi himself, presented with a chance to be "of use" in political service, resolves that he would prefer to be a tortoise dragging his tail in the mud (Graham 1989, 123). Better an earthy "low" existence than a "higher" life cut short, certainly in happiness but maybe also in duration; better to be useless than used up. But I think this reading of the useless tree, counting it as a thing that's right because it has found a way to last, thins the story out and makes it clear where it is really not. There is here something rooted in a funny style of mere prudence and something else that's more ambitious and elusive. The prudent part is easiest to see and sort into an order.

I think of this useless tree sometimes in faculty meetings. In university life, it is easy to see the value of being a little useless, for one who is too knotty or gnarly, too unreliable or prone to shirking, will not be asked to do the service work. Competence can be the enemy of peace and freedom, and that colleague always late or never finished may be on to something that we the worthy rest have missed—he is at least unbowed by the burdens felling others. So, too, my students readily find in this the stuff to generate an arresting pause to think: What if the modern processes of certification and credential accumulation through education are but ways to get yourself cut down? Much in my students' educational atmosphere enjoins them to become useful, to consider what employers want and how to shape themselves to suit. But what if that's just a way to say: Get soft and pliable, become a person who can be planed flat and set seamlessly inside the vast structure of capitalist and bureaucratic systems? Become, in other words, a useful board, so we can better situate you among others of your type—with each nailed firmly into one fixed spot, together you can hold it all in place. These are seditious thoughts provocative of much discomfort. Can we really laud *that guy*, the colleague who never shares the work? Can we really invite the debt-ridden student to scorn the link between schooling and career? I don't think these are the point, in fact, but the point is more unsettling still.

Human social structures conspire to make us useful, and they are at their most efficacious when they forestall and block our asking, useful *for what*? Rather than engage that vexing question, we instead cast an aggrieved and weary eye upon our free-riding colleague or regretfully capitulate to the reality that those with degrees will indeed make more money in the end. In short, our thinking conforms to the traps socially and culturally set for us—it stops where the boundaries are already laid and seem most firmly fixed. We see what "useful" means and capitulate—sometimes in resentment, sometimes in caution—because the trap, the system we inhabit, affords little sight of what might lie outside it. We each become a Sisyphus condemned to roll another institutional strategic plan or semester of courses up Useful Hill, only to begin all over again and call this sorry, repetitive, and meaningless process "life," for what else could we do? Drag our tails in the mud instead? The philosopher in me sees other options here. If human life is "really as stupid as this," I could always act as critic. I could stand apart and call it all a farce, or head out beyond established bounds to seek new territories where I might find or make some meaning. That is, I could let go rolling up the stone in favor of a "useless," nihilistic idle, or I could settle into inquiry about the *truly* useful in a bid to find the rocks that I might roll with some existential authenticity and purpose. These look like ways to step outside the trap, to reject the constrictions and confinement of those things we are socially trained to call "useful." But neither these, nor any decisive command to "drag your tail in the mud," are what Zhuangzi offers, and the person in me likes him for that.

2.3. Traps and Traps

There is sometimes in the *Zhuangzi* a kind of skepticism without limit. If you see a trap and know it for a trap, then what? Beware another trap, he seems to say. This is most evident in a story the text tells of a time when Zhuangzi himself struggles with being both philosopher and person. In it, Zhuangzi is engaging in a little poaching, hoping to hunt for game where he should not (Graham 1989, 118). He spies a magpie and is caught by its air of close attention, by its vulnerability to his bow while its sights are fixed elsewhere. The magpie is arrested in its spot because it has spied a bit of prey, a mantis. The mantis is unaware of the magpie because it, in turn, has its eyes focused on prey, a cicada nearby. Zhuangzi, watching all, uneasily marvels, "It is inherent in things that they are ties to each other, that one kind calls up another." Zhuangzi then casts aside his bow just as the gamekeeper closes in on him, hurling curses in pursuit. Zhuangzi escapes to home but there descends into a gloom. "I forgot what could happen to me," he remarks. Presumably, like the magpie and the mantis, he "[forgot] at the sight of gain that [he] had a body of [his] own." He counted himself the predator when he was also prey. This story, like most told in the *Zhuangzi*, does not have a clean and tidy point, but the person in me finds in it a remark upon philosophy and what it can do to we who practice it. Put plainly, the hunt for understanding can make us miss the traps life sets for us, can make us think we are but predators when we too are also, always, prey.

Zhuangzi's glum reaction to his near capture for poaching indicates a trouble common to philosophy, or perhaps just to philosophers. Aware that the prevailing understandings of some matter are not right or true, we seek a different prospect for a new perspective, we hunt for new and better understanding. We seek the sort of thing that Zhuangzi saw, how this connects to that, how systems work and hang together in ways that, once we see them, we can say. But as Zhuangzi was when poaching, so we are with our philosophies. We are in the world and of it—we too should be uneasy just upon a sight of how things may knit together, for our sight will fail to include us in the scene. Forget this at your peril. Thus I worry at the "lesson" I derive from thinking of the useless tree. I can see that the culture's compulsory usefulness may straighten what is better bent and coercively compel us to live against our finer interests, and I can see that uselessness may have better "uses." Yet even as I see and say this, I wonder if I have landed in another trap, one made more exquisite because it vainly counts itself a kind of freedom. The worry is that I see the trap of usefulness, but fail to notice I am also in it. The predator of usefulness is on me, even as I tout the value of being a little useless. I am not being clear, so let me be less fanciful, let me talk more like a philosopher and less like a confused person.

I believe Zhuangzi is onto something with his useless, thriving tree. Being maladaptive in a system that would cut you down were you better fitted to its values promises a kind of freedom. The trouble is that we philosophers are rarely like this tree, that philosophy cannot make us into trees. We are instead the ones who announce the logic of the tree and the illogic of the system it evades. We are critics of the system and, sometimes, builders of alternative systems. We take what passes for prevailing understanding and appraise it from what purports to be a posture outside, beyond, or simply *other* than that common understanding. We are the seers of the tree, the questioners and critics, the ones to spot and to announce the false or bad or wrong in how prevailing understandings work. I suspect that this is very *useful* to those systems we would seek to flee or wreck. Every effective system that would straighten people into useful shape needs a few who will decline. The iconoclast and rebel, the seeker and explorer—these too are everywhere found in systems that forbid them or discourage the "free" or "independent" thought. Whether we philosophers decline to be of use or earnestly seek to find the truly useful, we play a useful role for the system as a whole. I think of this sometimes when I am teaching *Zhuangzi*, when I detail the seditious thoughts therein.

My students find Zhuangzi deliciously rebellious and we, all of us, then play parts long sketched within the system: youth ready to explode the verities of a system they have not yet fully joined, me the aged philosopher "corrupting" them, the way philosophers are said to do. Philosophers, we philosophers are wont to say, will *question everything* and so we do, inviting students to do likewise. It is a tale as old as Socrates, but therein lies the problem. If we really are such a challenge and trial on the system, how is it we have lasted? Unlike the tree, we don't survive so long because we are useless to the system but because we sit inside it, useful in our way. I worry our survival owes to how we act like monkeys. This at least is how I often feel as I opine in class.

Zhuangzi tells a story of a monkey keeper making feeding arrangements for his monkeys (Graham 1989, 54). The keeper tells the monkeys that in allotting them their daily nuts, he will give them three shares in the morning and four at night. The monkeys are appalled and greet this news in outrage and fierce anger. So the monkey keeper answers their objections and offers instead to give them four shares in the morning and three at night. The monkeys are delighted. Without change "either in name or in substance," the monkeys can be shifted from disapproval to approval, from rage to delight. The monkey keeper discerns that little rearrangements can keep the status quo intact. Rebellion need not be resisted or combated where it can be quieted with mild gestures, movements that simulate difference yet leave the workings of the world as is, unamended and intact. Philosophy, I think, can be like this. It can be the four in the morning and three at night that calms unease and forestalls any real refusal of the systems we inhabit. It can be the slight rearrangement of the terms on which we live, just enough to do the trick and keep us all onside, accepting of the nuts we get. This sorry thought may not well attach to a purified conception of philosophy, that heady endeavor of "seeking wisdom" we romantically imagine for ourselves. But philosophy is practiced in a world and has something like "a body of its own," one made vulnerable by how readily we forget it.

Whether we are mere critics of the system or builders of a new and better system, we philosophers find what we are, and become what we are, in the world that we, like all the rest, inhabit. Our "innovation," if such it can be called, is to make ourselves a kind of counterbalance that keeps it all from tipping over. We are, in Zhuangzi's idiom, a *that* which stands in contrast to the wider culture's *this*, offering the promise of some truth we need the inspiration of the false to see, seekers of the right cast in relief against the wrong (Graham 1989, 53ff). And this transpires in a world not well made for "loving wisdom," but in a world we may nonetheless well serve. The youth we teach are provisioned with an interlude of "seeking wisdom" that lets them "question all" before they settle, all more snugly, in their place as useful, planed flat boards. We philosophers will go on professing to refuse, our refusals written up in academic papers that even other philosophers will not read. But still, we'll tote them up on a c.v., for this is how we seek our own professional advantage—it is the magpie in our sights. We—the iconoclasts and rebels, the seekers and explorers—will tamely gather annually in hotels, each to show what each has wrought by way of this year's never quite seditious wisdom. Still, together we will manage to count ourselves as predators, not prey, and it is just this fact that has us well and truly busted in the systems we purport to bust.

The stories Zhuangzi tells and that I here relate are by now a tangled mess. We philosophers are more flat boards, but ones who imagine ourselves too gnarly to be used, we are poachers eyeing prey with a predator unseen upon us, and we are monkeys fiercely dissenting for differences in nuts that really make no difference. Or, in my own idiom, we are the aggressively nippy lapdog that believes itself a fierce pit bull—domesticated creatures that, to be sure, no one wants to pet but also never to be truly feared, just that kind of dog to make itself absurd by snarling viciously while cosseted inside a tiny sweater. This cynical, despairing diagnosis of our state is why I find it so hard to write of Zhuangzi as a philosopher would—the irony of yapping out the critique while pretending not to yap is just too much—but it is also why the person in me revels to but read him. To critique as a philosopher is to fall into another trap, a bid to stand outside the system of my own profession, as if I am not also prey to the world it sits inside and helps sustain. But thinking of all this as but a person gives me a welcome chance to own that I just feel stupid. I can see the traps, but also see that there is no way to Bartleby about them, no way to proclaim plainly and with some success that "I would prefer not to." The traps are there, and I am in them, will or no. What, then, can one do? Zhuangzi does not pretend to have an answer, and here too resides a reason to find in him relief.

Zhuangzi is a philosopher without unambiguous solutions to the problems he espies. He speaks of sages who wander out beyond the bounds, but gives no settled plan or decisive way to seek such freedom—after all, wandering is not a thing one *plans*. His sages seem instead to revel in enrichments of confusion, in the simple fact that they are cast adrift on winds beyond their ken (e.g., Graham 1989, 82). They are unbothered by doubts and decline to have "too much respect for the undoubted" (Graham 1989, 63). In short, Zhuangzi is at ease with some stupidity, and it is this that most commends him to me, for it is this I find in shortest supply among philosophers. To be sure, in our institutionalized "corruption of the youth," we will laud Socrates's style of wisdom that has us, unlike others, aware of what we do not know. So, too, most of us can likely well provide robust, well-argued disputations that would favor intellectual humility. But let's face it, all such exercises are performed well-armored, with any vulnerable, living tissue of real confusion covered over with the heavy, protective plating of *reasons*. Worst of all, our humility and unknowing are all too often *confident*, yet more intricate ways of seeming "smart"—we style our humility to be knowing and clever. This is why it is hard to find another philosopher, as stupid as oneself, with whom to share a stupid word. This is perhaps why I find Zhuangzi's extensive, wild, and muddied ruminations about how to live so enchanting. They show something of what it's like to live and revel in confusion, to be a philosopher not "practicing humility," that altogether too leaden and self-serious "virtue," but lively in uncertainty or even a little drunk with it.

2.4. Flex, Not Fix

In one passage, Zhuangzi lauds a drunk who falls from a cart (Graham 1989, 137). The drunk, he notes, does not get injured the way a sober person might because "he rides without knowing it, falls without knowing it." Alcohol makes him all looseness and flex, and because he does not pinch and brace against the fall, he is unhurt.[8] Where many of our most vexing human troubles are concerned, we could all use a little drink. More exactly, we need less to brace ourselves with settled answers or studied ways to live than to find the flex that comes from drinking deep our own uncertainties. Though it is shot all through the text, Zhuangzi seems to model this most clearly when he turns to talk of death.

The standard scholarly philosophical picture would hold that Zhuangzi offers an account of death that counsels us against its badness, that he encourages an appreciation of death as a phenomenon unsevered from life and from the natural processes that we prize and indeed require if we are to access what we like in life.[9] But here is the trouble with making scholarly philosophical pictures of Zhuangzi's views: while this may serve as an adequate academic summary of

---

[8] Edward Slingerland offers a useful discussion of this passage with respect to *wuwei*, or effortless action, in Slingerland, *Trying Not to Try*, chapter 2.

[9] For an academic presentation of the tensions and apparent inconsistencies in Zhuangzi's views of death, see Amy Olberding, Sorrow and the Sage: Grief in the *Zhuangzi, Dao: A Journal of Comparative Philosophy* 6(4) (2007): 339–359.

"views" the text contains, in truth the text careens wildly. It has scenes of ribald, comic joy in dying that will shock and scenes to break one's heart with grief, and never does it say how all these scenes align together. Zhuangzi lauds as sages those who greet the deaths of friends with jokes and even some who sing merrily aside a dead friend's corpse (Graham 1989, 87–91). Even so, Zhuangzi passes the grave of his own dead friend, Huizi, in deep, abiding melancholy that they can no longer share a word. Zhuangzi standing next to Huizi's grave is the loneliest of men, a man bereft of joke or song because he is bereft of friend (Graham 1989, 124). Zhuangzi also speaks of his own wife's death by comparing it to a natural season that has passed, yet another turning in the lovely cyclic way of things (Graham 1989, 123–124). But he also says that when she died, he of course cried and wailed, as if sorrow was the only thing to feel. He largely rejects mourning and perhaps even burial itself, suggesting his students leave his corpse open to the air for birds to eat, rather than the more usual style that favors worms (Graham 1989, 125). But he also offers high praise for a fellow, Mengsun Cai, renowned for mourning well and in a wash of tears in a culture that would prize such practices (Graham 1989, 90). Mengsun Cai cries without real feeling but sometimes, Zhuangzi here suggests, one really ought to go along, just do as others do. In short, where action guidance is concerned, Zhuangzi is what most would call *inconsistent*.

There are ways to sort Zhuangzi's talk of death into a kind of order— to give to all the stories sense and purpose—but when we do this, we do it without Zhuangzi, for he declines to offer order, declines to settle on what is best to do. To the key questions on hand in all his talk of death—Should I find death a sorrow? Should I grieve my dead? Should I instead react to loss with joy or even joking?—he seems to offer an ambiguous, "Well, you could that." Yet lurking alongside a claim like this is also the addendum, "But you could also do something else." You could weep, or you could joke; you could mourn in the common ways that people do, or you could sing a jaunty tune; you could be haunted by a lonely thought, or you could celebrate the unsteady stuff of change. The options accumulate as a kind of catalog of maybe. Here then, I think, is the drunkard's flex, the uncertain sacralization of the stupid as a kind of looseness.

Zhuangzi looks like nothing so much as someone who is not settled on a single course, someone who never settles on the way because the ways will be as many as the circumstances that give rise to them. Ease with death and ease with our not knowing means never quite deciding on a course. The answer seems to be to have fewer settled answers, to not pin your life to ever seeking answers but instead allow yourself to wander around without them, to flit and see instead what this turns up. I expect that if we struggle for a "message" or a "point" in the text entire, it will look like this, like an abandonment of "messages" and of "points." And this is why the text can offer much to philosophers who would also and at once be people.

I am not a Zhuangist. I neither finally accept the "ways" that Zhuangzi offers, nor am I convinced by all he says. I am not inclined to practice philosophy as he does. I have, in short, objections. But I likewise find nowhere much to go with them. They too are not the point. Instead, Zhuangzi operates akin to friend, the one to whom one can carry disenchantment and disappointment in expectation of relief. Zhuangzi is sometimes called therapeutic, his joyful and lighthearted skepticism working as a sort of balm where hunts for certainty have done their worst.[10] Perhaps more basically than this, where ordinary life is concerned, Zhuangzi's catalog of "maybes" is a help. The human condition is irreducibly imperfect and, really, just a mess. It is so often doggedly confusing—not a thing to solve or to sort out with any fiercely reductive rigor. Where other philosophers have seen this, no others seem to celebrate it, to make it in fact the thing modeled in philosophy itself. The standard philosophical impulse—that compulsion to sort things out and lend them sense and order—is not an impulse I can always like. It is too often spare and mean in the enriching chaos of a life that one must live in some, and often great, confusion. Philosophy too often does not want us well with our confusions. Philosophy is too often fix when we need flex. It wants us smart, not stupid, but Zhuangzi lets me see this as the failing that it is. Zhuangzi makes me helpfully suspicious of myself, of all that I may be missing—even and *especially* when I am seeking to miss nothing, which is to say when I am being

---

[10] See, e.g., Lisa Raphals, Skeptical Strategies in the *Zhuangzi* and *Theaetetus*, *Philosophy East and West* 44(3) (1994): 501-526..

a philosopher. If I must be a philosopher, best to be reluctant and a bit unwilling with it. Best not to be too smart. To be stupid is, at least sometimes, what it means to be awake, to be alive. Perhaps it is in fact when we are at our best, if we could but learn to enjoy it.

Bibliography

Cook, Scott (ed.) (2003). *Hiding the World in the World: Uneven Discourses on the Zhuangzi*. Albany: State University of New York Press.

Coutinho, Steve (2015). Conceptual Analyses of the *Zhuangzi*. In Liu Xiaogan (ed.), *Dao Companion to Daoist Philosophy*. New York: Springer, 159–191.

Galvany, Albert (2009). Distorting the Rule of Seriousness: Laughter, Death and Friendship in the *Zhuangzi*. *Dao: A Journal of Comparative Philosophy* 8(1): 49–59.

Graham, A. C. (1989). *Chuang Tzu: The Inner Chapters*. Indianapolis, IN: Hackett.

Kidd, Ian (2019). Following the Way of Heaven: Exemplarism, Emulation, and Daoism. *Journal of the American Philosophical Association* 6(1): 1–15.

Kjellberg, Paul, and Ivanhoe, Philip J. (eds.) (1996). *Essays on Skepticism, Relativism, and Ethics in the Zhuangzi*. Albany: State University of New York Press.

Olberding, Amy (2007). Sorrow and the Sage: Grief in the *Zhuangzi*. *Dao: A Journal of Comparative Philosophy* 6(4): 339–359.

Raphals, Lisa (1994). Skeptical Strategies in the *Zhuangzi and Theaetetus*. *Philosophy East and West* 44(3): 501–526.

Slingerland, Edward. (2014). *Trying Not to Try: The Art and Science of Spontaneity*. New York: Crown.

3

Vasubandhu's *Viṃśatikākārikā*

Bryce Huebner

The *Treatise in Twenty Verses* (*Viṃśatikākārikā*) is a wild philosophical ride.[*] Over the course of just fifteen pages of translated text,
Vasubandhu explores numerous questions about perception, memory,
and causation; he argues that mereological simples do not provide a
plausible basis for metaphysical theorizing; and he attempts to demonstrate that our understanding of our own minds, as well as our attempts
to understand other minds, tends to reflect deep patterns of metaphysical confusion. The arguments for these claims are often complex. But
they always proceed in an analytical fashion, providing support for
contentious claims as well as responses to potential objections. Many
of these arguments will feel familiar to people who work within the
traditions that dominate European and North American philosophy
departments. But many of them explore metaphysical and phenomenological questions that are more distantly related to the concerns
that have commonly motivated philosophers working within these
traditions. For example, Vasubandhu appeals to karmic processes, and
to worlds populated by hell beings and hungry ghosts. And getting a
handle on these arguments requires learning to think differently about
philosophical claims. This can be a lot of fun, and it can help to open up
possibilities that are rarely explored in European and North American
philosophy departments.

That said, I will not offer a close reading of the *Treatise in Twenty
Verses* in this chapter, as the exploration of this text is more than half
the fun. Instead, I will attempt to guide readers who are not familiar

[*] I would like to thanks Eyal Aviv, Genevieve Hayman, and Sonam Kachru for many
helpful discussions of Vasubandhu's philosophical project; and I would like to thank
Ruth Kramer for numerous helpful comments on the claims that I make in this paper.

Bryce Huebner, *Vasubandhu's* Vimśatikākārikā In: *Neglected Classics of Philosophy*. Edited by:
Eric Schliesser, Oxford University Press. © Oxford University Press 2022.
DOI: 10.1093/oso/9780190097196.003.0004

with this text toward some of the interesting insights that emerge in thinking *with Vasubandhu* about the possibility that neither our epistemic nor conceptual practices reveal a world of persisting and determinate objects. As I read Vasubandhu, he seems to have held that people encounter the world from a partial and distorted perspective, which leads them to treat complex networks of causal phenomena as persisting subjects and determinate objects. He also seems to have held that differences in people's habits and histories lead them to experience the world differently; and he argued that our categorical understanding of the world obscures this fact, leading us to impose a concrete structure on experience, which extends far beyond what actually exists. Finally, Vasubandhu seems to have thought that *saying* anything about the non-conceptual structure of the world would impose distortions that would end up being difficult to unseat. I thus read him as defending a kind of quietist non-realism (compare Ram-Prasad 2013), and as disrupting the assumption that there are necessary connections between the world we experience conceptually, and the world that exists independently of our conceptualizations.

I will explore the implications of adopting this perspective through the lens of the *Treatise in Twenty Verses* in this chapter. But since many readers of this book will be unfamiliar with the work of Vasubandhu, it will help to say just a bit about who he was, and why he we should all pay more attention to his work. Here too, however, I want to suggest that our understanding of who Vasubandhu was is likely to reflect epistemic and conceptual practices that impose more structure than is actually available to us—so this introduction to Vasubandhu also helps to make one of the core points that I want to discuss in this chapter.

3.1. Who Was Vasubandhu?

The accounts of Vasubandhu's life that are preserved in Chinese and Tibetan texts suggest that he was a Buddhist monk from Gandhāra, who wrote during the fourth and fifth centuries CE (see Gold 2014, ch. 1). As a young monk, he learned the basics of the Vaibhāṣika-Sarvāstivāda system. But he was a voracious student, and he traveled to Kashmir to learn from the masters of this system. After several years of studying with them, he returned to Gandhāra, and began to lecture on all of the things he had learned—including the path to liberation, the nature and status of mental events, and the persistence of entities across time. He was an incredibly successful teacher, but his success was not without stress. The Kashmiri masters had not authorized him to teach, and they became very angry. But they quickly forgave him when they read his masterful summary of their system: *Verses on the Treasury of the Abhidharma* (*Abhidharmakośakārikā*). Vasubandhu's text became the focus of intense discussion and scrutiny, earning him an important place in the history of Buddhist philosophy.

But Vasubandhu was more concerned with getting things right than with winning approval. And his growing discomfort with the Vaibhāṣika system led him to compose a multi-volume commentary (*Abhidharmakośabhāsya*), which presented a robust overview and analysis of numerous different schools of Buddhist thought, and which articulated a novel philosophical framework centered on momentary events linked by chains of causal dependence. The Vaibhāṣika masters were not happy with this development. But this text has remained one of the most important texts on everything from Buddhist psychology to Buddhist ontology. Perhaps this reflects the fact that Vasubandhu was a court tutor, who needed to teach a wide variety of perspectives. Or perhaps it reflects the fact that he was a skilled debater, who took part in many public discussions of Buddhist thought (though he apparently refused repeated demands for public debate by the Vaibhāṣikas). But in any case, the depth and breadth of this text could have easily been the end of Vasubandhu's story.

Things appeared to be going beautifully for Vasubandhu. But his half-brother, Asaṅga, was becoming increasingly worried about Vasubandhu's rejection of the Mahāyāna framework, and more specifically about his rejection of the *Bodhisattvayāna* ideal of seeking liberation for the benefit of all sentient beings. Asaṅga was a meditative virtuoso, and one of the founders of the Yogācāra tradition. In his own work, Asaṅga attempted to show that conceptual experience reflects a process of cognitive construction, not an encounter with a preexisting world. Like most people who are exposed to this position, Vasubandhu was skeptical. But after studying Asaṅga's writings, and learning from Asaṅga's best students, he accepted this philosophical approach. And toward the end of his life, he wrote several polemical pieces defending the hypotheses we identify as central to Yogācāra thought, including the *Treatise in Twenty Verses*.

The texts that are attributed to Vasubandhu thus represent three distinct traditions: Vaibhāṣika, Sautrāntika, and Yogācāra. In each case, the texts display a sophisticated ability to synthesize theoretical frameworks, and to figure out where alternatives succeed and fail. But the breadth of these perspectives is incredible; it is roughly like suggesting that a single philosopher wrote all of the psychological and metaphysical texts that we ascribe to Locke, Hume, and Kant! That said, there is a high degree of theoretical unity to these texts (Gold 2014); and the story about his three conversion experiences offers a fairly plausible explanation of his development from a more realist to a more constructivist understanding of human psychology. But academic debate persists over whether the name "Vasubandhu" refers to a single philosopher, or something more like a philosophical workshop organized around a distinctive network of themes and concerns.[1]

As Maria Heim (2013, 10) suggests, attributions of authorship in Buddhist traditions were commonly made to support claims to authenticity and status, with attributions of unified authorship to multiple texts signaling that such texts could be, and should be, read together. Treating the texts that are attributed to Vasubandhu as a unified body of knowledge would have allowed subsequent philosophers to highlight specific possibilities, and to suggest specific interpretations of his arguments. But pre-modern Buddhist scholars are unlikely to have been particularly concerned with the forms of stylistic or thematic unity that worry us now. In general, appeals to historical accuracy reflect the presence of technologies for tracking and recording things, and for treating those things as permanently existing features of our world. But such assumptions would have been at odds with the concerns of the Buddhist philosophers who were thinking about the arguments that Vasubandhu made—they would have been more concerned to use specific texts to illuminate one another, in the service of pursuing individual or collective liberation.

---

[1] For recent examples of the exemplary scholarship of this domain, compare Gold 2014 and Kapstein 2018 on the *Treatise on Three Natures*.

Oral cultures often rely on historical claims to legitimate and stabilize specific claims, in ways that render them credible, and that generate more robust experiences of we-feeling (Fields and Fields 2014, 177). It is easy to forget this, given our habituated understanding of the history of philosophy. And learning to treat authorship as a status, which reflects the values and interests of people who have attributed it, is likely to require stepping back from our deeply embedded tendencies to assume that there must be a determinate person, with determinate characteristics, who wrote a particular text. But as the arguments in the *Treatise in Twenty Verses* suggest, the human tendency to hold fast to preconceived assumptions can obscure possibilities, by leading us to act in ways that further entrench habituated patterns of ignorance.

The story of Vasubandhu's life is presented within a hagiographical context, which portrays him as a teacher who cut through the distortions that had accumulated within different philosophical traditions. Likewise, the story of his development reflects an ongoing attempt to solidify a network of normative philosophical commitments, which were shared by the people who were reading these texts, and an attempt to make the relationships between these philosophical frameworks intelligible. Finally, from the perspective of the arguments that are developed in the *Treatise in Twenty Verses*, the insight that can be drawn from the story of Vasubandhu's life is that reflecting on our philosophical commitments can help us to change how we experience the world, by disclosing possibilities that have been obscured by the historical situation where we find ourselves. Put somewhat differently, in paying attention to Vasubandhu's work, we can learn new ways of representing seemingly familiar arguments, on the basis of the information that is made available to us, by engaging with specific texts, which are situated within specific theoretical frameworks.[2]

---

[2] How much of what we take ourselves to know about the philosophical heroes in European cannon is hagiographical? We may not conceive of "our" philosophers as saints or sages, but which claims stick, and which claims we remember, plausibly reflects significant biases buried deep within our discipline. We only need to look as far as the debates over the authorship of the Shakespearean canon to know that such disputes do not lie far afield.

3.2. The *Treatise in Twenty Verses*:
The Opening Gambit

Whoever Vasubandhu was, he was concerned with the complexities and ambiguities that structure our everyday understanding of the world—and he wanted to show that the world we experience is merely one way of representing things, which has been shaped by patterns of ignorance (*avidyā*) as well as habitual assumptions about what the world must be like. And as I read his Yogācāra texts, they suggest that "our subjectivities and our object-worlds are shaped through and through by the past, that there is an ego-identification with the cognitive organ such that we mistake the causes of our experience for our object world itself, rather than the forces of the past, and that these first two features are shared among a group of beings" (Brennan 2019, 285). We can see what this amounts to by considering the opening claim from the *Treatise in Twenty Verses*: everything that can be experienced as part of a world is just the presentation of content.[3] The delicious Thai food I crave, as well as the pad krapow tofu that I eat, are mere presentations (*vijñapti*). And the arguments in the *Treatise* are intended to show that speculative claims about a world existing beyond these presentations will always be explanatorily superfluous.

As Vasubandhu puts the point at the beginning of the opening verse: when we posit a world existing beyond our experience, we make the same mistake that a person with an inflamed eye would make if they claimed that the floaters in their visual field existed beyond their experience of them. This argument may seem strange, but I recently had serious allergies, which caused swelling in my left eye. For a couple of weeks, I saw floaters everywhere I went. And when I would drink coffee or tea, it would seem like they were swimming in my cup. On at least a couple of occasions, I took a second look—with my non-swollen eye—to make sure that there weren't any "things" swimming in my coffee. And since I was thinking about this chapter, I began to realize that my actions were driven by presentations of things that had no existence beyond my current experience.

---

[3] Throughout this chapter, I rely upon Silk's (2016) critical edition of the text. In-text citations refer to verse numbers in the *Treatise*.

Intriguingly, the experienced realism of such presentations can be far more pronounced than my own experience of floaters in my coffee. For example, realistic hallucinations often emerge in the context of visual impairments (Abbott et al. 2007; Schadlu et al. 2009); and there are reports of blind people who experience fully elaborated visual worlds (Jones 2018, 181ff.). Critically, Vasubandhu would probably suggest that such experiences should not be dismissed, or treated as failures of a normally functioning cognitive mechanism. He would probably interpret these phenomena as consistent with the processes that generate typical experiences, in the context of differences in embodiment, as well as differences in contextually salient information. And like many cognitive scientists, he would probably treat such experiences as further evidence that the mind can construct nonexistent phenomena in response to changes in the eye. This claim might seem strange if we assume that experience *tracks* a preexisting world. But if we understand experience as reflecting the mind's best guess about the causes of its current state, these experiences will be predictable effects of these differences in embodiment and context (Seth and Tsakiris 2018).

Of course, even if our experience of the world is just presentation of content, we will still need to explain why people with typically functioning eyes experience things differently than people with visual impairments. And we still need to explain why the world we experience typically seems to consist of preexisting spatiotemporal objects with their own causal powers. These are the issues that the next section of the text attempts to addresses.

3.3. Dreams

Across numerous philosophical traditions, dreams have been evoked to clarify the claim that minds have the capacity to construct complex networks of cognitive phenomena. So, it should come as no surprise when Vasubandhu suggests that dreams routinely depict nonexistent objects, occurring in specific places, at specific times, and possessing specific causal powers (3ab). As I read him, Vasubandhu has two reasons for appealing to dreams in this context: first, dreams reveal that the mind is able to construct the reality it encounters; and second, dreams reveal that the mind is able to model numerous different kinds of experiences within a merely virtual domain. Most dreams depict a world that is populated by objects with identifiable causal proper- ties (Windt 2015); and the dream-self is often experienced as just one self among many dream characters (Windt 2018, 7). Of course, there is substantial variability in the kinds of dreams that people experi- ence. Moreover, some dreams lack visual characteristics altogether; and there may even be dreamed experiences of formless realms, which are nonetheless witnessed from a subjective perspective (Windt et al. 2016). Each of these phenomena suggest that dreaming is a construc- tive process, which generates immersive spatiotemporal hallucinations (Windt 2015). And this is precisely what Vasubandhu wants to show with this case.

Of course, dream objects lack many of the causal powers that are displayed by apparently real objects (*Treatise* 4ab). Drinking a cup of dream coffee will not satisfy my waking thirst, and it will not in- crease my waking energy levels. Far more generally, the effects of dream behavior do not carry over directly into waking life. But there are connections between dreams and embodied experience. In light of his position as a male-identified monk, Vasubandhu found the appeal to nocturnal emissions striking in this regard.

A review of recent empirical literature, however, suggests that there are many other, more interesting ways for dreams to affect embodied agents (Windt 2018, 13–14). Experiments with lucid dreamers re- veal that eye saccades, heart rates, respiration rates, first-clenching, and twitching muscles track experienced dream activity; and targeted wake-up experiments suggest similar connections in non-lucid dreamers. More strikingly, while movement is typically inhibited during REM (rapid eye movement) sleep, people with REM beha- vior disorder (RBD) often engage in goal-directed actions that accord with their dream activities. Embodied experience also seems to shape subjective experience in dreams. Experiments using misting devices and blood pressure cuffs, for example, have shown that sensory phe- nomena are commonly incorporated into dreams as unrelated objects (e.g., waterfalls, strange shoes, or broken legs), as the mind attempts to accommodate incoming sensory information in light of whatever model it is constructing (Windt 2015, 359). Finally, phantom limbs will often be experienced in dreams for decades after the loss of a limb, but often without the unpleasant sensations that are present in waking life, and often as movable, whereas they are experienced as paralyzed in waking life (Windt 2018, 8).

Across each of these cases, the mind attempts to balance numerous factors to produce a representation of a body in a world.[4] This process yields simulations that are anchored to preexisting expectations, as well as currently available sensory information. But in the absence of robust and persistent perceptual inputs, the constraints that would usually shape perceptual expectations are relaxed (Hobson and Friston 2012; Windt 2018). This is probably why the existing data have failed to demonstrate any clear or reliable mapping between dreamed and embodied experiences; instead, what they reveal is a continuous spectrum of possibilities, ranging from coarse-grained and minimal connections, to lucid experiences, to the forms of enactment that are observed in people with RBD (Windt 2015, 378). And none of these cases displays the full range of connections between action and intention that are distinctive of waking life (Windt 2015, 379).

Still, it is clear that dreaming draws upon whatever elements happen to arise in consciousness, whether they be sensory signals from the body, memories of previous situations, or values and ideals that have been internalized over a person's life. Vasubandhu would be happy with this result. For him, the ability to represent a world is supported by a dynamic process where seeds of past experience (*bīja*) produce experimental fruit (*phala*) through a complex network of situationally and contextually relevant causes. Put differently, he seems to have held that our experience of the world reflects an ongoing dynamic process,

---

[4] There are complicated questions about the ontological status of "mind" in Vasubandhu's framework. The *Treatise in Twenty Verses* opens with the claim that everything we experience is mere presentation, and in the opening verse of the prose commentary, Vasubandhu makes it clear that this is equivalent to saying that what we experience is nothing but thought, mind, or consciousness. I take the critical upshot to be that we can't get outside of the constructed nature of experience, which is the output of various mental processes. In some Yogācāra texts, it is suggested that we can come to see our understanding of mind as merely a way of presenting things. But this opens up difficult questions about what is doing the constructing. Addressing this issue would require diving far more deeply into Yogācāra ontology than I have the space to do here—though this is an issue I intend to address in my future research.

where actions shape what we experience, and where experience shapes what we perceive, remember, and imagine. What we are typically aware of is the output of this ongoing dynamic process; and this is why we can never be directly aware of the world so long as we rely upon past experience to make sense of our current state.

Of course, Vasubandhu acknowledges differences between dreaming and waking life. And he concedes that it would only be reasonable to characterize experiences as dreamlike if they could be compared to an awakened state (*Treatise* 17cd). So in the remainder of the text, he elaborates upon the suggestion that our conceptual experience of the world is conditioned by habituated forms of ignorance—and he attempts to show that the same processes that construct dreams are operative in constructing everyday experience. For Vasubandhu the difference between waking and dreaming experience is simply that the construction of everyday experience is "reined in" by interpersonally structured networks of causes and conditions. Put much too simply, he argues that human experience is filtered through patterns of attunement to things that typically matter to humans, things that matter to the people who surround us, and things that matter to us as individuals (cf., Huebner 2018; Markus and Kitayama 2010; Todd and Manaligod 2017). And importantly, he holds that we can awaken from the shared illusions that emerge in this context.[5] While his own understanding of this claim depends upon normative commitments that readers of this chapter might not share, I think that his suggestion that we can awaken from habituated forms of ignorance is worth taking seriously (for example, see McRae 2019).

To see what this amounts to, we must turn to another of Vasubandhu's examples, which clarifies the ways in which facts about our history lead us to project problematic normative assumptions onto world. It might not be immediately obvious how Vasubandhu's claim that all pretas (hungry ghosts) experience the same world is relevant to questions about the construction of human experience. But understanding what this claim amounts to can help us understand why it is so difficult to awaken from habituated forms of ignorance.

---

[5] This should be unsurprising: "Buddha" literally means "one who woke up."

3.4. Hungry Ghosts and Hell Guardians

According to Buddhist tradition, pretas are supernatural beings that are usually invisible to us. They wander through the same realm as us, but encounter a *world* that is far more disgusting. Where we see delicious foods, they see putrid filth; where we see drinkable water, they see rivers filled with pus, urine, and feces; and where we see comfortable clothing and warm blankets, they see painful and uncomfortable materials. Vasubandhu holds that such experiences result from the fruition of morally similar actions (3bd; cf., *Petavatthu*). And this holds the key to understanding the nature of habituated ignorance. Their world, as well as their identity as pretas, has been shaped by habituated cravings; and their current form of embodiment leads these pretas to track affordances that perpetuate their own suffering. Consequently, some of them wander the world in search of food, water, and clothing, because they denied such things to others in a previous birth; and others experience insatiable urges to consume disgusting things, because they forced someone to do so in a previous birth.

This seemingly exotic example reflects Vasubandhu's suggestion that experience is always constructed by a process that is anchored to habituation (Kachru 2015; Prueitt 2018; Tzohar 2017). Critically, Vasubandhu seems to hold that: (1) humans (like pretas) are the kinds of entities that track particular kinds of affordances, on the basis of habituation to action; and (2) sharing a world is sharing such affordances, while inhabiting different worlds is a matter of tracking different affordances. As other Vaibhāṣika and Yogācāra philosophers have noted, this kind of habituation to a world is pervasive: where an ascetic sees a corpse as something to meditate upon, a lustful man experiences a desirable woman, and a dog experiences food (for discussion of this case, see Prueitt 2018; Yamabe 2003). And I contend that while we have all been born into a human realm, our understanding of what the world affords is continually shaped by social and material structures that we both create and inhabit. People are rewarded for forms of social engagement that accord with local norms, and they are criticized for acting in ways that are socially deviant. As a result, they learn to categorize information in ways that are culturally sanctioned; and since culturally deviant forms of categorization are rarely reinforced, psychological processes tend to reflect the worlds, contexts, and social systems that people are chronically immersed in (Reber and Norenzayan 2018). We see the effects of this fact across numerous social and political divides, where people seem to perceive different things when presented with identical stimuli.[6]

Yu Luo and Jiaying Zhao (2019) have found, for example, that people who identify as liberal attend to the rising phase of a temperature curve, and are more likely to give a higher estimate of global temperature change, than people who identify as conservative. More strikingly, they show that increased attention to periods of rising temperature makes liberals more willing to sign climate change petitions, and more willing to donate to environmental organizations. By contrast, conservatives are more willing to engage in such behaviors when the flat phase of a temperature graph is highlighted. In parallel, Phia Salter and colleagues (2018) have shown that there is a similar connection between the world that people experience, and the way that they conceptualize racial categories. For example, ignorance about the significant historical effects of racism leads White American students to perceive less racism in US society than the Black students at the same university (Bonam et al. 2019). In part, this is probably because presentations of Black history at majority White high schools tend to focus on individual achievements, while downplaying the significance of racial barriers (Salter and Adams, 2016). In part, this is probably a result of the patterns of socialization that lead people to adopt "colorblind" ideologies.[7] And, perhaps most critically, this is partly the result of the material structure of the spaces that people tend to

[6] As Jay Van Bavel and Andrea Pereira (2018, 213) note, "US Democrats and Republicans strongly disagree on scientific findings, such as climate change or economic issues (such that Republicans show much more optimistic economic expectations than do Democrats after the election of Donald Trump in 2016), and even on facts that have little to do with political policy, such as crowd sizes. For instance, supporters of Donald Trump were more likely than supporters of his political opponent (Hillary Clinton) or non-voters to mistakenly identify a photo of the inauguration of President Barack Obama in 2009 as being that of the Donald Trump inauguration in 2017."

[7] Both the prevalence of this term and the way that it is used unreflectively reveal another deep pattern of bias. I won't focus on this here, but I will flag the issue as just one more way in which our understanding of the world is shaped by habituated patterns of ignorance.

move through, and the ways that they tend to interact in social spaces; and in the United States, it is common for White people to primarily move through material and social environments that reflect their own interests and perspectives (Moore 2008).

Returning to the *Treatise in Twenty Verses*, things are far worse for the beings who inhabit Buddhist hells (*Treatise* 4cd; cf., Sayādaw 2016, 80ff). Here, shared forms of embodiment and habituation yield shared experiences of hell guardians. But these experiences are complete mental fabrication—according to Vasubandhu, hell guardians are impossible. Nonetheless, the experience of hell guardians is real enough to affect a hell being's ongoing suffering! This case might seem irrelevant to the current discussion. But as Barbara Fields and Karen Fields (2014) convincingly argue, the races we find it easy to perceive and track, as well as the racialized structure of the world we all inhabit, are sustained through active patterns of social ignorance. They contend that racial categories are called into existence through forms of "racecraft," which conjure racialized phenomena into existence (compare Headley 2004). While people "see" races, and treat race as a property they can possess, the experience of being a racialized subject or encountering racialized situations is the result of a dynamic process of habituation, which organizes and perpetuates numerous patterns of suffering.

We learn which racial categories to use through exposure; and in internalizing a model of the racialized landscape, it becomes easy for us to assume that we know how people are racialized, and how we should identify ourselves. There are numerous forms of ongoing social feedback that shape our understanding of space as racialized, making it easy for us to cling to assumptions about what races are. And over time, the resulting assumptions organize our understandings of ourselves, and our understanding of one another. Put bluntly, the structure of our world is the outcome of a dynamic and ongoing process, which sustains a tacit understanding of the racialized identities by providing an organizing structure for interpreting the films we watch and the books that we read in racialized or politicized terms, which anchor our biases to specific religious or cultural identities. Through this process, we internalize both an understanding of ourselves, and an understanding of our social world. And as we attempt to navigate racially structured worlds, we construct practical expectations about the people we tend to interact with.[8]

The implication is twofold: our "cultural worlds" are organized to facilitate context-specific ways of perceiving and acting in the world; and our actions in the world are organized to maintain the structure of our social context, by promoting the preferences, practices, and actions that are most consistent with our understanding of things (Salter et al. 2018). We expect some "kinds" of people to be more distant or hostile than they are—and when we do, we might interact with them in ways that evoke further discomfort. We come to expect others to be friendlier or more helpful than they are—and when people violate such expectations, we might feel confused or rejected. And from inside the resulting worldview, it will often be difficult to know which of our experiences reflect social illusions, and which reflect genuine facts about the world.

Fortunately, since such assumptions are dynamically constructed, they can also be dismantled and reconstructed. Doing so is never easy. It requires developing an embodied and habituated understanding of the assumptions that undergird our self-understanding, as well as our understanding of what is possible. Sometimes, we can do this by cultivating a richer awareness of our expectations, or by softening our tendency to assume that people possess stable and persisting character traits (Barrett and Dunne 2018; cf., Stone et al. 2010). But where ongoing forms of oppression support entrenched expectations, the production of real and lasting change is likely to require transforming the material and social structure of the world that we are attuned to. Figuring out what such changes are likely to require necessitates a search for novel ways of breaking down our reliance on "the false

---

[8] Sally Haslanger (2019, 20) worries about the cost of adopting an anti-realist approach to race. "Not only would we have to claim that our attributions of race to individuals are false, but that the historical, symbolic, explanatory, practical, and epistemic roles of race are all founded on illusion." I cannot address this worry in detail here. But I think that the Yogācāra tradition provides a way of understanding how our practical activities can be driven by illusory assumptions, which reflect habituated patterns of ignorance (for further discussion, see Huebner 2019). According to this framework, racist and racializing practices exist, and we will converge upon a representation of the world as racialized where our evolutionary histories and patterns of socialization converge—but the races we perceive will still lack the kind of existence we commonly attribute to them.

beliefs and misunderstandings that inform our everyday sense of reality" (McRae 2019, 44). And in thinking with Vasubandhu, we might develop novel tools for understanding the mechanisms that underlie racecraft and related phenomena, as we come to an embodied awareness of what it means to see that all perception is habituated hallucination, which is governed by interpersonal processes that lead people in similar social positions to hallucinate in similar ways.[9]

3.5. Merely Representations?

Against this backdrop, I contend that Vasubandu wants to make it clear that realists have a lot of work to do, if they want to demonstrate that the world of persisting subjects and objects that we typically experience is necessary to explain why experience has the characteristics it does. In the remainder of the text, he attempts to show: (1) that every *claim* we make about the world reflects an ill-fated attempt to properly characterize a dynamic flow of momentary events; (2) that stable and persisting "objects" only exist as presentations (*vijñapti*); and (3) that it would be a mistake to reify such presentations, and to suppose that such objects are necessary to support and justify our conceptual practices (Tzohar 2017, 338). Summarizing, we might say that Vasubandhu held that every claim we make about external objects depends on our history, our embodiment, and the strategies we take up in exploring the world—and there is no way to demonstrate that such explorations track a preexisting world that lies beyond our highly conceptualized experience. Indeed, even if we encountered Kantian things-in-themselves, we couldn't know that we had—and this is why we should recognize that the world "is appearances all the way down" (Daston 2019, 65).

It should come as no surprise, then, that Vasubandhu is commonly understood to be a metaphysical idealist (Carpenter 2014; Kellner and Taber; Schmithausen 2005). He might be. But his arguments appeal to embodiment, history, and intersubjective agreement; and they

---

[9] I am currently working on a book that will address some of these issues.

generate interpersonal stability without appealing to a god or an objective perspective that reveals a single correct way of describing the world. I have no idea if such a position can be made plausible; but it is an interesting suggestion, and—to the best of my knowledge—one that has yet to be explored by people working in contemporary philosophy departments.[10] Regardless of whether this hypothesis can be made to work, attempting to think it though has the potential to decenter some of the path-dependent assumptions that have structured Western idealism, while offering novel insights that go beyond what has been said in existing interpretive traditions (cf., Siderits 2019).

But maybe this is the wrong approach altogether. Perhaps Vasubandhu is an epistemological idealist (Gold 2014), or a skeptic about metaphysics (Mills 2017), or a phenomenologist (Lusthaus 2014; Garfield 2015). Whatever the case may be, a plausible understanding of his position is likely to require reshaping the way we ask and answer metaphysical questions. I think that the resulting view is something more like a kind of pan-illusionism, which holds that everyday cognition delivers a partial and distorted view of the world, which misrepresents complex networks of causal phenomena as the subjects and objects that we routinely experience. If I had a different history, or a different set of habitual dispositions, I might have even written a chapter that focused on these issues. But for now, I will leave that project to someone else (see Huebner, Kachru, and Aviv forthcoming).

3.6. What Is a Neglected Philosophical Classic?

Against this backdrop, I would like to close by asking: What makes the *Treatise in Twenty Verses* a neglected philosophical classic?[11] Buddhist philosophers and scholars of Buddhism have studied and discussed this text for roughly 1,500 years. Such discussions had an enormous impact on philosophical traditions that emerged in India, Tibet, and China; and the text continues to be discussed by numerous

---

[10] For a view that comes closer to this position, see Yetter-Chappell (2017).

[11] For further discussion of the criteria that I discuss in this paragraph, see Schliesser (2017, xxiv).

contemporary philosophers, including many who are writing in English. Someone who skillfully engaged with the style and substance of this text would be treated—at the very least—as an advanced student in Buddhist philosophy. And as I have attempted to show in this chapter, this text has the potential to capture the interest of a wider philosophical audience. In a sense, it is obvious that this text is a philosophical classic—so much so that it might seem that this chapter has had the incoherent goal of showing that a widely read and highly influential work of philosophy is also a neglected classic. But critically, the *Treatise in Twenty Verses* is rarely taught in *philosophy departments* in Europe and North America.

This is not particularly surprising. We learn which texts are part of the philosophical canon through exposure; and in internalizing a model of the philosophical landscape, it becomes easy to assume that we know which things deserve to be read and which things we can safely ignore. Numerous forms of ongoing social feedback then shape our understanding of the discipline of philosophy, making it easy to cling to our assumptions about what philosophy is and what it should be. And over time, the resulting assumptions come to organize our understandings of ourselves, and our understanding of one another *as philosophers*. The structure of our discipline is thus the outcome of a dynamic and ongoing process, which sustains a tacit understanding of the identity "academic philosopher" by providing an organizing structure for the texts we read, the arguments we take seriously, and the people we see as making interesting and valuable philosophical claims (and as readers of the text will quickly learn, this is the kind of cognitive process that is described in the *Treatise in Twenty Verses*).

Fortunately, since such assumptions are dynamically constructed, they can also be dismantled and reconstructed. Doing so will never be easy, as it will require developing a deep understanding of the impermanence of the assumptions that undergird our self-understanding as philosophers, as well as our understanding of which issues are worth taking seriously. And this will require learning how to treat the boundaries around our discipline as reflections of collective ignorance (Dotson 2013; Olberding 2017). But this is precisely the kind of path that the arguments in the *Treatise in Twenty Verses* are designed to help us along—and it is also one of the things the story of Vasubandhu's life can help us understand. I think that getting more people to read and think about this text has the potential to help us collectively discover new and interesting ways of thinking about the shape of our discipline. Indeed, existing engagements with this text suggest a way of moving toward a more cosmopolitan approach to philosophy, which has the potential to reveal novel perspectives on intriguing philosophical questions.[12] Just as critically, this text "contains many subtleties that have never been noticed, let alone discussed" (Kellner and Taber 2014, 734). Sadly, there are many complexities that I have been unable to address; but I hope that others will find ways of approaching this text from a more cosmopolitan perspective, which draws upon insights from contemporary philosophy as well as the perspectives that are present in the *Treatise in Twenty Verses*. There are good translations of the text, as well as numerous excellent secondary sources to provide insight and guidance along the way. And there is plenty of work left be done in exploring the details of this text!

Bibliography

Abbott, E. J., Connor, G. B., Artes, P. H., and Abadi, R. V. (2007). Visual Loss and Visual Hallucinations in Patients with Age-Related Macular Degeneration (Charles Bonnet Syndrome). *Investigative Ophthalmology & Visual Science*, 48(3), 1416–1423.

Barrett, L. F., and Dunne, J. (2018). Buddhists in Love. *Aeon*. https://aeon.co/essays/does-buddhist-detachment-allow-for-a-healthier-togetherness

Bonam, C. M., Nair Das, V., Coleman, B. R., and Salter, P. (2019). Ignoring History, Denying Racism: Mounting Evidence for the Marley Hypothesis and Epistemologies of Ignorance. *Social Psychological and Personality Science* 10(2): 257–265.

Brennan, J. C. (2019). A Buddhist Phenomenology of the White Mind. In McRae, E., and Yancy, G. (eds), *Buddhism and Whiteness*. Lanham, MD: Rowman & Littlefield, 277–292.

Carpenter, A. (2014). *Indian Buddhist Philosophy*. London: Routledge.

Daston, L. (2019) *Against Nature*. Cambridge, MA: MIT Press.

---

[12] For intriguing suggestions about what this might look like in this context, compare Gleig (2019), on the idea of enlightenment beyond The Enlightenment, and Thompson (2020, 165ff.) on cosmopolitanism as an alternative to Buddhist naturalism.

Dotson, K. (2013). How Is This Paper Philosophy? *Comparative Philosophy* 3(1): 121–121.

Fields, K. E., and Fields, B. J. (2014). *Racecraft*. London: Verso Trade.

Garfield, J. L. (2015). *Engaging Buddhism*. Oxford: Oxford University Press.

Gleig, A. (2019). *American Dharma*. New Haven, CT: Yale University Press.

Gold, J. (2014). *Paving the Great Way*. New York: Columbia University Press.

Haslanger, S. (2019). Tracing the Sociopolitical Reality of Race. In Glasgow, J., Haslanger, S., Jeffers, C., and Spencer, Q. (eds.), *What Is Race? Four Philosophical Views*. New York: Oxford University Press, 4–37.

Headley, Clevis. (2004). Delegitimizing the Normativity of "Whiteness": A Critical Africana Philosophical Study of the Metaphoricity of "Whiteness." In Yancy, G. (ed.), *What White Looks Like: African American Philosophers on the Whiteness Question*. New York: Routledge, 107–142.

Heim, M. (2013). *The Forerunner of All Things*. New York: Oxford University Press.

Hobson, J. A., and Friston, K. J. (2012). Waking and Dreaming Consciousness. *Progress in Neurobiology* 98(1): 82–98.

Huebner, B. (2018). Picturing, Signifying, and Attending. *Belgrade Philosophical Annual* 31: 7–40.

Huebner, B. (2019). The Interdependence and Emptiness of Whiteness. In McRae, E., and Yancy, G. (eds.), *Buddhism and Whiteness*. Lanham, MD: Rowman & Littlefield, 229–252.

Huebner, B., Kachru, S., and Aviv, A. (forthcoming). The Magic of Consciousness: Sculpting and Alternative Illusionism. In Beiweis, S. and Shani, I. (eds.), *Consciousness, Nature, and Ultimate Reality: Cross-Cultural Perspectives*. London: Bloomsbury.

Jones, A. (2018). *Beyond Vision*. Montreal: McGill-Queen's Press-MQUP.

Kachru, Sonam. 2015. *Minds and Worlds*. Ph.D. dissertation, University of Chicago.

Kapstein, M. T. (2018). Who Wrote the Trisvabhāvanirdeśa? *Journal of Indian Philosophy* 46(1): 1–30.

Kellner, B., and Taber, J. (2014). Studies in Yogācāra-Vijñānavāda Idealism I. *Asiatische Studien-Études Asiatiques* 68(3): 709–756.

Luo, Y., and Zhao, J (2019). Motivated Attention in Climate Change Perception and Action. *Frontiers in Psychology* 10: 1541. doi:10.3389/pfsyg.2019.01541

Lusthaus, D. (2014). *Buddhist Phenomenology*. London: Routledge.

Markus, H. R., and Kitayama, S. (2010). Cultures and Selves. *Perspectives on Psychological Science* 5(4): 420–430.

McRae, E. (2019). White Delusion and *Avidyā*. In McRae, E., and Yancy, G. (eds.), Buddhism and Whiteness. Lanham, MD: Rowman & Littlefield, 43–60.

Mills, E. (2017). External-World Skepticism in Classical India. *International Journal for the Study of Skepticism* 7(3): 147–172.

Moore, W. L. (2008). *Reproducing Racism*. Lanham, MD: Rowman & Littlefield.

Olberding, A. (2017). Philosophical Exclusion and Conversational Practices. *Philosophy East and West* 67(4): 1023–1038.

Prueitt, C. (2018). Karmic Imprints, Exclusion, and the Creation of the Worlds of Conventional Experience in Dharmakīrti's Thought. *Sophia* 57(2): 313–335.

Ram-Prasad, C. (2013). *Advaita Epistemology and Metaphysics*. London: Routledge.

Reber, R., and Norenzayan, A. (2018). Shared Fluency Theory of Social Cohesiveness. In Proust, J., and Fortier, M. (eds.), *Metacognitive Diversity*. Oxford: Oxford University Press, 47–67.

Salter, P. S., and Adams, G. (2016). On the Intentionality of Cultural Products. *Frontiers in Psychology* 7: 1166. doi:10.3389/fpsyg.2016.01166

Salter, P. S., Adams, G., and Perez, M. J. (2018). Racism in the Structure of Everyday Worlds: A Cultural-Psychological Perspective. *Current Directions in Psychological Science* 27(3): 150–155.

Sayādaw, Mahāsī (2016). *Manual of Insight*. Somerville, MA: Wisdom Publications.

Schliesser, E. (2017). On Being a Classic in Philosophy. In Schliesser, E. (ed.), *Ten Neglected Classics of Philosophy*. New York: Oxford University Press, xiii–xxvi.

Schmithausen, L. (2005). *On the Problem of the External World in the Ch'eng Wei Shih Lun* (Vol. 13). Tokyo: International Institute for Buddhist Studies.

Schadlu, A. P., Schadlu, R., and Shepherd, J. B. (2009). Charles Bonnet Syndrome. *Current Opinion in Ophthalmology* 20(3): 219–222.

Seth, A. K., and Tsakiris, M. (2018). Being a Beast Machine: The Somatic Basis of Conscious Selfhood. *Trends in Cognitive Sciences* 22(11): 969–981.

Siderits, M. (2019). Review of Graham Priest's *The Fifth Corner of Four: An Essay on Buddhist Metaphysics and the Catuṣkoṭi*. NDPR. https://ndpr.nd.edu/news/the-fifth-corner-of-four-an-essay-on-buddhist-metaphysics-and-the-catuskoti/.

Silk, J. A. (2016). *Materials Toward the Study of Vasubandhu's Viṁśikā*. Harvard Oriental Series. Cambridge, MA: Harvard University Press.

Stone, D., Heen, S., and Patton, B. (2010). *Difficult Conversations: How to Discuss What Matters Most*. New York: Penguin.

Thompson, E. (2020). *Why I Am Not a Buddhist*. New Haven, CT: Yale University Press.

Thera, Ven. Kiribathgoda Gnanananda. (2015). *Stories of Ghosts from the Petavatthu*. Toronto: Mahamega.

Todd, R. M., and Manaligod, M. G. (2017). Implicit Guidance of Attention. *Cortex* 30(1): e1–8.

Tzohar, R. (2017). Imagine Being a Preta. *Sophia* 56(2): 337–354.

Van Bavel, J. J., and Pereira, A. (2018). The Partisan Brain. *Trends in Cognitive Sciences* 22(3): 213–224.

Windt, J. M. (2015). *Dreaming*. Cambridge, MA: MIT Press.

Windt, J. (2018). Predictive Brains, Dreaming Selves, Sleeping Bodies. *Synthese* 195(6): 1–49. doi:10.1007/s11229-017-1525-6.

Windt, J. M., Nielsen, T., and Thompson, E. (2016). Does Consciousness Disappear in Dreamless Sleep? *Trends in Cognitive Sciences* 20(12): 871–882.

Yamabe, N. (2003). On the School Affiliation of Aśvaghoṣa. *Journal of the International Association of Buddhist Studies* 26(2): 225–254.

Yetter-Chappell, H. (2017). Idealism without God. In Goldschmidt, T., and Pearce, K. L. (eds.), *Idealism*. Oxford: Oxford University Press, 66–81.

4

Hōnen's *Senchaku-Shū*

Yumiko Inukai

Who is Hōnen? Hōnen is a Japanese Buddhist monk who founded the Pure Land ("Jōdo" in Japanese) School as an independent sect of Buddhism in Japan in the twelfth century CE, and wrote its doctrinal text, the *Senchaku Hongan Nembutsu Shū* (*Senchaku-Shū* hereafter), in which the teachings of the nembutsu (the recitation of the name of Amida Buddha, *"Namu Amida Butsu"*) are presented.[1] There is no need to argue the importance and significance of Hōnen and his *Senchaku-Shū* in the history of Japanese Buddhism. It is not amiss to say that Hōnen's insistence on the exclusive adherence to the nembutsu was revolutionary in marking the departure from the earlier teachings of Japanese Buddhism, although the basic Pure Land thoughts that focus on Amida Buddha's Original Vow and various practices involving Amida Buddha (e.g., the visualization of Amida) had been brought to Japan before Hōnen. The *Senchaku-Shū*, written in 1198, is a seminal text in which Hōnen offers the arguments for his exclusive selection of the nembutsu, and yet it has not drawn much attention from philosophers, unlike Dogen's texts. Here I discuss the ingenuity

---

[1] In the *Sutra of Immeasurable Life* (*Muryōjyu-kyō* in Japanese), Sākyamuni Buddha tells a story of a bodhisattva named Dhārmakara (*Hōzō Bosatsu* in Japanese), who would eventually become Amida Buddha. It is told that he made forty-eight vows not to enter into the final enlightenment until he created the Jōdo in which even the most sinful person would be reborn when he was still a bodhisattva. Among the forty-eight vows, the Eighteenth Vow is often called the "Original Vow" of Amida, which is the main focus of Jōdo Buddhism. The Original Vow is specifically about the nembutsu, according to which Hōzō Bosatsu would make sure, provided that he attains Buddhahood, that any sentient being will attain the rebirth in the Jōdo if they recite the nembutsu wholeheartedly. It is believed in the Pure Land thought that since Hōzō Bosatsu has already become Amida Buddha, this shows that his vows have already been fulfilled. Fulfilling his vows, Amida is believed to come to the practitioner of the nembutsu at her death to personally take her to the Jōdo, which is an immaculate realm free of any temptations and corruptions that are pervasive in our world.

Yumiko Inukai, *Hōnen's* Senchaku-Shū In: *Neglected Classics of Philosophy*. Edited by: Eric Schliesser, Oxford University Press. © Oxford University Press 2022. DOI: 10.1093/oso/9780190097196.003.0005

of Hōnen. The *Senchaku-Shū* is not just a religious text in which the primary practice of Jōdo Buddhism is expounded: rather, it is a hermeneutical text in which Hōnen provides his own interpretations of purposefully chosen passages from the principal texts of Jōdo Buddhism (i.e., *Sūtra of Immeasurable Life, Meditation Sūtra*, and *Amida Sūtra*) and comments on them in order to systematically advance and support his distinctive view and his deliberate selection of the nembutsu.

The title of the text, *Senchaku Hongan Nembutsu Shū*, literally means "Passages on the Selection of the Nembutsu in the Original Vow."[2] The text is primarily to explain reasons for *selecting*, among all other practices, the nembutsu as the only efficacious practice for all, including both monks and laypeople. Emphasizing the significance of the nembutsu being *selected* by Amida, Sākyamuni, all buddhas of the six directions, and some Pure Land scholars whom he considers as authoritative, Hōnen attempts to show that there is strong justification for the nembutsu as a right practice. While the nembutsu was *chosen*, other practices were *rejected* by those wise, adept, compassionate beings who had already gone through the variety of arduous Buddhist practices and study because its superiority was clear to them. Hōnen takes pains to explain the meaning of "select" and of Amida's selection in chapter 3, and Sākyamuni's entrustment of the nembutsu in chapter 12, of the *Senchaku-Shū*. In his response to the question of why Sākyamuni explained various practices, both contemplative and non-contemplative, when he would recommend only the nembutsu to transmit for the future, Hōnen explains that Sākyamuni had to explain all possible practices in order to reveal the superiority of the nembutsu. It would not be enough for the nembutsu to be simply recommended even by Sākyamuni as a right practice without explanation. Selecting the nembutsu and rejecting and abandoning other practices could be done only if Sākyamuni had good *reasons* to do so in comparing them. The nembutsu being *selected* over all other practices entails its being truly established as the sole practice for all. In the final chapter of

---

[2] Most of the passages quoted from the Senchaku-Shū are taken from *Hōnen's Senchakushū*, translated and edited by Senchakushū English Translation Project (Honolulu and Tokyo: University of Hawaii Press and Sōgō Bukkyō Kenkyūjo, 1998), unless indicated otherwise.

the *Senchaku-Shū*, Hōnen states, "Considering the broad intent of the three [Pure Land] sutras, I can conclude that the most fundamental notion of all is to select the nembutsu from among the many forms of practice."[3] It is of the utmost importance to Hōnen that the selection of the nembutsu and his teachings of it are all well-grounded, which is demonstrated in the structure of the *Senchaku-Shū*. Hōnen begins each chapter with quotes from the Pure Land sutras and Shan-tao's (*Zendō*) commentaries, and follows by ingeniously explaining and arguing his own views of the nembutsu, showing that his views are textually grounded. Moreover, he raises critical questions himself regarding the quoted passages to expound them even further by answering them. Hōnen thus provides reasons for his selection of the nembutsu quite systematically in the *Senchaku-Shū* with each chapter.

It is evident that Hōnen possesses solid and vast knowledge of Buddhist teachings and scriptures, on which he bases his teachings of the nembutsu. What is more interesting and intriguing, however, is that Hōnen's distinctive views of the nembutsu are more deeply grounded in the genuine convictions he arrived at through his personal experiences rather than through texts and scriptures. The reason for *his* selection of the nembutsu ultimately comes from his deep, intimate realization of his own being. Interestingly, Hōnen does not even mention his own personal experience as one of the reasons for his selection of the nembutsu at all; yet, it is clearly reflected in the psychological condition that Hōnen requires the practitioner to have for her recitation of the nembutsu to be proper and worthwhile. He maintains that the practitioner must undergo a profound psychological journey in which she first realizes herself as an incompetent, confused, ordinary person and sincerely feels hopeless and helpless to escape from this corrupt world on her own. Note that the critical self-realization is not of oneself as interdependently existing, or being merely conventionally constructed out of various components (as some other Buddhists might say about the self).[4] Rather, in Honen's teachings, it is the realization of oneself

---

[3] *Hōnen's* Senchakushū, 145.

[4] There are at least three key ideas that most of the Buddhist philosophers hold with regard to the "self," although the details of their views may not be exactly the same. They are: (1) the self lacks substantiality or independent/intrinsic existence; (2) the self has something to do with an aggregate made up of the processes that involve five

merely as the *human*, understood as a being who is filled with desires, attachments, and destructive emotions, lacking sufficient capacities to eliminate them by her effort. This genuine self-realization is the necessary first step for the practitioner to begin to recite the nembutsu properly. Thus, for Hōnen, the efficacy of the nembutsu is not derived merely from Amida's grace and compassion. A close reading of the *Senchaku-Shū* reveals that Hōnen's nembutsu is not a simple recitation of the name of Amida Buddha. It requires specific conditions of the practitioner's inner states and involves a psychological process, ultimately effecting the spiritual transformation of her*self*. The ingenuity of Hōnen's teachings of the nembutsu in the *Senchaku-Shū* is that refraining from directly and explicitly urging practitioners to focus on the psychological components, he offers a seemingly easy, simple method any person could use to achieve what Dōgen famously says in *Genjōkōan*: "To study the Buddha Way is to study the self. To study the self is to forget the self."[5]

My purpose in this chapter is not to show the significance and relevance of Hōnen's arguments and ideas to contemporary philosophy. Rather, it is to show how intriguing and astute Hōnen is, especially with regard to his sole endorsement of the nembutsu and his insight into its psychological implications. My aim is twofold: I show (1) how Hōnen's teachings of the nembutsu are informed by his personal experience of himself, and (2) that Hōnen places much weight on the psychological process of the nembutsu practitioner and that this psychological process is in fact a process in which the practitioner's sense of the *self* becomes transformed to the point where she "forgets herself," which is

elements—material form, consciousness, sensation, perception, and volition; and (3) an aggregate cannot be considered as a unitary, singular entity. In a Pali canon, "The Questions of King Milinda" (*Milindapañha*), questions of the self are posed and discussed in the conversation between a monk, Nāgasena, and a king, Milinda. Nāgasena explains that the name "Nāgasena" is just a useful, practical denotation, which, nonetheless, is related to the five aggregates in some way. Later Buddhist philosophers came to different views about how the referent of the name relates to the five aggregates, how *real* the referent of the name may be considered, etc., and began to make a finer distinction between the concept of the "self" and the concept of the "person." For extensive discussions of the Buddhist ideas of the self/person, see Siderits, *Personal Identity and Buddhist Philosophy: Empty Person* (London: Routledge, 2015).

[5] Dōgen, *Genjōkōan*, trans. Bret W. Davis, in Edelglass, W., and Garfield, J. L. (eds.), *Buddhist Philosophy: Essential Readings* (New York: Oxford University Press, 2000), 256

the crucial goal of various Buddhist practices after all.[6] The *Senchaku-Shū* is a text that represents the personal experiences and insights of Hōnen, who underwent very common aspects of human life: failure and disappointment. It is a text written by a genuine human for the purpose of helping all humans.

4.1. Realization of Oneself as an Ordinary Person

Hōnen goes far beyond any other Buddhist monk in his conception of the nembutsu: the nembutsu is the *only* practice that is efficacious for all people, whether they are monks or ordinary laypeople who have or have not committed any evil acts.[7] This radical endorsement of the nembutsu was the key to establishing Jōdo Buddhism as a separate, independent sect in Japan, despite various oppositions to Hōnen's distinctive views of the nembutsu from the already established Buddhist institution in Japan. Hōnen was well-known for his vast knowledge of Buddhist teachings and his ability to debate.[8] However, the strength of his conviction about the legitimacy of the nembutsu did not come merely from his intellectual acumen or firm understanding of Amida's Original Vow. It was derived from the depth of his affectively infused realization that he, Hōnen himself, could be saved only through the nembutsu: it was a profoundly *personal* conviction. It is quite interesting and illuminating to trace Hōnen's psychological journey leading up to his encounter with the Pure Land thoughts, especially those

[6] D. T. Suzuki argues for a similar point in Part II of his essay, The Koan Exercise, appearing in his *Essays in Zen Buddhism*, second series (New Delhi: Munshiram Manoharlal, 2008), 186, 192. He offers his analysis of the nembutsu in terms of the psychological transformative effect on the nembutsu practitioner, arguing that the mechanical recitation of the nembutsu could elicit some kind of psychological experience.

[7] See footnote 12 for a brief explanation of the Buddhist categorization of evil acts. Persons who have committed evil acts are called *akunin*, and the view that even *akunin*s can be saved by Amida's grace as long as they recite the nembutsu wholeheartedly prior to their death is called *Akunin-Shōki*. The notion of *Akunin-Shōki* is often attributed to Shinran, the first disciple of Hōnen, who founded the *Jōdo-Shinshū* (Shin Buddhism) in Japan. But it is undeniable that Hōnen believes that the efficacy of the nembutsu applies to *all* people, including *akunin*s.

[8] It is recorded that, in 1186, Hōnen engaged in a day-long debate with a number of Buddhist scholars, which is often called "Ōhara-dangi." It is said that at the end of the debate, they were all convinced and started to recite the nembutsu.

expounded in Zendō's commentaries. It reveals that the encounter was indeed a pivotal, transformative "conversion" experience for Hōnen, which involved a critical recognition of the nature of *himself,* shaping various aspects of his distinctive conception of the nembutsu.

There are several biographies of Hōnen,[9] which attest that he diligently and rigorously practiced and studied the precepts and scriptures of various Buddhist sects at Mount Hiei for about thirty years. Yet, he experienced what we often experience in life: failure due to his limited capacity. A dramatic episode of his realization is recorded in his disciple Benchō's commentary on the *Senchaku-Shū,* called *Tetsu Senchaku Hongan Nembutsu Shū:*

> I have realized that I have not attained a single precept in *kai-gyo,* or achieved concentration in *jyo-gyo,* or attained the right wisdom to eliminate *bonno* and realize the truth in *e-gyo.* . . . Furthermore, the mind of the *bonbu* is easily distracted by things around it like a monkey, and it is indeed scattered everywhere, easily perturbed, and unable to concentrate. How could I attain wisdom that removes *bonno*? How could I sever the fetters created by evil deeds and *bonno* without the sword of immaculate wisdom? Without severing those fetters, how could I liberate myself from the bondage of transmigration of birth and death?[10]

Kai-gyō (practice of observing precepts), *jyō-gyō* (practice of achieving concentration), and *e-gyō* (practice of attaining wisdom) comprise the Buddhist threefold practice called *Sangaku* (Three Learnings).[11] Hōnen openly confessed that he was unable to achieve even a fraction of the *Sangaku* despite his long, earnest practice and study. His mind, like a monkey, was wavering, disconcerted, and easy to be upset so that

---

[9] To name only a few, *Genkū shōnin shinikki* (before 1256), *Daigobon Hōnen shōnin denki* (circa 1242), and *Chionkōshiki* (circa 1224).

[10] *Jōdo-shū Seiten,* edited by Jōdo-shū Seiten Kankō Iinkai (Tokyo: Jōdo-shū Shuppan, 2009), vol. 3, 284; my translation.

[11] Sangaku encompasses the Eight-Fold Path, which is the fourth of the Four Noble Truths that are believed to be the Buddha's first teachings right after his enlightenment. The Eight-Fold Path comprises right speech, right conduct, right livelihood (*kai-gyō*), right effort, right mindfulness, right concentration (*jyō-gyō*), right view, and right resolve (*e-gyō*).

it could not settle itself (failing in *jyō-gyō*). Without being able to concentrate in the mind, he could not attain wisdom to remove passions and desires that block his liberation (failing in *e-gyō*). He still therefore remained an ignorant person who is likely to commit "evil deeds" by being motivated by self-serving desires and reactive emotions (*bonno*) (failing in *kai-gyō*).[12] Failing in all the three aspects of the Buddhist practice, he realized he was just an ordinary person (*bonbu*) after all.

The Japanese term *bonbu* refers to an ordinary human in Hōnen's teachings, as well as in Buddhism in general, in contradistinction to *shō-nin*, referring to a master who has achieved wisdom and virtue. We all are basically *bonbus*, who are filled with desires, attachments, aversions, and various reactive emotions like anger and jealousy (*bonno*), which all relate to what Buddhists consider ignorance, or "primary confusion," as Garfield aptly calls it.[13] *Bonno* points to the affective aspects of the human. Buddhism tends to underscore *bonno* as distinctively human characteristics, and they are taken to be the fundamental causes of our suffering. The existence of rationality in human beings is not denied, but it is generally argued in Buddhism that the root of *bonno* is one's ignorance of the true nature of things in the world, including oneself. Thus, *bonbu* is an ordinary human who is ignorant and thereby governed by desires, attachments, and emotions, and this is exactly how Hōnen ended up recognizing himself, despite his extensive, intense practice.[14]

---

[12] In Buddhism, "evil deeds" are sometimes categorized into two groups: (1) five deadly transgressions (*go-gyakuzai*), and (2) ten evil actions (*jyū-aku*). Five deadly transgressions include: matricide, patricide, killing an arhat, injuring a buddha, and causing schism in the Buddhist community. Ten evil actions include: killing, stealing, sexual misconduct, lying, slandering, harsh speech, frivolous speech, covetousness, ill will, and holding wrong views.

[13] Ignorance, or "primal confusion," in Buddhism is not just being ignorant of some truths; rather, as Garfield explains, referring to the fourteenth–fifteenth century Tibetan philosopher Tsongkhapa, it is "the positive superimposition of a characteristic on reality that it lacks" (2015, 9). Instead of seeing things as they are, that is, interdependent and impermanent, we, ordinary persons, see objects as independent and permanent with intrinsic natures in themselves, and situate ourselves in the center of a world in which those objects exist distinctly from us as well. Buddhist philosophers consider this outlook we take up as the source of *dukkha* (which is often translated as suffering and sorrow).

[14] Hōnen attributes greed, anger, and ignorance to a *bonbu* as his essential characteristics in *Shichikajō no Kishōmon* (*Seven Article Pledge*). *Shichikajō no Kishōmon* in

Recognizing the limitations of himself as a *bonbu*, Hōnen fell into despair:

How sad this is. How sad. What can I do? What can I do? Someone like me does not have what it takes to master the *Sangaku*. I have asked various wise people and visited scholars in order to find other teachings appropriate for my mind and practices feasible for me, but no one could teach or direct me.[15]

He realized that the present state of the world would not help either. It was widely acknowledged among Buddhists at this time that the current historical period was considered as the Age of the Final, Degenerate Dharma (*Mappo*), when the Buddha's teachings were already too distant and thus became quite difficult to master, and people's capability of Buddhist practices had declined greatly. As the world in which he and all other humans were already struggling and suffering was itself a corrupted one at this Age of the Final Dharma, Hōnen felt deep despair and sadness over our hopeless situations. Nonetheless, Hōnen did not give up: still seeking to find the way of salvation, "in the meantime, I entered the repository of Buddhist texts in despair and studied the sutras in grief."[16] This is exactly when he encountered the ideas of the nembutsu that were espoused in Zendō's commentary. Although he had read Zendō before, he was now convinced that the sincere and wholehearted nembutsu is the only way of liberation for himself and all *bonbu*s.

Nowhere in his anecdote did he appeal to the depth of his understanding of the efficacy of the nembutsu or the power of Amida's grace. The overwhelming despair prepared Hōnen psychologically to be able to sincerely appreciate the deep meaning of the nembutsu and its aptness as a practice for all *bonbu*s. Deeming the *Sangaku* too difficult to master due to the limitations of a *bonbu*, Hōnen *rejected* the *Sangaku* as

---

Hōnen, Nihon no Meicho, vol. 5, edited by Yoshitaka Tsukamoto (Tokyo: Chūō-kōron Sha, 1971), 245.

[15] *Jōdo-shū Seiten*, vol. 3, 284; my translation.
[16] Ibid., vol. 3, 284–285; my translation.

an inadequate and ineffective method and *selected* the nembutsu as the only efficacious practice for himself, and for all.[17]

4.2. Psychological Conditions and Transformation of the Nembutsu Practitioner

Hōnen's recognition that he was simply a *bonbu* was not merely a self-deprecating one: it was a sincere acceptance of himself as human. It is clear from his narrative that reading and understanding the Buddhist texts, as well as practicing, did not lead him to this awareness. The real failure and his agonizing despair over it were necessary to induce this recognition, which in turn brought him to the absolute faith in the grace of Amida. This is a critical point at which Hōnen practically surrenders himself to the compassionate power of Amida, instead of believing that he would be capable of achieving the "immaculate wisdom" to liberate himself by his own power. This is why the nembutsu practice is regarded as the "Other-Power" method, in contrast to the "Self-Power" method. The notion of the Other-Power method, strictly speaking, seems to go entirely against what Śākyamuni Buddha supposedly said: "you must be your own lamps, be your own refuges. Take refuge in nothing outside yourselves. Hold firm to the truth as a lamp and a refuge, and do not look for refuge to anything besides yourselves."[18] What Hōnen discovered in his struggle is exactly his inability to do what the Buddha is saying here, which led

---

[17] Hōnen took Zendō's position on the nembutsu as authoritative and his endorsement of it as grounding its legitimacy. In response to questions of why he uses only Zendō's writing to support his own teachings of the nembutsu, Hōnen answers in chapter 16 of the *Senchaku-Shū*, "Master Shan-tao was a man who did indeed achieve *samādhi* [a state of mind in which the mind is perfectly calm and free from various thoughts so that it is able to see things as they are]. We rely on him because there is evidence that he achieved *samādhi*, according to the method." *Hōnen's* Senchakushū, 148. Although Hōnen dismisses *samādhi* as a state of mental concentration required to attain liberation, he still considers it a sign of spiritual elevation.

[18] William Theodore de Bary (ed.), *The Buddhist Tradition: In India, China & Japan* (New York: Vintage Books, 1972), 29. This passage appears in the *Mahāparinibbāṇa Sutta* (the Discourse of the Great Passing-Away) which records the last days of the Buddha. Although its authenticity is not clear, the idea expressed in this particular passage is reflected in the teachings of the Buddha.

him to the method of absolute faith in the power of something besides himself—Amida. Wouldn't this be a problem? Hônen indeed attempts to show that the nembutsu is a legitimate Buddhist practice, regardless of its Other-Power reliance. He argues in chapter 11 of the *Senchaku-Shû* that it is clearly stated in the *Meditation Sutra* that Sākyamuni Buddha praises the nembutsu practitioners over practitioners of other practices; and in chapter 12, he further discusses another passage from the *Meditation Sutra*, which states that the Sākyamuni Buddha entrusted only the nembutsu to his disciple Ānanda. Although Hônen's apparent attempt in the *Senchaku-Shû* is largely to show that the legitimacy of the nembutsu is attested in the primary sutras, he also sees the nembutsu as a practice that helps the practitioner to transform her sense of the self spiritually when it is performed properly.

In chapter 8 of the *Senchaku-Shû*, entitled "Passages That Show That Those Who Practice Nembutsu Should Certainly Possess the Three Kinds of Mind [*Sanjin*],"[19] Hônen explains the kinds of mindset that the practitioner must have for the recitation of the nembutsu to be proper. Elsewhere, Hônen makes an explicit statement about the necessity of a particular psychological condition in the proper nembutsu, which he calls *Anjin*:

> Regarding the practice that must be performed once one entered the Gateway of the Jōdo, the mind and practice must appropriately fit together. That is, they are called *Anjin* and *Kigyo*. *Anjin* refers to a condition of the mind.[20]

It is clear that Hônen does not think that a mere verbal utterance of "*Namu Amida Butsu*" would be sufficient to count as the practice; both

---

[19] *Hônen's* Senchakushû, 99.

[20] *Jôdo-shû Ryaku Shô* (*Summary of the Jôdo Viewpoint*), in *Hônen, Nihon no Meicho*, vol. 5, 260; my translation. *Kigyô* is a Japanese term referring to an actual recitation of the nembutsu that Tao-Ch'o (*Dôshaku*) distinguishes in his *Collection of Passages on the Land of Peach and Bliss* (*Anraku-Shû*) between the Gateway of the Holy Path (*Shôdô-mon*) and the Gateway of Jōdo (*Jôdo-mon*). *Shôdô-mon* is a path to the attainment of enlightenment by doing rigorous Buddhist practices like those which Hônen did at Mount Hiei, whereas *Jôdo-mon* is a path to the rebirth in Pure Land (*jôdo*) by doing the nembutsu practice. In chapter 1 of the *Senchaku-Shû*, Hônen begins with a passage from the *Anraku-Shû* in which those two gateways are contrasted, arguing the Gateway of Holy Path should be rejected and the Gateway of Jōdo followed.

internal (*Anjin*) and external (*Kigyō*) conditions must properly be present together in the recitation of the nembutsu. Notice, however, that this clear statement of the requirement of *Anjin* and the descriptive title of chapter 8 seem to be in conflict with Hōnen's emphasis on the universal accessibility of the nembutsu. He clearly states in chapter 3 of the *Senchaku-Shū* that the easiness of the nembutsu was the reason for its selection by Amida:

> It is therefore clear that since the nembutsu is easy, it is open to everyone, while the various other practices are not open to people of all capacities because they are difficult. Was it not in order to bring all sentient beings without exception to birth that he [Dharmākara] in his original vow cast aside the difficult practice and selected the easy one? If the original vow required us to make images of the Buddha and to build stūpas, the poor and destitute would surely have no hope of birth. . . . If the original vow required us to have wisdom and intelligence, the dull and foolish would surely have no hope for birth. . . . Further, if the original vow required us to observe the precepts and abide by the monastic rules, those who have broken the precepts and those who have never undertaken them would surely have no hope of birth. . . . For this reason, the Tathāgata Amida . . . moved by impartial compassion and wishing to save all beings universally . . . selected the single practice of reciting the nembutsu.[21]

Amida chose the nembutsu because it is available to any human equally, regardless of economic and social status, intellectual abilities, and moral character. But if a proper mental condition is required for the nembutsu to be proper and worthwhile, we would be unlikely to practice even the nembutsu properly, given that we are all confused, distracted, and weak-minded *bonbus*. Nonetheless, it is also repeatedly insisted in the *Senchaku-Shū* that the nembutsu must be recited *single-mindedly and wholeheartedly*. It will be clear, once we explore Hōnen's view of *Anjin*, that it neither involves mental absorption (like sitting meditation) nor requires the attainment of knowledge of Buddhist

[21] *Hōnen's* Senchakushū, 77–78.

teachings. It is important to remember that Hōnen intimately realized the impossibility of achieving mental concentration and attaining such knowledge as he and all humans are *bonbus* with insuperable limitations. Just as Hōnen himself did, *Anjin* can be acquired by the practitioner through affectively infused, personal experiences that are quite common to all humans in this earthly life: failures, a strong sense of limitations, and feelings of hopelessness and helplessness.

Anjin has three aspects, which are together called *Sanjin* (meaning literally "three minds"): (1) the truly authentic mind (*shijō-shin*), (2) the mind of deep faith (*jin-shin*), and (3) the mind that dedicates one's merit toward rebirth in the Jōdo with a resolution to be reborn there (*ekōhotsugan-shin*). First, to have the truly authentic mind (*shijō-shin*) is for one to be truthful to one's inner state and express it outwardly as it is; in other words, one's outward appearance is in accord with her inner, psychological states. Hōnen states:

> that which is called the sincere mind is the mind that is truly genuine. Its characteristics are as described in a passage quoted earlier. Thus, in the passage, "[one should not] outwardly manifest the aspects of being wise, good, and diligent while inwardly embracing vanity and falsehood." The word "outwardly" is the opposite of "inwardly." That is to say, one's outward aspect is not in accord with one's inner heart. In other words, outwardly one is intelligent, but inwardly one is foolish ... outwardly a person is good while inwardly he is evil ... a person outwardly gives the appearance of diligence whereas inwardly his mind indulges in sloth. If one were to turn around that which is outside and put it inside, then surely one would possess what is essential for liberation.[22]

Hōnen emphasizes the importance of the total correspondence between outward expressions and inward states in his explanation of *shijō-shin*. What is exhibited through this correspondence is how *true* the practitioner is to herself. The truly authentic mind (*shijō-shin*) is the fundamental mental framework required in the proper recitation

---

[22] Ibid., 111–112.

of the nembutsu, where proper inner states such as beliefs, convictions, and intentions come to be outwardly expressed truthfully with *shijō-shin* in the nembutsu. Thus, the *shijō-shin* does not provide the practitioner with *what* to do or *what* characters to cultivate, but rather *how* to do things. Importantly, particular inward states which are to be expressed through *shijō-shin* in the proper nembutsu are specified by *jin-shin* and *ekōhotsugan-shin*.

After presenting a long quote from Zendō's commentary on the *Meditation Sūtra*, Hōnen only highlights the importance of faith and lack of doubt involved in the mind of deep faith (*jin-shin*):

> One ought surely to know that it is through doubt that one is held fast within the house of birth and death, while it is through faith that one can enter into the castle of *nirvana*. By establishing the two aspects of faith [inherent in the profound mind], the birth of all nine levels of people is definitely assured.[23]

The two aspects of faith in the *jin-shin* are succinctly explained in Zendō's quote:

> The first is to believe resolutely and deeply that one is actually a guilty *bonbu* who has always been tumbling and transmigrating for countless kalpas and unable to attain liberation by oneself. The second aspect is to believe resolutely and deeply that Amida, through the Forty-Eight Vows, embraces and leads sentient beings and believe without doubt or even without wondering that those who entrust themselves to the power of these Vows will certainly attain rebirth in the Jōdo.[24]

They are: (1) self-acceptance of one's own wickedness and of one's incapability of attaining liberation by one's own effort, and (2) unwavering faith in Amida's Vows and the power of Amida's Vows to bring about the liberation of all nembutsu practitioners. The first aspect (1) is of the profound recognition of oneself as a *bonbu*: one is filled with

[23] Ibid., 112.
[24] *Jōdo-shū Seiten*, vol. 3, 140–141; my translation.

bonno that inexorably governs her life and, what is worse, she is incapable of eliminating her bonno to liberate herself on her own. This is exactly what Hōnen realized about himself after thirty years of rigorous study and practice at Mount Hiei. The second aspect (2) is of the absolute faith in Amida's Vows: one must believe that Amida's Vows are all effective at this point, including the Eighteenth Vow (i.e., Amida's Original Vow), so that there is no doubt that all those who wholeheartedly entrust themselves to Amida's grace will attain rebirth in the Jōdo without fail. These two aspects are intimately related, according to Hōnen, in that the first one is necessary for the second one to be firmly held. Unless one truly realizes and sincerely accepts herself as a *bonbu*, she would still be deluded to think that she has the capacity to achieve liberation by her own effort. Even if she might turn to Amida then, her faith would not be a wholehearted, unshakable one. The absolute acceptance of oneself as a helpless *bonbu* and the complete faith in Amida's power must be genuinely and resolutely held in the heart of the practitioner: the slightest doubt about either would keep her in the cycle of birth and death.

Finally, the mind that dedicates one's merit toward rebirth in the Jōdo with a resolution to be reborn there (*ekōhotsugan-shin*) is an aspect of the mind in which one brings the purpose of rebirth in the Jōdo to the main focus of her life by dedicating all the merits of her past, present, and future acts to it. To have the *ekōhotsugan-shin* is to

> take delight in the merits of the good achieved by one's physical, vocal, and mental acts of the past and the present in and beyond this world and by all the other *bonbus*' and Holy beings' physical, vocal, and mental acts in and beyond this world, dedicate all these merits to the rebirth in the Jōdo with the truly authentic and profound mind, and wish to be reborn in the Amida's Jōdo.[25]

Everything in one's life should always center around rebirth in the Jōdo, which means that her life comes to be organized and built entirely for the sole purpose of it. Even the merits of other people's acts,

---

[25] Ibid., 146; my translation.

as well as acts of Holy beings, should be taken delightfully for the purpose of the rebirth in the Jōdo. The *ekōhotsugan-shin* goes beyond the recitation of the nembutsu to involve every aspect of the practitioner's conduct and that of all the other beings in the past, present, and future.

How do the three aspects of the mind work together to constitute the psychological condition of the practitioner in the proper recitation of the nembutsu? The practitioner first must reject the possibility of liberating herself by her own power by way of the sincere acknowledgment of her *bonbu*-ness. This self-recognition is a necessary starting-point for the nembutsu to be recited with proper mindset. As a result, the practitioner completely surrenders herself to accept the grace of Amida wholeheartedly. The *jin-shin* consists in these two steps. The absolute faith in Amida becomes the stable anchor of her entire frame of mind, and her whole life comes to be organized and lived for the purpose of the rebirth in the Jōdo (*ekōhotsugan-shin*). This whole mental, psychological development is to be expressed outwardly in her behavior, most importantly, in the vocal recitation of the nembutsu (*shijō-shin*). It is important to note that the *Sanjin* does not comprise a step-by-step psychological process of the nembutsu practitioner, except that one aspect of the *jin-shin*, the self-recognition of being a *bonbu*, is a critical precondition for the genuine entrustment of herself to Amida's power. But, the rest of the *Sanjin* can become more and more profound through the repeated *practice of* the nembutsu to the point where the recitation of the nembutsu comes to reflect the profound acknowledgment of oneself as a *bonbu* (i.e., "knowing oneself") and the absolute surrendering of oneself and one's self-seeking desires and attachments (i.e., "forgetting oneself").

Hōnen's conception of the nembutsu is far more complex than the common view of the nembutsu as an easy, faith-oriented spiritual practice. First, for Hōnen, reciting the nembutsu is an act that is not limited to the vocal utterance of "*Namu Amida Butsu.*" The nembutsu practitioner must go through a psychologically transformative journey that Hōnen himself took. The journey begins with the hardest and most critical step: self-realization. The practitioner has to realize the nature of herself as a *bonbu* who is essentially confused, distracted, and filled with desires and negative emotions like anger, greed, and jealousy (i.e., *bonno*). This realization, if sincere and thorough, is accompanied with unbearable feelings of hopelessness and helplessness that she could not escape from this corrupt world by her own effort. In this abyss of despair, the practitioner truly understands the compassion and power of Amida's original vow, and surrenders herself to Amida's grace. Holding absolute faith in Amida firmly in her heart, she makes an unwavering commitment to rebirth in the Jōdo, directing her life for this purpose. This is when her utterance, "*Namu Amida Butsu*," becomes genuinely single-minded and wholehearted. Reciting the nembutsu is a dynamic, emotionally infused process in which the practitioner transforms herself from being a *bonbu* to being a spiritually grounded person.

Second, the efficacy of the nembutsu reaches beyond the realm of spirituality in Hōnen's understanding of it. The *Sanjin* encompasses the practitioner's mindset not only in the act of reciting the nembutsu, but in any act: behavioral, verbal, and mental. The one aspect of the mind of deep faith (*jin-shin*) is specifically about Amida's original vow. But the other part, about the sincere self-realization and acceptance of one's nature as a *bonbu*, must have various psychological effects, one of which is to dishearten oneself so much so that she completely entrusts herself to Amida as her guide and savior. As Hōnen's experience indicates, such realization is the greatest, humbling experience for oneself. This initial, humbling self-realization must bring her to the depth of her own being, affecting her overall outlook toward her *self* and her own life, which is reflected in the *ekōhotsugan-shin*. But, the *ekōhotsugan-shin* is not just about the recitation of the nembutsu: it is about *everything* that one does in life, as well as other people's acts. Thus, being completely true to oneself (*shijō-shin*) with the unshakable *jin-shin* and the *ekōhotsugan-shin* at the center of one's heart, one's mind is firmly settled (not distracted by *bonno* like the mind of *bonbu*), and one rearranges one's entire life, acting resolutely for the purpose of the rebirth in the Jōdo. *That* would be an ethical, unselfish life.

Furthermore, Hōnen conceives the act of reciting the nembutsu as building a direct, personal connection with Amida. In chapter 7 of the *Senchaku-Shū*, entitled "Amida's light embraces only the nembutsu practitioner,"[26] Hōnen explains by quoting Zendō that the practitioner

---

[26] *Jōdo-shū Seiten*, vol. 3, 136; my translation.

comes to be embraced by Amida's light in the present life by establishing various karmic relations with Amida by reciting the nembutsu.[27] What meaning does it have to be embraced by Amida's light? The *Sutra of Immeasurable Life* (*Muryōjyu-kyō*) says: "Those who are embraced by the light of Amida in this world eliminate their greed, anger, and ignorance, become flexible both physically and mentally, leap for joy and happiness, and develop the good heart."[28] The practitioner loses the essential negative aspects of being a *bonbu*, that is, the *bonno*, (i.e., greed, anger, and ignorance), which is tantamount to losing her *bonbu*-ness. By way of reciting the nembutsu with the *Sanjin*, therefore, the practitioner indeed transforms herself from a *bonbu* to a being without *bonno*.

The recitation of the nembutsu, in Hōnen's view, is not a cry for help or forgiveness. When it is done properly, as he sees it, it is a culmination of the practitioner's journey of self-discovery and self-transformation, although Hōnen does not say so explicitly. The superiority of the nembutsu to other Buddhist practices does not consist merely in its easiness; more importantly, it is a practice accessible to all by which we, *bonbu*s, can still eliminate the *bonbu*-ness that binds us to this corrupt world without rigorously striving to do so. That is where the genius of Hōnen lies. "Knowing oneself" sincerely as a *bonbu* brings her to the firm understanding of, and the absolute faith in, Amida's grace and the nembutsu selected by Amida; through the single-minded and wholehearted recitation of the nembutsu, she then "forgets herself" as a *bonbu*, being embraced by Amida's light. It is particularly interesting that the *self* that must be genuinely realized to begin the transformative journey of one*self*, in Hōnen's view, is a being with limitations, ignorance, and emotions, that is, what it is to be *human*. The indispensable

---

[27] There are three types of the karmic relations: (1) *shin-nen* (interaction of personal closeness), (2) *gon-nen* (interaction of intimacy), and (3) *zōjō-en* (interaction of increasing merits). A personal closeness is established between Amida and the practitioner by the nembutsu as Amida hears, sees, knows, and remembers the practitioner's utterances, actions, beliefs, and thoughts of Amida (*shin-nen*); Amida appears before the practitioner when she recites the nembutsu with sincere desire to see Amida (*gon-nen*); and Amida removes all the wrongdoings of the practitioner and ensures that she will be reborn in the Jōdo by actually coming to take her to the Jōdo at her death (*zōjō-en*) if she single-mindedly and wholeheartedly recites the nembutsu.

[28] *Jōdo Sanbu-kyō* (first volume), edited by Hajime Nakamura, Kyōshō Hayashima, and Kazuyoshi Kino (Tokyo: Iwanami Shoten, 2007), 171; my translation.

self-discovery in the practice of the nembutsu is not what we really are or what we are ultimately not, metaphysically speaking. But, in the end, whatever the self really is, the nembutsu practitioner loses her *self*. Just as Dogen uses the metaphor of the reflection of the moon in water to refer to the attainment of enlightenment in *Genjōkōan*,[29] Hōnen ends the *Senchaku-Shū* by saying, "The nembutsu practice can be compared to the reflection of the moon in water: it freely rises up [to the moon] or [the moon shines] down [on the water]."[30] Through the nembutsu, Amida and the practitioner come together.

Bibliography

Andrews, Allan A. (1987a). The Senchakushū in Japanese Religious History: The Founding of a Pure Land School. *Journal of the American Academy of Religion* 55(3): 473–499.

Andrews, Allan A. (1987b). Pure Land Buddhist Hermeneutics: Hōnen's Interpretation of *Nembutsu*. *Journal of the International Association of Buddhist Studies* 10(2): 7–25.

Benchō (1996). *Tetsu Senchaku Hongan Nembutsu Shū*, ed. Jōdo-shū Seiten Kankō Iinkai in *Jōdo-shū Seiten*, Vol. 3. Tokyo: Jōdo-shū Shuppan.

Dōgen (2009). *Genjōkōan*, ed. Edelglass, W., and Garfield, J. L., trans. Bret W. Davis. In *Buddhist Philosophy: Essential Readings*. New York, Oxford University Press.

Garfield, J. L. (2014). *Engaging Buddhism: Why It Matters to Philosophy*. New York: Oxford University Press.

Hōnen (2009). *Senchaku Hongan Nembutsu Shū*, ed. Jōdo-shū Seiten Kankō Iinkai. In *Jōdo-shū Seiten*, Vol. 3, Tokyo: Jōdo-shū Shuppan.

Hōnen's Senchakushū (1998). Trans. and ed. Senchakushū English Translation Project. Honolulu and Tokyo: University of Hawaii Press and Sōgō Bukkyō Kenkyūjo, 1998.

Hōnen's Senchakushū (1971a). *Jōdo-shū Ryaku Shō (Summary of the Jōdo Viewpoint)*, ed. Yoshitaka Tsukamoto. In *Nihon no Meicho: Hōnen*, Vol. 5. Tokyo: Chūō-kōron Sha.

Hōnen's Senchakushū (1971b). *Shichikajō no Kishōmon (Seven Article Pledge)*, ed. Yoshitaka Tsukamoto. In *Nihon no Meicho: Hōnen*, Vol. 5. Tokyo: Chūō-kōron Sha.

---

[29] *Buddhist Philosophy*, 257.
[30] *Hōnen's* Senchakushū, 153.

James, William (1985). *The Varieties of Religious Experience*. Cambridge, MA: Harvard University Press.

Jōdo-shū no Oshie: Rekishi, Shisō, Kadai (1984). Ed. Chion-in Jōdoshū-gaku Kenkyūjo. Kyoto: Chion-in Jōdoshū-gaku Kenkyūjo.

Shimizu, Tōru (1975). Hōnen-shōnin no Ningen-kan [Hōnen's View on Human]. In Chion-in Jōdoshū-gaku Kenkyūjo (ed.), *Hōnen Bukkyō no Kenkyū* [*Inquiry concerning Honen's Buddhism*]. Tokyo: Sankibō Busshōrin, 173-200.

Siderits, Mark (2015). *Personal Identity and Buddhist Philosophy: Empty Person*. London: Routledge.

Sūtra of Immeasurable Life (*Muryōjyu-kyō*) (2007). Ed. Hajime Nakamura, Kyōshō Hayashima, and Kazuyoshi Kino. In *Jōdo Sanbu-kyō*, Vol. 1. Tokyo: Iwanami Shoten.

Suzuki, D. T. (2000). *Essays in Zen Buddhism*, second series. New Delhi: Munshiram Manoharlal.

Takahashi, Kōji (1975). Hōnen no Nembutsu-zanmai ni tsuite [On Honen's Nembutsu-samadhi]. In Nippon Bukkyō-gakkai (ed.), *Bukkyō niokeru Shinpi Shisō* [*Mystical Thought in Buddhism*]. Kyoto: Heirakuji Shoten, 175-188.

Takahashi, Kōji (2004). *Hōnen no Shūkyō*. Tokyo: Jōdo-shū Press.

Tōdō, Kyōshun (1976). Hōnen-shōnin tosono Ibun nimirareru Zanmai nitsuite [On Honen and Zanmai seen in his Writings]. In Nippon Bukkyō-gakkai (ed.), *Bukkyō niokeru Zanmai Shisō* [*Views on Zanmai in Buddhism*]. Kyoto: Heirakuji Shoten, 227-240.

Tōdō, Kyōshun (2001). *Senchaku-shū Koza*. Tokyo: Jōdo-shū Press.

Unno, Mark (1989). The Nembutsu as the Teaching of No-teaching: The Natural Unfolding of Compassion-Wisdom. *The Pure Land: New Series* 6: 45-65.

5

Sor Juana's "Let us pretend
I am happy"

Lisa Shapiro

5.1. Introduction

Sor Juana Inés de la Cruz, while widely recognized as a premier author of colonial Spanish literature,[1] has certainly been neglected as a

---

[1] Most famously, the Nobel laureate Octavio Paz wrote a book about her, *Sor Juana Inés de la Cruz, o, La trampas de la fe* (1983), translated as *Sor Juana, Or the Traps of Faith* (1990). Canal Once and Bravo Films produced a period bio-series about her, *Juana Inés*, that was completed in 2016 and was acquired by Netflix in 2017. Her life is in many respects well-suited to a bio-pic.

Sor Juana's biography has from the beginning been a bit of a hagiography. It is largely founded on Diego Callejo's "Aprobación," the permission to publish Sor Juana's *Fama y obras póstumas* (Madrid: Manuel Ruiz de Murga, 1700), which makes a dramatic story of her life. This "Aprobación" was published as a self-standing annotated work by Ermilo Abreu Gómez in 1936, and was reissued in 1996. Scholarship since the mid-twentieth century, and in particular the ground-breaking work of Paz, corrected some errors of fact and discovered new material. Sor Juana was born in 1648 as Juana Inés de Asbaje y Ramírez, the illegitimate daughter of a Spanish father and a Creole mother, in New Spain, the Spanish colony that is now Mexico. She was raised on the farm of her maternal grandfather in San Miguel Nepantla, near what is now Mexico City. She was a precocious child, learning to read early. In 1656 (age eight), she was sent to Mexico City to live with a maternal aunt and her husband, where she learned Latin. She also learned Nahuatl, the Indigenous Aztec language (though she may have learned that language at San Miguel Nepantla). With her Latin, she was able to read philosophy and theology, and she gained a reputation for her intelligence, as well as for her beauty. In 1664, at age sixteen, she was presented to the court of the viceroy, and she was admitted to the service of Doña Leonor Carreto, Marquesa de Mancera, the vicereine. In 1669 she entered the Convent of the Barefoot Carmelites, but she stayed only a few months before moving and taking vows at the convent of Santa Paula of the order of San Jerónimo. There she had the freedom to pursue her studies in a range of areas, including philosophy, the natural sciences, and music, at least until she was reprimanded by the Bishop of Puebla (see n. 17). In 1695, the convent was visited by an epidemic, and Sor Juana contracted the disease while tending to her ailing sisters. She died in April 1695. Emilie Bergmann, "Sor Juana Inés de la Cruz," *Oxford Bibliographies*, 2018, is not only helpful regarding sources for biographical

Lisa Shapiro, *Sor Juana's "Let us pretend I am happy"* In: *Neglected Classics of Philosophy*.
Edited by: Eric Schliesser, Oxford University Press. © Oxford University Press 2022.
DOI: 10.1093/oso/9780190097196.003.0006

philosopher, though that ground is shifting.[2] To consider her as a philosopher, a reader faces (at least) one significant challenge. Though she is interested in canonical philosophical issues, she explores these issues through non-canonical genres, including poetry and expository letters. As contemporary philosophers, or at least contemporary historians of philosophy, we are not unfamiliar with interpreting letters, which often blend personal and philosophical matters and move from topic to topic. Philosophical correspondence was often circulated, if not published, and figures importantly in understanding philosophers of the past. However, we are not trained to read poetry.[3] Upon reflection, at least some of us can point to examples of philosophers whose work (or at least some of it) takes the form of a poem—Parmenides, Lucretius (*De Rerum Natura*), Margaret Cavendish (see *Poems and Fancies*), Bernard de Mandeville (*Fable of the Bees*), and Alexander Pope (*Essay on Man*)—but in considering these works, we rarely if ever take into account their poetic form. Either we simply ignore that the philosophical work is a poem, as is the case typically with Parmenides and Lucretius, or we count the poem as a work of philosophy only because it is accompanied by other discursive texts that expand on the themes contained in the poem, as with Cavendish and Mandeville.

information, it is an extraordinary resource for finding information about literary scholarship on Sor Juana.

[2] The neglect of Sor Juana by philosophers is certainly the case within Anglophone philosophy, but I think it has also been true within Spanish-language philosophy. See recent articles: Laura Benítez, Sensibility and Understanding in the Epistemological Thought of Sor Juana Inés de la Cruz, in Eileen O'Neill and Marcy P. Lascano (eds.), *Feminist History of Philosophy: The Recovery and Evaluation of Women's Philosophical Thought*, 75–96.; Sergio Armando Gallegos-Ordorica, Sor Juana Inés de la Cruz on Self-Control, *Philosophy Compass* (2020); and Gallegos-Ordorica and Adriana Clavel-Vásquez, The Socratic Pedagogy of Sor Juana Inés de la Cruz, in Karen Detlefsen and Lisa Shapiro (eds.), *The Routledge Handbook of Women and Early Modern European Philosophy* (London: Routledge, forthcoming); and Virginia Aspe Armella, *Approaches to the Theory of Freedom in Sor Juana Inés de la Cruz*, transl. E. Norvelle and M. Murgia (Aliosventos Ediciones, 2018).

[3] I want to emphasize that this is true of contemporary philosophers and historians of philosophy, but it may well not have been true of philosophers of other periods. The philosophers of the late seventeenth and early eighteenth centuries noted in the examples that follow wrote philosophical poetry, and they no doubt read the poems of Racine, Donne, Milton, and Dryden, not to mention Dante Alighieri. Similarly, in the nineteenth century, philosophical poets such as Goethe were widely read and influential. Thanks to Eric Schliesser for highlighting the distinctiveness of our current way of doing philosophy.

That few might take Pope's *Essay on Man* as a work of philosophy shows how we contemporary philosophers don't know what to do with a poem.

In this chapter, I propose to consider just one of Sor Juana's poems: "Let us pretend I am happy."[4] The poem on its face offers a series of skeptical arguments that undermine the possibility of knowledge. In section 5.2, I articulate this core argument. I argue that unlike her contemporaries, Sor Juana does not think skeptical challenges can be answered by a recognition of the limits of human understanding. The interpretive question then is whether she thinks there is a response to skepticism, and if so, what it is. In section 5.3, I consider what is distinctive about poetry as a form of representing one's thoughts, and I suggest that Sor Juana's choice of poetry as the genre to express her philosophy should be factored into our interpretation. In section 5.4, taking into account its poetic form, I argue that Sor Juana aims to temper our natural desire to pursue knowledge, to avoid its excesses, through affective elements of the poem itself. By tempering our epistemic desires, it is possible to move beyond skepticism. I further suggest that in the poem Sor Juana presents a conception of thought as essentially affective, and that account of the nature of thought makes poetry a particularly appropriate genre for her philosophy.

5.2. The Argument of "Let us pretend I am happy"

The poem "Let us pretend I am happy" was likely written in the period 1680–1690, during which Sor Juana wrote extensively, and, in particular, wrote poems and plays. During this time, she received the patronage of the viceroy and vicereine, Tomás de la Cerda, Marqués de la Laguna, and Maria Luisa Manrique de Lara y Gonzaga, Marquesa de la

---

[4] I refer to the poem, as is customary, by its first line. It is also identified by its number in the modern edition of her collected works (much as are Shakespeare's sonnets). Note that the sequence in the *Obras completas* is an editorial decision and does not reflect original publication order. The translation I have used (Grossman) identifies the poem by its genre, as Ballad 2, or in Spanish, *Romance 2*. The genre is composed of an indefinite number of stanzas, with lines of eight syllables, with the odd lines unrhymed, and the even lines using an assonant rhyme.

Laguna and Condesa de Paredes. This poem originally appears in Sor Juana's first volume of poetry, *Inundación castálida*, published in 1689 under the sponsorship of the Condesa de Paredes upon her return to Spain.[5] I want to begin by offering a straightforward reading of "Let us pretend I am happy" as a skeptical argument against the possibility of knowledge.[6] While I will go on to complicate the reading, the central argument provides the scaffolding on which the complications hang.

The body of the poem presents as a series of skeptical arguments. The first is an argument from the diversity of opinions. People have differing opinions about one and the same thing: about the color of objects, about whether they are attractive or anger-inducing, about whether a task eases the labor or increases it, about whether an event is cause for joy and laughter, or sadness and suffering. Each can defend their own position with reasons.

A proof is found for everything	Para todo se halla prueba
a reason on which to base it;	y razón en qué fundarlo;
and nothing has a good reason	y no hay razón para nada
since there is reason for so much.	de haber razón para tanto.

All people are equal judges;	Todos son iguales jueces;
being both equal and varied,	y siendo iguales y varios,
there is no one who can decide	no hay quien pueda decider
which argument is true and right.	Cuál es lo más acertado.

Because rational capacities are equally distributed, and yet each person is different, no one has the epistemic standing to be a judge and

---

[5] A second volume of her works, *Segundo volumen*, was published in 1692; this includes a particularly philosophical 950-line poem, *Primero Sueño*, which she describes as her best work. A third volume, *Fama, y obras póstumas*, was published in 1700, after her death.

[6] Benítez (2019) simply maintains that the poem presents a skeptical argument. This section can be read as a defense of that reading. Gallegos-Ordorica and Clavel-Vázquez (forthcoming) argue that Sor Juana deploys a Socratic pedagogy, and one might read Sor Juana as positioning herself as a Socratic figure in this poem. Socrates, in the early Platonic dialogues, is forthright about the limits of his knowledge, and yet nonetheless is positioned as both wise and content. I leave it to other readers to explore this potential reading.

arbitrate the differences of opinion: there is no basis on which to determine which is more certain.

While Sor Juana's argument appeals to a dispute between Democritus and Heraclitus over the causes of joy (laughter) and sadness (tears), the argument seems to allude to the Second and Third Modes of suspension of judgment in Sextus Empiricus's *Outlines of Pyrrhonism*.[7] In the second mode, Sextus argues that the differences in standards of perceptions between different communities of human beings are so significant that there is no basis for asserting the true esssences of things, and so we must suspend judgment. And in the Third Mode of suspension of judgment, Sextus aims to undermine the epistemic authority the dogmatists assign to themselves to settle the essences of things, for even among the dogmatists there are differences in perceptions of sensible things, and there is no stable basis for allowing one individual's perceptions to carry the day. Even a designated wise person will themselves be party to the disagreement, and so not able to judge disinterestedly.

The poem then pivots sharply from these third-personal considerations to a perspective that is at once both second and first personal, and to a second skeptical argument. The opening of the poem, "Let us pretend I am happy/melancholy Thought" initiates a self-reflective conversation between herself and Thought, which can only be her own thoughts. At this point in the poem, Sor Juana asks what basis "you" have for playing the judge and deciding the case, and it is clear she is asking this question of both Thought and herself. And she chides herself at her own mistaken assumption of authority, her choice of the "bitter" option. For to assume the role of judge is to overvalue the power of one's own reason. Just as do people's opinions, one can reason to opposite conclusions.

| Discursive reason is a sword | El discurso es unacero |
| quite effective at both ends: | que sirve para ambos cabos: |

---

[7] While it has long been acknowledged that there are strands of skepticism in Sor Juana (see Paz 1983 and 1990, for example, as well as Benítez 2019), it is not clear whether she read Sextus herself, though some versions of his works were recovered and accessible from the sixteenth century forward, and were influential on, among others, Montaigne.

| with the point of the blade it kills | de dar muerte, por la punta, |
| the pommel on the hilt protects. | Por el pomo, des resguardo. |

At issue, again, is the basis for the authority of one set of reasons over another. The same tools that draw inferences from a set of premises can be used to raise objections to those very premises. And from contrary premises, they reason to different conclusion. Reasoning itself is a tool as much for building a body of knowledge, as for bringing it tumbling down. Yet, Sor Juana recognizes that the reason at play here is simply discourse, and these are "specious reasons [*discursos sutiles*]" rather than knowledge;[8] "true knowledge consists only in choosing salutary virtue [*que el saber consiste solo en elegir lo más sana*]."[9] Just as there are conflicting standards between individuals, so too within oneself, sets of reasons can come into conflict. One set of reasons is able to tear down what another set has built because there is no internal authority privileging one set of reasons over another. What is missing is a clear standard of truth that can direct and guide reason.

To bring home this point, Sor Juana turns to consider the interpretation of omens to illustrate how the pursuit of knowledge by reasoning goes awry. Omens purport to foretell what is as yet unknown: if we were only able to understand what they mean, we would have knowledge. Yet these interpretations are indeterminate, with nothing to settle whether they are correct or misguided but the unknown future itself. Interpreters of omens are also in a bind. If they make predictions that are too bold, their authority will be undermined when what is predicted does not come to pass. Yet if they acknowledge their ignorance, they find themselves in exactly the same position as those who turn to them, and so likely without work.

Sor Juana does not draw the analogy out fully. If she did, it would go like this: It is part of our nature to seek knowledge, and in doing so we strive to grasp truth. Yet, as we make claims, we have no standards by which to judge them other than the whole of the world, something of which we are ignorant. Nonetheless, the

---

[8] "No es saber, saber hacer discursos sutiles, vanos."
[9] A better literal translation would simply be "choosing the most healthy," but in what follows the poem slides into clearly moral language. The translator anticipates this.

pursuit of knowledge continues. We can make claims about the nature of the world, but we will find our authority undermined when we are ultimately confronted with countervailing evidence. Yet we cannot refuse to make any claims at all, for then we would not be true to our nature; instead of seeking knowledge, we would be still. The challenge for those pursuing knowledge is finding the middle ground:

For knowledge is also a vice:	También es vicio el saber,
if it is not constantly curbed,	qui si no se va atajando,
and if this is not acknowledged,	cuando menos se conoce
the greater the havoc it wreaks;	es más nocivo el estragon;
and if the flight is not brought down	y si el vuelo no le abaten,
fed and fattened on subtleties	en sutilezas cebado,
it will forget the essential	por suidar de lo curioso
for the sake of the rare and strange.[10]	Olvida lo necessario.

One might expect the poem to end here, while the poet affirms her pursuit of knowledge, while resolving to remain within the limits of human understanding.

This theme proliferates throughout early modern philosophy.[11] Descartes's *Meditations* may begin with a series of skeptical arguments that result in radical skepticism, but meditation by meditation some ground is won back, yet all the while attentive to the limits of human rational capacities. The Fourth Meditation, even as it sets out the method for avoiding error, makes a point of both recognizing the limits of finite human understanding and resting content with those limits.[12] And the Sixth Meditation concludes by acknowledging "all the errors

[10] It is hard to translate poetry, but Sor Juana's emphasis on what is necessary to knowledge is lost by shifting the order of the lines.

[11] I do not know whether Sor Juana was familiar with either Descartes or Locke; my point here is that the theme of achieving knowledge within the limits of human understanding proliferates in the period. See the discussions in section 5.4, n. 12, and n. 29 for further discussion of possible connections between Sor Juana and Descartes.

[12] "I have no cause for complaint on the ground that the power of understanding or the natural light which God gave me is no greater than it is; for it is in the nature of a finite intellect to lack understanding of many things, and it is in the nature of a created intellect to be finite" (AT 7:60; CSM 2:42).

to which my nature is liable," even while it also contains within it the resources for correcting and avoiding those errors (AT 7:89; CSM 2 61). Locke too is cognizant of the limits of human understanding, and in the Introduction to his *Essay Concerning Human Understanding* he frames his project as one of "search[ing] out the *Bounds* between Opinion and Knowledge" (ECHU 1.1.3), and he proposes to "discover the Powers [of the understanding]; *how far* they reach; to what things they are in any Degree proportionate; and where they fail us . . . [so that we will] be more cautious in meddling with things exceeding its Comprehension; . . . stop, when it is at the utmost Extent of its Tether; and . . . sit down in a quiet Ignorance of those Things, which, upon Examination, are found to be beyond the reach of our Capacities" (ECHU 1.1.4).

Yet Sor Juana does not end this poem with a similar positive affirmation of human capacity for understanding with a recognition of its limits. Instead, she offers vivid images of unchecked natural excess. An unpruned tree compromises the fruit and leaves the tree barren; a ship without proper ballast builds up so much speed that it undermines its stability, and that of its crew. We pursue knowledge inexorably, but then we are confronted with our failures.

What benefit to intellect	¿De qué sirve al ingenio
to gestate so many offspring,	el producer muchos partos,
if that multitude is followed	si a la multitude se sigue
by ill-fated miscarriages?	El malogro de abortarlos?

Sor Juana uses the Socratic metaphor of the art of philosophy as akin to that of a midwife to make vivid the pain of our epistemic failures. For what starts as a great joy—the gestation of a new life—ends in the tragedy not only of the still birth, but the real risk these failed pregnancies pose to the life of the mother: "the one who gestates will be left if not dead, then gravely injured." Further she takes the common philosophical trope of the light of the intellect to compare the intellect to a fire, but one that "consumes more matter the brighter the fire appears." The implication is that there will soon be no fuel left to burn and the fire will extinguish itself.

Sor Juana's point is twofold. First, we have a natural desire to know more, and insofar as this desire is natural, it is always present.[13] The second point follows from the conclusion of the second skeptical argument, which, recall, argues that we do not contain within ourselves the standard of truth that can guide our reason. Without the standard, our intellect has no way of demarcating its limits. Without this check, so long as we persist in our desire to know, our intellect does not have the capacity to rein itself in and exercise self-restraint. The comparison with Descartes and Locke is stark. Descartes and Locke are optimistic about the force of self-understanding to properly modulate our epistemic ambition, to enjoin us to self-discipline so to allow us to expand what we know. Unlike her near contemporaries, Sor Juana sees the desire for knowledge, once it takes hold, as overwhelming.

This pessimistic note that the search for knowledge will ultimately engulf us in flames is not, however, the end of the poem. Nor is this extended skeptical argument all there is to the poem, as attention to its first line indicates. "Let us pretend I am happy" addresses the central philosophical issue of achieving happiness from its very first line. The argument of the poem starts from the assumption that happiness is achieved by acquiring knowledge, as is evident from the way the first stanza continues:

Let us pretend I am happy	Finjamos que soy feliz
melancholy Thought, for a while;	triste pensamiento, un rato
perhaps you can persuade me, though	quizá prodréis persuadirme,
I know the contrary is true:	aunque yo sé lo contrario.

Melancholy though she is, he wants to persuade herself—to know of herself—that she is happy. However, as the poem continues, as we have just seen, the reason for her unhappiness is laid bare in a series of skeptical arguments: knowledge is elusive. Insofar as she cannot persuade herself that she has any knowledge, she cannot persuade herself she is happy. And thus, happiness too is elusive and cannot

---

[13] Aristotle opens Book 1 of his *Metaphysics* by asserting, "All men by nature desire to know" (980a22).

be feigned. The poem concludes, to find happiness we need to learn
how not to know:

Oh, if there were only a school	¡Oh, si como hay de saber
or seminary where they taught	hubiera algún seminario
classes in how not to know	o escuela donde a ignorar
as they teach classes in knowing.	se enseñaran lòs trabajos!
How happily the man would live	¡Qué felizmente viviera
who with languid circumspection	el que, flojamente cauto
would simply laugh at the menace	burlara las amenazas
of the influence of the stars!	del influjo de los astros!
Let us learn about not knowing	Aprendamos a ignorar,
O Thought, for we then discover	pensamiento, pues hallamos
That for all I add to discourse	que cuanto añado al discurso,
I usurp as much from my years.	Tanto le usurpo a los años.

That is, Sor Juana concludes by asserting the negation of the basic assumption: to achieve happiness we have to learn to *not* know.[14]

One way to read this conclusion is to take the poem to be leveraging
its core skeptical arguments to present a *reductio ad absurdum*; having
demonstrated that the search for knowledge both leads to happiness
and leads to unhappiness, we must reject its basic premise that knowledge is necessary to achieve happiness in favor of its contrary. This
conclusion would seem to align with the epithet of the poem: "She
acknowledges the excesses of a good deal of erudition, which she fears
is useless even to learning and injurious to living."[15] However, on this

---

[14] Gallegos-Ordorica and Clavel-Vásquez (forthcoming) argue that Sor Juana is here
deploying complex irony.
[15] "Acusa la hidropesía de mucha ciencia, que teme inútil aun para saber, y nociva para
vivir." The translation obscures the reference to dropsy. This reference is additional cir-
cumstantial evidence that the poem is a critique of Descartes, for in the Sixth Meditation
dropsy presents a final skeptical challenge to the meditator, an example of how our very
nature can mislead us. Descartes responds that it is sufficient that our nature is that most
conducive to our self-preservation, and affords us the means to correct for any natural
errors. I point to a divergence between Sor Juana and Descartes above, and say more
about how her account is different from Descartes's in section 5.4 of this chapter. See also
n. 29. Also, "erudition" does not adequately capture "ciencia," which refers to scientific
(that is, well-ordered) knowledge.

reading it remains unclear what we are to do with our natural desire for knowledge. Surely, were we to attend classes in not knowing, we would find ourselves just as unhappy, as we would not be realizing one of our fundamental human desires: to pursue knowledge.

There is, however, another possibility. We can read Sor Juana as recognizing that since reason has no authority to instruct us in the limits of our understanding, the only way that we can reign in our natural desire for knowledge is to cultivate an opposing desire. Her call for classes in how not to know is not for lessons designed to imbue either an understanding of the limits of human rational capacities or a skeptical resignation to the impossibility of knowledge. Rather, "learning about not knowing" would involve cultivating those opposing desires that would serve to restrain the very human desire for knowledge.[16]

In section 5.4, I will consider this second possibility in more detail, but first I want to turn to consider the poetic form in which the argument I have been outlining appears.

5.3. Poetic Form

Critical attention to Sor Juana's *romances* has been, quite understandably, from a literary perspective. In Spanish poetry, sixteenth- and seventeenth-century ballads derive from narrative popular songs in the medieval oral tradition, and they preserve the function of celebrating momentous events, that is, of providing exaggerated representations in order to honor the occasion and its central personae. In the mid-seventeenth century, the particular form also underwent a transformation, starting with Louis de Góngora, whom Sor Juana herself acknowledges as an influence,[17] and continuing with Sor Juana herself. Antonio Alatorre describes her as "the most representative poet of the Spanish Baroque, and its most obvious culmination."[18] Sor Juana

---

[16] Sorana Corneanu in her *Regimens of the Mind: Boyle Locke, and the Early Modern Cultura Animi Tradition* (Chicago: University of Chicago Press 2011)argues that early modern epistemology requires that the mind be set in order, and a substantial part of that involves a proper regulation of the passions.

[17] Sor Juana introduces her "El Sueño" (First I Dream) as in imitation of Góngora.

[18] Antonio Alatorre, *Avatares barrocos del romance*, 342, quoted in Rocío Quispe-Agnoli, Sor Juana's *Romances*, in Emilie L. Bergmann and Stacey Schlau

retains some aspects of the classical ballad, sometimes representing and praising particular individuals. However, in other poems she uses the form to fashion a representation of herself.[19] While fitting "Let us pretend I am happy" into this way of understanding Sor Juana's use of the ballad form presents a bit of challenge,[20] there is a more general point about Sor Juana's poetry that is particularly apt for considering this particular poem as a piece of philosophy.

It is clear is that for Sor Juana, poetry was a self-conscious stylistic choice. In her *Response of the Poet to the very eminent Sor Filotea de la Cruz*, in which she responds to the admonition of the Bishop of Puebla to stop pursuing her intellectual activities and stop writing poetry,[21] she asserts that her nature compels her to seek knowledge[22] and that she expresses whatever knowledge she obtains through poetry.

Stephen M. Hart,[23] in noting that a number of Sor-Juana's poems are thematized by the distinction between appearances and reality, homes in on Poem 145, which, he argues, contrasts the form of representation proper to a painting from that proper to a poem. A painting can easily misrepresent its subject, through "fallacious syllogisms of colour" and other modes of deceiving our senses. A poem, however, is capable of a more veridical representation and so is better able to convey truth.

(eds.), *The Routledge Research Companion to the Works of Sor Juana Inés de la Cruz* (London: Routledge, 2017), 152–163.

[19] See Quispe-Agnoli 2017, 155.
[20] Quispe-Agnoli (2017) suggests that Sor Juana is interested in representing the challenges of her own fame in the poem (see p. 152). This strikes me as a misreading, but he seems drawn to it to justify Alfonso Méndez Plancarte's categorization of the poem as Ballad.
[21] In 1690, Sor Juana was reprimanded for her pursuit of worldly knowledge by the Bishop of Puebla, don Manuel Fernández de Santa Cruz, using the pseudonym Sor Filotea. Her reply, the *Response of the Poet* (*Respuesta a sor Filotea*), of 1691, perhaps Sor Juana's most well-known work, is a rhetorically complex feminist tract, in which Sor Juana defends her lifelong pursuit of knowledge while demonstrating her knowledge of the natural sciences, poetry, and the classics. In 1693 she appears to have signed a general confession, and in 1694 she renewed her vows. In part to address the troubled finances of the convent caused by a series of natural disasters, she sold much of her extensive library and musical and scientific instruments.
[22] She writes, for instance, that as a child "my desire to learn was stronger in me that the desire to eat" (*Selected Works*, 2014, 162).
[23] Stephen M. Hart, Sor Juana Inés de la Cruz, in Stephen M. Hart (ed.), *The Cambridge Companion to Latin American Poetry* (Cambridge: Cambridge University Press, 2018), 99–112; see in particular 105–107.

What distinguishes the representations of a painting from that of a poem such that poems are more veridical? Hart's arguments draw on readings of a series of love poems, and it is important that what is represented in these poems is the love of the poet for their subject. In writing a poem about the beloved, the poet not only represents discursively the beloved's lovable qualities, she also is able to represent those qualities through the poem's expression of love. In this way, by expressing poetically the poet's love for those qualities, the poem makes veridical the poem's representation of the object as lovable: insofar as its qualities are loved, the object is indeed lovable. The way in which a poem folds an emotional expression into its representation provides a way to understand this distinction between paintings and poems.

We might think of a painting as representing its subject in a disinterested way.[24] A painting represents sensible qualities of objects, and in particular their shape and color. A painting aims to depict the real qualities of things. While it may well evoke emotions in us, it does not do so by representing those emotions, but rather through its first-order representation. For instance, a portrait depicts the facial features of an individual we know, and in being reminded of that person, our feelings toward them come to the surface. The portrait itself represents neither our affective relation to that person nor that of the painter, nor does it aim to do so.

A poem, on the other hand, by its very design, expresses the emotions of its author, communicates those emotions to its readers, and evokes in them similar emotions.[25] Karen Simecek sums this up nicely: "one

---

[24] I don't myself endorse this account of the way paintings represent, but this model does help in drawing the contrast between paintings and poems.

[25] I rely on contemporary discussion to clarify what is particular to the poetic form, and one might object that this is potentially anachronistic. I cannot settle this one way or the other here, but let me make two points. First, T. S. Eliot in his essay "The Metaphysical Poets" (*Times Literary Supplement*, October 20, 1921, 669–670) argues against reading poets such as John Donne as severing the rational from sensibility and rather that these poets were "at best, engaged in the task of trying to find the verbal equivalent for states of mind and feeling" and that the best English and French poets of the seventeenth and nineteenth centuries "have the same essential quality of transmuting ideas into sensations, of transforming an observation into a state of mind." Second, Plato famously alludes in *Republic* X to the "ancient quarrel" between poetry and philosophy (607b5–6), and this issue of poetry and rhetoric comes up elsewhere in that dialogue as well as in others (*Ion*, *Phaedrus*, and *Gorgias*). I do not want to pretend to interpret Plato

of the things we look to poetry for is a form of expression and a space for affective response alongside cognitive engagement."[26] Unlike an essay, or even a narrative, a poet attends to language, selecting words not only for what they denote, but also for their connotations, and for how they sound.[27] A poem discursively represents things imagistically, but also, through the very words it uses in its imagistic representations, it also expresses the feelings those things evoke. Those words have connotations, and through those connotations evoke similar feelings in the poem's readers. The feelings a poem evokes are not mediated through its representation; a reader does not first form an image of the poem's subject and then respond to that image. Rather, the feelings are folded into the representation itself. In this way, Simecek argues, poems are essentially perspectival, "captur[ing] a particular complex orientation (a general evaluative attitude) towards experience, which act as a 'tool for thinking', since such an orientation will govern how we go about making sense of our experience as well as directing the thoughts and feelings we have in response to what we experience."[28] A poem simultaneously represents the world and situates us within it, stirring us both to understand and to be moved by it.

I suggest that we understand Sor Juana's choice of poetry to present her ideas, including her philosophy, as connected to the way poetry folds affect into its representations, as well as to the way it aims to evoke affects in its readers. With regard to "Let us pretend I am happy," we can ask: Why should Sor Juana have expressed her views about human desire for knowledge as a poem? How does the poem incorporate affect in its argument? How does it convey affect to its readers? What

---

here, but it is commonly held that for him, poetry not only misrepresents its objects but actively encourages that misrepresentation through the manipulation of emotions. So even this criticism of poetry depends on understanding poetry as carrying emotional force. Theorists of poetry seem to agree that poetic representations essentially involve emotions. They disagree about (a) how poetry involves emotions and (b) whether the evoking of emotions can ever be good. Thanks to Eric Schliesser for pressing this point.

[26] Karen Simecek, New Directions for the Philosophy of Poetry, *Philosophy Compass* 14 (2019): e12593. https://doi.org/10.1111/phc3.12593.

[27] Again see Eliot's short essay "The Metaphysical Poets" for a similar analysis.

[28] Karen Simecek, Poetry, Emotion, and the Perspectival View, *British Journal of Aesthetics* 55(4) (2015): 501. doi:10.1093/aesthj/ayv041. Simecek is drawing on the work of Elisabeth Camp here.

philosophical work are those affective dimensions doing? I do not mean to imply that poetry is the only genre of writing that leverages affective responses. My concern is not why Sor Juana chose poetry over any other genre, but rather what she gains by doing philosophy in poetry.

5.4. Poetic Form and the Philosophical Argument

In the second reading of the conclusion of "Let us pretend I am happy" that I offered in section 5.2, I have already suggested one role of affect. For Sor Juana, we have a natural desire for knowledge, which, if it remains unchecked, will move us to excess. In her view, this epistemic desire cannot be countered by an understanding of our limits, but only by a contrary desire—a desire to not know. Given the understanding of poetic form I articulated in section 5.3, we can see how emotions function within the argument of the poem and read the conclusion of the poem as signaling that the poem itself is designed to cultivate in us that contrary desire.

Sor Juana escalates her skepticism to challenge the authority of her own reason to determine what is true through the use of emotionally evocative language. She presents discursive reason as a double-edged sword invoking the fear of battle, but also the judiciousness felt in making decisions with real consequences. She invokes Icarus's ill-fated flight too close to the sun, and along with it the hubris that drove him there, the shame of the fall, and the grief of his father, Daedalus. She describes scholarship "fed and fattened on subtleties [*en sutilezas cebado*]," invoking an image of fattened animals unable to move and thrive, just as the scholars "forget the essential for the sake of the rare and strange [*por cuidar de lo curioso olvida lo necessario*]." She thus invokes feelings of lethargy, loss, and disorientation. She suggests that our search for knowledge requires pruning, as does a tree to bear fruit, evoking the joy of harvesting fresh fruit, and the disappointment when the trees are barren. She reminds us of the need for ballast to maintain stability in a ship, just as a knowledge seeker needs to have something to keep herself in check, evoking the thrill of moving swiftly through waves, as well as the terror at the threat of capsizing. These metaphors build to the poem's conclusion, where the intellect is compared to a fire that is all-consuming and that serves as a forge to transform its own weapons against itself.

It is important to recognize that it is not that the poem offers skeptical arguments that then raise emotions in the reader, but rather that the skeptical arguments themselves are full of emotions. The same desire for knowledge that leads to skepticism, as I argued earlier, also generates a set of increasingly negative emotions. These negative emotions effectively work to counter the desire for knowledge, serving to temper the impulse that can lead to useless and injurious erudition. They thus offer an introductory class in how not to know. With her epistemic impulses in check, the poet can be happy, and "simply laugh at the menace/of the influence of the stars! [*burlara las amenazas/del influjo de los astros!*]." She thus recalls the illustrative case of the interpretation of omens; she is now so comfortable with the indeterminacy of our ability to predict that she can laugh.

However, I also want to suggest that the poem makes a more fundamental point about the connection between affect and understanding, alongside its core skeptical argument. The first line of the poem, and thus its nominal title, "Let us pretend I am happy," recalls the end of Descartes's First Meditation.[29] There, though he realizes that he has reason to take all his former beliefs to be doubtful, he nonetheless falls back into his old habits of belief and to break these habits he proposes to "deceive myself, by pretending [*fingam*; *feignant*] for a time that these former beliefs are utterly false and imaginary" (AT 7:22). Sor Juana's opening word, "Finjamos," is the same root. Yet while the Descartes's meditator proposes to feign a belief is false, Sor Juana proposes to feign an opposing affective state.

---

[29] I draw on Descartes to help develop this part of my reading of Sor Juana. Though I have no evidence that she would have been familiar with the *Meditations*, it is not entirely implausible. Sor Juana was incredibly well read, and her interest in natural philosophy might well have led to her encountering Descartes. Nonetheless, another possible influence is Teresa of Ávila, a Carmelite nun, writing a century earlier, who advocated ascetic practices. The connection would be complex, as Sor Juana left a Carmelite order because of its austerity, and I cannot explore this connection here. Christia Mercer has argued that Descartes's malicious demon derives from Teresa's *Interior Castle* in Descartes' Debt to Teresa of Ávila, or Why We Should Work on Women in the History of Philosophy, *Philosophical Studies* 174 (2017): 2539–2555.

While she is melancholy, she proposes to pretend to be its opposite, happy. While Descartes's readers often ask whether it is possible to deceive oneself to take what one believes to be true to be false, at least the meditator simply takes his former beliefs to be true out of habit. Sor Juana *knows* she is really melancholy. The poem thus immediately confronts the reader with a question: Is it possible to deceive oneself about what one is feeling? If we know we are feeling one way, can we pretend to feel something we are not, especially when what we are feeling is the contrary?

The opening stanza of the poem effectively notes that if she were to pretend convincingly that she is happy, she would contravene what she currently knows: that she is not happy. But of course if she and her Thought are successful in pretending, she would be happy. This possibility can be seen as affirming the basic assumption of the relation between knowledge and happiness: if she were to persuade herself of something, she would know it, and insofar as she has acquired knowledge, she would be happy. If she were to persuade herself of her own happiness, that very truth would be self-affirming: she would know herself to be happy, and in knowing this fact about herself, she would further affirm her happiness. The question then is whether she can even acquire that first bit of knowledge.

The second stanza proposes a common strategy:

for since on mere apprehension	que pues solo en la aprehenión
they say all suffering depends,	dicen que estiban los daños,
if you imagine good fortune	si os imagináis dichoso
you will not be so downcast.	No series tan desdichado.

It is easy to read this stanza as simply invoking a neo-Stoic truism that to be happy one only needs to think happy thoughts.[30] However, the structure of the poetic phrasing equivocates between the apprehension of a thought associated with happiness (or suffering), on the one hand, and the apprehension of suffering (or happiness), on

---

[30] Descartes writes something similar in correspondence with Elisabeth. See his letter of May or June 1645 (AT4: 218ff). Elisabeth does not find this advice particularly helpful. See her letter of June 22, 1645 (AT4:233ff).

the other. The former sense points to the neo-Stoic truism. The latter sense, however, invokes Descartes's *cogito*. For Descartes, whether my thoughts are true or false, "'I am, I exist' is necessarily true whenever it is put forward by me or conceived in my mind" (AT 7:25; CSM 2:17). From here Descartes's meditator begins the slow road to answer the radical skepticism of the First Meditation, coming to see that this necessary truth implies she exists insofar as she is thinking and so that she is a thinking thing. The *cogito* is, I think, best understood as an exercise of mere apprehension. It does not matter what the meditator is thinking *of*, only that she has a thought. Essential to having a thought, for Descartes, is just the awareness of its object. The assertion "I am, I exist" is meant to capture that bare awareness, an awareness that is contained in every other thought.

Sor Juana here, in invoking a "mere apprehension," effectively suggests that the awareness proper to thought ought not to be understood as an assertion, but rather as a feeling, be it suffering or happiness. The neo-Stoic truism depends on it being the case that no matter what we think, our thoughts come with affect. I can make myself happy by thinking happy thoughts, precisely because thoughts *are* happy or sad. On this reading, then, Sor Juana presents, right at the beginning of the poem, what might be regarded as an affective equivalent to Descartes's *cogito*: Whether what I imagine is happy or sad, in having the thoughts I do, I am experiencing feelings, and so I am essentially a feeling thing. This essential affective dimension of thought explains how reasons move us: reason affords us standards of truth and so knowledge, but it is because we feel the force of reason that we are moved to seek them.

In the next stanza, she pleads for her "understanding [to] allow me to rest a while [*Sirvame el entendimiento alguna vez de descanso*]," wanting to be free from the force that propels her to keep wanting to know more. Tellingly, however, what keeps her understanding from resting are the first set of skeptical arguments from the diversity of opinions. This might seem to undermine my reading, as it is not contrary feelings but contrary reasons that moved the understanding in opposite directions—"a proof is found for everything [*Para todo se halla preuba*]." However, we can read these skeptical arguments as arising from our affect-driven impulse to pursue knowledge. In a search for conclusive reasons, we find ourselves moved first in one direction, then the other.[31]

This reading also allows us to better understand why Sor Juana does not go the direction of Descartes and Locke, using reason to discover the limits of our understanding. Insofar as our thought is essentially affective, there is no disinterested affectless vantage point from which to grasp the limits of the understanding. We can only strive to counter our passion for knowledge with other countervailing emotions. As already noted, the poem moves from a direct presentation of opposing opinions to use metaphors and images designed to evoke associated emotions in the reader. These affective responses reach a crescendo. Just as the poem imagines our intellect as a fire consuming all around it, burning bright but destroying everything, so too do the emotions the poem evoke in us leave us spent, and the desire for knowledge is somewhat dissipated. With emotions damped down, the rhythm of the poem settles into its conclusion, with a request for classes in not knowing.

The threat of skepticism is answered not through reason, but rather by cultivating a properly balanced affective profile. It would not be inappropriate to characterize this balanced affective profile as virtue, a mean between the desire to know and the desire to not know. In order to know, we must strive for virtue; but it is also through virtue that we will in fact achieve happiness. Pretending we are happy is not a matter of pretending we are virtuous, but rather trying to pretend we are happy forces us not only to confront the excesses of our desire for knowledge, but also to understand our nature as a *feeling*, thinking thing.

Finally, this reading also helps us to understand why Sor Juana expresses her philosophy poetically. Insofar as she takes thought to be essentially affective, to express those thoughts she requires a medium through which that affective dimension is adequately represented. Poetry is a particularly effective genre of writing for enfolding emotions into its representations.

---

[31] As Descartes puts it in the Fourth Meditation: "although probable conjectures may pull me in one direction, the mere knowledge that they are simply conjectures, and not certain and indubitable reasons, is itself quite enough to push my assent the other way" (AT 7:59; CSM 2: 41).

Bibliography

Aristotle ([1924] 1984). *Metaphysics*. Ross, W. D. (trans.). In *The Complete Works of Aristotle*, Vol. 2. Barnes, Jonathan (ed.). Princeton, NJ: Princeton University Press.

Aspe Armella, Virginia (2018). *Approaches to the Theory of Freedom in Sor Juana Inés de la Cruz*. Norvelle, E., and Murgia, M (trans.). Zibatá, Mexico: Aliosventos Ediciones.

Baillet, Adrien ([1692] 1946). *Vie de Monsieur Descartes*. Paris: La Table Ronde.

Benítez, Laura (2019). Sensibility and Understanding in the Epistemological Thought of Sor Juana Inés de la Cruz. In O'Neill, E., and Lascano, M. P. (eds.), *Feminist History of Philosophy: The Recovery and Evaluation of Women's Philosophical Thought*. Cham: Springer, 75–96.

Bergmann, Emilie (2018). Sor Juana Inés de la Cruz. *Oxford Bibliographies*.

Callejo, Diego (1700). Aprobación. In Sor Juan Inés de la Cruz, *Fama y obras póstumas*. Manuel Ruiz de Murga.

Corneanu, Sorana (2011). *Regimens of the Mind: Boyle, Locke, and the Early Modern Cultura Animi Tradition*. Chicago: University of Chicago Press.

Descartes, René (1996) *Oeuvres completes*. 11 vols. Adam, C., and Paul Tannery, P. (eds.). Paris: Vrin. Cited internally as "AT volume number: page number."

Descartes, René (1984). *The Philosophical Writings of Descartes*. Vol. 2. Cottingham, J., Stoothoff, R., and Murdoch, D. (trans. and eds.). Cambridge: Cambridge University Press. Cited internally as "CSM 2: page number."

Eliot, T. S. (1921). The Metaphysical Poets. *Times Literary Supplement*, October 20, 1031, pp. 669–670.

Gallegos-Ordorica, Sergio Armando (2020). Sor Juana Inés de la Cruz on Self-Control. *Philosophy Compass* 15(10): 1–10. https://doi.org/10.11111/phc3.12699.

Gallegos-Ordorica, Sergio Armando, and Clavel-Vázquez, Adriana (forthcoming). The Socratic Pedagogy of Sor Juana Inés de la Cruz. In Detlefsen, K., and Shapiro, L. (eds.), *The Routledge Handbook of Women and Early Modern European Philosophy*. Ed. New York: Routledge.

Hart, Stephen M. (2018). "Sor Juana Inés de la Cruz." In Hart, Stephen M. (ed.), *The Cambridge Companion to Latin American Poetry*. Cambridge: Cambridge University Press, 99–112.

Juana Inés de la Cruz, Sor (1976). *Obras Completas*, 4 vols. Méndez Plancarte, A., and Salceda, A. G. (eds.). Mexico: Fondo de Cultura Económica.

Juana Inés de la Cruz, Sor (2014). *Selected Works*. Grossman, Edith (trans.). Alvarez, Julia (intro.). New York: W. W. Norton.

Juana Inés de la Cruz, Sor (1997). *Poems, Protes, and a Dream*. Sayers Peden, Margaret (trans.). New York: Penguin.

Locke, John (1975). *An Essay Concerning Human Understanding*. Nidditch, P. H. (ed.). Oxford: Oxford University Press. Cited internally as "ECHU Book. Chapter. Paragraph."

Mercer, Christia (2017). Descartes' Debt to Teresa of Ávila, or Why We Should Work on Women in the History of Philosophy. *Philosophical Studies* 174: 2539–2555.

Paz, Octavio (1990). *Sor Juana, or the Traps of Faith*. Sayers Peden, Margaret (trans.). Cambridge, MA: Harvard University Press.

Quispe-Agnoli, Rocío (2017). Sor Juana's *Romances*: Fame, Contemplation, Celebration. In Bergmann, E. L., and Schlau, S. (eds.), *The Routledge Research Companion to the Works of Sor Juana Inés de la Cruz*. London: Routledge, 152–163.

Sextus Empiricus (1985). *Selections for the Major Writings on Scepticism, Man & God*. Hallie, P. P. (ed.). Etheridge, S. G. (trans.). Indianapolis, IN: Hackett.

Simecek, Karen (2019). New Directions for the Philosophy of Poetry. *Philosophy Compass* 14: e12593. http://doi.org/10.1111/ph3.12593.

Simecek, Karen (2015). Poetry, Emotion, and the Perspectival View. *British Journal of Aesthetics* 55(4): 501. doi:10.1093/aesthj/ayv041.

6

Anton Wilhelm Amo

*Treatise on the Art of Soberly and Accurately
Philosophizing (1738)*

Justin E. H. Smith

6.1. An Introduction to Anton Wilhelm
Amo's Oeuvre

Anton Wilhelm Amo was born around 1700 in Axim, in present-day
Ghana, and died in the same country at some point in 1752 or later.[1,2]
From 1707 to 1747, he lived in Germany, and from 1729 made a se-
ries of contributions to German jurisprudence and philosophy at the
Universities of Halle, then Wittenberg, then Jena.

In 1729 Amo defended a thesis in law at Halle, entitled *De jure
Maurorum in Europa* [*On the Right of Moors in Europe*]. Though this
work has often been said to be "missing," it is more likely that it never
existed as a written text in the first place. In early eighteenth-century
German universities, it was common for the defense of a thesis to un-
fold as an event without an accompanying text, and so, while we know
from short summaries what Amo said at this event, more or less, it is
quite likely that what he said is all that ever existed of the work. Further
research may prove this conjecture wrong.

---

[1] Special thanks to Victor Emma-Adamah, Paulin Hountondji, Dwight Lewis,
Stephen Menn, and Enrico Pasini, for their long and various contributions to my understanding of Amo's life and work.

[2] For an extensive account of Amo's biography and the contexts of his intellectual
development, see Stephen Menn and Justin E. H. Smith, Introduction, *Anton Wilhelm
Amo: Philosophical Dissertations on Mind and Body* (Oxford: Oxford University Press,
2020). The reader is referred to this work for further bibliography as well, which is
omitted here in view of limited space.

Justin E. H. Smith, *Anton Wilhelm Amo* In: *Neglected Classics of Philosophy.* Edited by: Eric Schliesser,
Oxford University Press. © Oxford University Press 2022. DOI: 10.1093/oso/9780190097196.003.0007

There are in any case three extant texts by Amo, all of which are contributions to philosophy rather than law. Two of them were published as dissertations accompanying disputations—thus, as texts that supplement events—at the University of Wittenberg in 1734. The first is entitled *Dissertatio inauguralis philosophica de humanae mentis apatheia* [*Inaugural Philosophical Dissertation on the Impassivity of the Human Mind*]. Amo is identified as both the author of this text and as its defender at the corresponding event. The work is an argument for a radical sort of dualism, going far beyond what Descartes permitted, by holding that the very idea that the soul might undergo any passions at all is, strictly speaking, incoherent. The *Impassivity* is the most thoroughly studied of Amo's three works, and has the virtue of succinctness and formal rigor. It is followed just one month later by a second philosophical work, the so-called Meiner dissertation, or, more correctly, the *Disputatio philosophica continens ideam distinctam eorum quae competunt vel menti vel corpori nostro vivo et organico* [*Philosophical Disputation Containing a Distinct Idea of Those Things That Pertain Either to the Mind or to Our Living and Organic Body*].[3]

These two philosophical works are vastly outweighed, in scope and aims, by a third and final work on logic, along with some rhetoric, hermeneutics, and diverse related topics, published four years later in 1738: the *Tractatus de arte sobrie et accurate philosophandi* [*Treatise on the Art of Soberly and Accurately Philosophizing*].

Amo had already drafted at least some version of this work as early as 1734, at the time of the publication of the two dissertations on mind and body. We know this because he refers to his *Logic* at least once in the *Impassivity*: in treating the distinction between what may be "logically" attributed to a sensation and what may be "physically" attributed to it, Amo remarks that he will "explain about these matters in our *Logic*."[4] And indeed this is what he

---

[3] The reason for the frequent misattribution of this work to a certain Johannes Theodosius Meiner is simple. Meiner was Amo's student, and defended the work at the event that corresponded to the text, thus earning the most prominent place on the title page of that text.

[4] Anton Wilhelm Amo (1734), *Dissertatio inauguralis philosophica de humanae mentis apatheia* (hereafter *Apatheia*), Wittenberg: Ex Officina Schomachiana, Chapter 1, Member 2, §1., Note 1, 11; in Burchard Brentjes (ed.), *Antonius Guilielmus Amo Afer aus Axim in Ghana. Student, Doktor der Philosophie, Magister legens an den Universitäten*

does.[5] In the *Treatise*, in turn, Amo makes repeated references back to the *Impassivity*[6] and to the Meiner dissertation.[7] In sum, it is wholly fitting to see Amo's three philosophical works as, if not a trilogy, then at least as a threefold manifestation of one and the same unified philosophical project, with abundant cross-references and evident intertextuality. Unlike the two earlier works, however, the *Treatise* is not a dissertation, and does not seem to have been the textual component of any official passage from one institutional rank to a higher one. Nonetheless, as we will see, Amo plainly hoped that this work would help him to gain a secure university position, a hope that would remain mostly unfulfilled throughout the remainder of his career in Germany.

6.2. The Origins of the *Treatise*

While we do not know what the state of the *Treatise* was in 1734, we have strong evidence that it existed as a complete manuscript by 1736. The recent discovery of a letter in an Estonian archive,[8] written by Amo's own hand in German, reveals that the philosopher was, as of March 24, 1736, living in the village of Wildenhain, near Torgau in southeastern Saxony. The letter is addressed to an unnamed but evidently very important personage, and it indicates in format and style

Halle, Wittenberg, Jena, 1727–1747. Dokumente / Autographe / Belege (hereafter DAB) (Halle: Martin-Luther-Universität Halle-Wittenberg, 1968), 22.

[5] Anton Wilhelm Amo, *Tractatus de arte sobrie et accurate philosophandi* (hereafter *Tractatus*) (Halle : Ex Officina Kitleriana, 1738), General Part, Chapter 4, "De Sensione logice considerata," 41 / DAB 107.

[6] Amo, *Tractatus*, General Part, Chapter 1, §7, Note, 4 / DAB 70, refers back to *Apatheia*, Chapter 1, Member 1, §1., Note 2, 4 / DAB 14; *Treatise*, Special Part, Section 1, Chapter 2, Member 2, Note 2, 70 / DAB 136, refers back to *Apatheia*, Chapter 2, Sole Member, 15 / DAB 25.

[7] Amo, *Tractatus*, General Part, Chapter I, §7, Note 2, 5 / DAB 71, refers back to Anton Wilhelm Amo, *Disputatio philosophica continens Ideam distinctam eorum quae competunt vel menti vel corpori nostro vivo et organico* (hereafter "the Meiner dissertation") (Wittenberg: Literis Vidvae Kobersteinianae, 1734), Chapter 1, Member 2, Section 2, 8–9 / DAB 42–43; *Tractatus*, Special Part, Section 1, Chapter 1, Member 2, §5, 59 / DAB 125, refers back to the Meiner dissertation, Chapter 2, Member 2, §1 and §3, 8–9; DAB 42–43; and *Tractatus*, Special Part, Section 1, Chapter 5, Member 1, §4, Note, 87 / DAB 153, refers back to the Meiner dissertation, Chapter 2, Member 2, §6, 13 / DAB 47.

[8] Friedrich Ludwig Schardiuse autograafide kollektsioon, No. 3115, University of Tartu Library. I thank Dwight Lewis for alerting me to this document's existence.

that its purpose is something like that of a cover letter in a job application. This is a significant discovery for more than one reason. In the letter Amo refers to the "academy" to which the recipient belongs. Ordinarily we might interpret this term as part of a rhetorical inflation of the status of the person to whom the letter is sent, who might otherwise be a mere university professor or possibly something even lower. However, we are able to determine something more about the likely addressee of the letter by considering the collection in which it was found. The letter was in fact bequeathed to the University of Tartu in 1852 by Friedrich Ludwig Schardius, who had been the librarian of the St. Petersburg Academy of Sciences, founded in 1725 after a long planning phase in which G. W. Leibniz, among others, was centrally involved. The Schardius collection also includes a number of other letters to known St. Petersburg academicians, many of them sent by prominent Halle professors, not least by Christian Thomasius, Christian Wolff, and Georg Ernst Stahl. Thus, we may assume with high probability that Amo was at the time seeking some sort of position in the new Russian capital. This effort would be unsuccessful, but what is most interesting for our purposes is the reference Amo makes, without further clarification, to "the enclosed" [*inliegendes*]. The context suggests that what was enclosed was a "writing sample," one that would showcase his freshest and most mature contribution to philosophy; the timing suggests that the sample was what would two years later be published as the *Treatise*.

We do not know what Amo was doing in Wildenhain, or why he was unable to travel to Russia. What we do know is that by July 21, 1736, he would arrive instead at the University of Jena, where he enjoyed his longest stretch of employment, if always precarious and conditional upon continued success. Amo gained a particularly strong supporter in the dean of the faculty of philosophy, Friedrich Andreas Hallbauer, who wrote a note to his colleagues on June 29, two days after Amo's initial introduction, presenting various options for the "nostrification," or the transfer of credentials from one university to another, of this impoverished philosopher: "[H]e would either have to be nostrified at no cost," Hallbauer writes, "or the cost should be suspended until such time as he gains earnings here; or he should be permitted to teach provisionally, until we can see whether he receives steady applause [*applausus*], in which case he should be allowed to be officially nostrified."⁹

On March 4, 1737, as we read in the archives of the University of Halle, "Mister Amo submitted his work on logic to the censor's office" [*M. Amo scriptum logicum censurae submisit*].¹⁰ A key stage in the genesis of the work has now been completed. The *censura* in fact functioned more as an official rubber-stamping, making sure that everything had been done in the proper format according to the proper conventions, than as "censoring" in the narrow contemporary sense of the suppression of free thought. But whatever the university was watching out for, Amo got his work past some official body within it, and in 1738 the work was finally published. The fact that the work passed the *censura* in Halle and was published there, rather than in Jena where he was at the time working and residing, indicates that although he continued to move around, Halle, where he had first gone to study in 1727, remained the center of his professional life.

The *Treatise* could not have been widely studied or commented on in the initial years following its publication. The only known copy of the first edition is in the library collection of the University of Erlangen, and there is no reason to believe that it ever existed in more than perhaps a few dozen copies. The *Treatise's* publisher in Halle, Johann Gottfried Kittler (in Latin Kitlerius), established himself as a Halle printer only in 1731, taking over the established press of Johann Christian Hermann that year. He would go on to publish works of prominent Halle figures such as Thomasius, alongside many more "neglected" works of "neglected" authors, such as, in 1736, the *Dissertatio philosophica de veritate unica* [*Philosophical Dissertation on the Sole Truth*], the text corresponding to a thesis defended by Samuel Christian Harras, which defense was presided by Christopher Andrea Büttner—to pick somewhat at random a perfectly obscure, yet also fairly comparable, dissertation published at Halle around the time of Amo's own work. As with Amo's dissertations, it would take some textual analysis to determine which of these two was the author of the work, or indeed whether both of them were.

---

⁹ Universitätsarchiv Jena: Bestand M 97 Dekanatsakten III Bl. 63r. / DAB 277.
¹⁰ Universitätsarchiv Halle: Rep. 21 Abt. III Nr. 261, 83 / DAB 59.

The philosophical aims and import of Amo's first two works have by now been fairly well studied, and opinions differ as to how original and valuable they are.[11] Some scholars have come away from their close reading of Amo's two philosophical dissertations of 1734 with the firm conviction that they are noteworthy among the countless other such publications of their kind from the same time and place, as providing, in particular, a novel and bold variation on the Cartesian dualist program, in consequence of a well-argued derivation of philosophical conclusions from widely shared premises. But what about the *Treatise*? Let us turn now to the work itself, in order to be able to begin to answer this question in an informed way.

6.3. The Scope, Aims, and Sources of the *Treatise*

6.3.1. General Considerations

The *Treatise* is far too compendious and wide-ranging for us to survey all of the many topics discussed in it; simply to reproduce its table of contents would take up more space than we have. But we may at least touch on a number of its noteworthy elements.

Its full title, to begin, is worth citing: *The Guinea-African, Master of Philosophy and the Liberal Arts, Anton Wilhelm Amo's Treatise on the Art of Soberly and Accurately Philosophizing, In Accordance with His Academic Lessons, With an Added Succinct and Diligent Treatment of Criticism, Interpretation, Method, the Art of Disputation, and Other things that are Learned from Logic.*[12] This description suggests that the topics covered in the work overlap at least partially with those

---

[11] See, e.g., Burchard Brentjes, *Anton Wilhelm Amo: der schwarze Philosoph in Halle* (Leipzig : Koehler & Amelang, 1976); Yawovi Emmanuel Edeh, *Die Grundlagen der philosophischen Schriften von Amo. In welchem Verhältnis steht Amo zu Christian Wolff, dass man ihn als 'einen führnehmlichen Wolffianer' bezeichnen kann?* (Essen : Die blaue Eule, 2003); Victor Emma-Adamah, *Anton Wilhelm Amo (1703–1756): An African-German Philosopher of Mind*, MA thesis, University of Free State, Bloemfontein, South Africa, 2015; Paulin J. Hountondji, *Un philosophe africain dans l'Allemagne du XVIIIe siècle* (Paris: Presses Universitaires de France, 1970); Kwasi Wiredu, Amo's Critique of Descartes' Philosophy of Mind, in Kwasi Wiredu (ed.), *A Companion to African Philosophy* (Cambridge: Blackwell, 2004), 200–206.

[12] Amo, *Tractatus*, Title Page / DAB 60.

of the courses he had been teaching most recently. In fact, as we will see, the title's suggestion is borne out in the work, which gives signs of functioning as a sort of manual that Amo used to supplement the courses he taught, and that he hoped others might begin to use as well for such purposes now that it had been published. Moreover, the two-part structure of the title suggests that we may be reading two treatises fused together, with everything in the "added treatment" being added sometime later than 1734. The concrete evidence for this is that the references in the *Impassivity* and the Meiner dissertation to what Amo calls there his "*Logic*" are to early parts of the *Treatise*, well before the "added treatment." The later parts of the *Treatise* are more eclectic, and less systematic, and give the impression much more of the sort of survey of sundry topics that Amo would have been required to provide in his teaching at Jena.

Again, *The Treatise* belongs to a different genre than the two 1734 works: it is large and ambitious, rather than tight and focused. The work, 208 pages long, is divided into a relatively short "General Part" with five chapters,[13] and a longer "Special Part" with four sections,[14] the first of which has five chapters, the second of which six, the third of which eight, and the fourth of which three. As in the two 1734 dissertations, the chapters are divided into "Members" [*Membra*], and the members into numbered articles or sections marked with a § symbol. The work is highly formalized, and the prose that is found within any section seldom dilates beyond the single observation that Amo believes must be made at that place. He allows himself somewhat looser reflections mostly in the "Notes" that sometimes appear at the end of sections, akin to the "Scholia" that follow the propositions in Spinoza's *Ethics*.

6.3.2. Mapping Amo's Sources

In all three of his philosophical works, Amo chooses his philosophical sources out of a mixture of philosophical affiliation, institutional

---

[13] Amo, *Tractatus*, 1–53 / DAB 67–119.
[14] Amo, *Tractatus*, 54–208 / DAB 120–274.

expediency (the need to reference certain luminaries and to avoid others), and, finally, convenience—turning to whatever works may have been at hand or regularly accessible, under circumstances we will likely never be able to reconstruct with complete precision. It is nonetheless useful to survey his references, thereby locating the work within a sort of bibliographical map, and seeing more clearly what the motivation may be behind many of Amo's concerns and claims. This map, once drawn up, places Amo in a peculiar country, with unexpected neighbors.

Amo cites classical Greek authors (Aristotle,[15] Epictetus[16]); classical Roman authors (Augustine,[17] Aulus Gellius,[18] Cicero,[19] Ovid,[20] Seneca,[21] Varro[22]); a surprising number of medieval and late Scholastic authors working in a broadly Catholic ecclesiastical tradition, including Thomas Aquinas,[23] the Brussels neo-Scotist philosopher Jean Gabriel Boyvin (1605–1681),[24] François Crespin (also known as Franciscus Bonae Spei, 1617–1677);[25] a number of modern German authors, particularly those working within the Lutheran tradition, including Christian Thomasius,[26] Daniel Friedrich Jahn,[27] Adam Rechenberg,[28] Johann Burkhard Mencke,[29] Nicolaus Hieronymus Gundling,[30] and of course Philipp Melanchthon, who was the sixteenth-century philosopher and theologian largely responsible for adapting Lutheran dogma into a vast intellectual program to be implemented in university

---

[15] Amo, *Tractatus*, 43, 151–52, 201–202 / DAB 109, 217–218, 267–268.

[16] Amo, *Tractatus*, 129, 146 / DAB 195, 212.

[17] Amo, *Tractatus*, 200 / DAB 266.

[18] Amo, *Tractatus*, 17 / DAB 83.

[19] Amo, *Tractatus*, 10, 16, 25, 32, 44, 166, 172, 201–202 / DAB 76, 82, 91, 98, 110, 232, 238, 267–268.

[20] Amo, *Tractatus*, 45 / DAB 111. Amo does not mention Ovid by name in his quotation of the *Metamorphoses*.

[21] Amo, *Tractatus*, 172 / DAB 238.

[22] Amo, *Tractatus*, 199 / DAB 265.

[23] Thomas is generally cited by Amo via the abridgments in the work of Augustinus a Virgine Maria, the reference for which will be given below.

[24] Amo, *Tractatus*, 56 / DAB 122.

[25] Amo, *Tractatus*, 55 / DAB 121.

[26] Amo, *Tractatus*, 22, 193 / DAB 88, 187.

[27] Amo, *Tractatus*, 171 / DAB 237.

[28] Amo, *Tractatus*, 32 / DAB 98.

[29] Amo, *Tractatus*, 22 / DAB 88.

[30] Amo, *Tractatus*, 181 / DAB 247.

education. Thomasius and Gundling were closely associated with the University of Halle, and were Amo's contemporaries. Amo was almost certainly a disciple of Thomasius in at least some capacity, and Gundling for his part had explicitly mentioned Amo's *Impassivity* in a 1736 work compiling recent academic news from around Germany.[31] Much of Amo's German citation network is, so to speak, in the family: Rechenberg was married to Thomasius's sister, for example.

Amo also refers once to the Genevan theologian and philosopher Jean Le Clerc (1657–1736), a systematic philosopher who summarizes post-Cartesian schools of thought clearly while representing none of them, and who had been an important sounding-board for Amo's own views in the *Impassivity*.[32] He cites Francis Bacon one time as well,[33] the only reference to any English philosopher in any of Amo's writings. He cites the Bible a dozen times. In all, one gains a sense of Amo as a widely read philosopher, who is not afraid to cite from diverse traditions to support his own views, without concern that a citation from an author implies any further agreement with the author beyond what is explicit in the citation. This said, his comfort and familiarity with Catholic authors, writing as he is at the very heart of the Lutheran movement, is striking. Could Amo have hoped to engage more fully, in subsequent work, in a project of irenic reconciliation, of the sort to which Leibniz had devoted so much effort before him? One may only speculate.

Most of these authors receive no more than one citation. The Scholastic author Augustin de la Vierge Marie (Augustinus a Virgine Maria, d. 1689), a Breton Carmelite priest based in Tours, is cited a number of times, but these are references to his *Philosophiae Aristo-Thomisticae cursus* [*Course of Aristo-Thomistic Philosophy*],[34] which turn out to be direct or nearly direct quotations, variously, of Aristotle or Thomas. Epictetus is cited twice (we know from an entry by Amo in a Jena student's *Stammbuch* in 1736 that Amo was a great admirer of Epictetus: he chose to quote the ancient Stoic in a friendly

---

[31]   See Nicolaus Hieronymus Gundling (1736), *Vollständige Historie der Gelahrtheit*, Part Four, Leipzig, 5601 / DAB 51.

[32]   Amo, *Tractatus*, 162, 169 / DAB 228, 235.

[33]   Amo, *Tractatus*, 197 / DAB 263.

[34]   See Augustinus a Virgine Maria, *Philosophiae Aristo-Thomisticae cursus* (Leiden: H. Boissat & G. Remus, 1664), 4 volumes.

dedication[35]); Thomasius, whom Amo likely knew personally, is quoted three times; and Cicero is cited a total of nine times, with seven of these being references to *De officiis* [*On Duties*].

But Cicero comes in only in second place (not counting the Bible). Amo's most important resource for the *Treatise* is the work of Pierre de Saint-Joseph (Petrus a Sancto Josepho Fuliensi, 1594–1662), a member of the Cistercian abbey of Feuillans [*Congregatio Beatae Mariae Fuliensis*] in southern France. Saint-Joseph was a prolific author, who might also be said to be "neglected," if not by Amo, who cites him a total of fourteen times in the *Treatise*. Saint-Joseph was the author of several treatises of systematic theology and philosophy, to many of which he gave the title *Idea*, for example the *Idea theologiae moralis* (1652), the *Idea theologiae speculativa* (1652), the *Idea philosophiae naturalis, seu Physica* (1654), the *Idea philosophiae moralis, seu Ethica* (1654), the *Idea philosophiae universalis, seu Metaphysica* (1654), and the *Idea philosophiae rationalis, seu Logica* (1655).[36] For Saint-Joseph, philosophy consists in four parts (a "quadruplex Philosophia," in his own words): the universal, natural, moral, and rational, which may also be called, respectively, "metaphysics," "physics," "ethics," and "logic." Amo cites Saint-Joseph's physics, metaphysics, and most of all—not surprisingly given the subject of the *Treatise*—his logic.

Given Amo's overwhelming reliance on the philosophical works of Saint-Joseph, it is worth briefly summarizing his predecessor's project and method. Saint-Joseph defines logic as "a certain habit of the mind, by which all the operations of our intellect are directed in order towards knowing the truth."[37] Logic, however, Saint-Joseph continues, "is not wisdom, as it does not in itself treat of the most ancient and most worthy things."[38] Amo never says anything that similarly aims as it were to put logic in its place. This is not surprising. His *Treatise* is not conceived as part of a larger project covering all the different areas of philosophy. The *Treatise* is rather Amo's most comprehensive

[35] Thüringer Universitäts- und Landesbibliothek Jena St. 83: Bl. 210v.

[36] Pierre de Saint-Joseph, *Idea philosophiae rationalis, seu, Logica* (Cologne: Apud Constantinius Munich, 1655). Here we give only the bibliographical information for Saint-Joseph's *Logic*. In what follows, we will be citing from the second edition, published in Paris in 1659 by Georgius Iosse.

[37] Saint-Joseph, *Idea philosophiae rationalis*, Prelude, Article 1, 1.

[38] Saint-Joseph, *Idea philosophiae rationalis*, Prelude, Article 3, Praemonitum 6, 3.

statement of his philosophical project, and for that reason it is more ambitious than a typical work on logic, and consistently avoids limiting logic's scope or importance. Amo does, however, explicitly cite, on two occasions, the "Praemonitum" that immediately precedes the one cited just above,[39] in which Saint-Joseph distinguishes between metaphysics and logic, and also, more importantly for Amo, refers to logic as both an "art" and as a "habit," through which a person may cultivate the proper disposition of mind.

Amo is diligent about citing his sources. He often quotes Saint-Joseph verbatim, implying full agreement with his predecessor's view. Thus in the Second Member of Chapter One, Section One, of the Special Part, "On Representation," Amo follows the author of the *Idea* in asserting that "[t]hree acts or degrees of our cognition are commonly assigned, of which the first is called simple apprehension, the second judgment, and the third discourse."[40] Amo's work follows roughly the same order and progression as Saint-Joseph's; with two exceptions, his citations of the *Idea of Rational Philosophy* advance to ever later parts of the book, as we advance through Amo's own book. Thus in the Member 2 of Chapter 4, Section 3 of the Special Part, "On Regular and Simple Syllogisms," Amo refers to Book 2, chapter 2, article 2 of the *Idea*, where Saint-Joseph observes that "an enunciation is commonly divided into simple and composite."[41] In Member 4 of Chapter 4, Section 3 of the Special Part, "On Regular Composite Syllogisms," Amo cites Saint-Joseph's *Idea*, Book 3, chapter 5, article 4, "On Hypothetical Copulative and Disjunctive Syllogism." Curiously, Amo gives the same example of such a syllogism, identifying it as an enthymeme, but he removes Saint-Joseph's stock individual, Plato, and replaces him with the fictional Titius: "Titius is wealthy and learned; therefore he is wealthy, or, therefore he is learned."[42] Did Amo wish to avoid speaking of Plato here? He never mentions him anywhere else in his work. Yet, again, we may only speculate.

---

[39] Amo, *Tractatus*, 23, 49 / DAB 89, 115.

[40] Amo, *Tractatus*, 55 / DAB 121; citing Saint-Joseph, *Idea philosophiae rationalis*, Prelude, Article 9, Observandum 3, 27.

[41] Amo, *Tractatus*, 153–154 / DAB 219–220; citing Saint-Joseph, *Idea philosophiae rationalis*, 188.

[42] Amo, *Tractatus*, 167 / 233; citing Saint-Joseph, *Idea philosophiae rationalis*, 286.

6.3.3. Accurate, Sober, and Comprehensive

Chapter 1 of the General Part is devoted to "intention," which Amo defines as "that faculty of an intelligent substance that determines, having cognized a thing, either to act or to disregard it, in view of the conscious end it has."[43] This broad definition means that many topics indeed can fall under the scope of a treatment of intention. Member 5 of the same chapter is concerned with "learning in general," which Amo sees as a further development of his treatment of intention, as "the intention of the learned person is the intellection of intelligibles according to themselves. The objects are the things of divine and human intention, particularly as concerns the intention of the philosopher."[44] The ends of learning, we discover in Member 8, are threefold: "self-conservation, perfection, and eternal happiness of the mind."[45]

Amo goes on to offer a division of the different "orders of the learned," which correspond roughly to the divisions of the faculties in a university: theology, jurisprudence, medicine, and philosophy, "to the latter of which science [mathesis] may be added." Already in the first chapter, we see clearly that Amo conceives of "logic" in an expansive sense, one that is not so unusual in the early modern period, that includes much broader questions of the organization of learning both at an institutional and at a conceptual level. More than this, Amo's division here is plainly focused on the local Halle context (though he is at the time at Jena), where medicine, law, theology, and philosophy are the four prominent faculties of the university. Amo is known to have had relations with members of all four of them, and in this light his division reads almost as a sort of brochure for the university, a pitch for the variety of course offerings and the benefits that taking them might confer.

After giving a brief summary of law, medicine, and theology, Amo moves on to treat of "mathesis,"[46] promising that philosophy, the one discipline not summarized here, will get extensive treatment

---

[43] Amo, *Tractatus*, 68–69 / DAB 134–135.
[44] Amo, *Tractatus*, 10 / DAB 76.
[45] Amo, *Tractatus*, 14 / DAB 80.
[46] Amo, *Tractatus*, 19 / DAB 85.

throughout the *Treatise*. Mathesis, for Amo, includes both pure and mixed mathematics, the latter of which includes, for example, astronomy, mechanics, chronology, hydrometry, and architecture, which may be civil, military, or naval.[47] This division is more or less conventional, and calls to mind in particular the schemes for a division of the sciences that Leibniz had been actively proposing to Peter the Great and his councilors in the planning stages for the opening of the St. Petersburg Academy of Sciences. Here, anyhow, Amo is not only reflecting the organization of his own university, but is also envisioning larger and more ambitious institutions, perhaps with an eye to joining one of them in particular, in faraway Russia.

The one place in Amo's entire surviving corpus where we find an explicit mention of Leibniz is in Member 14 of Chapter 1, "Of Curious Learning." The context is one of at least moderate disparagement. Amo calls Leibniz a "polyhistorian," alongside others such as Hugo Grotius, Hermann Conring, and Julius Caesar, which is to say a person who has "(i) adequate knowledge of all letters, which they call 'the humanities'; (ii) practical knowledge of the special superior faculties of the sciences."[48] Such polyhistory is not necessarily bad on Amo's view, but one must be careful, for, as he notes, citing Seneca's second letter to Lucilius, "The man who is everywhere is nowhere."[49] A truly pernicious variety of polyhistory, by contrast, as Amo goes on to note, is the sort that concerns itself with unuseful things only for pure delectation of the mind; the sort that encourages perfunctoriness; the sort that engages with objects it is impossible to know; and the sort that dabbles in impious matters, such as "black kaballah, the magical arts, excavations of treasures by means of the magical arts," etc.[50]

It is likely that Amo had met Leibniz when the former was a boy at the court of Wolfenbüttel and the latter was an elderly philosopher and diplomat on one of his regular visits. However, not just in his specific philosophical commitments, but indeed in his general philosophical disposition, Amo is no Leibnizian. While Leibniz too disdained the

47   Amo, *Tractatus*, 19 / DAB 85.
48   Amo, *Tractatus*, 21 / DAB 87.
49   Amo, *Tractatus*, 21 / DAB 87.
50   Amo, *Tractatus*, 21 / DAB 87.

credulity of those who become too wrapped up in natural magic and alchemy, even here he tended to think that one must pay at least some attention, since even fools may have real insights on occasion. Leibniz did not shy away from curiosity, but allowed himself to range widely. Amo, by contrast, is a cautious and rigorous thinker, holding forth only on what he is certain he knows, and presenting his philosophy in a rigorous and focused way. He is comprehensive, in part because he must be in order to succeed as a teacher; but his philosophical spirit is first and foremost one of sobriety and accuracy, not of curiosity and self-dispersion.

Chapter 2 is "On Philosophy," which Amo defines as "a habit of the intellect and of the will, by which we continually undertake to determinately and adequately know the things themselves, to the extent possible with certainty; and by means of the application of this sort of cognition, the perfection of man gains in possible increments."[51] As to its divisions, the first and most basic is between speculative and practical philosophy, the former consisting in turn in three branches: ontology, which deals with being in general; physics, which treats of bodies; and pneumatology, which studies spirits. Practical philosophy is divided into logic, ethics, and natural theology, the last of which is "the habit of the contemplative intellect and the will, by which the mind . . . , arguing from the existence, origin, and essence of the world to the existence and essence of God, and to the dependence of man on him, deduces the duties that are naturally owed to him."[52]

This is a curious division for a number of reasons. One is that if the Treatise is a work of "logic," as Amo calls it, it turns out that part of logic consists in classifying logic alongside other branches of learning besides logic. Logic is then inherently meta-logical in a way that, say, pneumatology is not meta-pneumatological. Another curious point is Amo's classification of logic among the practical branches of philosophy, closer to ethics than to the various speculative domains. This is a somewhat, though not completely, original move on Amo's part. It was of course common to describe logic as a "habit" (as we have seen in Saint-Joseph), an "art," or a "discipline." Pierre Gassendi, for

[51] Amo, Tractatus, 24 / DAB 90.
[52] Amo, Tractatus, 30–31 / DAB 96–97.

example, describes logic as a directing of the intellect toward the pursuit of truth, but he sees it as one branch of a twofold art, the other being ethics or morals, which directs the will toward the pursuit of the good.[53] And the *Port-Royal Logic*, similarly, conceives this subject as at least in part devoted to thinking clearly about concepts in order to make clear distinctions. Gassendi, the Port-Royal authors, and Amo alike are far from the common view from the nineteenth century on of logic as concerned with the structure of facts in the world, rather than as a human project of ordering our thoughts that is closely aligned with pedagogy. Since Amo's basic division of philosophy is into the "speculative" and the "practical," rather than into the "theoretical" and the practical, it is not so surprising that logic must fall into the "practical" domain: it cannot be speculative, since it does not aim to produce new positive knowledge about the world. It is nonetheless surprising to find it described as practical; while logic is a "habit" for Amo, the benefit of cultivating this habit is mostly cognitive and intellectual. We pursue it, he explains "in order that (1) we should understand intelligible beings determinately and adequately; (2) we should acquire the habitual perfection of the intellect in knowing things according to themselves."[54]

Having taxonomized philosophy and determined logic's place within it, Amo goes on in Chapter 3 of the General Part to treat of "Things Considered Logically," beginning with "Being and Its Principle" in Member 1. A "principle" in Amo's technical sense is either real or actual, on the one hand, or formal, on the other. These two terms have storied and complex histories in philosophy, but in general we may expect that a formal principle is what makes a given individual thing the sort of thing it is, while a real principle is what ensures that that thing exists at all as a thing, or *res*. Yet Amo's explication of this distinction defies any easy attempt to fit it into this broad historical pattern. For him, a real principle is that from which a being "has its origin, existence, and essence,"[55] and this is the case in a twofold sense, either for spirits or for bodies. A formal principle is "that mode of acting, by which a being acquires diverse determinations and modifications, or

---

[53] See Pierre Gassendi (1658), *Syntagma Philosophicum*, vol. 2: *Logica*, Proemium.

[54] Amo, *Tractatus*, 30–31 / DAB 96–97.

[55] Amo, *Tractatus*, 33 / DAB 99.

its specific difference."[56] The real principle constitutes the genus of a given being, while the formal principle constitutes the species. Could Amo mean these terms here in a hierarchical sense, where the genus is a broader category in which several different species can coexist? In a subsequent note, Amo explains that it is with respect to the formal principle that we seek answers to the questions "(a) Of what sort? (b) How? (c) To what extent, or for how long? (d) How many times? (e) What is the being formally? (f) Of what genus is it? Of what species? What sort of individual is it?"[57] At first glance, we are dealing here with something like an enumeration of the different ways "in which being is said," akin to Aristotle's categories. But if the formal principle "constitutes the species," as Amo has already said, it is odd that one should, as Amo states in (f), consider this principle in order to determine both the genus and the species of a given being, as well indeed as determining its individuality; and it is at least tautological, if not confused, to say, as Amo does in (e), that it is the formal principle that tells us what the being is formally. While the principle of charity in interpretation restrains us from concluding as much with any certainty, it may be that Amo has simply gone too fast in this section, and has gotten lost in the conceptual distinctions he has attempted to lay out.

Chapter 4 of the General Part is concerned with "Sensation Considered Logically." Sensation is not, obviously, a part of logic as we conceive it, yet here we see the unity of Amo's philosophical project and the continuity of the *Treatise* with his earlier works. For Amo, sensation is "the sensible quality present in the sensory organs," and it may be considered in a threefold way: "physically, morally, and logically."[58] Physically, a sensation is either agreeable or disagreeable; morally, "habitual sensations" or customs are to be judged in terms of whether they are good or bad; logically, a sensation is judged according to whether it is present or absent in the organs of memory and sense. "Present" and "absent" function for Amo in what we might call his "logic of sense" in the same way "true" and "false" do in standard logic. Amo does not have much more to say about this distinction, but it is intriguingly

---

[56] Amo, *Tractatus*, 33 / DAB 99.
[57] Amo, *Tractatus*, 34–35 / DAB 100–101.
[58] Amo, *Tractatus*, 41 / DAB 107.

original, and unlike his discussion of real and formal principles, does not appear mired in confusion.

Chapter 5 concerns the three faculties of the mind: "intellective act, will, and effective act." The existence of these faculties is inferred from their respective effects: cognition; deliberation and choice; and action or omitting to act. Amo goes on to provide an analysis of will, the second of the three faculties, and it is worthy of particular mention. He defines it as "the act of the mind by which it determines things that are cognized, so as to act or omit to act in accordance with a known end."[59] The will has both moral and physical dimensions. Its physical features are "(a) sensitive appetite; and (b) natural instinct, manifested as motile causes."[60] Appetite is "that sensible quality that comes forth in the longing for edible things, towards the conservation and delectation of the body," while instinct is "the innate propensity, sensed in the heart, by which we give ourselves to those things which are agreeable."[61] This is, at the very least, a further indication of Amo's distance from Leibniz, who appropriated the concept of *appetitus* for a philosophical application rather far from the physiological sensation of hunger, which application in turn seems far from Amo's concerns here.

The sixth and final chapter of the General Part is on "Truth and Falsehood in Respect of a Thing," and it contains only three members: the first, on "truth in general," the second "on falsehood," and the third "on truth and falsehood as concerns our mode of knowing." He explains that truth is either objective or intentional. Objective truth is either real or sensual: again, the preoccupation with sensation is seldom far from Amo's mind, even in his engagement with what are sometimes seen as more basic philosophical concepts such as being and truth. Intentionally considered, in turn, truth is either logical, moral, or pragmatic. Logical truth is the agreement of a cognition with the thing of which it is the cognition. Moral truth is made possible by the presence of will, and it manifests itself as justice and virtue. Pragmatic truth, finally, is truth the reality of which necessarily brings about an effect when it is applied.

[59] Amo, *Tractatus*, 44 / DAB 110.
[60] Amo, *Tractatus*, 44 / DAB 110.
[61] Amo, *Tractatus*, 44 / DAB 110.

Truth is said for Amo, too, in many ways, and none of these basic varieties of truth seems to have any precedence over the others.

So much, as Amo would say, for the General Part. There follows the longer Special Part, to which we cannot do anything close to full justice here. The reason for this separation, into general and special, is far from self-evident. The Special Part is separated into four sections: one on "the momentary intellective act prior to reflection, and on representation and attention"; a second on "reflection, contemplation, and deliberation"; a third on "momentary effects and operations of the mind after reflection"; and, finally, a fourth on the art of disputation.

Section 3, Chapter 4, "On Syllogisms," is a particularly lively survey of this core element of rote learning in the standard university curriculum going back to the Middle Ages. This chapter again shows the close link of much of Amo's work in the *Treatise* to his life as a teacher, and one gains insights here into the talent he must have had in this career. Amo presents the standard tables of the various syllogistic figures, using the traditional names "Barbara," "Celarent," "Darii," "Festino," and so on, each one encoding in the sequence of its three vowels a given order of universal or particular, and negative or affirmative, propositions, as one moves from the major premise to the minor premise and on to the conclusion of the syllogism. This is dry material, but necessary for any student who aspires to think soberly and accurately.

Like many other modern philosophers who engage with logic and see it as a tradition not totally distinct from classical rhetoric, Amo also spends some time dealing with the various species of fallacy and sophism, and much like Gassendi, he seems to appreciate the potential for humor they often contain. It is not hard to picture him presenting the "Fallacy of Composition" to his class, just as he does in the *Treatise*:

> This goat is yours.
> This goat is a mother.
> Therefore, this goat is your mother.[62]

---

[62] Amo, *Tractatus*, 173 / DAB 239.

The joke works better in Latin, where there is no difference between "your" and "yours," and no indefinite article that appears in the second premise only to fall out in the conclusion. In any case, it is clear that Amo liked the joke, that he understood the fine line between logic and what the ancients often denounced as "fallacy-mongering," and that he was not afraid to monger fallacies a bit himself in order, perhaps, to get his "student evaluations" up, as measured on the scale of loudness of post-lecture *applausus*.

6.4. Conclusion

Historians of philosophy in general are not trained in even the most elementary distant-reading corpus analysis, in taking the broad measure of how many works of a certain sort were produced in a certain region in a certain span of time. Scholars of, say, eighteenth-century English novels, do not happen upon a single forgotten work from the time and place that interests them, discover that it is interesting and revelatory, and then go on to ask why it has been "neglected." They do not do this because they know how massive the corpus is. Without such knowledge it is impossible to say anything meaningful about whether a work has been *unduly* neglected. The present author has devoted considerable time to understanding Amo's work and its sources and context, and in hindsight finds this time well spent. But in part this finding has to do with the conviction, only deepened through the study of Amo, that minor figures are particularly valuable for the way they shine light on the time and place in which they are working. Amo is rightly considered a minor figure, not very different in his intellectual output from many other young men who received MA degrees in philosophy in Lutheran Germany in the eighteenth century. All the more reason to study him.

Amo's work is interesting and revelatory, both because it tells us quite a bit about the intellectual world he inhabited in early eighteenth-century Germany, and because it is a testament to the life and existence of a remarkable individual. Should it be, as it were, de-neglected? Certainly, if that is what we decide at present is best. But this *is* a choice, a constructive act, and not a correction of the record to accommodate a preexisting but unrecognized fact of the matter.

One way to go about making this choice is to ask: Who would benefit most from reading this work? The answer that immediately presents itself is: Any student in an introductory survey course in philosophy—who happens to be enrolled at the University of Jena or Halle circa 1738. Beyond this, the work will be of interest to any scholar specialized in the exceedingly narrow subject of academic philosophy in Saxony in the early eighteenth century. And it will be of at least some interest to anyone wishing to learn about the biography of a particularly remarkable African in early modern Europe. But Amo's life would have been worthy of study no matter what the quality of his philosophical work had been, so it would be useful, if we do choose to de-neglect his work, to find something intrinsic to it that makes it philosophically interesting beyond the circumstances of its origin. This might be something determined not by the quality of the work in achieving its own goals—correctly delineating the tables of syllogistic forms and so on—but rather by its genre: that is, this work might be of interest to the extent that it is a work of African philosophy.

But is it? There is not a single sentence in the extant works of Amo that indicates any interest in grappling with questions of African identity, or in reflecting on the differences between philosophical traditions in different parts of the world. We might suppose that an interest in such questions could be found in the "missing" treatise, the 1729 legal dissertation on the right of "Moors" in Europe. But even here we must be careful not to speculate. For one thing, again, it is likely that there never was such a treatise, but only an oral defense of a thesis. This thesis, moreover, was likely drawn from topics covered by Johann Peter von Ludewig in lectures attended by Amo in the law faculty at Halle earlier in the fall semester of 1729. In these lectures, von Ludewig discussed the *Corpus juris civilis* that had been the basis of the transmission of Roman Law into the Holy Roman Empire, and that had included considerable discussion of Justinian's enfeoffment of African or "Moorish" kings following the Vandalic War of the sixth century CE, which had certain legal implications for high-ranking Africans traveling in Europe in late antiquity.[63] In other words, even

---

[63] See Johann Peter von Ludewig, *Vita Iustiniani atque Theodorae Augustorum nec non Triboniani. Iurisprudentiae iustinianae proscenium* (Halae Salicae: Impensis Orphanotrophei, 1731), 377.

this work, which likely no scholar has read since 1729, and which seems at first glance to concern questions that would be especially suitable for an African philosopher to take on, might simply have been the result of a topic assigned by a mentor, based on the widespread interest in the Halle legal faculty in understanding the legacy of Roman law in contemporary Germany.

If we agree with Paulin Hountondji, any work of philosophy written by an African is a work of African philosophy, whether it is about Thomistic metaphysics, modal logic, or whatever. Hountondji resorts to this definition in order to avoid the alternative view, according to which African philosophy is "ethnophilosophy," embedded in traditional cultures and waiting for "extraction" by suitably trained (i.e., inevitably Europeanized) experts.[64] If Hountondji is right that Amo's work is African philosophy, on this narrow definition, then we might also combine his insight with a notion introduced by Liam Kofi Bright, and say that the *Treatise* is an early representative of the genre of "formal Africana philosophy." But if we reject Hountondji's definition—and the reader is free to decide whether to do so or not—then we must admit that there is nothing intrinsic to the work at all warranting the appellation "African." Africa comes up exactly once in the work: on the title page, in the identification of Amo as a "Guinea-African." This identification was likely less salient to a contemporary reader than it seems to be to us. It was common to identify largely unknown authors by reference to their place of origin, and the title pages of many books of a similar sort give the name of the author along with his hometown. Thus Harras's *On the Sole Truth*, to which we have already alluded, published by the same press as the *Treatise* was one year earlier, informs us that its author (or perhaps only its defender) hails from Sylda in the Southern Harz.

If the *Treatise* is not a work of African philosophy, there is only one thing left for it to be, at least if we limit ourselves to geographical designations: a work of German philosophy. Amo could have been no older than seven when he arrived in Germany; certain idiosyncrasies

---

[64] Paulin Hountondji, *African Philosophy: Myth and Reality*, 2nd ed., trans. Henri Evans, with Jonathan Rée (Bloomington: Indiana University Press, [1976] 1996), 111–130.

of his Latin syntax reveal an author at work whose native language, for all practical purposes, is German. More expansively, the *Treatise* is a work of academic Latinate German philosophy in the modern Lutheran university tradition, closely reflecting the curricula in place at the universities of Halle, Wittenberg, and Jena, and with a curious admixture of French Catholic late Scholasticism. A neglected classic? Again, the choice is ours to make.

Bibliography

Amo, A. W. (1734). *Disputatio philosophica continens Ideam distinctam eorum quae competunt vel menti vel corpori nostro vivo et organico.* Wittenberg: Literis Vidvae Kobersteinianae.

Amo, A. W. (1734). *Dissertatio inauguralis philosophica de humanae mentis apatheia.* Wittenberg: Ex Officina Schomachiana.

Amo, A. W. (1738). *Tractatus de arte sobrie et accurate philosophandi.* Halle: Ex Officina Kitleriana.

Augustinus a Virgine Maria (1664). *Philosophiae Aristo-Thomisticae cursus.* 4 vols. Leiden: H. Boissat & G. Remus.

Brentjes, B. (1968). *Antonius Guilielmus Amo Afer aus Axim in Ghana. Student, Doktor der Philosophie, Magister legens an den Universitäten Halle, Wittenberg, Jena, 1727–1747: Dokumente/Autographe/Belege.* Halle: Martin-Luther-Universität Halle-Wittenberg.

Brentjes, B. (1976). *Anton Wilhelm Amo: der schwarze Philosoph in Halle.* Leipzig: Koehler & Amelang.

Edeh, Y. E. (2003). *Die Grundlagen der philosophischen Schriften von Amo. In welchem Verhältnis steht Amo zu Christian Wolff, dass man ihn als 'einen führnehmlichen Wolffianer' bezeichnen kann?* Essen: Die blaue Eule.

Emma-Adamah, V. (2015). *Anton Wilhelm Amo (1703–1756): An African-German Philosopher of Mind.* MA thesis, University of Free State, Bloemfontein, South Africa.

Gassendi, P. (1658). *Syntagma Philosophicum,* vol. 2: *Logica.* Leiden: Anisson.

Gundling, N. H. (1736). *Vollständige Historie der Gelahrtheit.* Leipzig.

Hountondji, P. J. (1970). *Un philosophe africain dans l'Allemagne du XVIIIe siècle.* Paris: Presses Universitaires de France.

Hountondji, P. J. ([1976] 1996). *African Philosophy: Myth and Reality,* 2nd ed. Trans. Henri Evans, with Jonathan Rée. Bloomington: Indiana University Press.

von Ludewig, J. P. (1731). *Vita Iustiniani atque Theodorae Augustorum nec non Triboniani. Iurisprudentiae iustinianae proscenium.* Halle: Impensis Orphanotrophei.

Menn, S., and Smith, J. E. H. (2020). Introduction. In *Anton Wilhelm Amo: Philosophical Dissertations on Mind and Body.* Oxford: Oxford University Press.

Saint-Joseph, P. de (1655). *Idea philosophiae rationalis, seu, Logica.* Cologne: Apud Constantinius Munich.

Wiredu, K. (2004). Amo's Critique of Descartes' Philosophy of Mind. In Wiredu, K. (ed.), *A Companion to African Philosophy.* Cambridge: Blackwell, 200–206.

7

On Mary Shepherd's *Essay upon the Relation of Cause and Effect*

Jessica Wilson

7.1. Overview

Mary Shepherd (1777–1847) was appreciated in her day by those who knew her—geologist Charles Lyell said of her that she was an "unanswerable logician, in whose argument it was impossible to find loophole or flaw"; William Whewell, inventor and exemplar of the term "scientist," used one of her two treatises in a course at Cambridge; the poet Samuel Taylor Coleridge drafted a poem describing her as "a desperate scholar," which any true philosopher will take as a great compliment. Her work later fell into obscurity, however.[1] Recently, Shepherd's work has gotten a bit more attention, both as offering certain novel criticisms of the doctrines of Berkeley and Hume (see Atherton 1996 and Rickless 2018) and with an eye to considering certain of her positive views (see Bolton 2010; LoLordo 2019; Boyle 2020; and Landy 2020). This recent activity is all to the good, but Shepherd remains almost criminally underrated.

For one thing, Shepherd doesn't just criticize the doctrines of Berkeley and Hume—in my estimation she decimates them, politely but ruthlessly, with the skill of a surgeon who is not taking any chances that whatever-it-is might survive. Some commentators have suggested that certain of Shepherd's arguments are not entirely successful. This would not be surprising, if true—few arguments are

---

[1] See Bolton 2021 and the introduction to Boyle 2018 for further biographical details about Shepherd.

Jessica Wilson, *On Mary Shepherd's* Essay upon the Relation of Cause and Effect In: *Neglected Classics of Philosophy*. Edited by: Eric Schliesser, Oxford University Press. © Oxford University Press 2022. DOI: 10.1093/oso/9780190097196.003.0008

completely airtight—but I'm more convinced by her than by them.[2] Even more deserving of attention and appreciation are Shepherd's positive views about the nature of reality and our access to it—views which are not just novel and interesting but considerably more plausible than those of her opponents, and which are as relevant as ever so far as explorations into our options in contemporary metaphysics and epistemology are concerned. Either of Shepherd's two major works—the 1824 *Essay upon the Relation of Cause and Effect, Controverting the Doctrine of Mr. Hume, Concerning the Nature of that Relation*[3] (henceforth: ERCE), or the 1827 *Essays on the Perception of an External Universe, and Other Subjects Connected with the Doctrine of Causation*[4] (henceforth: EPEU)—would do by way of illustrating the importance of her work. Here I'll focus on her first treatise and the accounts of the epistemology and metaphysics of causation that she advances therein.

After a brief setup, I canvass certain of Shepherd's trenchant objections to Hume's argumentation; I then present the positive core of her response to Hume, which consists in providing novel accounts of how reason alone or reason coupled with experience can justify, first, that every effect must have a cause, and second, that it is necessary that like causes produce like effects. Among other contributions, here Shepherd provides a distinctively metaphysical argument for the claim that nothing can begin to exist "of itself" (going beyond an appeal to the Principle of Sufficient Reason, in particular), and leverages difference-making considerations to make the case that a single "experimentum crucis" can justify causal belief (anticipating Mill's "method of difference"). I close by highlighting salient features of

---

[2] For example, Atherton (1996) levels several complaints about Shepherd's critique of Berkeley's idealism, but as Rickless (2018) shows, these complaints are undeserved. The only flaw Rickless identifies in Shepherd's critique is the non-injurious one according to which her charge that Berkeley's main argument for idealism equivocates on "perceive" would be better framed as involving an equivocation on "perception by sense"; this tweak aside, it remains that "Shepherd has identified, at least in general terms, both the location and the essential nature of the problem with [Berkeley's] argument," and more generally that "no philosopher, none of [Berkeley's] contemporaries and no other successor of his over the course of three centuries, was able to get as close as she did to the nub of the issue" (329).

[3] See McRobert 2000, vol. 1.

[4] See McRobert 2000, vol. 2, and Lolordo 2020.

Shepherd's metaphysics of causation, whereby causation is singularist and local (anticipating Ducasse and Anscombe) and involves synchronic interactions (anticipating Mill's and certain contemporary accounts), and according to which objects are essentially characterized by their causes and effects (anticipating contemporary causal or dispositional essentialist positions).[5]

7.2. The Project and Its Stage-Setting

Shepherd presents her project in ERCE as primarily critical of Hume's doctrines concerning causation, and in particular of his views and argumentation according to which neither reason nor experience, individually or together, can justify the beliefs that, first, "it [is] necessary [that] every thing whose existence has a beginning should also have a Cause," and second, that "such particular Causes must necessarily have such particular Effects," so that the only basis for such beliefs lies in "custom acting on the imagination," which latter position forms the basis for Hume's "constant conjunction" (or "regularity") account of causation. While (as we'll see) Shepherd criticizes many specific aspects of Hume's argumentation, her primary line of objection involves showing, as per her positive views of the matters at hand, how either reason alone or reason coupled with experience can justify the beliefs in question, in a way that in turn supports her original and very different account of causation, as well as certain concomitant views

---

[5] See Fantl 2016 for nuanced discussion of Shepherd's anticipation of certain contemporary accounts of objects and properties. Attention to Shepherd's second treatise suggests other views for which she deserves historical credit, including the view, commonly attributed to Russell ([1912] 1967), that the existence of a mind-independent external world is supported by an inference to the best explanation of the pattern of our experiences. As Shepherd summarizes the line of thought, "the readiness [. . .] to appear when called for by the use of the organs of sense, mixed with the reasoning, that the organs of sense and mind being the same, a third set of objects is needed in order to determine those perceptions in particular which are neither the organs of sense nor mind in general, forms together the familiar reason, (the superinduced sensation,) which yields to all,—infants, and peasants, as much as to wise men, the notion of the continual existence of objects unperceived" (EPEU 15). As Atherton (1996) puts it, "The idea is that various relations among our sensations constitute a proof there are external existences, because, roughly speaking, the existence of the sensations we experience, related as they are, could not be explained unless external bodies existed" (350).

(which I unfortunately will not have space to discuss here) pertaining to the uniformity of nature and the practical question of what guides human expectation and action.[6]

Before getting to (certain of) Shepherd's critical and constructive views, I'll highlight two ways in which she perspicuously sets the stage for her discussion, which will also serve to remind the reader of certain of Hume's lines of thought.

7.2.1. The Import of the Project

Prior to presenting Hume's doctrines, Shepherd registers that she will not be completely adhering to his request, in the *Essays*, to ignore the previous *Treatise* as a product of his "juvenile" reasoning. One difference between these works is that in the *Treatise*, Hume explicitly considers what justification there might be for the belief that "every thing whose existence has a beginning should also have a Cause," as well as the belief that "such particular causes must necessarily have such particular effects," whereas in the *Essays* only the latter belief is explicitly treated. As Shepherd notes, however, Hume's reasons for rejecting the two beliefs in the *Treatise* were ultimately of a piece. In the *Treatise* Hume first argues, on grounds that he can conceive otherwise, that the need for a new existence to have a cause is not justified by reason:

The separation [. . .] of the idea of a cause, from that of a beginning of existence, is plainly possible for the imagination, and consequently the *actual* separation of these objects is so far possible, that it implies no contradiction, nor absurdity, and is, therefore, incapable of being refuted by any reasoning, from mere ideas; without which it is impossible to demonstrate the necessity of a cause. (*Treatise*, §1.3.3.3)

---

[6] As LoLordo (2019) puts it, "Like Reid and Kant, Shepherd aims to refute Hume by providing a better alternative" (1).

This much leaves open whether the belief in the necessity of a cause might arise from "observation and experience"; and in the *Treatise* Hume registers that he will "sink this question in the following: Why we conclude that such particular causes must necessarily have such particular effects? Because the *same answer will serve for both questions*" (§1.3.3.9). And as above, Hume's answer is ultimately that neither belief is justified, and that commitment to each is ultimately due to a kind of psychological projection born of customary experience.

Now, notwithstanding that Hume restricts his focus to the second question in the *Essays*, Shepherd argues that he continues to be committed to the first belief's being unjustified:

> "That Cause and Effect are distinct and separable;" so "that any object may be conceived, as therefore capable of beginning its own existence," must be considered as among the notions adopted in the *Essays*: what else is the meaning of such propositions as these: "There appears not throughout all nature, any one instance of connection, as conceivable by us;" "one event follows another," "but we never can observe any tye between them, etc." Indeed, the not admitting any "relations of ideas," or "any reasonings a priori," (so as to be capable of supporting the idea of CAUSATION as a creating principle absolutely necessary in the universe) is but repeating "the juvenile ideas" of the Treatise, and casting them anew in these later pieces. (38–39)

Correspondingly, Shepherd observes, Hume's reasons for rejecting necessary causal connections in the *Treatise* serve just as well— assuming they go through—to undercut the reasons for thinking that every beginning of existence must have a cause. And this in turn, she observes, undercuts the primary reason to believe in God, as the requisite first or primary cause of all else. So while taking the *Essays* in isolation from the *Treatise* might suggest that Hume's focus in his later work pertains just to a somewhat abstruse issue in the metaphysics of causation (albeit one having import for our practical deliberations), Shepherd flags that a key motivation for the existence of some eternally existing generative principle—God, on the usual construal—is also at stake.

7.2.2. The Presentation of Hume's View

Shepherd's exegesis of Hume's position receives a dedicated chapter, largely in the form of linked direct quotes from the *Treatise* and the *Essays*.[7] Why so much direct quotation? As she observes:

> In every controversial work, much obscurity appears in an author's arguments, on account of the opinions of his adversary not being distinctly understood; owing either to partial quotation, or mistaken statement: I therefore mean to obviate all chance of any misunderstanding on that ground, by giving the adversary's opinions upon the controverted doctrine in his own words; taking care to leave out only extraneous matter, and to alter the arrangement in such a manner as to form at once a clear and concise, a fair and intelligible view of the whole subject. (7)

I highlight this exegetical strategy since it is evidence of her general dialectical perspicuity. Shepherd was well aware that as a woman aiming—somewhat unusually for the time—to criticize a prominent male figure, and moreover as regards a view that was "rampant [and] widely spread,"[8] mere paraphrase of Hume's view would have offered the opportunity for others to dismiss her work from the get-go as missing the target, somehow or other. Smart indeed, then, for Shepherd to let Hume perform his own exegesis, such that there is really no denying that he offered the arguments and held the views which will be the subject of her critique.

7.3. A Few Representative Objections

I next canvass a few of the objections that Shepherd directs at specific aspects of Hume's discussion, to give the reader a feel for the

---

[7] Shepherd does similarly in presenting Berkeley's views in EPEU.

[8] As Robert Blackey put it in his *History of the Philosophy of Mind*: "When [Shepherd] undertook a public refutation of these erroneous notions on cause and effect, it must be remembered it was at a time when they were most rampant, and widely spread over the northern parts of Britain in particular" (1848, v. 4, 43).

remarkable precision and incisiveness characteristically on display in her work. These objections include:

1. That Hume's glosses on the topic at hand make no sense as they stand, and must be revised:

   "To make any meaning whatever of the proposition, "We may imagine causes to exist separate from their effects;" the objects we call *causes* are not to be imagined as *causes*, but may be supposed *not to cause any thing*, but to exist without *determining their own effects*, or *any others*; that is, causes and their effects are so evidently distinct, that they may be imagined to be unconnected objects, that are *not causes and effects*, and to exist separately without a contradiction, though they are named expressly as signs of the ideas we have, that they are necessary to one another." (33)

2. That Hume's statement of the second question—"Why we conclude that such particular Causes must necessarily have such particular Effects?"—is also inapt:

   "The question, however, ought to stand thus, "why LIKE CAUSES must necessarily have LIKE EFFECTS?" because what is really enquired into, is the general notion of necessary connexion, between all like Cause and Effect; and by thus putting the question respecting particulars only, although they might be included in an universal answer, yet no answer applicable to them MERELY, could authorize an universal axiom. The manner of stating the enquiry in the Essays, is also too vaguely expressed, (although it be evident that it is the general relation which is enquired into). Mr. Hume says, "we will now enquire, how we arrive at the knowledge of Cause and Effect." (*Essays*, Sec. 4. P. 27) *It ought to be stated*, how we arrive at the knowledge of the *necessary connexion*, between *like* Cause and Effect?" (40)

3. That in the course of discussing the second question, Hume shifts to a different question:

   "If it should be asked, (as Mr. Hume presently does,) how is it known when objects are similar upon any two occasions; the "sensible qualities may be the same, and not the *secret powers, upon which the Effects depend?*" I answer, this is to *shift* the question from the examination of *like Causes supposed*, to the consideration of the *method whereby their presence* may be *detected.*" (60)

4. That Hume errs in supposing that whatever he can conceive (e.g., there being a new existent without a cause, or some similar cause producing a different effect) is genuinely possible:

"Mr. Hume makes also a great mistake in supposing because we can conceive in the fancy the existence of objects contrary to our experience, that therefore they may really exist in nature; for it by no means follows that things which are incongruous in nature, may not be contemplated by the imagination, and received as possible until reason shows the contrary." (83)

5. That Hume's argument that the belief in necessary causal connection is justified by custom, not reason, proceeds by assuming what it is to be proven:

"The sum of Mr. Hume's argument is, that we knowing nothing of the "secrets of nature," we cannot know there is really a necessary connection between objects; but *imagining* there is [such a connection], this *imagination* arises, from a CUSTOMARY OBSERVATION, of *the invariableness of their antecedence and subsequence*;—which invariableness, however, does not prove, that each connexion may be more than an *insulated causal event*; not obligatory in nature; therefore *other subsequent* events might, without a contradiction, be imagined to happen after *similar antecedents*, and a *different order of events* might be supposed in the "course of nature."

Now shortly the whole of this reasoning the *possibility of nature altering her course*, is but a circle! For the argument is invented to show that CUSTOM *not* REASON, must be the only ground of our belief in the relation of Cause and Effect.— But it is *impossible to imagine such a change in nature*, unless *reason* were previously excluded as the principle of that relation;—*and it is impossible to exclude reason as the principle of that relation*, except by supposing *that nature may alter her course.*" (86–87)

6. That "Mr. Hume's three definitions of the relation of Cause and Effect are, in many respects, faulty, and not borne out by his own arguments" (64). To start, his first, "constant conjunction," definition is unsupported by lights of his own argument:

"He defines a Cause "an object followed by another, and where all the objects similar to the first are followed by objects similar to the second."—Now if he means an object that will in *future*, as in *past* times, be always followed by another; an *invariable* necessity in the antecedent to be followed by its subsequent, his whole argument tends to prove the *contrary*, and to show that experience has power to answer for the *past* only, and cannot for the future." (64)

7. That his second, counterfactual, definition is not a mere "in other words" variation on the first, and in any case is again unsupported by his previous argumentation:[9]

"He goes on to say, "or in other words, where if the first object had not been, the second had never existed;" but this idea expresses a much stricter necessity of connexion than does the relation of any number of objects, which had only followed each other in *past time*, however often their antecedency and subsequency had been repeated. Such a necessity is contradicted the whole way by the argument. It is quite another sentiment, from that which arises from the ideas of always *before* and *after*. That which requires another object to its existence, must be

---

[9] Shepherd also observes that by Hume's lights (though, given her causal essentialist view of objects, not her own) "[t]he second definition is also erroneous, because although similar causes must have similar effects, yet diverse causes may produce the same effects also—therefore the second object might exist without the first, by the operation of any other cause efficient to it" (67).

necessarily connected with it; and I contend that it is so connected [. . .]. But Mr. Hume says, it is only connected, as an invariable subsequent, must always be understood to require its invariable antecedent.—But I retort, Why does the definition assume more than the argument can possibly bear out?" (64–66)

8. That Hume's first definition of causation, as well as his third, "association of ideas," definition, fails to provide sufficient conditions on causation:

"In every just definition, the ideas that are included in the terms, must not suit any other object. Now many objects are invariably antecedents and subsequents, that are not Causes and Effects [. . .]. (67)

[T]hat the thought always being carried by the appearance of one object to the idea of another, proves nothing but an accidental though strong association of ideas; and is in like manner objectionable, on account of suiting other objects than the thing defined. Every Andrew is not necessarily "Simon Peter's Brother," although my thought always recurs to that idea, upon every mention of the name of Andrew." (68)

9. That Hume's account of causation as (merely) involving certain associations of ideas is circular, since his theory of ideas assumes that impressions cause ideas:

"[Hume claims that] "Every idea is copied from some preceding impression (idea being an Effect *derived* from impression as its Cause). In all single instances of the operation of bodies there is nothing that produces, nor consequently can suggest the idea of necessary connection. But when *many* instances appear, we *feel* a new impression, a customary connexion in the thought, between one object and its usual attendant."

Now this method of placing the argument is but the statement of *another circle*; for *causation* is used as the very principle which lies at the foundation of the whole system;

and afterwards we are desired to search for the *impression*, which is the CAUSE of that EFFECT, viz. the *idea causation*." (90–91)

Shepherd doesn't belabor these objections, since she has bigger fish to fry; indeed, as in the case of the terminological infelicities, she sometimes mentions Hume's failings only to fix them up on his behalf. Nonetheless, many are individually quite devastating. That Hume "switches the question" from an investigation into the grounds for believing that like Causes produce like Effects to an investigation into the grounds for believing that superficial appearances of objects or events are tracking the same "secret powers"—i.e., into an investigation into how one knows whether some state of affairs is in fact a "like Cause"—is problematic, not just because it changes the subject, but because we *don't* believe the revised claim. Everyone will agree that what *appear* to be like Causes might not produce like Effects, so that, e.g., what superficially appears to be bread might fail to nourish us, and so on. That Hume assumes that his off-the-cuff conceivings infallibly track genuine possibility is also problematic, given the heavy weight these conceivings must bear in his argument; I'm inclined to agree with Shepherd that the only way for these conceivings to do the work that Hume needs them to do is if the conclusion that they are supposed to establish (namely, that the beliefs in question are not justified by reason) is tacitly assumed. Shepherd is kind to Hume in calling his definitions of causation "multiply faulty": jointly inequivalent, individually problematic, and extending far beyond anything that Hume's argumentation could be reasonably taken to have established, they are a mess. Perhaps most devastating is Shepherd's charge that Hume's account of causation as involving an association of ideas is fatally circular, in that Hume's account of ideas crucially relies on a causal relation—the one holding between impressions and ideas—that in the nature of the case cannot be analyzed in the terms of his account.[10]

---

[10] This objection (#9, above) is closely associated with one according to which Hume's definition is extensionally incorrect, since it can't handle the case of an impression causing an idea.

Even independent of Shepherd's positive arguments to come, it is striking how careless she reveals Hume's argumentation to be.

7.4. On the Justification for the Claim That Every New Existent Must Have a Cause

In this and the next sections we turn to Shepherd's positive views, which constitute the constructive core of her critique of Hume.

7.4.1. The Initially Empty World Thought Experiment

Having highlighted the continuing import of Hume's doctrines to the question of whether every beginning of existence has a cause, Shepherd directs her attention to undercutting Hume's claim that this belief is not justified by reason, by means of the following thought experiment:

> Let the object which we suppose to begin its existence of itself be imagined, abstracted from the nature of all objects we are acquainted with, saving in its capacity for existence; let us suppose it to be no effect; there shall be no prevening circumstances whatever that affect it, nor any existence in the universe: let it be so; let there be nought but a blank; and a mass of whatsoever can be supposed not to require a cause START FORTH into existence, and make the first breach on the wide nonentity around; now, what is this starting forth, beginning, coming into existence, but an action, which is a quality of an object not yet in being, and so not possible to have its qualities determined, nevertheless exhibiting its qualities? If, indeed, it should be shown, that there is no proposition whatever taken as a ground on which to build an argument in this question, neither one conclusion nor the other can be supported; and there need be no attempt at reasoning. But, if my adversary allows that, no existence being supposed previously in the universe, existence, in order to be, must begin to be, and that the notion of beginning an action (the being that begins it not supposed yet in existence), involves a contradiction in terms; then this beginning to exist cannot appear but as a capacity some

nature hath to alter the presupposed nonentity, and to act for itself, whilst itself is not in being. The original assumption may deny, as much as it pleases, all cause of existence; but, whilst in its very idea, the commencement of existence is an effect predicated of some supposed cause, (*because the quality of an object* which must be *in existence* to possess it,) we must conclude that *there is no object which begins to exist, but must owe its existence to some cause.* (35–36)

Here we see Shepherd addressing, in bracing fashion, the question of what it would be for something to come to exist, stripping away all extraneous features in a way that serves, in turn, to provide the basis of a distinctively metaphysical argument for the claim that everything that begins to exist must have a cause.

I'll say more about Shepherd's argument shortly, but to start it's worth noting the originality and potential dialectical force of her approach. As Shepherd points out, in considering Hume's first question, Clarke and Locke "felt the involved absurdity so great, that they passed over the first question as too ridiculous, probably, to consider formally" (37). In other words, Clarke and Locke took for granted as intuitively obvious that everything that begins to exist must have a cause, which in turn put Hume in position to accuse them of begging the question, and so engaging in "fallacious" reasoning. Relatedly, though the further theistic upshot of Shepherd's argument is in the tradition of arguments for the existence of God that appeal to the truth of the claim that "nothing comes from nothing" or *ex nihilo nihil fit* (what Schliesser 2021 calls a "weak-ish version of the [Principle of Sufficient Reason] PSR"), Shepherd neither takes this claim for granted nor supports it by appeal to explanatory considerations of the sort operative in the PSR. Rather, and very roughly, she supports this premise on grounds that for something to come to exist there must first be an action of its beginning to exist, but in the case at hand—a case to which Hume is clearly committed—there is nothing available to perform the action at issue.

To expand on and assess this line of thought, it's first useful to register that it takes the form of a reductio, as follows:

1. An object—say, *X*—could begin to exist without a cause. (Assumed for reductio)

2. If X could begin to exist without a cause, then X could begin to exist in an initially empty universe U.

3. Therefore, X could begin to exist in an initially empty universe U. (1, 2)

4. X's beginning to exist in U is an action.

5. An action is a quality of an existing object.

6. Therefore, X's beginning to exist in U is a quality of an existing object. (4, 5)

7. Since U is empty prior to X's existing, no object exists in U to possess the quality of X's beginning to exist—not an entity besides X, for there are no such entities, and not X, for X does not yet exist. (3)

8. Therefore, it is not the case that X's beginning to exist in U is a quality of an existing object. (7)

9. An object could not begin to exist without a cause. (1, 6, 8)

How does Shepherd's reductio fare? To start, as she notes, her argument requires that "no existence being supposed previously in the universe, existence, in order to be, must begin to be."[11] In other words, it has to be, first, possible that there is a universe that is initially completely empty and which later contains some existent, and second, that in such a case said existent must at some point "begin to be." Hume is clearly committed to there being a universe that is initially empty and later comes to contain something, as a concomitant of his view that all goings-on are "entirely loose and separate." It is moreover plausible that for something to come into existence, it must begin to be—that is, begin to exist. There is initially nothing; later there is something; at some point, the latter entity must begin to exist. So far, so good. Next, it is also plausible that any such beginning to exist would be an action of some sort—at least in a lightweight sense of "action" as involving some kind of happening. Perhaps the weakest premise in Shepherd's argument involves the claim that the action of the new existent's beginning to exist must be "a quality of an existing object." As Fantl (2016) wonders, "Why suppose that beginning to exist is an action of an object at all?" (98). Why couldn't a beginning to exist just happen, so to speak,

---

[11] Note that Shepherd here flags that her argument generalizes to address not just new objects, but new existents of any ontological category.

without some existing object performing the action? Fair enough, but I think a closer examination of what Shepherd is getting at here shows that her argument doesn't require that the action at issue be performed by an object possessing some quality, and indeed goes through even if this action rather involves—or just is—an existing (objectless) event or other feature of reality. For her purposes, all that is required is that any kind of happening—whether object-involving action or objectless event—requires that *something* exist to perform the action or constitute the event of the happening. *Something* has to exist for there to be an action or event of "starting forth," *something* has to exist for there to be "the first breach on the wide nonentity around."[12] That much seems plausible, however: How could there be a happening (action, event) without something existent to perform or constitute the happening? But then the problem remains that in the empty world scenario, nothing exists to perform or constitute X's beginning to exist—not some existent besides X, since by assumption there aren't any other existents, and not X itself, since by assumption X doesn't yet exist.

I think what Shepherd is getting at here is the metaphysical reasoning underlying the intuitive supposition that "nothing comes from nothing." Anything that comes into existence has to begin to exist—there has to be a transition from the state of nonexistence to the state of existence of the entity in question. But if there really is nothing, there isn't anything to perform the associated action, constitute the associated event—except, perhaps, the something itself, which doesn't make sense, since by assumption it doesn't yet exist. As she puts it: "every

---

[12] The revised argument would then read:
1. An object—say, X—could begin to exist without a cause. (Assumed for reductio)
2. If X could begin to exist without a cause, then X could begin to exist in an initially empty universe U.
3. Therefore, X could begin to exist in an initially empty universe U. (1, 2)
4. X's beginning to exist in U is a happening (action, event).
5. A happening (action, event) requires that an entity exist to perform or constitute the happening.
6. Therefore, X's beginning to exist in U requires an existing entity. (4, 5)
7. Since U is empty prior to X's existing, no entity exists in U to perform or constitute X's beginning to exist—not an entity besides X, for there are no such entities, and not X, for X does not yet exist. (3)
8. Therefore, it is not the case that X's beginning to exist in U requires an existing entity. (7)
9. An object could not begin to exist without a cause. (1, 6, 8)

mind feels it so, because it perceives that an *alteration* could not begin of itself" (67).

One might wonder if this line of thought has been empirically undercut by contemporary science. Don't virtual particles "pop" into existence in a way, making room for something to begin to exist without having any cause? No, for such a case isn't one where nothing exists. On the contrary: the field and the laws of physics (whatever those are, exactly) serve as an existent basis for the coming-to-be of the virtual particles. Similar observations are commonly made in discussions of cosmology. Supposing the universe had a beginning, then what came before that? Could the universe have come from nothing? Even those thinking that there is a sense in which this makes sense qualify that the laws of physics (some kind of existent, however characterized) were still (somehow) around, as in a recent article on the topic:

> Although a universe, in Vilenkin's scheme, can come from nothing in the sense of there being no space, time or matter, something is in place beforehand—namely the laws of physics. Those laws govern the something-from-nothing moment of creation that gives rise to our universe, and they also govern eternal inflation, which takes over in the first nanosecond of time. (Nadis 2013)

The brilliance of Shepherd's case lies in her explicitly specifying— what Hume must grant, on pain of undercutting his supposition that "everything is entirely loose and separate"—that in the case at issue, *nothing whatsoever* exists, prior to the purportedly uncaused new existence.

7.4.2. Further Considerations

How might Hume respond? Shepherd's positive answer to the question "why we believe that every new existence has a cause" involves unpacking the concept of a new existent in a way that reveals the need for a cause via the connection to something needed to initiate "starting forth" or "beginning to exist," which need in turn reveals that the assumption that a new existent doesn't have a cause leads to contradiction. All this is in line with Hume's own methodology, according to which justification that proceeds by means of "reason" involves there being "relations between ideas" of the sort leading to "contradiction [or] absurdity" under the assumption that the relations aren't in place. That Hume can "conceive" of there being a new existent without a cause doesn't count for much in the face of these considerations (as per Shepherd's objection #4, above). Indeed, she might point to the fact that it is crucial, in order to appreciate the relation existing between the ideas of a new existent and a cause, to consider the sort of case at issue in her thought experiment. Otherwise, there is a danger that any purported "conceiving" of a new existent coming to be without a cause might be tacitly a conceiving of a new existent coming to be with some unknown cause. So far, so bad for Hume.

That said, if Hume or others fail to find her argument convincing, Shepherd offers as backup the consideration—going beyond anything Locke or Clarke registers—that she is as much within her rights to maintain that it is necessary that every new existent has a cause as Hume is within his rights to maintain the contrary. As above, Hume complains against Locke and Clarke that their claims that it would be absurd to suppose that a new existent could lack a cause beg the question against his claim to the contrary, and hence count as "fallacious" reasoning. As Shepherd correctly notes, however, Hume doesn't provide any substantive independent reason in support of his view that an existent *doesn't* require a cause beyond his finding this claim intuitively plausible, and hence he is "begging the question" against those who find the claim absurd just as much as vice versa: "yet his own argument, the whole way, consists in the possibility of imagining an effect 'non-existent' this minute and 'existing the next;' and does not himself consider any other 'sort of being possible.'"

Given the preceding considerations, she concludes with a request:

Before I proceed further, I wish my reader to grant the proposition, "That a Being cannot begin its existence of itself;" because I mean to make use of it in my further reply to Mr. Hume's doctrines; and, unless this step is allowed, I can make no further progress in this argument. (39)

As above, the proposition is metaphysically defensible (as per her thought experiment) and independently plausible (as per the "nothing comes from nothing" intuition that even scientists accept). Moreover, and in any case, its endorsement isn't on any *worse* ground, epistemically speaking, than Hume's denial. Shepherd is admirably clear about the fact that she will making heavy use of this proposition in what follows—a fact which may itself lend further support to the proposition, insofar as it leads to a metaphysics and epistemology of causation that is considerably more plausible than one based on its rejection.

7.5. On the Justification for the Claim That Like Causes and Effects Are Necessarily Connected

Shepherd next turns to considering the question (clarified, as above) of "how we arrive at the knowledge of the *necessary connection* between *like* Cause and Effect" (40), registering that "it is my intention to shew [. . .] that it is Reason, and not Custom, which guides our minds in forming the notions of necessary connexion, of belief and of expectation" (42). Her argumentation presses Hume in ways that hit the sweet spot of originality and plausibility, and which moreover have important ramifications for the epistemology and metaphysics of causation, as well as for the metaphysics of objects.

Her offensive strategy proceeds in two steps. First, she argues, relying in part on the foundational premise (motivated by her previous reductio) that "a being cannot begin its existence of itself," that experience of constant conjunction is not required for us to believe that a causal relation is in place. Rather, via an "*experimentum crucis*," where "a single experience [. . .] awakens in the mind the required process of reasoning," we can come to believe that a particular object in certain circumstances causes a given effect. Second, she argues that we are justified in believing that a "like" object in "like" circumstances will produce a "like" effect. Let's walk through this reasoning more slowly, in Shepherd's words.

7.5.1. The Experimentum Crucis Argument

As regards the first step, she says:

> Objects which we know by our senses do begin their existences, and
> by our reason know they cannot begin it of themselves, must begin
> it by the operation of some other beings in existence, producing
> these new qualities in nature, and introducing them to our observa-
> tion. The very meaning of the word Cause, is Producer or Creator;
> of Effect, the Produced or Created and the idea is gained by such an
> observance of nature, as we think is efficient in any given case, to
> an *experimentum crucis*. Long observation of the invariableness of
> antecedency, and subsequency, is not wanted; many trials are not
> wanted, to generate the notion of producing power.
>   One trial is enough, in such circumstances, as will bring the mind
> to the following reasoning.
>   Here is a new quality, which appears to my senses:
>   But it could not arise of itself; nor could any surrounding objects,
> but one (or more) affect it; therefore that one, (or more) have
> occasioned it, for there is nothing else to make a difference; and a dif-
> ference could not *"begin of itself."* (43–44)

Shepherd illustrates the line of reasoning here with the case of the eye:

> This is an argument, which all persons, however illiterate, feel the
> force of. It is the only foundation for the demonstrations of the labo-
> ratory of the chymist; which all life resembles and so closely, in many
> instances, that the philosopher, and the vulgar [...] each knows that
> in certain given circumstances, the closing of the Eye will eclipse the
> prospect, of nature; and the slight motion of reopening it, will restore
> all the objects to view. Therefore, the Eye (in these circumstances,) is
> the Cause or Producer of vision. ONE trial would be enough, under
> certain known circumstances. Why? not from "custom," because
> there has been one trial only; but from Reason, because vision not
> being able to produce itself, nor any of the surrounding objects by
> the supposition; it is the Eye which must necessarily perform the op-
> eration; for there is nothing else to make a difference; and a different
> quality could not "begin its own existence." (44–45)

Hence reason, aided by experience, suffices to determine a cause–effect relation in a given case—even if only one instance of the relation (one "trial") has been experienced. Somewhat more formally, we are justified in accepting the following form of reasoning, leading to knowledge of causes even in the absence of experience of customary conjunction of the cause and effect types in question:

1. Upon introducing object or event A (and no other object or event[13]) into circumstances K not including object or event B, B comes to exist.
2. Either K caused B, B caused itself, or A caused B.
3. K didn't cause B.
4. B didn't cause itself (a different quality could not "begin its own existence").
5. A (understood as occurring in K) caused B.

As a general corollary:

1. Customary conjunction is not required to be justified in believing in the holding of a causal relation between objects or events A (or A-in-K) and B.

Before proceeding to the second stage of Shepherd's argument, let us pause to appreciate that Shepherd here advances what Mill ([1843] 1973) later describes as the most "potent" of his famous methods for determining cause–effect relations—namely, the "method of difference," according to which "[i]f an instance in which the phenomenon under investigation occurs, and an instance in which it does not occur, have every circumstance save one in common, that one occurring only in the former; the circumstance in which alone the two instances differ, is the [. . .] cause, or an indispensable part of the cause, of the phenomenon" ([1843] 1973, Ch. VIII, §1). Like Shepherd, Mill highlights not just the method but the fact that its use is ubiquitous in both science and everyday life:

---

[13] Thanks to Martha Bolton for flagging the need for this qualifier.

It is scarcely necessary to give examples of a logical process to which we owe almost all the inductive conclusions we draw in daily life. When a man is shot through the heart, it is by this method we know that it was the gunshot which killed him: for he was in the fullness of life immediately before, all circumstances being the same, except the wound. ([1843] 1973, Ch. VIII, §1)

More generally, in Shepherd's discussion we see an explicit identification of difference-making as key to the epistemology of causes—a methodological approach arguably tacitly operative in motivating and testing Newton's theory of gravity (see Smith 2014). All this points not just to the historical importance of Shepherd's understanding of the epistemology of causation, but also to its independent plausibility. In addition to prefiguring the most important of Mill's methods, Shepherd's reasoning here serves as the basis for her distinctively *singularist* metaphysical account of causation—an account not unlike one which Mill also endorsed, several decades later.

7.5.2. Necessary Connection and the Foundational Principle

To return to the thread: thus far, Shepherd has argued that attention to difference-making considerations can serve as a basis for "single case" causal inference. Granting this much, what justifies the further belief that causal relations are necessary?

Ingeniously, it is again the proposition that "a being cannot begin its existence of itself" that does the heavy lifting here. For suppose that, as a result of an *experimentum crucis*, we come to realize that a given object or event of type A in circumstances of type K (for short: A-in-K) causes an object or event of type B. What guarantees that another object or event of type A in circumstances of type K will cause an object or event of type B? Shepherd points out that—on the assumption that the case at hand really is one involving a "like cause" (that is, one involving an object or event of type A introduced into circumstances of type K)—the foundational principle ensures that an object or event of type B will ensue. For if B were not to occur, then this would count as a difference from (and associated new quality in) a state of affairs in which B was present, either involving an object or event D different from B, or as involving simply the absence of B. Such a difference could not "begin of itself," however, and so must have been caused or produced by something besides an A-in-K. But the assumption of the antecedent goings-on being "like" the ones which previously caused B rules out that any other goings-on are available to produce such a different effect. Consequently, reason, assisted by experience, serves to justify the proposition that like causes necessarily produce like effects. As Shepherd puts it, continuing on from her example of the eye:

> It is this sort of REASONING UPON EXPERIMENT, which takes place in every man's mind, concerning every affair in life, which generates the notion of Power, and necessary Connexion; and gives birth to that maxim, "*a like Cause must produce a like Effect.*" The circumstances being supposed the same on a second occasion as on a former one, and carefully observed to be so; the Eye when opened would be expected to let in light, and all her objects. "I observe (says the mind) in this or any other case, all the prevening circumstances the same as before; for there is nothing to make a difference; and a difference cannot arise without something to occasion it; else there would be a *beginning of existence* by itself, which is impossible." (45)

Somewhat more formally:

1. Upon introducing object or event A (and no other object or event) into circumstances K not including object or event B, B comes to exist, and we are thereby justified in believing that A-in-K caused B.
2. It is not necessary that like Causes produce like Effects. (Assumed for reductio)
3. If it is not necessary that like Causes produce like Effects, it could turn out that upon introducing an object or event of type A into circumstances of type K, no object or event of type B comes to exist.
4. It could turn out that upon introducing an object or event of type A into circumstances of type K, no object or event of type B comes to exist. (2, 3)

5. The failure of an object or event of type B to occur in the second scenario is a difference which could not "begin of itself." (A different quality could not "begin its own existence")
6. But by the assumption of the case as one involving a "like Cause," there is nothing else in the second scenario to serve as the cause of the difference.
7. It could not turn out that upon introducing an object or event of type A into circumstances of type K, no object or event of type B comes to exist. (5, 6)
8. It is necessary that like Causes produce like Effects. (4, 7)

As a corollary:

1. Customary conjunction is not required in order to be justified in believing that it is necessary that like Causes produce like Effects.

Shepherd summarizes by highlighting the "compound" nature of the justification at issue, as drawing from both reason and experience:

> It is this compound idea, therefore, the result of the experience of what does take place upon any given trial, MIXED with the reasoning that nothing else could ensue, unless on the one hand, *efficient causes were allowed for the alteration*; or, on the other, that things could "alter their existences FOR THEMSELVES"; which generates the notion of *power* or 'producing principle,' and for which we have formed the word. (45–46)

7.5.3. Further Considerations

How might Hume respond? As above, Shepherd has provided a basis in reason for the claim that it is necessary that every new beginning have a cause, and relatedly (given the parameters of the motivating case) that nothing can begin to exist "of itself." Now, the first step of her strategy, whereby she makes a case that we can have knowledge of a causal relation after experience of a single instance by means of what is effectively the method of difference, involves an observation of the sort that Hume allows—namely, one which involves resemblances or failures of resemblance. The pattern at issue is one where initially, circumstances K do not include some goings-on B, and later, circumstances K do involve some goings-on B, with the only difference being the introduction of object or event A into the circumstances. In such a case, the observation of a failure of resemblance is reasonably seen—as Mill, himself an empiricist, acknowledges—as providing an experiential basis for taking A to be a partial or complete cause of E.[14] Shepherd prefigures and expands on this line of thought, noting that given the foundational principle that nothing can come to exist of itself, it's not an option to maintain that the difference consisting in the presence of A had nothing to do with the difference consisting in the presence of B, with B simply being responsible for its own "coming to be." So far, so bad for Hume.

To be sure, such judgments are fallible, but that's a different issue.[15] Indeed, as discussed above, in the course of Hume's discussion he switches from the question of why we believe that like causes and like effects are necessarily connected to the quite different question of how we come to believe that superficial appearances of objects or events are tracking the same "secret powers." If one holds the original question properly fixed, Shepherd's considerations come into play, to establish a justificatory basis, in "reason aided by experience," for believing the claim at issue:

> When the *secret powers*, and sensible qualities, are known, or *supposed the same*, the conclusion is demonstrative; *so must be the Effects*. (61–62)

That said, one might wonder if Hume can respond by denying that for an object or event to be "like" the original A, the secret powers as well as the sensible qualities must be "supposed the same."[16] Rather,

---

[14] Interestingly, prior to reading Shepherd I had argued that a Humean could accept singularism about causation on the basis of observations of comings-to-be of resemblances or failures of resemblance; see Wilson 2009.

[15] Moreover, it need not be obvious what exactly the difference maker is as regards a given effect; as regards such cases, Shepherd observes (note, p. 44): "When more trials are needed than ONE, it is in order to detect the circumstances, not to lay a foundation for the general principle, that a LIKE Cause repeated, a LIKE Effect will take place."

[16] Thanks to Martha Bolton for suggesting this response.

Hume might continue, the characterization of an object or event of type *A* need advert only to its sensible qualities, with its "powers" being understood in deflationary terms of extrinsic regularities; or (as a variation on the interpretation advanced in Strawson 1992) said characterization might also advert to "secret powers"—but only of a contingent variety.

Either way, Shepherd has a response. As against the first suggestion, she can reply that a deflationary view of powers (or causation) as a matter of extrinsic regularities is motivated only on the assumption that one cannot be justified in believing in a given causal relation in the single case; but as per the *experimentum crucis* argument, this assumption is false. As against the second suggestion, she can reply that if an object or event of type *A* has certain "secret" powers, then some explanation for the modal status of those powers as necessary or contingent is required. If the powers are part of the nature of objects or events of type *A*, then this would explain the powers' being necessary. What would explain their being contingent? Hume's story here will again appeal to regularities: our only access to causal facts proceeds via regularities (he will say), but different regularities will generate different powers. And here again, Shepherd will observe that as per the *experimentum crucis* argument, there is no motivation for taking what causes what to be a matter of regularities, and hence no motivation for taking the powers of objects or events to be contingent.

Given that she has previously undermined Hume's motivations for taking the powers of objects and events to be contingent, it is reasonable (and non-question-begging) for Shepherd to understand what it is to be a like Cause as she does—in which case "reason aided by experience" (and most saliently the foundational principle that nothing can begin "of itself") kicks in to justify the claim that it is necessary that like Causes produce like Effects.

7.6. The Metaphysics of Causation

As in Hume's discussions, Shepherd's account of the justification of certain causal beliefs is associated with a metaphysical account of causation. Here I must be brief, due to limitations of space; but the view is so interesting it's worth putting on the table, if only as a teaser.[17] To start, causes and effects are defined as follows:

> A Cause [...] is such action of an object, as shall enable it, in conjunction with another, to form a new nature, capable of exhibiting qualities varying from those of either of the objects unconjoined. This is really to be a producer of new being.—This is a generation, or *creation*, of qualities not conceived of, antecedently to their existence;—and not merely [as on Hume's view] an "idea always followed by another," on account of a "customary association between them."
>
> An Effect is the produced quality exhibited to the senses, as the essential property of natures so conjoined. Necessary connexion of cause and effect is the obligation qualities have to inhere in their objects, and to exhibit their varieties [...] Power is but another word for efficient cause, or "productive principle;" and signifies the *property* which lies in the *secret nature of objects*, when unobserved by the senses, and which determines the qualities that can be exhibited to them upon every new conjunction. (63–64)

Shepherd's account of causation has (at least) four distinctive metaphysical features, each of which marks an important point of contrast with Hume's account(s).

First is that causation is a *singular, local* phenomenon (as later advanced in, e.g., Ducasse 1926 and Anscombe 1971). On Hume's view, whether an object or event A causes another object or event B is not a matter of (just) the holding of certain facts in the vicinity of A and B, but is rather a matter of non-local facts about whether goings-on of type A (or A-in-K), located at other parts of space and time, stand in certain relations of temporal priority and spatial contiguity to goings-on of type B, either for a given "experiencer" or (on the sort of objective construal that contemporary neo-Humeans typically endorse) as holding throughout all spacetime. By way of contrast, for Shepherd, whether A (A-in-K) and B are causally related is a local, singular matter; and notwithstanding that the necessary connection between

---

[17] For a much more developed and very illuminating exposition of the details of Shepherd's account of causation, see Bolton 2010.

cause and effect types has implications for what happens when "like Causes" occur in other parts of spacetime, these other occurrences do not help constitute the holding of any given instance of the relation.

Second is that causation is a *synchronic* phenomenon: causes and effects occur at the same time. This metaphysical "take" on causal relations is consonant with Newton's studied neutrality on the operation of forces, which made room for causes and effects (as in the case of gravitational interactions) to be synchronous (and was later advanced in Mill 1843). Notwithstanding this Newtonian imprimatur, one of Hume's legacies, nearly universally encoded in contemporary accounts of causation of whatever stripe, is that this relation is diachronic. Of course, as Shepherd acknowledges, we can and do speak of an object or event existing prior to an effect as "the cause" or "a cause." On her view, however, this designation signifies just that the temporally antecedent object at issue is one of those objects or circumstances that, when conjoined with some others, constitutes a new nature with new qualities—i.e., the effect:

> "*Antecedency* and *subsequency*," are therefore immaterial to the proper definition of Cause and Effect; on the contrary, although an object, in order to act as a Cause, must be in Being antecedently to such action; yet when it *acts as a Cause*, its *Effects* are *synchronous with that action*, and are *included in it*; which a close inspection into the nature of cause will prove. Each conjunction of bodies, (now separately in existence, and of certain defined qualities,) produces upon their union those new natures, whose qualities must necessarily *be in*, and *with them, in the very moment of their formation*. Thus *the union of two distinct natures*, is the *cause, producer or creator* of another [. . .] the cause has not acted, is not completed, till the *union* has taken place, and the new nature is formed with all its qualities, *in*, and *about it*. (49–50)

Indeed, cause and effect are ultimately just different construals of one and the same state of affairs:

> Effects are nothing but those same conjunctions of qualities, which in other words are admitted as similar causes, in the supposition of

the question. The objects (whose *union is necessary* to a given result,) must certainly exist, *antecedent* to such an union. But it is *in their UNION*, there exists those *newly formed objects*, or masses of qualities called *Effects*, which are therefore *identical* with the *similar cause*; for in *this union*, Cause and Effect are *synchronous*, and they are but different words for the same *Essence*. (57)

For example, while we may speak of the fire as a cause of the discerptibility of the wood, in fact it is the union of fire and wood that is both cause and effect:

Fire and wood must be antecedent to combustion, no doubt; but in the *union of Fire and Wood*, there exists immediately *combustion* as a new event in nature; —also in this union exists the similar *cause* allowed by the *data*, whilst combustion is also termed the *Effect* of the union of Fire and Wood [. . .]. (57)

Third is that causation is something like the coming-to-be-instantiated of a new property (or properties) upon the coming together—the "union"—of distinct objects or events. This is a fascinating idea! While it might be cashed out in various ways, one clear connection is to contemporary accounts on which causation involves the mutual manifestation of powers or dispositions (see, e.g., dispositional or powers-based accounts along the lines of Martin 1993 and Williams 2019). Here again, Shepherd was early on the scene in identifying a new position in causal-metaphysical space.

Fourth is that causation is deeply implicated in the *natures* of the objects or events involved:

If then an existence now in being, conjoined with any other, forms thereby a new nature, capable of exhibiting new qualities, these new qualities must enter into the definition of the objects; they become a part of their natures; [. . .] the new qualities, that are named effects, are expected without a doubt to arise upon every such conjunction; because, they as much belong to this newly combined nature, as the original qualities did to each separate nature, before their conjunction. (47)

In advancing the thesis that the effects associated with an object are essential to it, Shepherd aims to undercut the distinction between the supposed properties or qualities of an object and its effects. For example, on her view, the discerptibility of a fire is just as essential to it as its involving a flame or having a certain color. Yet again, we have in Shepherd's work a clear precursor to salient contemporary views (as per, e.g., Shoemaker 1980 and Bird 2007) on which powers or dispositions are essential to objects or the features they possess.

7.7. Concluding Remarks

Here I have only had opportunity to briefly outline some of the main critical observations, argumentative strategies, and positive views manifest in Shepherd's ERCE. But this much suffices, I warrant, to show that she is an intellectual force to be reckoned with, deserving of far more scholarly attention than she has been given thus far. Those teaching modern philosophy would do well to include Shepherd on their syllabi, if for no other reason than to give students a sense of how someone sharp (sharper than Reid, for example) might go about skewering Berkeley's idealism or Hume's empiricism. Shepherd's critique of Hume in particular is also of great contemporary interest, reflecting that Hume's legacy—that is, a worldview on which not just causes but everything is foundationally disconnected (as per "Hume's Dictum"), and causes and laws are mere systematizations of patterns in the contingently sprinkled arrangement of little bits—continues to play a large and influential role in contemporary analytic metaphysics.[18]

Positive alternatives are needed. Contemporary metaphysicians resisting Hume's siren call in favor of views on which causal relations are necessary, dispositions are essential to objects and properties, and powers are foundational in the order of metaphysical explanation, often cite Aristotle as their philosophical forebear. That's fine, but I suggest that in Shepherd non-Humeans have their true forebear: someone whose positive accounts of the epistemology and metaphysics of

---

[18] See Wilson 2010 for discussion. As I observe in Wilson 2016, Hume's legacy has generated "decades of laboring in the imaginary legoland of Hume's Dictum" (100).

causation (and of objects) are clear precursors of various contemporary non-Humean accounts, and who more generally offers a cohesive, powerful, and scientifically informed vision of natural reality as deeply and essentially causally interconnected.[19]

Bibliography

Anscombe, G. E. M. (1971). *Causality and Determination*. Cambridge: Cambridge University Press.

Atherton, Margaret (1996). Lady Mary Shepherd's Case against George Berkeley. *British Journal for the History of Philosophy* 4(2): 347–366.

Bird, Alexander (2007). *Nature's Metaphysics: Laws and Properties*. Oxford: Oxford University Press.

Blackey, Robert (1848). *History of the Philosophy of Mind*. Vol. 1–4. London: Trelawney Wm. Saunders.

Bolton, Martha, "Mary Shepherd," *The Stanford Encyclopedia of Philosophy* (Spring 2021 Edition), Edward N. Zalta (ed.), https://plato.stanford.edu/archives/spr2021/entries/mary-shepherd/.

Bolton, Martha (2010). Causality and Causal Induction: The Necessitarian Theory of Lady Mary Shepher. In Allen, K., and Stoneham, T. (eds.), *Causation in Modern Philosophy*. London: Routledge, 242–262.

Boyle, Deborah (2018). *Lady Mary Shepherd: Selected Writings*. Exeter, UK: Imprint Academic.

Boyle, Deborah (2020). Mary Shepherd on Mind, Soul, and Self. *Journal of the History of Philosophy* 58 (1): 93–112. https://doi.org/10.1353/hph.2020.0005.

Ducasse, C. J. (1926). On the Nature and Observability of the Causal Relation. *Journal of Philosophy* 23: 57–68.

Landy, David (2020). A Defense of Shepherd's Account of Cause and Effect as Synchronous. *Journal of Modern Philosophy* 2(1): 1. https://doi.org/10.32881/jomp.46.

Lolordo, Antonia (2020). *Mary Shepherd's Essays on the Perception of an External Universe*. New York: Oxford University Press.

LoLordo, Antonia (2019). Mary Shepherd on Causation, Induction, and Natural Kinds. *Philosophers' Imprint* 19: 1–14.

Martin, C. B. (1993). Power for Realists. In Campbell, K., Bacon, J., and Reinhardt, L. (eds.), *Ontology, Causality, and Mind: Essays on the Philosophy of d. M. Armstrong*. Cambridge: Cambridge University Press, 175–186.

---

[19] Thanks to Martha Bolton, Catharine Diehl, Eric Schliesser, and an anonymous referee for helpful comments.

McRobert, Jennifer (2000). *Philosophical Writings of Mary Shepherd*, Vols. 1 and 2. Bristol, UK: Thoemmes Press.

Mill, John S. ([1843] 1973). *A System of Logic*. Toronto: University of Toronto Press.

Nadis, Steve (2013). What Came Before the Big Bang? *Discover*, October 2013. https://www.discovermagazine.com/the-sciences/what-came-before-the-big-bang.

Rickless, Samuel C. (2018). Is Shepherd's Pen Mightier Than Berkeley's Word? *British Journal for the History of Philosophy* 26(2): 317–330. https://doi.org/10.1080/09608788.2017.1381584.

Russell, Bertrand ([1912] 1967). *The Problems of Philosophy*. Oxford: Oxford University Press.

Schliesser, Eric (2021). "Newton's Modal Metaphysics and Polemics with Spinozism in the General Scholium." In Schliesser, Eric. *Newton's Metaphysics: Essays*. Oxford University Press, 198–221.

Shoemaker, Sydney (1980). Causality and Properties. In van Inwagen, P. (ed.), *Time and Cause*. Dordrecht: D. Reidel, 109–135.

Smith, George E. (2014). Closing the Loop: Testing Newtonian Gravity, Then and Now. In Biener, Z., and Schliesser, E. (eds.), *Newton and Empiricism*. Oxford: Oxford University Press, 262–351.

Strawson, Galen (1992). *The Secret Connexion: Causation, Realism and David Hume*. Oxford: Oxford University Press.

Williams, Neil (2019). *The Powers Metaphysic*. Oxford: Oxford University Press.

Wilson, Jessica M. (2009). Resemblance-Based Resources for Reductive Singularism. *The Monist* 92: 153–190.

Wilson, Jessica M. (2010). What Is Hume's Dictum, and Why Believe It? *Philosophy and Phenomenological Research* 80: 595–637.

Wilson, Jessica M. (2016). Three Barriers to Philosophical Progress. In Broderick, D., and Blackford, R. (eds.), *Philosophy's Future: The Problem of Philosophical Progres*. Wiley-Oxford: Blackwell, 91–104.

8

Ida B. Wells-Barnett's *The Red Record*

Liam Kofi Bright

8.1. Introduction

Ida B. Wells-Barnett's *The Red Record* is an argument against lynching as a means of enforcing law and order in the United States. It is not, merely, a condemnation of lynching; it is an argument, with structure purporting to logically interlink premises so as to support a conclusion. It thus adduces reasons against a practice that many would say is totally unreasonable—and, indeed, so evidently unreasonable that the point scarcely needs to be argued. But argue it Wells-Barnett did, and the focus of my investigation in this chapter shall be on what her argument is supposed to achieve and why she has arranged it in the manner she did.

It is not the case that extra-judicial killing has vanished as a method of enforcing a social order. The lynch-mobs of Wells-Barnett's day may have disappeared, but as I write this essay the United States—and much of the world beyond—is once more in uproar as footage of the extra-judicial murder of a black man, accused of a most trivial crime, came to light. This the latest of many such outrages in recent years. Perhaps as you read this chapter a similar uprising shall be in process, or you will remember when recently it was—or anticipate it soon being so again. Under such circumstances Wells-Barnett's work will always seem pertinent. It is thus no coincidence that as the specter of police violence toward African Americans has haunted American public life and political discourse, Wells-Barnett received a posthumous Pulitzer Prize (Silkey 2020). More broadly, brute force and associated intimidation are central methods of racial oppression, and likely to be with us so long as any sort of domination continues to blemish the earth. By offering a detailed, well researched, examination of a particularly stark

Liam Kofi Bright, *Ida B. Wells-Barnett's* The Red Record In: *Neglected Classics of Philosophy*.
Edited by: Eric Schliesser, Oxford University Press. © Oxford University Press 2022.
DOI: 10.1093/oso/9780190097196.003.0009

example of such evil, Wells-Barnett has offered future generations much data and a plausible analysis of said data to build upon.

However, beyond being informative about its first-order subject matter, Wells-Barnett's text, and Wells-Barnett herself, give us exemplars, respectively, for how to do socially relevant scholarship, and how to be an activist-scholar. The central tension I explore in this regard is the relationship between being persuasive to a hostile audience, on the one hand, and doing work according to epistemic standards one endorses oneself. These are tensions any activist-scholar must navigate. I argue that through her style of work she realized a kind of epistemic self-determination that should be considered an admirable trait for scholar activists. Before explaining this, however, a summary of what this neglected classic actually says.

8.2. A Brief Survey of *The Red Record*

Published in 1895, *The Red Record*'s main goal is to press the case against lynching as a form of upholding justice. That lynching is unethical may seem so obvious as to not need serious defense, and we shall return to this thought in the conclusion. But Wells-Barnett addresses this herself within *Red Record*. She says that any Christian who knew the facts of the case would certainly oppose lynching (Wells-Barnett 2002a, 151; henceforth all page number citations without attribution are to this text)—though as we shall see, there are dramatic ironies within the text on this point. But she also opens the text by recounting that at the time she writes, African Americans were the subject of such dreadful propaganda that many thought even mass lynching might be justified against them. For the charge was being made by defenders of this violence that lynching was the only way to prevent black men from raping white women, and the heinousness of the latter crime (60), as well as white Southern men's investment in the welfare and honor of women (62), justified this measure. So she takes her goal to at least be substantial in the following sense: people are disposed to disbelieve her conclusion, and she has work to do in swaying them.

Her argumentative strategy is itself simple yet effective. She begins by presenting some statistics on the prevalence and spread of lynching in 1894, and the causes behind each case as reported by the *Chicago Tribune*. Immediately this makes the point that in most of these cases no rape was even alleged by the people involved at the time, undermining the propagandistic argument made on behalf of lynch law by its retrospective defenders. However, while this is often the point the book is remembered for (and even then, often not properly credited; Harris 2003, 217), the bulk of the book goes beyond making this simple point. Wells-Barnett spends the substantial middle portion of the book going through principles one might wish a fair or decent judicial system to satisfy, and arguing that examination of how these lynchings have worked in practice violate all of them in an often horrific manner. The principles Wells-Barnett argues are violated are as follows: one ought differentiate between those who are and are not mentally capable of culpability, which lynch-mobs routinely fail to do; due process is a requirement of an adequate system of justice, but since lynch-mobs make a mockery of this, they clearly often target people who did not commit the crime in question; there must be proportionality between crime and punishment, but since lynching is applied to such a wide variety of cases this is impossible; and most basically of all, punishment should not be applied where there is no crime even alleged, and yet lynch-mobs sometimes target such innocents. Each of these sections works by Wells-Barnett briefly introducing the central theme, then proceeding to go through various cases wherein the principle in question is manifestly violated in a horrific manner—always using white-owned newspapers for their reports on events.

What follows is a rather interesting chapter in itself, the central message of which can be described as: lynching as a practice facilitates a pernicious ideology. This is an ideology in the sense of a set of claims people are widely aware of and which can permissibly be appealed to in legitimizing their actions or legitimizing the social order more broadly (see Táíwò 2018). Wells-Barnett argues that those familiar with the facts on the ground know full well that in many cases of alleged rape, there are "voluntary and clandestine" relationships going on between black men and white women. But given the anti-black racial prejudices of the day and the general desire of powerful Southern whites to maintain the subordination of blacks, it would be extremely inconvenient to acknowledge that such voluntary unions occur with reasonable frequency. As such, the papers do not report honestly on what is going on. Lynching evidently serves as a powerful and shocking deterrent to such unions; it murders and thereby silences the black man involved, while often gaining the participation of the white woman involved, whose reputation now depends on denying the voluntary nature of the union. And finally, by perpetuating the line that such cases are invariably rape, it has "the effect of fastening the odium upon the race of a peculiar propensity for this foul crime" (109). As such, establishing the practice of lynching serves to establish something like the claim "black people are monstrous rapists who may, perhaps must, be violently suppressed if peace is to be had" as a publicly available justification for action (see also Wells-Barnett and Le Vin 1899, 1). Needless to say, this general disdain for black people further legitimizes our subordination.

All this being argued, Wells-Barnett rounds the book out by pressing her case that something must be done about all this, reiterating that mealy-mouthed compromises with lynching's justifications are unacceptable, and calling upon those who read to get involved in the campaign against lynching. In words we shall return to, Wells-Barnett is quite specific about what those who have been persuaded should do. "The very frequent inquiry made after my lectures by interested friends is 'What can I do to help the cause?' The answer always is 'Tell the world the facts.' When the Christian world knows the alarming growth and extent of outlawry in our land, some means will be found to stop it" (151). *Red Record* is thus simultaneously an act of telling the world the facts and an inducement to pass this information on. It will be important later on that the audience for the latter inducement, and hence the presumed audience for the text, seems to be white Americans. This because in the midst of calling the reader to anti-lynching action, Wells-Barnett says one ought to "[t]hink and act on independent lines in this behalf, remembering that after all, it is the white man's civilization and the white man's government which are on trial" (149). The apparent meaning of this is an appeal to the reader's sense of investment in the good name of the white man's civilization and government. I will hence presume that Wells-Barnett had an intended audience of white people, and white Americans especially, since at other times she refers to America as "our community and country" (148).

Here, then, is what Wells-Barnett has established by the end of *Red Record*. The defenses offered of lynching do not stand up to scrutiny when examined in light of the facts as reported by white-owned newspapers. Further, those very same sources make it clear that the prevalence of lynching is leading to the flagrant violation of important principles that any decent system of justice must satisfy. Finally, by perpetuating the pernicious ideology surrounding black people and their propensity to crime, lynching and the stories given in its defense serve to justify the brutal subordination of black people, all based on a lie. Since error and deception are so key to both how lynching is maintained and justified, and also part of the pernicious effect it has on the world, exposing the truth is a natural method of fighting it. This is what Ida B. Wells-Barnett has done, and she exhorts you, the reader, to do likewise.

Red Record is a work of naturalistic applied ethics, or applied politics, or even in some sense applied legal philosophy. The great strength of the book is to blend together careful empirical investigation, self-conscious carefulness about the evidential sources used during that empirical investigation, and explicit moral reasoning in light of plausible general principles. In addition to the first-order facts about lynching, its history and effects, that one gains from this text, it also presents a model of applied philosophy that can fruitfully serve as a methodological paradigm for contemporary work.

To help draw its methodological interest out, I shall in the remainder focus on one of the methodological peculiarities of this work—ought Wells-Barnett to have restricted her evidence base to only the pronouncements made by white-owned newspapers and white journalists? There is something at least prima facie odd about this, given that, first, this is strictly a subset of the evidence she possesses and thus might be felt to violate intuitive principles of good reasoning that are often thought essential for confirming one's claims (Good 1967). And, further, it is not just a subset of her evidence, but a subset which—as we shall see—she quite avowedly does not trust. I shall refer to this restriction of her sources to white newspaper sources as Wells-Barnett's evidential self-limitation. And I shall simultaneously address two questions—one, a hermeneutic question, why did she do this, and two, a normative question, can it have been a good idea to do as much?

I shall claim that this was in fact a good strategy on her part, both in light of her own projects and also normative goals we might endorse, and understanding why helps us see why her work can serve as a model for applied work in the future.

8.3. A Rhetorical Counter to Epistemic Injustice?

There is an immediately apparent answer to our question, and one indeed suggested by the text. Wells-Barnett draws upon white-owned newspapers and white journalists because she expects them to be trusted in a way that she does not expect black people in general, or herself as a black woman in particular, to be trusted. She thus tries to persuade her largely white audience by means of sources they will be inclined to believe. If one conceives of the text as primarily in the business of persuading people so as to rouse action, this would then justify the evidential self-limitation to untrustworthy white sources.

I shall argue that there is something to this interpretation, but dramatic ironies in the text and others of her writings complicate the story. The rhetorical advantages of appealing to white authors are indeed noted by Wells-Barnett. But her method's justification ultimately lies in its epistemic features. This epistemic justification for her evidential self-limitation, I will argue, allows Wells-Barnett to realize ideals of self-determination.

That is not to say that Wells-Barnett does not clearly appreciate the rhetorical advantage of appealing to the words and work of white journalists. Wells-Barnett says when introducing the statistics she shall be working from that

> [t]he purpose of the pages which follow shall be to give the record which has been made, not by the colored men, but that which is the result of complaints made by white men, of reports sent over the civilised world by white men in the South. Out of their own mouths shall the murderers be condemned. For a number of years the *Chicago Tribune*, admittedly one of the leading journals of America, has made a speciality of the compilation of statistics touching upon lynching. The data compiled by that journal and published to the

world January 1, 1894, up to the present time has not been disputed. In order to be safe from the charge of exaggeration, the incidents hereinafter reported have been confined to those vouched for by the *Tribune.* (Wells-Barnett 2002a, 68)

It is evidently significant that her choice of sources means the condemnation comes out of their own—presumably, saliently, white—mouths, and that she cannot be charged with exaggeration. Further, throughout the text, Wells-Barnett makes a point of noting her sources, and frequently draws attention to the fact that it is white journalists she quotes or white editors who approved certain stories, etc. She even quite explicitly calls back to this rationale later, saying, "Lest it might be charged that any deeds of that day are exaggerated, a white man's description which was published In the white journals of this country is used" (78). Likewise, she later notes that a "white person's word is taken as absolutely for as against a Negro" (120) when discussing a case wherein intervention by white people vouching for a black person's claims saved them from lynching.

In contemporary terminology, Wells-Barnett might be thought of as here preempting a sort of testimonial injustice or epistemic violence. For an example of how this might be spelled out, Kristie Dotson points out that "to communicate we all need an audience willing and capable of hearing us" (2011, 238). To display such a willingness and capacity to listen is linguistic reciprocation. She then says that epistemic violence occurs just in case there is "a refusal, intentional or unintentional, of an audience to communicatively reciprocate a linguistic exchange owing to pernicious ignorance" (2011, 238). Being systematically subject to such violence is one form of epistemic oppression (Dotson 2014).

With this in hand, one can say that Wells-Barnett anticipates that her audience will not be willing or capable of hearing her out. This because as a black woman she was subject to epistemic oppression. As such, she cannot expect reciprocation, and must take steps to avoid epistemic violence she would otherwise be subject to. To this end, she has her point made "out of the mouths" of white men, who are more likely to get a fair hearing. If one sees in *The Red Record* the primary goal as being to rouse action, the rhetorical goal of actually receiving uptake is very important to her purpose. The urgency of achieving this goal, and the fact that it requires reciprocity, would then justify the epistemic sacrifice of not using all her available evidence, and relying upon untrustworthy sources.

If this were all there was to say on the matter, it could still hold lessons for contemporary activists or activist-scholars. For, the epistemic ju-jitsu involved in turning the words of "the malicious and untruthful white press" (Wells-Barnnet 2002b, ch. 4) against white supremacy is an example of what can be gained by judiciously engaging with the source material one's opponents are working from. However, a fuller examination of the text and surrounding context makes this rhetorical reading of the text unlikely. For a key part of the text is that plenty of white people are in fact aware of these events and have not changed their minds about what is going on. For instance, as she notes:

> In July of this year, 1894, John Paul Bocock, a Southern white man living in New York, and assistant editor of the New York Tribune, took occasion to defy the publication of any instance where the lynched Negro was the victim of a white woman's falsehood. Such cases are not rare, but the press and people conversant with the facts, almost invariably suppress them. (108)

Mr. Bocock is evidently supposed to be aware of the falsehoods he is perpetuating by this conduct. However, he simply does not care, and goes on perpetuating his lies. It might be thought that he is unusually malicious, but then Wells-Barnett expressly says that such cases are not rare and that others like him invariably behave in the same way.

One might instead think that the problem is especially with Southern as opposed to Northern whites, and the hope is that the latter can be persuaded to act against the former. As we shall see, there is good evidence that Wells-Barnett thought that something like this might work. But her preferred mechanism for bringing this about was not likely to be moral suasion toward the Northern whites. Some background to this is—by the time Wells-Barnett wrote *The Red Record* she had experienced censorship, and indeed threats of violence and destruction of property, owing to her own efforts to expose lynching through a black press in Memphis (Hardin and Hinton 2001). In light of this, she had taken to giving speaking tours. Most pertinently, as she discusses in chapters 7 and 8 of *The Red Record*, she had given speeches in Britain. What's noticeable for our purposes is that she had been acutely aware that these had met with more success than her attempts to sway white Americans (Zackodnik 2005). She would indeed contrast the reception she got in Britain and America as being to the latter's discredit (Ochiai 1992, 371; Appiah 2011 defends the efficacy of persuading people that international good name or national honor depends upon ending some grave injustice).

In fact, in chapter 7 she answers the charge that it is unpatriotic of her to try to appeal to support for the anti-lynching cause from England and elsewhere abroad. Against this she argues that there has been up to now little evidence that Americans are all that concerned to do anything about lynchings, even when the facts are made apparent to them—though it should be noted that she expresses hope that this is in the midst of changing (125). She prefaces her response to the charge of unpatriotic behavior by saying, "If America would not hear the cry of men, women and children whose dying groans ascended to heaven praying for relief . . ." then no fair-minded person could begrudge her going abroad. And she then says:

> If stating the facts of these lynchings, as they appeared from time to time in the white newspapers of America—the news gathered by white correspondents, compiled by white press bureaus and disseminated among white people—shows any vindictiveness, then the mind which so charges is not amenable to argument. (121)

In short, it seems that it is not only Southern whites but (white) Americans more generally that Wells-Barnett was wary of actually being persuaded of the evils of lynching by being made aware of the facts. But, I have argued above, white Americans seem to be the intended audience of *The Red Record*. I thus doubt that seeking a rhetorically effective strategy can be the justification for the evidential self-limitation. Wells-Barnett could well, of course, have reasonably hoped that some in her intended audience would be persuaded, and was aware of what we would now call her epistemic oppression and how it affected her epistemic and rhetorical situation. But given her pessimism about white America's reaction to the facts even when they are known, I deny that it was her motivation to ensure she was believed on this point. Even if she were believed, white America's interest in perpetuating the suppression of blacks may induce many to simply ignore the facts. I thus see Wells-Barnett as appreciating a point that Du Bois famously only came to much later in his career (Du Bois [1944] 1990, 41), and I think there are better justifications available for her evidential self-limitation.

To summarize the results of this section, Wells-Barnett might plausibly be making use of only white evidential sources for rhetorical reasons, to overcome prejudice. This could be justified on the grounds of noting the urgency of persuading people given the drastic evil of lynching, and a plausible analysis of the epistemic oppression of black women in Wells-Barnett's own circumstance. However, this would rely on believing that white Americans would, if faced with the facts, change their mind and change behavior. There is some material in the text to support this. But on the whole, *The Red Record* contains too many passages evincing skepticism about the degree to which acquaintance with the facts changes minds in white America, and the broader context of Wells-Barnett's own writings suggest this was not something she had much faith in. As such it would be preferable to seek an alternative justification of *The Red Record*'s evidential self-limitation.

8.4. Statistical Virtues

I shall offer a rationale for Wells-Barnett's evidential self-limitation that stresses its epistemic rather than rhetorical virtues. It is a speculative account of Wells-Barnett's rationale, but I claim that it is consistent with the text and features of her practice as an activist-scholar.

The key point is an elaboration of Wells-Barnett's remarks when she notes that her goal is to ensure that she cannot be charged with "exaggeration." What is underlying this is presumably the following: the white press is not just unreliable, but would make all their errors in the same direction. They were going to err on the side of attributing more, and more extreme, crime to black people, and less brutal and more well justified acts to white people. So by examining their records and basing her claims only upon what she finds there, Wells-Barnett will certainly avoid any risk of over-playing her hand. In fact, presumably, she draws attention to this security from charge of exaggeration precisely because the opposite is likely to be true—by drawing from this source she is likely to be understating, and it is likely to be more difficult to prove that lynching is a great injustice to black people, and that white lynch-mobs are acting with totally unjustified brutality. I will argue that the central epistemic virtue of *The Red Record* as a text comes from thinking through what is gained by avoiding "exaggeration" in this particular manner.

Wells-Barnett arranged her evidence such that her central claims, I shall argue, passed a severe test. To see what this means and why it should be considered epistemically beneficial, it will be necessary to take a brief detour through contemporary philosophy of science.

Explicit discussion of the epistemic ideal of what we should now call *severe testing* can perhaps be traced to Popper (1959), and is related to the error theoretic perspective of Neymann and Pearson. But is nowadays typically associated with the work of Mayo and Spanos (2006). Mayo and Spanos were engaged in the project of trying to show that classical statistical methods were an epistemically well-justified way of carrying out ampliative or inductive inference. Mayo and Spanos succinctly tell us what it is to pass a severe test as such:

> A hypotheses H has severely passed a test to the extent that H would not have passed the test, or passed so well, were H false. (Mayo & Spanos 2006, 350)

Mayo and Spanos then develop a number of technical proposals designed to show how classical statistical methods can ensure that inductive reasoners carry out severe tests. Space will not permit going into too much detail as to why one might find more severe tests attractive. (For a book length elaboration and defense of the ideal of severe testing, see Mayo 2018. For a good technical introduction as to how statistical severity relates to philosophical theories of evidence, see the discussion in Fletcher and Mayo-Wilson 2019). The intuition, however, is clear enough—a hypothesis that has passed a severe test is one which we probably would have gotten rid of were it false. The fact that we find ourselves still warranted in holding on to a severely tested hypothesis thus gives us some security in taking it as the basis for further action.

Return now to Wells-Barnett's use of data and reports from white journalists. I claim that this evidential self-limitation meant that her hypothesis passed a more severe test than it might otherwise have done. Of course this discussion must remain at a broad qualitative level, but none the less I think the central lines of argument are clear enough that Wells-Barnett can safely be said to have secured this methodological virtue for her thesis. It would be anachronistic in the extreme, of course, to suggest that Wells-Barnett argued this way in order to (de dicto) secure for herself the epistemic good of severe testing. Rather, my contention is that it was in order to secure the underlying intuitive epistemic goods which the technical machinery for implementing severe tests is meant to capture.

Wells-Barnett is advancing the central claims that, first, most lynching does not even purportedly respond to allegations of rape. And, second, that a number of core principles which must be satisfied by a decent system of justice are flagrantly violated by lynch-mobs. While she does make use of statistical information here, her method of validating these claims are largely informal, and in principle she has many choice points and (what we now call) researcher degrees of freedom available to her (cf. Simmons et al. 2011). There is some reason to worry that she will be able to prove her central claims too easily, by cherry-picking sources or drawing upon the interpretations of events from persons who already agree with her.

Wells-Barnett's evidential self-limitation immediately cuts down on this freedom, and does so in a way that apparently stacks the deck against her. By this choice she's only allowed to draw from a source which, were there evidence that lynching was in fact usually a response to alleged rape, would be keen to document and advertise as much. And, likewise, given how keen the malicious and untruthful white press was to defend Southern whites, if there was evidence that lynch-mobs had behaved judiciously, it would be here. But this is just to say, if her claims were false, she would be unlikely to have been able to support them by appeal to these evidential sources. Her claims would not have passed the test of these evidential sources if they were false; but they have, and hence have passed severe tests. And by restricting herself to such sources and generally avoiding supplementing them with other news sources, Wells-Barnett ensures that only claims that pass severe test are allowed in—for the simple reason that it was only the severe tests that they were put to, only the kind of evidence base which would have caught them out were they false, which did the work in validating them.

Not only is the epistemic self-limitation thus seen to be an epistemically defensible procedure, it is also in line with what might be expected of Wells-Barnett's general beliefs. Indeed, I shall argue in the next section that this way of justifying her procedure also allowed her to avoid a certain kind of mental domination. The repeated emphasis on avoiding exaggeration can be seen as a reference to the fact that her evidence source will, if anything, push in the other direction from her central claims. As just argued, this plausibly generates severe tests for her claims. Yet it might be thought odd that, unlike the previous suggestion, this rationale for the evidential self-limitation does not involve consideration of what will prompt action in the audience; its attraction lies entirely in terms of the epistemic good of passing severe test. But I shall argue that this is not so odd in light of Wells-Barnett's statements on the intrinsic good of truth seeking.

For instance, in an essay from Christmas of 1895 on the role of women as a force for social good, she wrote that ". . . it is not queens, conscious of power . . . but yet the many workers and artists who minister to their love of the truthful and the beautiful, that most possess this influence for good" (Wells-Barnett (2002a), 181). Here she is directly saying that those who work out of the love of what is truthful are those who will bring about social change. That latter is, of course, a pragmatic good; but it is secured by being the sort of woman who loves truth in an intrinsic fashion. Note that the language here could be read as suggesting that one needs both the epistemic and aesthetic concerns to be a good activist—this might then in turn suggest a close alliance between the rhetorical and epistemic purposes of the text. I shall return to this in the conclusion.

Whatever her thoughts on the love of beauty, the importance of the love of what is truthful was always clear. It can also be seen in the opening to her narration in *Lynch Law in Georgia*, where she says, "[w]e submit all to the sober judgement of the Nation, confident that,

in this cause as well as all others, 'Truth is mighty and will prevail'"
(Wells-Barnett and Le Vin 1899, 1). And all this is consonant with the
closing chapter of *The Red Record* when, encouraging readers to spread
the word and change public opinion on lynching, she advises that they
"let the facts speak for themselves, with you as their medium" (148).
Recall also the advice to tell the world the facts as being the central
take-away for readers. Here, again, there is a suggestion that good will
come from the epistemic achievement of being a medium through
which facts may speak.

There is no doubt a tension here between these pronouncements
and her distrust in her white readership, and before concluding I shall
explore that tension. But for now, suffice it to note that Wells-Barnett
seems to think that an intrinsic concern for the truth is admirable,
and that work produced in line with that intrinsic concern can change
the world. It thus seems plausible that the fact that the epistemic self-
limitation would secure an epistemic good would be in itself enough to
explain Wells-Barnett's own adoption of the procedure; she wrote for
truth, not just for direct persuasiveness.

To summarize the argument of this section, I sought a rationale for
the epistemic self-limitation that was not directly tied to the good of
ensuring that white people came to see the facts. This was found in
noting that Wells-Barnett's mode of argument ensures her central
claims have passed severe tests, an intuitively desirable epistemic property nowadays studied by philosophers of statistics. Not only does this
provide an attractive epistemic rationale for Wells-Barnett's evidential
self-limitation, but Wells-Barnett herself suggests that it is important
for her mode of activism that her texts be epistemically well motivated.
It thus seems to suffice as a motive for her work that it would be epistemically virtuous to proceed as such, without it necessarily having the
sort of direct rhetorical or practically persuasive advantages that were
claimed for the former rationale.

8.5. Lessons for a Scholar-Activist

Wells-Barnett was an activist and an intellectual. As Collins puts
it, "[u]nlike contemporary distinctions made between intellectual

production and activism, Wells-Barnett managed to do both" (2002, 9). Guided by Collins's contextualization of Wells-Barnett's work, I have been trying to draw attention to the interplay between Wells-Barnett's urgent need to persuade and spur action, on the one hand, and her high epistemic purpose and reverence for truth seeking as an admirable goal in itself, combined with a realistic understanding of how much she could hope to sway white Americans in any case, on the other. These were not strictly separable features of her work. In this section I explain this feature of Wells-Barnett as a scholar-activist in more detail, and draw out an explicit moral for contemporary readers. What exactly is the relationship between the attempt to be persuasive to a white audience who cannot be trusted to care, and the attempt to do work according to plausible epistemic standards?

Wells-Barnett is part of an African American intellectual tradition which places great stock in the importance of "describ[ing] the truth of Black lives in a way that gives agency to African Americans" (Collins 2002, 15). She had a central moral proposition that she hoped both to prove and encourage belief in—as she put it in the introduction to the 1892 text *Southern Horrors*, "The Afro-American is not a bestial race. If this work can contribute in any way towards proving this, and at the same time arouse the conscience of the American people to a demand for justice . . . I shall feel I have done my race a service" (Wells-Barnett 2002b, 26). Note, again, that proving the point and persuading people to take action toward justice are both listed as goals for her work—but clearly separated, at least analytically, in how Wells-Barnett describes her own purpose for work. She hopes to persuade, but recognizes this as a distinct goal from trying to do good work according to her own epistemic standards. This analytic separation allowed Wells-Barnett to generate a mode of scholar-activism that encourages mental self-determination as a step along the path to general liberation.

Wells-Barnett can plausibly be seen as a forerunner to the militant African-American movement of the 1960s (Curry 2012). In memorable words found in *Southern Horrors*, she said that African Americans could learn from both the failures of the justice system to protect Black people and the success of some people in fighting off lynch-mobs. As she put it:

The lesson this teaches and which every Afro-American should ponder well, is that a Winchester rifle should have a place of honour in every black home, and it should be used for that protection which the law refuses to give. When the white man who is always the aggressor knows he runs as great risk of biting the dust every time his Afro-American victim does, he will have greater respect for Afro-American life. The more the Afro-American yields and cringes and begs, the more he has to do so, the more he is insulted, outraged and lynched. (Wells-Barnnett 2002b, 52)

And this is far from the only time one sees Wells-Barnett expressing such radical sentiments. She also advocated labor radicalism to force Northern capital to intervene against Southern whites:

In the creation of this healthier public sentiment, the Afro-American can do for himself what no one else can do for him. The world looks on with wonder that we have conceded so much and remain law-abiding under such great outrage and provocation. To Northern capital and Afro-American labor the South owes its rehabilitation. If labor is withdrawn capital will not remain. The Afro-American is thus the backbone of the South. A thorough knowledge and judicious exercise of this power in lynching localities could many times effect a bloodless revolution. The white man's dollar is his god, and to stop this will be to stop outrages in many localities. (Wells-Barnnett 2002b, 50)

I note in passing that whereas here Wells-Barnett suggests an idolatry of mammon that is typical of the white man, in *The Red Record* it is specifically the Christian world that she says will be moved to act by being presented with the facts.

And she presciently advocates a public transport boycott in the American South as a way of garnering support (Wells-Barnett 2002b, 51), before summarizing her point thusly:

The appeal to the white man's pocket has ever been more effectual than all the appeals ever made to his conscience. Nothing, absolutely nothing, is to be gained by a further sacrifice of manhood and self-respect. By the right exercise of his power as the industrial factor of the South, the Afro-American can demand and secure his rights, the punishment of lynchers, and a fair trial for accused rapists. (2002b, 51)

What one finds in these extracts from *Southern Horrors* again and again is a clear sense that it is only by standing up for ourselves, by engaging in "self-help," as one of *Southern Horror's* chapters is called, can we hope to secure justice. Her emphasis is on African-American self-liberation. I believe this same spirit can be seen as underlying the model of the scholar-activist in *The Red Record*.

For what one gains from this sort of epistemically conscientious scholar-activism is a sense of mental self-determination. We are doing our thinking for ourselves when we concern ourselves with what actually constitutes a good argument for our claims, rather than what would be persuasive to a hostile audience. The latter grants anti-Black racists a subtle but pervasive power, as even when reasoning for ourselves we are orienting ourselves around them, their standards, what they should be likely to believe. Wells-Barnett makes the best case she can because that matters to her; but by serving as a medium for the facts in this way, by evincing a love of what is truthful, she is also self-empowering—generating knowledge in a fashion that is acceptable to her, and useful to her projects insofar as knowledge of our power assists in the judicious exercise of said power. She did not spurn assistance from sympathetic whites where she could get it (King 2004, 127) and did clearly make strategic use of allies in Britain (Silkey 2015). But her methodological choices as a scholar-activist reflect her overriding concern that black people do for ourselves—we think for ourselves, according to standards that we ourselves endorse as reflecting our own love of the truthful. By such self-empowerment we may hope to win the future.

Wells-Barnett is nothing if not clear that there is, of course, a link between good knowledge and successful action. Schechter (2001) describes Wells-Barnett's intellectual style as that of a "visionary pragmatist," which accords well with the picture I have drawn here. So I am not saying that Wells-Barnett had a project of knowledge for knowledge's sake. In the end, the goal was to change the world and secure rights for Black people. The claim is simply that we shall achieve that worthy end best by becoming both materially and physically self-determined, and that involves due love for truth, and a well-grounded knowledge of the facts as they pertain to us. It requires that we make the best case we can for our claims, not in the hope that we will persuade thereby, but because we are working to our own standards, and are invested in securing both truth and our rights. It requires an epistemically conscientious form of scholar-activism, just like that of Ida B Wells-Barnett.

8.6. Conclusion

Wells-Barnett took the time to make a case against lynching. Ostensibly the text is written as if its audience is well-meaning American whites who might be persuaded that lynching is worth opposing if only the facts are properly presented to them. But it does not seem that she pinned her hopes for liberation from lynching upon persuading white readers that justice ought to be done. The goal of her work in *The Red Record* is not just to persuade anyone—either a white audience, or even herself—that lynching is really wrong and ought to be acted upon. The goal is to think for ourselves, to evince the love of truth by letting facts be known, and through knowledge to place ourselves in the position to take effective strategic action in securing our own liberation. This is not a total separation of rhetorical from epistemic aims, or a project of knowledge for knowledge's sake. As seen above, Wells-Barnett thinks that being the kind of person who seeks the truth—and, perhaps, who does so in combination with a love of beauty, presenting things in an aesthetically engaging manner—will be the sort of person who changes the world. And it is clear that if white Americans can be persuaded to take up the cause, Wells-Barnett will be happy for it. But the point is just that we should not orient our epistemic actions around these goals. What ought to determine our behavior is our own sense of what would constitute good inquiry. So while I think Wells-Barnett took both rhetorical and epistemic considerations seriously, my claim is that there was an order of priority between them, and should they ever come apart, then to secure mental self-determination the epistemic ought to

come first. All of us who would seek to not just interpret but change the
world can stand to learn from her work and example.[1]

Bibliography

Appiah, Kwame Anthony (2011). *The Honor Code: How Moral Revolutions Happen*. New York: W. W. Norton.

Collins, Patricia Hill (2002). Introductory Essay. In Ida B. Wells-Barnett (ed.), *On Lynching*, Amherst, NY: Prometheus Books, 9–24.

Curry, Tommy J. (2012). The Fortune of Wells: Ida B. Wells-Barnett's Use of T. Thomas Fortune's Philosophy of Social Agitation as a Prolegomenon to Militant Civil Rights Activism. In *Transactions of the Charles S. Peirce Society* 48(4): 456–482.

Dotson, Kristie (2011). Tracking Epistemic Violence, Tracking Practices of Silencing. *Hypatia* 26(2): 236–257.

Dotson, Kristie (2014). Conceptualizing Epistemic Oppression. *Social Epistemology* 28(2): 115–138.

Du Bois, W. E. B. ([1944] 1990). My Evolving Program for Negro Freedom. *Clinical Sociology Review* 8(1): 27–57.

Fletcher, Samuel C., and Mayo-Wilson, Conor (2019). Evidence in Classical Statistics. [Preprint] http://philsci-archive.pitt.edu/id/eprint/16191.

Good, Irving John (1967). On the Principle of Total Evidence. *British Journal for the Philosophy of Science* 17(4): 319–321.

Hardin, Robin, and Marcie Hinton (2001). The Squelching of Free Speech in Memphis: The Life of a Black Post-Reconstruction Newspaper. *Race, Gender & Class* 8(4): 78–95.

Harris, Paisley Jane (2003). Gatekeeping and Remaking: The Politics of Respectability in African American Women's History and Black Feminism. *Journal of Women's History* 15(1): 212–220.

King, Preston (2004). Ida B. Wells and the Management of Violence. *Critical Review of International Social and Political Philosophy* 7(4): 111–146.

Mayo, Deborah G. (2018). *Statistical Inference as Severe Testing*. Cambridge: Cambridge University Press.

Mayo, Deborah G., and Aris Spanos (2006). Severe Testing as a Basic Concept in a Neyman–Pearson Philosophy of Induction. *The British Journal for the Philosophy of Science* 57(2): 323–357.

[1] My thanks to Eric Schliesser, Kathleen Creel, Olúfẹ́mi O. Táíwò (the other one), Konstantin Genin, and Remco Heesen for comments on this chapter.

Ochiai, Akiko (1992). Ida B. Wells and Her Crusade for Justice: An African American Woman's Testimonial Autobiography. *Soundings* 75 (2/3) (Summer/Fall 1992): 365–381.

Popper, Karl (1959). *The Logic of Scientific Discovery*. New York: Basic Books.

Silkey, Sarah L. (2015). *Black Woman Reformer: Ida B. Wells, Lynching, and Transatlantic Activism*. Athens: University of Georgia Press.

Silkey, Sarah L. (2020). Ida B. Wells Won the Pulitzer. Here's Why That Matters. *Washington Post*, May 7, 2020. https://www.washingtonpost.com/outlook/2020/05/07/ida-b-wells-won-pulitzer-heres-why-that-matters/.

Simmons, Joseph P., Nelson, Leif D., and Simonsohn, Uri (2011). False-Positive Psychology: Undisclosed Flexibility in Data Collection and Analysis Allows Presenting Anything as Significant. *Psychological Science* 22(11): 1359–1366.

Schechter, Patricia Ann (2001). *Ida B. Wells-Barnett and American Reform, 1880–1930*. Chapel Hill: University of North Carolina Press.

Táíwò, Olúfémi O. (2018). The Empire Has No Clothes. *Disputatio* 10(51): 305–330.

Wells-Barnett, Ida B. ([1885] 1995). Women's Mission. In M. DeCosta-Willlis (ed.), *The Memphis Diary of Ida B. Wells*. Boston: Beacon Press, 179–182.

Wells-Barnett, Ida B. (2002a). Red Record. In her *On Lynching*, Amherst, NY: Prometheus Books, 55–152.

Wells-Barnett, Ida B. (2002b). Southern Horrors. In her *On Lynching*, Amherst, NY: Prometheus Books, 25–54.

Wells-Barnett, Ida B., and Louis P. Le Vin (1899). *Lynch Law in Georgia: A Six-weeks' Record in the Center of Southern Civilization, as Faithfully Chronicled by the "Atlanta Journal" and the "Atlanta Constitution": Also the Full Report of Louis P. Le Vin, the Chicago Detective Sent to Investigate the Burning of Samuel Hose, the Torture and Hanging of Elijah Strickland, the Colored Preacher, and the Lynching of Nine Men for Alleged Arson*. https://tile.loc.gov/storage-services/service/rbc/lcrbmrp/t1612/t1612.pdf.

Zackodnik, Teresa (2005). Ida B. Wells and "American Atrocities" in Britain. *Women's Studies International Forum* 28(4): 259–273.

9

The de Lagunas' *Dogmatism and Evolution*

Overcoming Modern Philosophy and Making Post-Quinean Analytic Philosophy

Joel Katzav

9.1. Introduction

Grace and Theodore de Laguna's joint 1910 monograph *Dogmatism and Evolution: Studies in Modern Philosophy* (*DE*) has been forgotten. I show, however, that it develops an important theory of judgment or, in contemporary terminology, epistemology. The theory rejects, and in doing so addresses challenges to, what the de Lagunas call "the dogmatism of rationalism and empiricism." Roughly, this dogmatism includes the dogmas that complex ideas are analyzable into simple ideas, that the relations simple ideas stand in are external, and that knowledge ultimately rests on judgments that are evaluated against experience individually, in single acts of infallible intuition. In rejecting the dogmas, *DE* rejects the analytic-synthetic distinction and the existence of infallible judgments, and proposes that judgments confront experience holistically, as parts of systems of judgments. *DE* also addresses challenges to other similarly holistic responses to dogmatism, including to Hegelian and pragmatist theories of judgment.

I show, further, that *DE* provides an important perspective on the history of modern philosophy. According to *DE*, this history involved the realization of the inadequacy of the dogmas of rationalism and empiricism, as well as of the analytic-synthetic distinction. George W. Hegel's and pragmatism's theories of judgment were responses to this realization, just as *DE* was. While *DE* explains how Hegel's system

Joel Katzav, *The de Lagunas'* Dogmatism and Evolution In: *Neglected Classics of Philosophy.*
Edited by: Eric Schliesser, Oxford University Press. © Oxford University Press 2022.
DOI: 10.1093/oso/9780190097196.003.0010

constitutes a response to dogmatism, *DE* is neither really explicit about how it or pragmatism constitute such responses, nor considers how later Hegelians, such as the de Lagunas' supervisor James E. Creighton, go beyond Hegel on this matter. Nevertheless, we will see that *DE*'s perspective can be straightforwardly extended to answer these questions.[1]

Finally, I argue that *DE* matters because its historical perspective can be extended to illuminate the development of mid-twentieth-century analytic philosophy. Willard V. Quine's 1951 paper, "Two Dogmas of Empiricism" (*TD*), rejects what he called "two dogmas of empiricism" and proposes a holistic epistemology. This rejection and positive proposal are usually supposed to lie behind *TD*'s revolutionary impact. But Quine's dogmas were part of what the de Lagunas, as well as the Hegelian Creighton, had targeted when rejecting dogmatism. And Quine's holism was close to the much earlier holism of Creighton, a position the de Lagunas also rejected. When viewed from the perspective of *DE*, *TD*'s real revolution lay in its relation to critical philosophy. Critical philosophy, roughly, aims to unpack, or examine the commitments of, established opinion. Speculative philosophy, of which *DE* is an instance, includes critical philosophy as a part, but also aims to go beyond science and common sense in teaching us about the world. What *TD* did was to contribute to narrowing down epistemology and metaphysics to critical epistemology and critical metaphysics.[2] *TD* also participated in the marginalization of philosophers who, like the de Lagunas, were speculative philosophers. Grace de Laguna surely recognized much of this as she stood opposite Quine during his first presentation of *TD* in 1950.

In section 9.2, I outline some key features of the de Lagunas' theory of judgment. In section 9.3, I present what *DE* tells us about how this theory of judgment goes beyond empiricism, rationalism, and Hegel's theory of judgment. In section 9.4, I present *DE*'s critical discussion

---

[1] According to *DE*'s introduction (*DE*, p. iv), the explanation for some of this lack of explicitness is that one of the authors—we are not told which one—had to withdraw from writing part III of the book, with the result that this part engaged less than adequately with parts I and II. Parts I and II present the de Lagunas' treatment of the dogmas and of Hegel, while their own position is mostly presented through criticism of pragmatism, in part III.

[2] Critical philosophy, as understood here, is not the Frankfurt School's critical theory.

of the pragmatist theories of judgment of William James and John Dewey; I also explain the roles of pragmatism and of Creighton's Hegelian theory of judgment in overcoming the dogmas of rationalism and empiricism. Section 9.5 illuminates mid-twentieth-century analytic philosophy. Section 9.6 is the conclusion.[3]

9.2. Some Key Features of the de Lagunas' Theory of Judgment

9.2.1. Holism and Fallibilism

According to the de Lagunas, ideas come in a variety of kinds. An image, for example, is an idea that represents specific circumstances, say, a specific chair from a specific perspective. A concept is an idea that is able to represent a single object in multiple circumstances and thus that can represent objects as such (*DE*, 165–166). The theory of judgment aims to describe the various kinds of ideas and to explain how those ideas that are characteristic of animals and early childhood, including images, evolve into those that come to be characteristic of humans as they mature, that is, into concepts, including the particularly sophisticated concepts characteristic of science, culture, and common sense (*DE*, 148–149, 165–166). The theory of judgment also includes a description of the evolving standards for the application of concepts in specific circumstances, that is, of the evolving standards for judgment. I here present some key aspects of the de Lagunas' view of concepts and the evolution of concepts, mostly leaving aside explanations for this evolution and leaving aside what the de Lagunas say about other kinds of ideas.

An important key to the de Lagunas' theory of judgment is their meaning holism regarding concepts, that is, their view that the meaning of a concept is partly fixed by its logical (deductive) relations to other concepts. As the de Lagunas put it,

---

[3] *DE* includes (p. 160) a potentially racist statement, though not one that explicitly identifies a particular race or that seems to express racial superiority or animosity.

the reference of a concept to a mode of conduct is never direct. The concept never directly bridges the gap between stimulus and response. On the contrary, thought is a long-circuiting of the connection, and its whole character depends upon its indirectness, its involution, if we may use the term. Though concepts, apart from the conduct which they prompt, mean nothing, yet their meaning is never analyzable except into other concepts, indirect like the first in their reference to conduct. (*DE*, 206)

When the de Lagunas say that a concept determines action indirectly, they mean that it determines action only as a function of relevant conditions. They add that the relevant conditions amount to what they call the "total situation," where a total situation includes relevant internal states of the organism, including judgments and interests, and external conditions (*DE*, 167). How one's concept of, say, one's coat guides one's behavior depends on external circumstances such as the weather, as well as on one's relevant judgments about the coat, the weather, and other matters, and on one's relevant goals.

Explicit in the preceding quote is the view that a concept's meaning has two components. It encompasses, in addition to the concept's logical relations to other concepts, the concept's role in guiding behavior, including not only overt behavior but also thought. The de Lagunas call the component relating to concepts' logical relations "content" and the component relating to behavior "import" (*DE*, 126, 139, 162–171, 190–194). In providing examples of the meanings of concepts, they tell us that the content of "toy" in the mouth of a three-year-old might be partly captured by "is bought by papa in a certain store" and the import of "toy" might partly be captured by its role in picking out toys (*DE*, 190). More interestingly, the de Lagunas write that "[o]n the side of content, evolution means a process of change distinguished by certain definite characteristics; on the side of import, it means no less than a whole new principle of classification, almost one might claim, of scientific procedure" (*DE*, 199).

The de Lagunas' view that the content of a concept correlates stimuli, behavioral responses, and goals indirectly via the concept's logical relations to other concepts goes along with the view that a concept's import is also not simply a matter of correlating stimulus and response. As the de Lagunas put it,

> [a] concept is never univocal in its reference to a mode of conduct; that is to say, its meaning is never limited to the correlation of a certain type of stimulus with a certain response. On the contrary, its import invariably embraces a variety of actions. (*DE*, 205)

Meaning holism regarding concepts implies, according to the de Lagunas, a variant of confirmation holism, that is, of the view that our concepts and judgments are tested by experience as systems rather than individually. Confirmation holism and the lack of univocity of concepts' relations to conduct imply, in turn, a variant of fallibilism, that is, of the view that all concepts and judgments are tentative. In light of meaning holism, the de Lagunas tell us that

> [e]very concept involves an indefinite number of problems; and these cannot be stated except in terms which themselves in turn involve indefinite series of problems. Nowhere is there an absolute given, a self-sufficient first premise. From this, as well as from the indirect and equivocal nature of the reference of thought to conduct, it follows that the confirmation or invalidation of a concept by the result of the conduct which it serves to guide can itself be no more than tentative. (*DE*, 206)

Because concepts are applied in logically interrelated clusters, any challenge to a judgment is, as a matter of logic, a challenge to the cluster to which it belongs. Similarly, because a concept has implications for conduct in a variety of circumstances, the success of a concept's application in any particular circumstance is, as it were, hostage to its application in other circumstances. An earlier judgment might, for example, have to be revised because of a later one. As a result, judgments are never evaluated in isolation. And since judgments are not evaluated in isolation, they are generally fallible. Fallibility is supposed to extend to mathematics and logic. The de Lagunas ask whether the concepts of number and the concepts of implication and inclusion it presupposes are final, and respond:

[t]his we see no sufficient reason to believe. On the contrary, the utterly unexpected development which the concept of number has recently undergone through researches in the theory of infinite numbers is an index of the possibilities which may yet be in store. Nothing could ever have seemed more necessary than that if $2X = X$, $X = 0$; and yet we know today that there is a distinct class of other roots. (*DE*, 159–160)

Elsewhere in *DE*, the de Lagunas claim something stronger than just the fallibility of all concepts and judgments. They claim that all concepts, including those of mathematics and logic, are ultimately evaluable in light of their success in guiding behavior and thus not solely on the basis of their content (*DE*, 137–139, 149, 198). Indeed, all concepts are ultimately evaluable in light of their role in guiding overt behavior:

[w]e must not, of course, fail to recognize that mental behavior can never become more than relatively independent of overt conduct. Its roots are in practical and social life, and the very condition of its health lies in an ever renewed contact with, and adaptation to, the changing phases of such life. (*DE*, 198)

The evaluability of concepts in light of behavior meshes with the de Lagunas' view that all concepts have import, but also with what they say about truth. They take the truth of judgments in general, including those of logic and mathematics, to be partly a function of success in guiding behavior (*DE*, 148–149). Judgments are, strictly speaking, never analytic in the sense of being true solely by virtue of meaning but are synthetic in the sense of being true partly in virtue of their success in guiding behavior.[4]

---

[4] The de Lagunas do not explicitly say that their claim that the truth of judgments depends on success in guiding behavior means that all judgments are synthetic. They would, however, have recognized this way of putting their position. Creighton, we will see, puts his related position in this way. More directly, as we will also see, the de Lagunas are explicit that they think that the distinction between the analytic and the synthetic depends on meaning atomism, a dogma they reject.

9.2.2.   Tempering Meaning Holism and Tempering the Implications of Meaning Holism

The de Lagunas are careful to temper their meaning holism, their confirmation holism, and the denial of the existence of truths that are true by virtue of meaning. With regard to meaning holism, their view is that our conceptual system is to some extent granular; some concepts are relatively closely interrelated when compared with others. Thus, while the content of a concept might be fixed by its logical place in our entire system of concepts, its content is largely fixed within a much more local cluster (*DE*, 200). Further, in the sciences,

> the process of integration and fixation of concepts has been carried farthest. Because the special science is so remote in its reference to common life and so entirely controlled in its progress by its own special end, it becomes a system relatively independent of the great body of cognitive experience. (*DE*, 200)[5]

Meaning holism is, for the de Lagunas, blunted in a further way. The development of each one of our relatively tightly knit clusters of concepts also includes the creation of new, relatively autonomous concepts. For the new concepts that are introduced into our system of concepts often bear few logical relations, and many contingent relations, to existing concepts (*DE*, 110–111, 161).

Similarly, the de Lagunas blunt confirmation holism. They recognize that the failure of the system of concepts in generating satisfactory behavior can, as far as logic is concerned, be due to any of the involved concepts, and thus can be due to commitments across different special sciences, or even across science and common sense. Nevertheless, they also see that the blame for such failure tends to be sought in a relatively circumscribed part of the system (*DE*, 152–153). The reason for a failed expectation regarding the time of the arrival of a bus is not, for example, sought in the assumptions of logic or physics. This is, on the de Lagunas' view, partly due to the purpose relativity of judgment. In order to reason, the de Lagunas argue, we inevitably make a variety of

---

[5] The de Lagunas classify physics as a special science.

assumptions, but which assumptions we make depends on the purpose of our reasoning and different purposes govern different instances of reasoning. As a result, standards of correctness for judgments vary with interests (*DE*, 153–155). Thus, for example, while a figure may, in some circumstances, count as a circle if our finest measurements show no deviation from the mathematical ideal of a circle, the degree of accuracy ordinarily required of a circle is no more than that it look circular to the unaided eye (*DE*, 150–151). Similarly, when economists assumed that people seek to gratify desires by the least exertion, all that was required was that the assumption hold other things being equal (*DE*, 159). But in mechanics, by contrast,

> there is no "other things being equal." The antecedent of each formula purports, at least, to set forth the precise conditions under which the consequent must follow. (*DE*, 159)

Now, since judgment is relative to purpose and purpose varies across domains of thinking, we evaluate claims in a given domain relatively independently of claims in other domains (*DE*, 152–153).

Importantly, while the purpose relativity of judgment blunts confirmation holism, evolution blunts purpose relativity. According to the de Lagunas, the development of relatively tightly knit systems of concepts and their associated standards of judgment brings with it, in some domains and especially in the mathematical sciences, an evaluation of judgments in increasingly large conceptual systems. And where judgment is increasingly systematic in this way, the application of concepts will become more conditional or indirect, that is, the appropriateness of the application of a given concept will depend on the applicability of larger clusters of related concepts (*DE*, 197–198). Further, judgment which is characterized by increasing systematicity and indirectness is also characterized by

> increasing definiteness and increasing universality, that is to say, by the greater and greater delicacy with which it is contradicted or confirmed by experience, and by its gradual transcendence of the limits of the particular interests and the particular occasion which have called it forth. (*DE*, 149–150)

A particularly high degree of indirectness and universality is found in mechanics and geometry:

> considerable alterations can be made in either and sufficiently compensated by corresponding alterations in the other. A non-Euclidean geometry, coupled with its appropriate non-Newtonian mechanics, can describe our world as exactly as the Euclidean can do. In short, geometry is recognizedly a branch of applied mathematics. (*DE*, 159)

Variation in definiteness of judgments is illustrated by the de Lagunas' already noted suggestion that the conditions in which mechanics' general judgments are supposed to hold are precisely specified, while those of economics are only supposed to hold other things being equal.

This brings us to blunting the rejection of the idea of truth by virtue of meaning. The de Lagunas think of the indirectness of concepts as the key evolutionary advantage of concepts. It is the conditionality of the applicability of concepts that makes uncovering the correct response to a novel situation something other than chance; the more conditional or indirect the concepts, the greater the ability to respond to diverse situations in different ways and thus to select an appropriate response (*DE*, 168–169). But the indirectness of concepts, they point out, means that thought has a structure of its own:

> with respect to thought and conduct it must be said that the very indirectness and equivocality of the reference of the former to the latter gives thought a character of its own, which is as independent of aught beyond as can well be imagined. (*DE*, 207)

The de Lagunas thus tie what they take to be the evolutionary advantage of concepts to the existence of conceptual structures that can be evaluated, by and large, independently of their impact on conduct and thus to something that comes close to analyticity, in the sense of truth by virtue of meaning.[6]

---

[6] The de Lagunas call formulae such as "7 + 5 = 12" analytic because they take them to be reducible to "statements of absolute identity" (*DE*, 159). Being reducible to an identity statement is accordingly an example of the kind of test of truth that, in their view, is close to being independent of experience.

9.3. Dogmatism and Hegel's Philosophy: A Nineteenth-Century Problem Situation

We can now consider the dogmas of rationalism and empiricism, and the story of the attempts to overcome them, first by Hegel and later by his followers, by the pragmatists and by the de Lagunas. This section focuses on rationalism and empiricism, and on Hegel's own position.

DE's discussion of rationalism and empiricism focuses primarily on three dogmas, as well as covers a corollary of these dogmas. The first dogma, call it "meaning atomism," is that ideas are either complex or simple, and that complex ideas can be analyzed into absolutely simple, and hence unanalyzable, ones. Empiricists held that psychological analysis, or dissection, of ideas of particulars would yield simple ideas. Rationalists, by contrast, thought that logical analysis, that is, an examination of the logical presuppositions of complex ideas, would yield simple ideas. The empiricist's simples were ingredients in ideas of particular objects, that is, sensations. The rationalist's simples were general ideas (*DE*, 30–33). The second dogma, call it "External Relations," is that the relations between simple ideas are independent of, i.e., not essential to, their natures or meanings (*DE*, 36). The third dogma, call it "Intuition," is that all knowledge ultimately rests on infallible intuitions of simple ideas. For rationalists, infallible intuition is provided by judgments affirming simple, general ideas. For empiricists, it is provided by judgments affirming simple sensations (*DE*, 25–33). According to the de Lagunas, the dogmas are closely related since, roughly, simple, logically independent concepts are required if infallible knowledge is to be possible (*DE*, 32–33). Indeed, we have seen that their own fallibilism is driven by the view that concepts have their meanings fixed, in part, by their logical interrelations.

The three dogmas bring with them, according to the de Lagunas, a number of corollaries. Of particular importance to what follows is a corollary that follows from meaning atomism's assumption that analysis yields simple ideas. The de Lagunas claim that "the very division of propositions into analytic and synthetic rests on this assumption," and do so, in part, on the ground that "no proposition could be determined as synthetic, unless a complete definition of its terms had exhibited their ultimate disparateness" (*DE*, 73). The idea here is that, unless we exhaustively analyze a proposition's concepts, we cannot determine what their mutual relations of implication are and thus determine whether the proposition is synthetic. So, meaning atomism provides the necessary basis for distinguishing between analytic and synthetic propositions.

One of the de Lagunas' key objections to dogmatism is that it takes the form of judgment to be fixed. Their view is that, in light of Charles R. Darwin's work on evolution, theories of judgment need to recognize, and empirically investigate, the past and future evolution of the form of judgment (*DE*, 19–20, 117–124). A second key objection to dogmatism—the final one to be summarized here—concerns relations between ideas. On the one hand, ideas without any interrelations are meaningless. On the other hand, it seems that dogmatists can admit no ideas of relations between ideas. Ideas of relations between ideas are complex and thus must, according to meaning atomism, be analyzable into constituent simple ideas. But no such analysis is possible, given External Relations. External Relations tells us that the meanings of simple ideas are independent of such ideas' interrelations, so that simple ideas imply nothing about their interrelations. Rationalists are, to be sure, willing to argue that inclusion is not a real relation and thus can still maintain that some ideas include others. But simple ideas can include no others, and thus remain unrelated to other ideas (*DE*, 36–42). Empiricists invariably admit some relations between simple ideas, despite their commitment to meaning atomism and External Relations (*DE*, 48–51).

After criticizing rationalism and empiricism, *DE* argues that Kant's, and his neo-Kantian followers', commitment to the analytic-synthetic distinction implies a commitment to simple ideas and thus to theories of judgment that fail in the way dogmatist ones do (*DE*, 73–80). A certain reading of Hegel is then identified as the main challenger to dogmatism.[7] On this reading, Hegel adopts the assumption, call it "Internal Relations," that a thing is wholly constituted by its relations to other things (*DE*, 88–91). It follows that ideas, which Hegel

---

[7] The de Lagunas recognize (*DE*, 148) other interpretations of Hegel, but are here interested in a standard interpretation.

supposedly identifies with concepts, are wholly constituted by their relations to their objects and to other ideas (*DE*, 92). Thus, contrary to
External Relations, no idea has a non-relational nature. And, contrary
to meaning atomism, ideas are generally analyzable in relational terms,
so that no idea is analyzable into unanalyzable ideas. Given that the
relations of an idea to its object will partly determine the idea's nature
and, accordingly, partly determine whether the idea will be true or not,
it seems the de Lagunas also imply that, for Hegel, the truth of an idea
is never entirely independent of how the world is and thus true just
by virtue of meaning. From their perspective, Hegel must reject the
analytic-synthetic distinction.

Intuition too must be given up with the adoption of Internal
Relations. Here, the de Lagunas attribute to Hegel a variant of their
own already mentioned argument for fallibilism; no finite, immediate
intuition could, given that the natures of ideas are relational and thus
that that their application is always indirect, serve as a sufficient basis
for judgment. Partly as a result, Hegel needs to find another basis for
judgment. His solution is to adopt an evolutionary form of confirmation holism according to which each judgment is evaluated in light of
its consistency with the entire system of thought (*DE*, 92–93, 99).

Hegel conceived of actuality as a system of internally related phenomena that is driven to change by internal contradictions. The
contradictions existing at any stage of the system's evolution are re-
solved in the stage they give rise to. Further, the phenomena at any
stage are subsumed in the subsequent stage, and their true nature is
fixed by their relations in the subsequent stage; the earlier stage is revealed as appearance (*DE*, 95–100). Such evolution occurs in parts of
actuality too. For example, the system of fundamental concepts we use
to interpret reality evolves, according to Hegel, due to internal logical contradictions. The true meaning of a concept in this system at
any time is fixed by a subset of its relations, specifically by its logical
relations to other fundamental concepts in the next, more consistent
stage of the system (*DE*, 100–102). In general, the *fully* true meaning
of an idea is fixed by its logical relations to ideas in the fully consistent
system of ideas (*DE*, 99).

A key problem the de Lagunas identify for Hegel's position is that
it does not subject the law of contradiction to evolution and indeed,

like rationalism, assumes this law is an infallible criterion of truth (*DE*, 105–106). Further, Hegel does not give empirically ascertained, contingent fact a role in explaining the evolution of concepts (*DE*, 117–119). Finally, Hegel's commitment to the idea that contradiction alone drives evolution comes with his recognition that actual history is only partially interpretable as being driven by this principle. Hegel must thus also suppose that history has entirely inexplicable, contingent elements (*DE*, 109). But the content of thought need imply nothing about any inexplicable, contingent historical elements. So Hegel seems to be committed to the view that thought is externally related to history, a commitment that is incompatible with his commitment to Internal Relations (*DE*, 110–111).

Thus, according to the de Lagunas, the nineteenth-century theory of judgment was in trouble. Dogmatist views of judgment, according to which judgment is ultimately based on intuition, were in trouble given their association with meaning atomism and External Relations. Such views of judgment were also in trouble because they were not evolutionary. At the same time, the leading evolutionary alternative to dogmatism, namely Hegel's philosophy, was also untenable. Its evolutionary epistemology did not extend to logic itself and thus was dogmatic, in the end. Further, its commitment to Internal Relations and to a corresponding, extreme form of holism led to inconsistency. The de Lagunas' own theory of judgment, however, avoids the troubles of dogmatism and of Hegel's evolutionism. The confirmation holism the de Lagunas adopt is not inconsistent in the way that Hegel's is. They treat logic as a fallible product of evolution, one that is ultimately also judged and explained by its role in guiding behavior. Similarly, they reject extreme forms of meaning holism, along with Internal Relations. They do this by taking concepts' meanings to depend on import in addition to logical relations, and by supposing the continued creation of new concepts that are largely related to existing concepts in contingent, and thus external, ways. Meaning holism is also limited because concepts cluster and judgment is contextual. At the same time, the de Lagunas reject meaning atomism, External Relations, and the problematic, non-holistic epistemology associated with these positions. Meaning atomism and External relations are rejected because, according to the de Lagunas, there are no simple, unanalyzable concepts.

All concepts have content and import as constituents, and are analyzable in terms of their logical relations and behavioral role.

9.4. Dogmatism, Pragmatism, and Hegelianism

9.4.1. The Pragmatist Response to Dogmatism and to Hegel

Let us see why the de Lagunas also think of pragmatism's theory of judgment—which for them is the theory of judgment found in the work of James and Dewey (*DE*, iii)—as a response to the failures of dogmatism and of Hegel's system, and also how the de Lagunas' position relates to pragmatism.

Pragmatism, as the de Lagunas understand it, assumes that ideas are practical. More explicitly, it assumes that the meaning of an idea is just its role in guiding overt behavior and that this role is just that of specifying what we are to do given our goals and the type of context we find ourselves in (*DE*, 126–127). In addition, the pragmatist holds that ideas are judged in terms of consistency with each other, and usefulness in guiding, overt behavior. When the interpretation of a new experience contradicts a body of ideas, the tendency is to reject the interpretation; and when an idea persistently fails, then not only it but also, in accordance with confirmation holism, ideas that harmonize with it are put in doubt (*DE*, 129). Here the de Lagunas note an anomaly in pragmatism, namely that it does not properly extend its view of meaning to the ideas of logic and mathematics. It states that, in these fields, an idea's meaning is also given by its role in guiding overt behavior. But, according to the de Lagunas, this claim is not substantiated. Pragmatism admits that judgments about ideas in logic and mathematics are to be made on purely a priori, intuitive grounds and thus entirely independently of the ideas' roles in guiding behavior (*DE*, 149).

Pragmatists follow Hegel in rejecting Intuition for the view that ideas are evaluated in an evolutionary and holistic way. True, pragmatists do not subject logic and mathematics to this evolutionary treatment, but they disagree with Hegel in supposing that experience and logic, rather than just logic, drives changes in our ideas. So pragmatists can suppose that logic too is subject to evolution; logic too can be properly conceived of as an instrument to be judged by its efficacy in guiding behavior in relation to experience. This, claim the de Lagunas, allows pragmatists to avoid reverting to dogmatism about logic and mathematics even if they have not chosen to do so (*DE*, 118, 202–204).

How the de Lagunas understand pragmatism's stance on the remaining dogmas requires some extrapolation from what *DE* explicitly states. Since pragmatism supposedly tells us that ideas can be analyzed in terms of their role in guiding overt behavior, extrapolation tells us that pragmatism is incompatible with the view that there are unanalyzable, simple ideas, and thus incompatible with External Relations and meaning atomism. Pragmatism also, since the analysis of meaning in terms of behavior is supposed to be a complete analysis, denies that ideas can partly be analyzed by specifying their logical relations to other ideas, contrary to Internal Relations. The analytic-synthetic distinction will have to be rejected if pragmatists are taken at their word and are supposed to think that all ideas are to be analyzed in terms of their roles in guiding behavior. With the rejection of Intuition, meaning atomism and External Relations, the pragmatist has avoided dogmatism and its challenges. With the rejection of Internal Relations, some of the challenges to Hegel's system are also avoided.

9.4.2. Objections to Pragmatism

As we have seen, the de Lagunas recognize that concepts do not directly link stimuli and response, even when goals are fixed. A concept only specifies behavior indirectly, as a function of circumstances broadly conceived, including which other concepts are in the agent's conceptual system. It is for this reason, recall, that they think that concepts have content. But then, contrary to the pragmatist theory of meaning, meaning cannot be explicated solely in terms of overt behavior; meaning cannot even be explicated in terms of import. This is the first of the de Lagunas' main criticisms of pragmatism (*DE*, 126–128).

A second main criticism of pragmatism (*DE*, 148–150) is that pragmatism fails to account for the fact that, in some domains, the evolution of concepts, and hence of judgment, is in the direction of increasing indirectness and decreasing context dependence. This objection can be read as the objection that pragmatists have failed to provide detail about the evolution of judgment, an objection to which Pragmatists could respond by filling in their position with relevant details. But the de Lagunas have a deeper objection here. Their claim is that the view that ideas are practical has little truth to it. The de Lagunas admit that there is truth in the claim that concepts are practical. Concepts' meanings do depend on their role in governing behavior, and the implications of a concept for behavior are context dependent. But concepts are indirect, and context dependent, to varying degrees, with some kinds of concepts, such as those of logic and mathematics, being highly indirect and context independent. As a result, it is more accurate to say that there are a variety of kinds of concepts, with varying degrees of practicality, and that many concepts are hardly practical at all.

The de Lagunas' above criticisms of pragmatism can be thought of as suggesting that it is an overreaction to the failures of dogmatism and of Hegel's system. The pragmatists avoid having to choose between dogmatism's External Relations and the Hegelian Internal Relations, but they do so by identifying meaning with a species of import and thus by ignoring the ineliminable role that content has in explaining human behavior. This blind spot, in turn, means that pragmatism fails to note the varying kinds of concepts, and corresponding kinds of judgment, that result from evolution and, accordingly, fails to see that there is little truth to the dictum that ideas are practical.

9.4.3. Creighton's Hegelian Response to Dogmatism

The de Lagunas and the pragmatists were not alone in responding to the challenges to dogmatism and to Hegel's system. Of particular interest here, partly because it makes more explicit the de Lagunas' Hegelian heritage and partly because it will later help illuminate Quine's *TD*, is Creighton's Hegelian response.

Creighton's theory of judgment is close to Hegel's theory, as presented by the de Lagunas. Most importantly, Creighton endorses a version of meaning holism that identifies meaning with content. For him, a concept's meaning is constituted by a system of judgments and thus by whatever other concepts are involved in those judgments (1898, 268–270). Further, Creighton's meaning holism comes with confirmation holism and the rejection of the analytic-synthetic distinction. In judgment, on his view, experience is brought "into relation with the facts which we already know, and is tested by them" (1898, 286). And because a judgment always involves bringing it into a relation with the rest of knowledge, judgment always adds to our knowledge, that is, is synthetic to some degree or another (1898, 280–282). Creighton states that "it was at one time supposed that analytic and synthetic judgments were entirely different in kind from each other," but adds that "this view is of course fundamentally different from the account of judgment which we have just given" (1898, 282–283).

Creighton was, however, aware of the kinds of challenges to Hegel put forward by the de Lagunas and responds to these. For example, he holds that the most general assumptions of all rational experience are justified only by their results and, accordingly, are criticized in light of experience. Such criticism results in a reinterpretation of our basic categories and forms of reasoning so that, contra Hegel, logic itself is not exempt from evolution (1913, 138).

Nevertheless, Creighton's position was, it is plausible to think, viewed as inadequate by the de Lagunas. For Creighton's insistence that judgment is evaluated in light of our entire system of judgments goes against the de Lagunas' contention that judgment is often properly local. Creighton does have a response to this contention, one he states in rebutting the pragmatist claim that judgment is always local. His response is that the local evaluation of judgment is merely a matter of expedience and thus a subject for psychology (1906, 489). For him, "the real locus of the logical problem . . . cannot be adequately defined except in the light of the object and end of experience as a whole" (1906, 489). The de Lagunas, however, would have responded that Creighton here fails adequately to take on board the evolving nature of judgment. Many kinds of judgment are still at a stage of evolution where their meaning is fixed in a relatively local way and so their evaluation should, as a matter of logic, be relatively local.

9.5. Dogmatism, Evolution, and Analytic Philosophy

9.5.1. "Two Dogmas of Empiricism" in Its Hegelian Context

What remains is to examine the place of Quine's TD in history. I will, in this section, look at TD in relation to dogmatism and Hegelianism. I will then, in the next section, use the distinction between speculative and critical philosophy to examine TD in the context of analytic philosophy.

TD is well known for its critique of what Quine took to be two dogmas of empiricism, as well as for its sketch of a holistic epistemology. The first of Quine's "dogmas" is reductionism, that is, the view "that each statement, taken in isolation from its fellows, can admit of confirmation or information" (1951, 38). The second dogma is "that there is a cleavage between the analytic and the synthetic" (1951, 38). These dogmas are included among the dogmas which are, much earlier, targeted by Creighton and the de Lagunas. Their criticism of Intuition includes criticism of the view that judgments are assessed individually. And they reject the existence of a sharp division between the analytic and the synthetic.

Quine replaces his dogmas with confirmation holism, which he describes as the view "that our statements about the external world face the tribunal of sense experience not individually but only as a corporate body" (1951, 38) and with the view that all statements depend on language and experience, and thus that all statements are, to some extent, synthetic (1951, 39). Quine also supposes that all statements are revisable in light of experience (1951, 40). These three positive theses were, as we have seen, defended by Creighton and the de Lagunas. Indeed, Quine's confirmation holism is close to Creighton's and is, like Creighton's, subject to the de Lagunas' worry that it does not adequately recognize the local evaluation of judgments. Quine himself later had similar worries about TD's holism (1991). The de Lagunas' sophisticated analysis of the varying degrees of indirectness of the contact of concepts with experience is absent from TD; it recognizes, but provides no insight into, the relatively non-empirical nature of some beliefs (1951, 40–41).

TD's position is thus a late, not very original, reversion to a Hegelian theory of judgment. This reversion is unlikely to be purely accidental. It is plausible that *TD* is, in part, a criticism of Clarence I. Lewis's pragmatist defence of the analytic-synthetic distinction (Morris 2018). Further, Quine's career starts in 1930s America and the de Lagunas' work was well known then (Katzav 2019), as was Creighton's (Auxier 2005) and, of course, that of the pragmatists.

9.5.2. "Two Dogmas of Empiricism" in Its Analytic Context

Speculative philosophy tends to encourage making claims that criticize, and go beyond, what is found in, or required by, established opinion, including science and common sense. In doing this, speculative philosophy aims to teach us about ourselves and our world. Importantly, the task of criticizing established opinion includes, as a proper part, engaging in critical philosophy. Examples of speculative philosophies are Hegelianism, the pragmatism of James and Dewey, and process philosophy. Critical philosophy, which includes analytic philosophy from the period 1940–1960, is epistemically conservative, that is, tends to discourage going beyond, or criticizing, some substantial portion of established opinion. Critical philosophy aims to elucidate, analyze, or determine the commitments of part, or all, of established opinion. Doing this may simply uncover aspects of existing, established opinion and its commitments, but may also involve reconstructing it and its commitments, while minimizing changes to them (Katzav 2018; Katzav and Vaesen 2017).

Creighton's vision for the theory of judgment exemplifies the speculative tendency. The theory of judgment, on his view, should offer an alternative interpretation of reality to the one offered by the special sciences. Developing this alternative requires critically evaluating the assumptions of the special sciences:

> in no case are the conclusions derived by employing the methods and assumptions which a special science finds adequate for its purpose to be accepted without modification or interpretation, as a direct description of the nature of reality. (Creighton 1919, 401)

Common sense, on Creighton's vision, seems to be touched on by philosophy only insofar as common sense finds its way into the special sciences (1919, 404–407).

(Grace) de Laguna's paper, "Speculative Philosophy" similarly takes "a critical examination of traditional belief and accepted common sense" (1951, 4) to be essential to speculative thought, and states that such thought goes beyond science in seeking to understand reality (1951, 16). *DE* itself is a speculative treatise. It is informed by Darwin's theory of evolution and by psychology, but ultimately aims independently to provide an evidential basis for a new evolutionary theory of judgment. *DE* does not exclusively or primarily bring out what is implicit in, follows from, or is required by, established opinion.

Quine's *TD*, by contrast, promotes a critical approach to philosophy. The positive picture of knowledge it offers, that is, its holism and opposition to the analytic-synthetic distinction, concerns the logical relations between judgments and evidence. No mention is made of the possibility of an evolutionary theory of judgment, never mind of the scientifically informed kind strived for by speculative philosophers such as the de Lagunas. If only by omission, *TD* thus gives "epistemology" something like the content of "logical analysis of confirmation," and contributes to transforming the import of "epistemology" by making epistemology's procedures more epistemically conservative and less empirical.[8] *TD*, to be sure, presents its case against the analytic-synthetic distinction as a "blurring of the supposed boundary between speculative metaphysics and natural science" (1951, 20). With the blurring of the distinction, all metaphysics supposedly becomes empirical. But *TD* tells us that metaphysics determines our ontological commitments by logically regimenting established scientific theories, and possibly also common sense, and seeing what the resulting regimentation quantifies over (1951, 43). So, Quine identifies the content and import of "speculative metaphysics" with that of something like "logical analysis of the ontology of established opinion." Further, the content of "logical analysis" is modified merely by the claim that, in unspecified circumstances, its

---

[8] Whether Quine's subsequent support for naturalized epistemology reverses these effects is not a question I address here.

procedure might be affected by empirical considerations; the import of "logical analysis" is not modified in any real way. Quine is, accordingly, primarily promoting a narrowing down of the content and import of "speculative metaphysics," one that excludes speculative philosophy and thus that makes philosophy a more epistemically conservative discipline. Further, while Quine's promotion of critical epistemology is done by omission, his promotion of critical metaphysics involves misrepresentation. At no point does *TD* make a case for critical philosophy; on this matter, *TD* is dogmatic.

Prior to publication, *TD* was presented at the 1950 American Philosophical Association Eastern Division meeting as part of a symposium about what were then the main trends in critical and speculative philosophy (Katzav and Vaesen 2017). Max Black, one of *the Philosophical Review*'s (*PR*'s) editors and the symposium organizer, wanted Quine to cover trends in critical philosophy and de Laguna to do the same for speculative philosophy (de Laguna 1950). Her paper was her already mentioned "Speculative Philosophy" and his was *TD*. The papers appeared in *PR* in 1951. Interestingly, she wrote Quine prior to the symposium, suggesting that they coordinate paper contents and extensively sharing her thoughts about her paper (de Laguna 1950). Quine's response is basically the abstract of his paper; he states his goal of rejecting the idea that statements can be tested individually and of rejecting the analytic-synthetic distinction (Quine 1950).

Black, and *PR*'s other analytic editors, had recently decided to exclude speculative philosophy from their journal, thus bringing to an end the openness to diverse philosophical approaches fostered by its earlier editors, including Creighton (Katzav and Vaesen 2017). And this marginalization, along with similar cases of marginalization at other prominent journals and institutions, including the journals *Mind* and *The Journal of Philosophy* and America's National Science Foundation, is plausibly part of what explains the eventual dominance of analytic philosophy in America and the amnesia about the work of philosophers such as Creighton and the de Lagunas (Katzav 2018; Katzav and Vaesen 2017; Vaesen and Katzav 2019). "Speculative Philosophy" thus can be thought of as representing the end of the tradition of speculative philosophy in *PR*. Indeed, her paper dutifully covers much of the canon of that tradition, including Dewey, Alfred

N. Whitehead, and Martin Heidegger. *TD*, on the other hand, was a dogmatic contributor to the marginalization of speculative philosophy. Further, *TD* was a key factor in determining the post-1950 trajectory of metaphysics (Glock 2008, ch. 2) and thus, not implausibly, in strengthening epistemically conservative, anti-speculative, relatively non-empirical metaphysics. Similarly, *TD*'s epistemology was influential (Elgin 2011), thus not implausibly playing a role in strengthening corresponding epistemology. That *TD* had the impact it had despite its unoriginal key claims is partly explained by the marginalization of speculative philosophy, including Quine's failure to acknowledge, never mind engage with, the work of speculative philosophers.

9.6. Conclusion

DE presents an intriguing picture of modern philosophy as the attempted overcoming of the dogmas of empiricism and rationalism, an attempt that includes Hegel's untenable, extreme form of holism. Filling in some of the details in the de Lagunas' story leads to thinking of late nineteenth- and early twentieth-century pragmatism and Hegelianism as still confronting the old dogmas, but also trying to avoid Hegel's extremism and, at the same time, to learn from Darwin. The de Lagunas themselves then appear to provide a moderate form of holism, one that avoids dogmatism and also takes on board the implications of the evolutionary nature of judgment. Further extending the de Lagunas' stories to the 1950s illuminates Quine's holism as a relatively unoriginal Hegelian form of holism, but as dogmatically tending to strengthen the epistemically conservative, anti-speculative tendencies in epistemology and metaphysics.

Bibliography

Auxier, R. A. (2005). Creighton. In Shook, J. R. (ed.), *The Dictionary of Modern American Philosophers*. Bristol: Thoemmes, 549–554.

Creighton, J. E. (1898). *An Introductory Logic*. New York: Macmillan.

Creighton, J. E. (1906). Experience and Thought. *The Philosophical Review* 15(5): 482–493.

Creighton, J. E. (1913). The Copernican Revolution in Philosophy. *The Psychological Review* 22(2): 133–150.

Creighton, J. E. (1919). *An Introductory Logic*, 3rd ed. New York: Macmillan.

De Laguna, G. A. (1950). Letter to Professor W. V. Quine, dated January the 24th, 1950. Correspondence with Grace De Laguna, W. V. Quine Papers, MS Am 2587, Item 293, Houghton Library, Harvard University.

De Laguna, G. A. (1951). Speculative Philosophy. *The Philosophical Review* 60(1): 1–19.

De Laguna, T. (1915). The Postulates of Deductive Logic. *The Journal of Philosophy* 12(9): 225–236.

De Laguna, T., and De Laguna, G. A. (1910). *Dogmatism and Evolution: Studies in Modern Philosophy*, New York: Macmillan.

Elgin, C. Z. (2011). The Legacy of Two Dogmas. *American Philosophical Quarterly* 48(3): 267–272.

Glock, H. (2008). *What Is Analytic Philosophy?* Cambridge: Cambridge University Press.

Katzav, J. (2018). Analytic Philosophy, 1925–1969: Emergence, Management and Nature. *British Journal for the History of Philosophy* 26(6): 1197–1221

Katzav, J. (2019). Theodore de Laguna's Discovery of the Deflationary Theory of Truth. *British Journal for the History of Philosophy* 27(5): 1025–1033.

Katzav, J., and Vaesen, K. (2017). On the Emergence of American Analytic Philosophy. *British Journal for the History of Philosophy* 25(4): 772–798.

Morris, E. (2018). Quine against Lewis (and Carnap) on Truth by Convention. *Pacific Philosophical Quarterly* 99(3): 366–391.

Quine, W. V. (1950). Letter to Grace A. De Laguna, dated February the 4th, 1950. Correspondence with Grace De Laguna, W. V. Quine Papers, MS Am 2587, Item 293, Houghton Library, Harvard University.

Quine, W. V. (1951). Two Dogmas of Empiricism. *The Philosophical Review* 60(1): 20–43.

Quine, W. V. (1991). Two Dogmas in Retrospect. *Canadian Journal of Philosophy* 21(3): 265–274.

Vaesen, K., and Katzav, J. (2019). The National Science Foundation and Philosophy of Science's Withdrawal from Social Concerns. *Studies in History and Philosophy of Science Part A* 78: 73–82.

10

B. R. Ambedkar on "Castes in India: Their Mechanism, Genesis and Development"

Meena Krishnamurthy

In 1913, at the age of twenty-two, B. R. Ambedkar arrived in New York City, ready to pursue an M.A. in Economics at Columbia University. He first presented "Castes in India: Their Mechanism, Genesis and Development" in Alexander Goldenweiser's anthropology seminar.[1] The paper was later published in *Indian Antiquary*.[2] Ambedkar begins the paper with the following remarks:

> The caste problem is a vast one, both theoretically and practically. Practically, it is an institution that portends tremendous consequences. It is a local problem, but one capable of much wider mischief, for "as long as caste in India does exist, Hindus will hardly intermarry or have any social intercourse with outsiders; and if Hindus migrate to other regions on earth, Indian caste would become a world problem."[3]

The caste problem was—and still is—an urgent global problem. As we know, it exists not only in India but also among the South Asian

---

[1] Ambedkar's "Castes in India" (hereinafter CI) was first presented as a draft at Alexander Goldenweiser's anthropology seminar at Columbia, in New York, on May 9, 1916. An annotated version of the essay was recently republished in Sharmila Rege (ed.), *Against the Madness of Manu* (New Delhi: Navayana, 2013), 77–108.

[2] Volume XLI, May 1917.

[3] Here Ambedkar quotes S.V. Ketkar, *History of Caste in India* (Ithaca, NY: Taylor and Carpenter, 1909), 4.

Meena Krishnamurthy, *B. R. Ambedkar on "Castes in India: Their Mechanism, Genesis and Development"* In: *Neglected Classics of Philosophy*. Edited by: Eric Schliesser, Oxford University Press. © Oxford University Press 2022. DOI: 10.1093/oso/9780190097196.003.0011

diaspora of the United Kingdom, Canada, Australia, and the United States. W. E. B. Du Bois and Jyotirao Phule argue that the caste problem and the race problem are one and the same.[4] Isabel Wilkerson makes related claims in her recent book *Caste*; and, in *The New Jim Crow*, Michele Alexander argues that the incarceration of poor people of color in the United States is tantamount to a new caste system.[5] The caste question, along with its genesis and evolution, was and still is an important concern within India and outside of it.

In "Castes in India," Ambedkar gives a pathbreaking account of the origin and evolution of caste in India. This relatively unknown scholarly essay served as the theoretical basis for what would later become his most famous work, *Annihilation of Caste*, which was a moral argument against the caste system.[6] I begin this chapter by explaining what caste is and why it originated, in Ambedkar's view. I also discuss the role that caste plays in the oppression of women in India. I argue that, in giving a causal explanation of women's oppression, Ambedkar departs from other important political works of the time, including Gandhi's, which all but ignores the oppression of women as an important form of social inequality. I discuss the philosophical lessons that we learn from reading Ambedkar's essay. Drawing on Charles W. Mills's criticisms of liberal political theory, I close the chapter by arguing that, because of the insights it offers, Ambedkar's "Castes in India" serves as an important corrective to the traditional canon in political philosophy.

10.1. Caste in India

Hindu society is classified into four Varnas, or castes: Brahmin (priests and teachers), Kshatriya (rulers and warriors), Vaishya

---

[4] W. E. B. Du Bois, Evolution of the Race Problem, *Proceedings of the National Negro Conference*, 1909, 142–158; Jyotirao Phule, Slavery, in G. P. Deshpande (ed.), *Selected Writings of Jotirao Phule* (Delhi: Leftword Books, 2002), 23–100.

[5] Isabel Wilkerson, *Caste: The Origin of Our Discontent* (New York: Random House, 2020); Michelle Alexander, *The New Jim Crow* (New York: The New Press, 2012).

[6] B. R. Ambedkar, *Annihilation of Caste* (New York: Verso, 2014); hereinafter "AoC." The speech was originally prepared in 1936 for the Annual Conference of the Jat-Pat-Todak Mandal of Lahore. Interestingly, the conference was canceled after the organizers came to know about the content of Ambedkar's speech.

(farmers, traders, merchants), and Shudra (laborers). The main castes are further subdivided into many smaller castes, or Jatis, including Adivasi (indigenous people, mostly of South India), Chandala (those who deal with corpses), and Dalit (meaning "broken," previously referred to as "Untouchables").[7] The Jatis are believed to lie outside the caste or varna system.

Following Sir H. Risley, Ambedkar takes for granted that caste is "a collection of families or groups of families bearing a common name which usually denotes or is associated with specific occupation" (CI, 6). He also thinks that caste is much more than this. Ambedkar's aim in "Castes in India" is to get clearer on the other essential features of caste, their origin and function. He begins his discussion of caste by canvassing other representative views of caste and by identifying what they "regarded as peculiarities of Caste" (CI, 7).

Some, such as Émile Senart, believe that "the idea of pollution" is essential to caste.[8] In India, Dalits are considered "polluted" or "unclean" and cannot touch or come into close contact with members of the other four castes—this is why they were traditionally referred to as "Untouchables." If Dalits do come into contact with members of a higher caste—if their shadow falls on a Brahmin, for example—the higher caste person must perform cleansing rituals to rid herself of the resulting "pollution."

While pollution may be an important part of caste, as it is practiced, Ambedkar rejects the claim that it is essential to caste. In his view, it is a contingent matter that caste is connected with pollution. In India, the highest caste is the priestly caste, and, he suggests, the "priest and purity are old associates" (CI, 7). Ambedkar concludes, "the idea of pollution" is associated with caste only because caste, in this instance, has a religious flavor. It originated from the *Laws of Manu*, which was a moral-religious legal code in India (around 200 BCE).

---

[7] The term "Dalit"—perhaps first used by Jyotirao Phule and later popularized by Ambedkar—is a relatively new term. Before 1935, the term "Depressed Classes" was used by the colonial government. After 1935, the term "Scheduled Castes" was and continues to be used for official matters. During the nationalist movement led by the Congress Party and Gandhi in the 1930s–1940s, the term "Harijans" was popularized. The term "Untouchable" was used throughout the twentieth century, but is no longer in use because of its pejorative connotation.

[8] Emile Senart, *Castes in India*, trans. Sir E. Denison Ross (London: Methuen, 1930).

Others, such as John Nesfield, hold that an essential feature of caste is the absence of social interaction. Caste limits social interaction to members of one's own caste.[9] Ambedkar suggests that this is the effect of caste, not its cause (CI, 8). It is the result of castes' "exclusiveness" (CI, 9). He argues that this natural consequence of caste, which was originally due to the exclusiveness of caste, eventually took on the character of a religious prohibition encoded in the *Laws*. Since it is something that only resulted later in the development of the caste system, Ambedkar does not see it as essential to the character of caste.

S. Venkatesh Ketar defines caste in relation to a system of castes: "caste" cannot exist without other castes, and there must be mechanisms to ensure that the boundaries between the different castes do not blur.[10] Ketkar suggests that the prohibition of intermarriage between castes and membership by autogeny are the two essential features of caste. Ambedkar argues—and sees this as his main contribution to the discussion of caste—that "these are but two aspects of one and the same thing, not two different things as Dr. Ketkar supposes. . . . If you prohibit intermarriage the result is that you limit membership to those born within the group" (CI, 10). In Ambedkar's view, intermarriage and autogeny are two different sides of the same coin.

10.1.1. Caste as Endogamy: The Problem of the Surplus Man and Woman

Ultimately, the only characteristic that can be considered "the essence of Caste," on Ambedkar's view, is "endogamy" (CI, 11). Caste is a social group that is enclosed through endogamy, where exogamy existed previously.

According to Ambedkar, the Indian population is a mixture of "Aryans" (Indo Europeans), "Dravidians" (Indigenous peoples of India), "Mongolians" (East Central Asians), and "Scythians" (Siberians) (CI, 5). These groups of individuals came with distinct cultural practices and beliefs. Over time, through constant contact and

---

[9] John Nesfield, *The Function of Modern Brahmins in Upper India* (Calcutta: 1887).
[10] S. V. Ketkar, *History of Caste in India* (Ithaca, NY: Taylor and Carpenter, 1909).

interaction, they came to share in a common culture. This is to say, in the Indian subcontinent, there was a long-standing history of exogamy (CI, 13).[11] Ambedkar believes there is a general human tendency toward exogamy; caste is "an artificial chopping off of the population into fixed definite units" (CI, 11). Having identified the essence of caste, Ambedkar seeks to explain how caste (as endogamy) came to be.

Why would endogamy be imposed on a previously exogamous society? Endogamy is necessary to maintain enclosure—the rigid boundaries—of caste, something that the caste system cannot exist without. Ambedkar argues that the central threat to the boundaries of caste is the problem of "the surplus man and surplus woman" (CI, 17). For caste to persist, men and women must marry and have children with individuals within their own caste. This requires an equal number of marriageable men and women within a caste. Parity is achieved only when husband and wife die at the same time. This raises problems, of course. The husband may die before the wife, leaving a surplus woman, or the wife may die before the husband, leaving a surplus man. If parity is not established, and the surplus man and woman cannot find suitable partners inside their caste, then they will be driven to marry and to have sex and children with people of other castes. This transgression—the creation of progeny, that is—blurs the boundaries of caste and threatens to undermine the entire system. This is why, according to Ambedkar, endogamy is imposed: it is an attempt to resolve the disparity between the number of marriageable men and women.

As Ambedkar notes, to ensure endogamy, the surplus woman must be "disposed" of. She was traditionally disposed of in two ways.[12] First, she was burned on the funeral pyre of her deceased husband—this is the practice of *sati* (CI, 19). *Sati* eliminates the two dangers that a surplus woman creates. If the surplus woman (a widow) isn't disposed of and remains in the group, she may marry outside the caste and violate

---

[11] In Ambedkar's mind, this is what distinguishes caste from race in the United States. In the United States, he argues, there was never a practice of exogamy between Black and white Americans (CI, 11). It was endogamous from the start. Ambedkar doesn't tell us what grounds the tendency toward exogamy, writing, "the prevalence of exogamy in the primitive worlds is a fact too well-known to need any explanation" (CI, 13).

[12] Though Ambedkar doesn't mention it, female infanticide is another mechanism to deal with the surplus of women.

endogamy, or she may marry within the caste, thereby reducing the number of men available for other potential brides and increasing competition among them. Burning the widow means she is "dead and gone"; the problem of remarriage inside or outside the caste no longer exists (CI, 20). Ambedkar notes that *sati* is very hard to put into practice, since most women will resist being thrown into a fire.

The second solution is to enforce widowhood on the woman for the remainder of her life (CI, 19). While it leaves open the possibility of remarriage and its problems for the caste system, it is more practicable. However, Ambedkar argues that this practice "fails to guard the morals of the group" (CI, 20). In contrast to the practice of *sati*, with enforced widowhood, the woman remains alive. Without the protection and social standing conferred to her by marriage, Ambedkar worries, that she may be a viewed as a source of "allurement" and left open to "immoral conduct" (CI, 20). Because of their vulnerable social positions, widows in India were and are more vulnerable to sexual harassment, rape, and forced prostitution than married women. Ambedkar suggests that this problem can to some extent be avoided by engaging in further immoral conduct: it can be avoided by degrading the widow to a condition where men are no longer "allured" (CI, 20). For example, widows were required to remove their jewelry and make up, and to shave their heads. This was done, in part, to make the widows less appealing to men. They were prohibited from attending weddings or other religious ceremonies, which often required ostentatious dress. They were also restricted, more generally, to staying inside the home. This way they could avoid the risk of attention from men. As Ambedkar concludes, the objectionable conditions that many widows in India faced are not natural; they are by design.

Because of patriarchy, the problem of the surplus man is much more difficult to solve. Ambedkar writes,

from time immemorial man as compared with woman has had the upper hand. He is a dominant figure in every group and of the two sexes has greater prestige. With this traditional superiority of man over woman his wishes have always been consulted. Woman, on the other hand, has been an easy prey to all kinds of iniquitous injunctions, religious, social or economic. But man as a maker of injunctions is most often above them all. Such being the case you cannot accord the same kind of treatment to a surplus man as you can to a surplus woman in a Caste. (CI, 21)

Ambedkar doesn't explain why or how men came to have superior social positions in Indian society. He takes this for granted and suggests that, because of this status, men will ensure that they are not treated as abjectly as woman are. Men's superior social position ensure that their voices are heard and that their interests are protected. This is why widowers are not subject to the same treatment as widows in India.[13]

Nevertheless, as important as the man is to a caste, endogamy is still more important—something must be done to solve the problem of the surplus man. One option is to require him, like the surplus woman, to be a widower. For some this will be easy enough, since they may be inclined toward self-imposed celibacy. However, given human nature, this policy is generally unrealizable. More importantly, as Ambedkar notes, it is also undesirable: celibacy means that the widower is no longer able to contribute to the numerical strength of his caste (CI, 23). It is the interest of the caste to keep him as "Grahastha (one who raises family)" (CI, 23). The solution, then, is to provide the surplus man with a wife, but this is difficult. In a caste that is thoroughly self-enclosed there are just as many marriageable women as there are men. The only way to provide the surplus man with a wife is to recruit one from those who are not yet of marriageable age. *Girl marriage* ensures that the surplus man is kept within the caste, and numerical reduction is avoided, while greater numerical strength of the caste is encouraged through procreation.

---

[13] Ambedkar assumes that, because men (unlike women) have a voice in how caste is arranged, the problem of surplus men is more difficult to solve than that of surplus women. One could argue that the problem of surplus men is also more difficult to solve because of the particular way that the elite caste in India is split between priests and warriors. In other societies, there have tended to be at least two other ways of solving the problem of surplus men (besides incarcerating them or finding other ways to get them killed): (a) send them away as colonists; (b) recruit them into an army. In both cases, there is a higher probability of the men dying or reproducing with foreign women (through enslavement or rape of those women). In the Indian case, (b) is not possible because Brahmins didn't typically enter the military. Fighting was traditionally left to the Kshatriya caste. This means that, in India, other ways of disposing of surplus men, outside of (a) and (b), must be found.

To summarize, in Ambedkar's view, the cultural practices of *sati*, enforced widowhood, celibacy, and girl marriage were created to solve the problem of the surplus man and woman in a caste and, ultimately, to maintain endogamy—which is the essence of caste.

10.1.2. Brahminism

Having explained the mechanisms of caste in India, one might wonder, why go to the trouble of solving the problem of the surplus woman and man in the first place? Why go to such lengths to maintain the rigid boundaries of caste? To answer this question, Ambedkar suggests we must consider the first caste to enclose itself and then explain how the others followed (CI, 32).

In Ambedkar's view, Brahmins were the originators of caste.

> The strict observance of these customs [of endogamy] and the social superiority arrogated by the priestly class in all ancient civilizations are sufficient to prove that they—the Brahmins—were the originators of this "unnatural institution" founded and maintained through these unnatural means. (CI 32)[14]

In creating "caste," Brahmins sought to protect their self-interest by entrenching a system that gave them "prestige" and "power" (CI, 32–42). Brahmins crafted religious philosophy, eventually encoded in the *Laws*, to justify and popularize the notion of a social hierarchy and their superior social position within it (CI, 29, 34).[15] What was unnatural was soon viewed as natural, leaving little basis for challenging the Brahmins' superior social status.

Despite this, Ambedkar argues, the Brahmins did not create the "caste system"—that is, the system of other castes and sub-castes. Their actions merely resulted in the creation of two castes: "Brahmins" and

---

[14] Cf., "it is the social system which embodies the arrogance and selfishness of a perverse section of the Hindus who were superior enough in social status to set it in fashion, and who had the authority to force it on their inferiors" (Ambedkar, AoC 5.8).
[15] As Ambedkar wrote, "this high-flown and ingenious sophistry indicates why these institutions were honoured" (CI, 29).

"non-Brahmins." The "non-Brahmins" subdivided further, which led to the formation of the many other castes in India. Two processes were at play.

The first process is "psychological" (CI, 41). Ambedkar argues that the non-Brahmin subdivisions became endogamous castes by wholeheartedly "imitating" the Brahmins.[16] These groups sought to secure social esteem for themselves through imitation. They, like the Brahmins, used religious philosophy to turn themselves into enclosed castes with superior social status, lesser than the Brahmins but higher than other castes (CI, 41).

Drawing on Walter Bagehot's work, Ambedkar argues that imitation is a "deep-seated" tendency among humans (CI, 41).[17] It is not voluntary, in his view, but is rather a subconscious drive seated in the most obscure parts of the mind (CI, 41). According to Gabriel Tarde's laws of imitation, Ambedkar argues that we tend to imitate those who are both most superior to us and nearest to us (i.e., those we see and interact with daily).[18] The Brahmins, with their God-like status in India, enjoy prestige and, given their priestly status, were a central part of most people's daily lives. Given this, it is not surprising that the other castes imitated the Brahmins by enclosing themselves.

Imitation is often an imperfect process. To ensure endogamy, the castes closest in status to the Brahmins, and who have the most familiarity with their practices, enforce the same social practices as Brahmins (CI, 43). Like the Brahmins, they insist on strict observance of *sati*, enforced widowhood, and girl marriage. However, the castes that are more distant in social status are those that depart more significantly from these practices and have less day-to-day to contact

[16] M. N. Srinivas's later work on Sanskritization also looked at the imitation of Brahmin behavior by upwardly mobile lower caste members. It was also criticized for its lack of engagement with Brahmins' unwillingness to accept non-Brahmins as their equals in the social interactions in workplace by blaming the victims. See his *Religion and Society among the Coorgs of South India* (Oxford: Clarendon Press, 1952).

[17] Here he follows Walter Bagehot, *The Works and Life of Walter Bagehot, vol. 8 (Physics and Politics, Currency Monopoly, and Essays)* ed. Mrs. Russell Barrington (London: Longmans, Green, 1915). https://oll.libertyfund.org/titles/bagehot-the-works-and-life-of-walter-bagehot-vol-8.

[18] Ambedkar draws on Gabriel Tarde, *Laws of Imitation*, trans. E. C. Parsons (New York: Henry Holt, 1903).

with Brahmins. Some of the lower castes have only girl marriage, for example.

The second process by which other castes are formed is "mechanistic" (CI, 44). Ambedkar argues that there is no such thing as a single "caste" but only "castes," which are plural in number. Consider the Brahmins. The Brahmins made themselves by closing themselves in and closing others out (CI, 44). In general, "if group a wants to be endogamous, Group b has to be so by sheer force of circumstance" (CI, 44). The process of endogamy necessarily leads to the creation of at least two groups.

Though he doesn't make this explicit, I would argue that there is a connection between the mechanistic and the psychological explanations of caste. It is the psychological process that drives Brahmins to engage in the mechanistic process in the first place.

Prestige and power—which the Brahmins seek—are positional goods. To secure prestige and the power that comes with it, one must have superior social status. To have superior social status requires that there is an inferior—someone to be superior in relation to. This means there must be at least one other caste that is inferior to the Brahmins. In the end, it is the psychological need for prestige and power that drives Brahmins to enclose themselves and, in turn, to create a non-Brahmin caste. Of course, the other non-Brahmin castes also wish to secure prestige and power. To the extent that they can, they imitate the Brahmins, securing as much prestige as possible. Ensuring that there are Dalit-like castes, which sit outside the caste (varna) system and necessarily have the least prestige among the groups, ensures that all other castes have at least some prestige, since they will always sit above at least one other group. This explains how the caste system in India originated and why it continues to persist today.

10.2. Other Views

While Ambedkar offers an insightful account of the origin of caste, the most original contribution of his essay is its account of women's oppression in India. While Ambedkar was not the first to try to identify the cause of women's oppression in India, his thinking surpasses some of most influential thinkers on the matter. To see that this is the case, I will lead you through a brief survey of historically important Indian thinkers on caste and women's oppression in India.

In her most well-known book, *The High Caste Hindu Woman*, Pandita Ramabai (1858–1922)—a renowned Sanskrit scholar, educational reformer, and political theorist—discusses the poor conditions of Brahmin women in India. Like Ambedkar, she focuses on the practices of *sati*, widowhood, and girl marriage and she links the oppression of women in India to the *Laws of Manu*. In her view, the *Laws* not only encourage and protect these oppressive practices but, perhaps more importantly, they also express "distrust and low estimate of women's nature and character in general."[19] For this reason, she argues that the law-giver Manu is "one of the hundreds who have done their best to make woman a hateful being in the world's eyes" (1909, 81). The *Laws* express contempt for women in India and they entrench the inferiority of women into the very normative structure of Hindu law and society. While she is very critical of this outcome, Ramabai suggests that it is rather difficult to ascertain the motives of those who wrote these horrible laws in the first place.[20]

Jyotirao ("Mahatma") Phule (1827–1890)—an anti-caste social reformer and political writer—would later ask, "what can have been the motives and object of those who wrote such cruel and inhuman 'Laws'?"[21] In answer, he argues, Brahmins are motivated by their own selfishness. They seek to create a system that benefits them as well as future generations of Brahmins. They began by creating the idea of the caste system and wrote books, such as the *Laws*, and devised mythology to legitimize this system and to thereby protect their own interests.[22][23]

According to Phule, Brahmins repressed resistance to their supremacy through two mechanisms: war (conquest) and ignorance.

---

[19] Pandita Ramabai, *The High Caste Hindu Woman* (New York: Fleming H. Revel, 1909), 80.

[20] Ibid, 100.

[21] Phule, Slavery, 30.

[22] Ibid, 36.

[23] Periyar E. V. Ramaswamy (1879–1973)—a Dravidian activist and political thinker—held something similar. He believed that a small number of individuals created caste distinctions so that they could dominate others.

According to Phule, when the Aryans, who later became the Brahmins, conquered the Indian subcontinent, they forced many of the original inhabitants to leave; and they killed and enslaved those who remained. To ensure the enslaved wouldn't revolt, the Brahmins used religion to convince them that "their slavery was justified even in the eyes of God."[24] Their religious treatises proclaimed that God had deliberately created the Shudras for the sole purpose of providing eternal service to the Brahmins.[25] This is how the Brahmins kept the Shudras ignorant of the immorality of the caste system (and of their own inherent equality). Despite this, he argues, some of the Shudras revolted against the despotic laws of the Brahmins. The Brahmins, he writes, responded by punishing the Shudras and dividing them into a further cast, "dictating that neither they nor their children should ever be touched by the other people."[26] This is how the Dalit caste was created and the practice of untouchability began, in Phule's view.

Influenced by Ramabai, Phule seeks to explain women's oppression through appeal to his general theory of conquest, violence, and caste. He argues that women were the primary victims of violence during the Aryan conquest.[27] They not only suffered violence firsthand ("blood oozing out of the gashes") but also secondhand through the death of their fathers, husbands, brothers, and children.[28] Later, extending his views to the more recent practices of child marriage and widowhood, Phule argues that girls continue to suffer greatly.[29] He notes that girl children are separated from their families at a young age (to live with their husband's families), are fed less than their boy husbands and, as a result, are stunted in growth; on top of this, they are loaded with work for days and nights. Phule worries that these terrible living conditions lead many young girls to commit suicide. He has similar views regarding widowhood. Like Ambedkar, he believes that widowhood left women open to sexual exploitation—either in the form of rape or

---

[24] Phule, Slavery, 37.
[25] Ibid, 37.
[26] Ibid, 45.
[27] Ibid, 42.
[28] Ibid, 43.
[29] Jyotirao Phule, Opinion from Jyotirao Govindrao Phulay on Note No. I by Mr. B.M. Malabari on Infant Marriage in India, in G. P. Deshpande (ed.), *Selected Writings of Jotirao Phule* (Delhi: Leftword Books, 2002), 193–194.

forced prostitution.[30] In some cases, this leads to unwanted pregnancy. In one case he discusses in detail, a pregnant widow, who was manipulated into sex by a Brahmin, killed her infant to avoid disgrace. She was arrested, tried, and found guilty and was sentenced to imprisonment for life. In Phule's view, her moral character was spoiled by both the Brahmin community and its pernicious laws. He doesn't trust Brahmins to end these practices of, what Uma Chakravarty would later call, Brahmanical patriarchy.[31] This is why Phule asks the British government to step in and to outlaw girlhood marriage and the exploitation of widows in India.

Gandhi departs from Ramabai and Phule's views on the conditions of women. While Gandhi campaigned against child marriage and argued for allowing widow remarriage, he was less critical of traditional widowhood than they were. Gandhi sees the widow—self-sacrificing and celibate—as a figure that all men and women should strive to emulate.[32] To the extent that Gandhi sees prostitution as a problem, he sometimes suggests that prostitutes have the choice to leave the profession and accuses them of preferring to live a life of ease. In his view, the only way forward was for prostitutes to "realize their dignity" and to "refuse to sell [their] honor."[33]

According to Gandhi, prostitution—like most other moral failings—results from lack of "self-control," the key to self-reliance and freedom. Prostitutes fell into "immoral" behavior because they fell prey to sexual desire and laziness.[34] On one hand, Gandhi attributes a significant

---

[30] Jyotirao Phule, Opinion from Jyotirao Govindrao Phulay on Note No. II, by Mr. B.M. Malabari on Enforced Widowhood, in G. P. Deshpande (ed.), *Selected Writings of Jotirao Phule* (Delhi: Leftword Books, 2002), 195–197.

[31] Uma Chakravarty, Conceptualising Brahmanical Patriarchy in Early India: Gender, Class, Caste and State, *Economic and Political Weekly*, April 3, 1993, 579–585.

[32] Ashwini Tambe, Gandhi's "Fallen" Sisters: Difference and the National Body Politic, *Social Scientist* 37(1–2) (2009): 21–38 at 25.

[33] Mohandas Karamchand Gandhi, *Collected Works of Mahatma Gandhi* (hereinafter "CWMG") (Delhi: Government of India, Publications Division, 1999), vol. 76, no 30, Meaning of Prohibition.

[34] In order to protect themselves, Gandhi urged every woman to pray when arising every morning: "God, keep me pure, give me the strength to preserve my chastity, strength to preserve it even at the cost of my life. With thee as my protector whom need I fear?" He claimed that "such a prayer made with a pure mind will surely protect every woman"; CWMG, Vol. 25, 437–438; quoted in Debali Mookerjea-Leonard, To Be Pure or Not to Be: Gandhi, Women, and the Partition of India, *Feminist Review* 94 (2010): 38–54 at 47.

sense of agency to these women by suggesting that their situation is the result of their own choices. Yet, on the other hand, he also engages in victim blaming and fails to acknowledge the broader conditions within which women made these choices. He largely ignores the conditions of material deprivation women (especially widows) found themselves in.[35] Many women were forced, by their circumstances or by men, into prostitution, rather than freely choosing it.[36] As Ashwini Tambe argues, Gandhi's approach to women's oppression is overly individualistic. This is why it misses the impact of broader social circumstances on women.

Ambedkar's own thoughts about the oppression of women build on those of Ramabai and especially Phule. Ramabai identifies the *Laws* as the central cause of women's oppression through their inferiorization of women. Phule explains why the *Laws* entrenched the oppression of women in the first place: to protect the self-interest of the Brahmins. This raises the question: Why does Brahmin self-interest take the form it does? Why does it result in practices of girl marriage, widowhood, and *sati* in India? Phule doesn't say, but this is the question that animates Ambedkar's discussion in "Castes in India." Ambedkar aims to build on Ramabai and Phule's work by delving deeper into the origin of these oppressive practices. As we know, the concept of endogamy—the very essence of caste, in Ambedkar's view—is central to his account. Endogamy ensures that caste boundaries are rigidly maintained, which ensures Brahmins' superior status.

Ambedkar's work is also a direct response to Gandhi's writings on women. Unlike Gandhi, Ambedkar did not believe that women voluntarily chose *sati*, widowhood, or girl marriage. Endogamy necessitated these practices, and Manu's *Laws* gave women little choice but

---

[35] On this see, Tambe, Gandhi's "Fallen" Sisters, 26, and Madhu Kishwar, Gandhi on Women, *Economic and Political Weekly* 20(40) (October 5): 1691–1702 at 1699.

[36] This may be because he believed that women ought to choose death rather than dishonor: "[women] must develop courage enough to die rather than yield to the brute in man. It has been suggested that a girl who is gagged or bound so as to make her powerless even for struggling cannot die as easily as I seem to think. I venture to assert that a girl who has the will to resist can burst all the bonds that may have been used to render her powerless. The resolute will give her the strength to die" (Gandhi, CWMG, vol. 76, no 30, 355–356; quoted in Mookerjea-Leonard, To Be Pure or Not to Be: Gandhi, Women, and the Partition of India, 48).

to follow them. He did not believe that internal change—developing the virtues of self-control and self-reliance—would improve women's lives. The problems that women and girl wives face have nothing to do with their own lack of moral virtue. Ambedkar, like Ramabai and Phule, felt that Brahminism and its *Laws* were the real problem. To improve the conditions of women, he argued that the caste system must be eliminated. Over time, he came to believe that Hinduism could not exist without Brahminism and its caste system. So, he came to advocate mass conversion to neo-Buddhism, which, in his view, is an anti-hierarchical religion.[37,38]

10.3. Lessons Learned

10.3.1. Causal Mechanisms Matter

Ambedkar—like the other Indian political thinkers we consider here—is primarily concerned with explaining the origin and evolution of the caste system and the poor conditions of women in India.[39] His interest in causation is not independent of his moral and political theorizing.

[37] Ambedkar publicly converted to Buddhism on October 14, 1956. He believed that some aspects of Buddhism were problematic and supported Navayana (neo)-Buddhism, which reinterpreted Buddhism to address social inequality. For his views on Buddhism, see B. R. Ambedkar, Aakash Singh, Rathore Verma, and Ajay Verma (eds.), *The Buddha and His Dhamma: A Critical Edition* (New Delhi: Oxford University Press, 2011).

[38] Ram Manohar Lohia, a socialist and independence activist, was greatly influenced by Ambedkar. However, he did not believe that Hinduism was unsalvageable. Instead, he believed that religious reform was essential to eliminating caste. He wrote: "Religion will also have to be cleared of its rubbish about castes" (see his *Caste System* [Hyderabad: Samta Vidyalaya, 1964], 141). Periyar was closer to Ambedkar in his views of Hinduism; he believed that Hinduism was nothing more than ideology and was used to oppress the Dravidians of South India. Periyar, in contrast to Lohia, was a "rationalist" and supported atheism.

[39] Causation is a long-standing concern in Indian philosophy. Classical Indian philosophers—in the Upanishads and Vedas—sought to identify the unitary cause of the origin of the complex universe. They were also concerned with the question of how action can lead to seen and unseen effects. These two interests were connected. Classical Indian thinkers believed that action, of the right sort, could lead to (or cause) spiritual liberation. In the hopes of attaining liberation, they sought to understand the nature of the world and how to navigate it. Understanding causation—the relation between cause and effect—was central to this project. Ambedkar's interest in causation continues in this Indian tradition, but instead of focusing on spiritual liberation, he is focused on social and political liberation. For an introduction to causation in Indian philosophy,

Understanding how the caste system arose and evolved over time is key, in his view, to analyzing why it is morally wrong and how it can be abolished. He has practical and theoretical reasons for thinking this. First, Ambedkar, like Phule, believes that people will be motivated to engage in action to abolish the caste system only after they understand how it works and what is morally objectionable about it.[40] Writing about the caste system—its origin and evolution—is central to his attempts to counter the Hindu ideology spread by Brahmins. Ambedkar writes to help Brahmins understand that caste is something created for and by Brahmins and other castes with superior social status. His hope is that this knowledge will motivate them to eliminate the caste system. One might wonder why the Brahmins need to be educated about the origin of the caste system, if they are its creators. While Dalits and other lower caste individuals can see through the ideology of Brahminism, because of their social position and experience, Brahmins believe their own spurious justifications of the caste system. Ambedkar wishes to help them counter this belief through his writings. Second, perhaps because of his training in sociology, Ambedkar believes we can only be sure of how to undo an injustice after we understand how it arises in the first place. In recognizing the role of endogamy in the caste system, and the role of ideology (perpetuated by *the Laws*), Ambedkar seeks to find a way to abolish the caste system.

10.3.2. Social, Not Natural

Through Ambedkar's analysis, we see that the caste system and the poor conditions of women are not natural. They are not the result of biology. They are the result of rules and practices designed by Brahmins and other high-caste Hindus. This is a claim that was worth establishing

see Roy W. Perrett, Indian Theories of Causation, in Edward Craig (ed.), *Routledge Encyclopedia of Philosophy Online*, Vol. 1 (London: Taylor and Francis, 1998), available at: https://www.rep.routledge.com/articles/thematic/causation-indian-theories-of/v-1.

[40] In fact, Ambedkar's thoughts in "Castes in India" serve as a basis for his later writings, including AoC, which outlines numerous moral criticisms of the caste system and a concrete plan for eliminating it.

then and reminding ourselves of now. Injustice is a social condition, not a natural one. As Ambedkar makes clear in his later work, in *Annihilation*, this claim has important moral consequences. The continued poor conditions of women, more generally, and of Dalits, more specifically, are not just the result of failing to help these individuals, a mere violation of a positive moral duty. Since they are the result of the purposeful actions of high-caste Hindus, the poor conditions of women and Dalits constitute a violation of a negative duty not to harm. This is an important moral conclusion because it makes clear who caused the harm of the caste system and who has a moral responsibility to make up for it.

10.3.3. Social, Not Individual

While the harm of caste impacts individuals, Ambedkar makes clear that the harm of caste accrues to individuals because of the social groups they belong to. The indignity and economic and sexual exploitation that widows experience is a function of their position in the social hierarchy of the caste system. It is largely a function of belonging to a high caste—being a Brahmin woman. Of course, lower caste women experience the worst of the caste system, but they do so in a way that is distinctive of their own caste. They experience poor treatment—economic and sexual exploitation, violence, and disrespect—at the hands of high-caste men and women.

10.3.4. Intersectionality Matters

In Ambedkar's view, we cannot understand the nature of the caste system and the harm that it gives rise to without considering how it intersects and interacts with patriarchy.[41] It is because of patriarchy that endogamy and Brahmin self-interest take the form that they do—i.e.,

---

[41] The term "intersectionality" was first used by Kimberle Crenshaw in Demarginalizing the Intersection of Race and Sex: A Black Feminist Critique of Antidiscrimination Doctrine, Feminist Theory and Antiracist Politics, *University of Chicago Legal Forum* 1(8) (1989): 139–167.

in establishing the practices of *sati*, widowhood, and girl marriage. Recall, Ambedkar says that, because of patriarchy (CI, 21), what can be done to women—namely, imposing celibacy, strict behavioral and aesthetic codes—can never be imposed on men. Patriarchy ensures that the most egregious harms of the caste system fall upon women.

10.4. A Corrective to Contemporary Liberal Political Philosophy

With these lessons in mind, it is clear that Ambedkar should be taken seriously as an important political philosopher who is worthy of study today—especially as a corrective to standard liberal political theory. To see why, consider the political philosophy of John Rawls, which has received significant attention (too much, in some people's view). Rawls's task in his most famous book, *A Theory of Justice*, and subsequent work is to identify the set of principles that would govern a just society.[42] Rawls begins by asking us to imagine ourselves in an original position, where we are to imagine ourselves behind a veil of ignorance. In this position, we have knowledge of general science and the social sciences and we know nothing specific about ourselves—we do not know our identity or social position, for example. We are asked to decide on the principles that it would be most rational to agree to from this position—these are the principles that will and ought to govern a just society. Rawls argues that we would select the *difference principle* to govern the distribution of primary goods such as income and wealth. The difference principle states that inequalities in primary goods are to be arranged so that they are to the (material) benefit of the least advantaged. Rational self-interested individuals would choose the difference principle because, once outside of the original position, it would ensure that, even if they happen to be among the worst-off members of society, they would be as well off as they could be.

Behind the veil, we know that material inequality might arise in the real world, but we lack a clear understanding of why or how it might do

[42] John Rawls, *A Theory of Justice* (Cambridge, MA: Harvard University Press. Revised edition, 1999).

so. Charles W. Mills has famously argued that, through these sorts of omissions and distortions, liberal theories, including those of Rawls, John Stuart Mill, and Thomas Hobbes, mystify the practices and structures that lead to inequality.[43] In particular, he argues, mainstream liberal theory omits imperialism and white supremacy from historical and contemporary representations of Europe and the Americas. Liberal theory functions to mislead people into accepting the status quo as legitimate. As a corrective, Mills suggests we need an account of how domination comes about and how it is reproduced. In identifying how the caste system arose, why it continues to persist, and how it causes objectionable (material) living conditions for women, Ambedkar does exactly this. He anticipates and gives a Millsian account of the oppression of woman and Dalits.

Why is this kind of project important? Getting clearer on the causes of inequality—in the ways Mills and Ambedkar would like us to—is important because it can lead us to new ideas about how to resolve social and economic inequality. Widows in India are often (but not always) living in poverty. Patrilocal residence—the custom of Hindu brides marrying into and living with their husbands' families—means that women sever ties with their own families. In many cases, this practice leaves women dependent on in-laws who don't want the burden of supporting the women after their husbands' death. Sometimes, family members also prevent the women from retaining possession of their husband's property, which makes living on their own almost impossible for these women.[44] Underlying these practices is the belief that women lack value after their husband's death and, in turn, that they are not entitled to care or property. Redistribution of wealth would certainly help in these cases. With greater income, these women would have greater economic security, for example; they may be better able to provide for their own basic needs and those of their children.[45] They may, in turn, be less likely to take up or be coerced into prostitution

---

[43] Charles W. Mills, *The Racial Contract* (Ithaca, NY: Cornell, 1997).

[44] This practice goes against customary law in India. The Hindu Succession Act (1956) states that widows who choose to remarry do have a right to their deceased husband's property.

[45] How much redistribution is supported by Rawls's difference principle is up for debate. I have argued that it would require significant redistribution. See Completing Rawls's Arguments for Equal Political Liberty and Its Fair Value: The Argument from Self-Respect, *Canadian Journal of Philosophy* 43(2) (2013): 179–205.

by their material circumstances. They may also be more able to cope with any debt that results from their husband's death (as in the case of death from chronic illness). However, in Ambedkar's view, redistribution of wealth and income would in itself be unlikely to solve many of the worst problems facing women in India, especially widows.[46,47] He would look at the India of today, where the middle class is exploding, and not be surprised by the fact that widows, no matter their class status, still experience stigmatization and social exclusion. As mentioned, in some cases, widows are still confined to their households and are excluded from attending social and religious events. Even today, the religious ideologies that support Brahmanical patriarchy (i.e., the *Laws*) still work to oppress women. Ambedkar, following Phule, would argue that, in addition to redistribution of wealth and income, Indians, and especially the Brahmins among them, need to be re-educated. We must use our new theories about domination, the caste system, and patriarchy to debunk the religious ideologies that support the caste system and the oppression of women. Without this, redistribution— no matter how significant—is unlikely to fundamentally improve the abject conditions of women.[48]

Furthermore, Ambedkar believes that, even with appropriate education, Brahmins may be unlikely to let go of their superior social position and the ideologies that support it. As I mentioned earlier, he argues that the only way forward is to opt out of Hinduism completely, its laws and ideologies, and to convert to neo-Buddhism. However, Ambedkar also knew that mass conversion among caste

[46] We see here some similarities to Susan Moller Okin's criticisms of Rawls in *Justice, Gender, and the Family* (New York: Basic Books, 1989). In her view, Rawls's theory of justice, in its original form, was unable to account for or overcome many of the injustices that women (in the United States) face.

[47] This is the beginning of Ambedkar's potential response to Lohia, who wrote: "Women must be given equal rights with men. Really speaking they must even get more if equality is to be obtained . . . these laws are not relevant for more than 80 per cent of India's women. . . . They have a meaning only for a few high-caste women in Brahmin, Bania, and Thakur homes . . . the act was good but incomplete and initiated by twice-born self-interest . . . the problem of the majority of Indian women is the lack of water taps and latrines" (Lohia 1964, 58–59). Ambedkar would argue that access to material goods isn't enough to establish social equality, which is of importance in addition to, and may even be necessary for, the kind of economic equality Lohia is concerned with.

[48] He also argued for inter-caste dining and marriage.

Hindus to Buddhism was unlikely. This is why he worked hard to ensure that the constitution and laws of independent (postcolonial) India contained concrete protections for women and Dalits. For example, Ambedkar drafted and sought to introduce The Hindu Code Bill, which, among other things, sought to change marriage laws— including marriageable age and rights to divorce for women[49]—and to give women the right of property (to her father's and husband's)— all of which had been denied by the *Laws*. In defending the new code, Ambedkar reportedly said,

> I should like to draw attention of the house to one important fact. The great political philosopher Burke who wrote his great book against the French Revolution said that those who want to conserve must be ready to repair. And all I am asking this House is: If you want to maintain the Hindu system, Hindu culture and Hindu society, do not hesitate to repair where repair is necessary. This Bill asks for nothing more than to repair those parts of the Hindu system which have become dilapidated.[50]

Ambedkar believes that, if it couldn't be abolished, then Hinduism must at least be repaired as far as possible. When the Bill initially failed to pass in 1948, Ambedkar resigned from the Cabinet. Later, in 1955, with some changes, his bill was passed as four separate bills.[51]

---

[49] In a similar vein, Periyar arranged many remarriages of widows, which he referred to as "self-respect marriages" (marriages carried out without a priest or religious rituals). He often asked the eldest widow in the family (widows were and still are viewed as a bad omen) to carry out the marriage ceremony.

[50] Quoted in Eleanore Zelliot, *Ambedkar Abroad*, Sixth Dr. Ambedkar Memorial Annual Lecture, Jawaharlal Nehru University, 2004, 15. https://www.jnu.ac.in/sites/defa
ult/files/6th%20Dr.%20Ambedkar%20memorial%20Lecture.pdf.

[51] As suggested earlier, another benefit of getting clear about the cause of inequality is that we can also get clearer about who has the moral responsibility to implement the solutions we come up with. While Rawls held that the duty to satisfy the difference principles (and to act in accordance with the policies that stem from it) is a duty that all citizens of a just society have to one another, Ambedkar would likely argue that, if particular groups of individuals have caused the inequality through practices of domination, then they have special duties to remedy it. Rawls cannot account for the existence of duties of repair that most of us would think that Indian Brahmins have toward Dalits and women. In this respect, Ambedkar's theory serves as a useful contrast to Rawls's liberal political theory and those like it.

In contrast to Ambedkar, contemporary liberal political philosophers have too often shied away from making concrete suggestions about law and policy. For Rawls, this is something that is done—through a process of reflective equilibrium[52]—only after the basic principles of justice have been decided upon. Following Rawls, mainstream (mostly American political) philosophers spent decades arguing about the right principles of justice, never quite making their way to concrete questions about appropriate policy and practice to overcome real and lived injustice. Today, things are changing in the United States. Even among those working in the mainstream, there is interest in social injustice, particularly as it relates to race, gender, sexual orientation, and class. Students, in particular, want to know how social injustices arise and how they ought to be combated. These young political philosophers could learn a few lessons—the importance of causation, social groups, and intersectionality—by studying Ambedkar's political philosophy, especially his essay on "Castes in India."

10.5. Conclusion

Ambedkar came to New York City and presented a sophisticated account of the origin and evolution of the caste system in India. He believed the oppression of women—through the practices of *sati*, widowhood, and girl marriage—played an essential role in the establishment and maintenance of the caste system by ensuring the rigid boundaries of caste. Unlike contemporary liberal political thinkers such as Rawls, Ambedkar looked at the world he found himself in and tried to explain how social and economic inequality arose. His ideas didn't stay in the ivory tower of academia. They motivated his own attempts to educate the masses and ultimately, as a writer of the

---

[52] The method of reflective equilibrium consists in working back and forth between our considered judgments or intuitions about what to do in a specific instance and the principles of justice that we believe ought to govern it. In working back and forth, we are supposed to decide what course of action (policy, practice) is the right one to take. Michael Della Rocca has argued that the method of reflective equilibrium has status quo bias built into it. See his The Taming of Philosophy, in Mogens Laerke, Justin H. Smith, and Eric Schliesser (eds.) (Oxford: Oxford University Press, 2013), 178–208. This may also explain why Rawls's method is unable to account for duties of repair (cf., fn. 51).

constitution, to change the laws of India. As Mills has argued, political philosophers of the Western tradition trade too often in abstract theories that have little to do with the important injustices we face. They render ideologies and practices of white supremacy, imperialism, and patriarchy invisible. Looking toward the work of Ambedkar and other Indian thinkers can help us out of the ivory tower and toward the real world, leading us to see things more clearly and to develop concrete solutions to the very real problems we face.

Bibliography

Alexander, Michelle (2012). *The New Jim Crow*. New York: The New Press.

Ambedkar, B. R. ([1917] 2013). Castes in India. *Indian Antiquary XLI, May 1917*. Reprinted in Sharmila Rege (ed.), *Against the Madness of Manu*. New Delhi: Navayana, 2013, 77–108.

Ambedkar, B. R. (2014). *Annihilation of Caste*. New York: Verso.

Ambedkar, B. R., Aakash Singh, Rathore Verma, and Ajay Verma (eds.). (2011). *The Buddha and His Dhamma: A Critical Edition*. New Delhi: Oxford University Press.

Bagehot, Walter. (1915). *The Works and Life of Walter Bagehot*, Volume 8: *Physics and Politics, Currency Monopoly, and Essays*, ed. Mrs. Russell Barrington. London: Longmans, Green. https://oll.libertyfund.org/titles/bagehot-the-works-and-life-of-walter-bagehot-vol-8.

Chakravarty, Uma. (1993). Conceptualising Brahmanical Patriarchy in Early India: Gender, Class, Caste and State. *Economic and Political Weekly* 28(14), 03 (April 3): 579–585.

Crenshaw, Kimberle (1989). Demarginalizing the Intersection of Race and Sex: A Black Feminist Critique of Antidiscrimination Doctrine, Feminist Theory and Antiracist Politics. *University of Chicago Legal Forum* 1(8): 139–167.

Della Rocca, Michael (2013). *The Taming of Philosophy*. Mogens Laerke, Justin H. Smith, and Eric Schliesse (eds.). Oxford: Oxford University Press, 178–208.

Du Bois, W. E. B. (1909). Evolution of the Race Problem. *Proceedings of the National Negro Conference*, 142–158. Reprinted: http://www.webdubois.org/dbEvolOfRaceProb.html, accessed April 6, 2022.

Gandhi, Mohandas Karamchand ([1958–1994] 1999). *Collected Works of Mahatma Gandhi* (cited as CWMG), Vols. 1–100 (E-Book or CD Rom version). Government of India, Publications Division.

Ketkar, S. V. (1909). *History of Caste in India*. Ithaca, NY: Taylor and Carpenter.

Kishwar, Madhu (1985). Gandhi on Women. *Economic and Political Weekly* 20(40) (October): 1691–1702.

Krishnamurthy, Meena (2013). Completing Rawls's Arguments for Equal Political Liberty and Its Fair Value: The Argument from Self-Respect. *Canadian Journal of Philosophy* 43(2): 179–205.

Lohia, Ram Manohar (1964). *Caste System.* Hyderabad: Samta Vidyalaya.

Mills, Charles W. (1997). *The Racial Contract.* Ithaca, NY: Cornell.

Mookerjea-Leonard, Debali (2010). To Be Pure or Not to Be: Gandhi, Women, and the Partition of India. *Feminist Review* 9: 38–54.

Nesfield, John (1887). *The Function of Modern Brahmins in Upper India.* Calcutta.

Okin, Susan Moller (1989). *Justice, Gender, and the Family.* New York: Basic Books.

Perrett, Roy W. (1998). Indian Theories of Causation. In Edward Craig (ed.), *Routledge Encyclopedia of Philosophy Online*, Vol. 1. London: Taylor and Francis. https://www.rep.routledge.com/articles/thematic/causation-ind ian-theories-of/v-1.

Phule, Jyotirao (2002). Opinion from Jyotirao Govindrao Phulay on Note No. I by Mr. B.M. Malabari on Infant Marriage in India. In G. P. Deshpande (ed.), *Selected Writings of Jotirao Phule.* Delhi: Leftword Books, 193–194.

Phule, Jyotirao (2002). Opinion from Jyotirao Govindrao Phulay on Note No. II, by Mr. B.M. Malabari on Enforced Widowhood. In G. P. Deshpande (ed.), *Selected Writings of Jotirao Phule.* Delhi: Leftword Books, 195–197.

Phule, Jyotirao (2002). Slavery. In G. P. Deshpande (ed.), *Selected Writings of Jotirao Phule.* Delhi: Leftword Books, 23–100.

Ramabai, Pandita (1909). *The High Caste Hindu Woman.* New York: Fleming H. Revel.

Rawls, John (1999). *A Theory of Justice.* Cambridge, MA: Harvard University Press. Revised edition.

Rege, Sharmila (ed.) (2013). *Against the Madness of Manu.* New Delhi: Navayana.

Senart, Emile (1930). *Castes in India*, trans. Sir E. Denison Ross. London: Methuen.

Srinivas, M. N. (1952). *Religion and Society among the Coorgs of South India.* Oxford: Clarendon Press.

Tambe, Ashwini (2009). Gandhi's "Fallen" Sisters: Difference and the National Body Politic. *Social Scientist* 37(1–2): 21–38.

Tarde, Gabriel (1903). *Laws of Imitation*, trans. E. C. Parsons. New York: Henry Holt.

Wilkerson, Isabel (2020). *Caste: The Origin of Our Discontent.* New York: Random House.

Zelliot, Eleanore "*Ambedkar Abroad,*" Sixth Dr. Ambedkar Memorial Annual Lecture, Jawahlal Nehru University, 2004. https://www.jnu.ac.in/sites/defa ult/files/6th%20Dr.%20Ambedkar%20memorial%20Lecture.pdf.

11

Civility, Silence, and Epistemic Labor in Audre Lorde's *Sister Outsider*

Serene J. Khader

In 2018, Michelle Obama said she could not forgive Donald Trump for having fomented the conspiracy theory that President Barack Obama had not been born in the United States. An editorial that immediately followed was entitled "Michelle Obama, Still Hating After All these Years" (Chumley 2018). When Christine Blasey Ford accused Brett Kavanaugh of having sexually assaulted her, a widely circulated op ed repeatedly contrasted Blasey's view with "objectivity" and "logic" and ended with speculation about Blasey Ford's mental health (Cherkasky 2018). A *Guardian* column written in response to public discussion of legislation that would protect trans people's rights in the United Kingdom assumed that trans women did not belong in women's prisons, but then went on to unselfconsciously tout the virtues of centrism, and distancing itself from the views of "both extremes" (Gleeson 2018).

All of these cases make something clear: calls to engage in civil, rational, public discussion can work to silence, rather than support, criticism of injustice. Such calls exert a particularly strong silencing effect on people from non-dominant groups. But much more remains to be said about why and how these calls to engage "rational" public discussion where we hear "both sides" undermine the pursuit of knowledge about social reality. Achieving justice requires an accurate understanding of society, and the workings of power within it—and some level of convergence on this understanding. It is difficult to arrive at such an understanding without the contributions of people in oppressed groups, whose social location enables them to shed light on, and theorize about, how society really works.

Serene J. Khader, *Civility, Silence, and Epistemic Labor in Audre Lorde's* Sister Outsider In: *Neglected Classics of Philosophy*. Edited by: Eric Schliesser, Oxford University Press. © Oxford University Press 2022. DOI: 10.1093/oso/9780190097196.003.0012

Calls to exercise the virtues associated with civility often back-fire, because our epistemic and communicative landscape is set up to impede the formulation and uptake of critical perspectives from the oppressed. Audre Lorde's *Sister Outsider* provides a sophisti-cated, conceptually rich, analysis of why this is the case. Originally published in 1984, this collection of essays and speeches should be regarded as a classic source on what is now called "epistemic oppres-sion" (Dotson 2014).[1] Lorde offers distinctive insights about why op-pressive conditions make knowledge of social reality hard to arrive at and communicate. Her work helps us see why advancing the interests of oppressed people depends on transforming our epistemic and com-municative practices—and reconceiving the norms that govern such practices. One of the book's contributions is a taxonomy of mechanisms that impede the creation and sharing of the type of social knowledge we would need to work toward a society without oppression.

I focus here on three particular sets of insights Lorde offers about how oppression impedes the attainment of knowledge about social reality and the formulation of insights about liberation: those about the epistemic and communicative mechanisms that force oppressed people into a "battle to preserve [their] own perceptions" (1984, 81); those about how what I call "unjust epistemic labor flows"; and those about the downsides of negative cultural attitudes surrounding anger. I assume in the following discussion that overcoming oppres-sion requires a somewhat accurate picture of social reality, that dom-inant understandings obscure the reality of oppression, and that it is difficult to arrive at a more accurate picture without the first-person perspectives of the oppressed.[2]

Audre Lorde was an activist, poet, and academic of the mid- and late twentieth century (De Veaux 2004). Given that self-naming was so im-portant for her work (as I will discuss below), it is unsurprising that she referred to herself by many labels, including Black, lesbian, feminist,

---

[1] Though I focus on the epistemic lessons of the text, they are only one small slice of what Lorde addresses in the book. For example, some essays offer critiques of US imperi-alism, and others offer theories about what it means to be multiply oppressed.

[2] The feminist philosophical tradition known as *standpoint epistemology* makes a more detailed case for this position: https://plato.stanford.edu/entries/feminist-social-epistemology/.

mother, poet, Zami (a Cariacou word for women who love women) (see Lorde 1983), and warrior. In addition to being a prose writer and a poet, Lorde was a committed political and academic activist who worked to transform institutions of knowledge so that women and women of color would be better represented in them. She was actively involved in the anti-war, civil rights, anti-apartheid, and AIDs justice movements, in addition to feminist struggles. With Barbara Smith, she founded Kitchen Table, a press devoted to publishing work by Black women.

Unlike most canonical Western philosophical texts, the pieces in *Sister Outsider* are not addressed to a general anonymous reader. They are by and large addressed to women who are active in the feminist movement, and in some cases, subgroups of feminist women, such as Black women or women of color. Though the text seeks to identify ways that oppressive structures like heterosexism, white supremacy, and patriarchy obscure the truth about social reality, Lorde's aim was clearly to confront her audience with the ways in which impediments to knowing the social world impeded genuinely liberatory political *action*.

11.1. Preserving Perceptions

In an interview with Adrienne Rich included in the book, Lorde describes her intellectual life as marked by a "battle to preserve my perceptions" (81). Though she uses the phrase autobiographically, it also encapsulates an element of her conceptualization of the general epistemic situation of oppressed people. For Lorde, oppressed people face limited conceptual and linguistic resources for describing social reality, their experiences, and their visions of liberation. Even when they manage to put these into language, they often remain illegible to members of dominant groups. I focus in this section on the first phenomenon and return to issues of legibility in the final section on anger.

Because liberation requires both self-knowledge by the oppressed and a somewhat accurate picture of social reality, Lorde describes oppressed people's desires for language as morally urgent. In her essay "The Transformation of Silence into Language and Action," Lorde describes "language and self-definition" as "needs" and analogizes the condition of lacking language to describe experiences of oppression to choking (45). The explicit thesis of her speech "Poetry Is Not a Luxury" is that political change cannot happen without the production of new and shared self-understandings by oppressed people. Overcoming oppression requires learning to "give name to the nameless" (37). Naming, for Lorde, is important for a specific political reason; it allows appropriate *evaluation*. Lorde analogizes language to light. The words we have affect "the quality of light by which we scrutinize our lives" (36).

The barriers to self-understanding and understanding social reality Lorde is interested in are distinct from the challenges to knowing ourselves that all of us face, or are susceptible to facing. It may seem initially that Lorde is merely describing universal difficulties for self-expression, but it is important to remember that the speeches and essays collected in *Sister Outsider* are always addressed to specific political audiences. When she discusses what "we" should do, she is referring to a specific "we" that shares an experience of oppression and struggle against it. As a result, most of the barriers to arriving at and communicating knowledge that Lorde describes track social group membership. For example, Lorde writes that Black people are often forced to see themselves through the lens of racist cultural imagery (43). She also argues that the only resources for self-understanding given by some white feminist texts to African women are those that associate them with extreme victimization, such as female genital mutilation (67–68).

Interestingly, Lorde suggests that there are two distinct ways by which our linguistic and conceptual repertoires can fail the oppressed who wish to describe their realities. I have focused so far on utter lack—the literal absence of words that would allow them to put their realities, and the social realities they testify to, into language. When Lorde speaks of naming the nameless, she often refers to pain, anger, and fear whose sources and characters are difficult to articulate. But dominant understandings can have shortcomings besides literal gaps. Lorde often suggests that existing language, rather than providing no words at all, provides words that *distort*, or as Lorde describes it, "misname" (120). To return to Lorde's metaphor about light, available linguistic resources may offer a certain light with which to evaluate reality, but it is a light that makes it difficult to see what is wrong with the status quo, as well as what possibilities for transcending it are.

Lorde offers one example of how an inadequate conceptual repertoire distorts, rather than leaves an absence, in her discussions of Black women's difficulties understanding one another in a racist and sexist world. In the oft-quoted "The Master's Tools Will Never Dismantle the Master's House," Lorde identifies the problem as being forced to use "the tools of a racist patriarchy to examine that patriarchy" (111). The conceptual resources available under oppressive conditions get in the way of questioning the acceptability of those conditions. Black women need to be able to direct their anger at unjust social structures rather than at one another, but this is difficult to do "when we are surrounded with synonyms for filth" (161). Similarly, she argues a world with more value for love, care, and eroticism would be more just to women and lesbians, but feminists often are among the most reluctant to mine these for liberatory resources (100). Lorde's explanation of this feminist missed opportunity is that our existing language for describing eroticism deforms it by associating it with servitude to and dependence on men. Women's eroticism toward, and love and care for, other women could create the basis for solidarity and challenge racist and capitalist structures, but it is difficult for this potential to be actualized when the word "eroticism" is linked to men's use of women, both sexually, and, in the psychoanalytic tradition, as sources of nourishment.

It may seem that what Lorde is describing is the presence of bad ideas, rather than the absence of the right language. But Lorde is partly concerned with the associations that words and concepts carry, and the way they are often difficult to extricate from certain conversations or ways of seeing the world. We may be able to literally say that we should think the erotic differently, but this does not change the fact that nurturance and love are coded as feminine roles within a gendered hierarchy. It is difficult to speak of the erotic without calling to mind images of women being used, such as images from misogynistic pornography and the nursing breast. In Lorde's words, the erotic conjures images of women being "kept in a distant/inferior position and psychically milked" (54).

If it is true that dominant concepts come with associations that are difficult to break, funneling liberatory ideas through widely available concepts will often force the oppressed to speak in distortions and approximations. To borrow Lorde's own light metaphor, there will be cases where using the concepts of the dominant refract the perceptions of oppressed people to the point of unrecognizability. Worse still, it may risk blocking the truth, as Lorde says anti-Black and anti-woman images do to Black women, who, in her words, are forced to encounter one another through "coated in stereotypes" (170). In Lorde's view, women and other oppressed individuals need to question "not only the truth of what we speak, but the truth of the language by which we speak it" (43).

This is why, regardless of whether the problem is lack or distortion, liberation depends on oppressed people inventing new words and concepts. Lorde holds that the arts, and linguistic art in particular, are essential to social change, because they are one site of the creation of a new imaginary. Lorde explicitly distinguishes creative uses of language from concepts and ideas. Poetry allows for combining words in meaningful ways that are not yet concepts, and from these linguistic forms, ideas can spring (37). As Lorde puts it, poetry is the "light within which we predicate our dreams, first made into language, then made into idea, then into tangible action" (37). The denial of opportunities to make art, and to engage in the self-exploration, to oppressed individuals are one cause of the inadequacy of dominant linguistic and conceptual repertoires. Oppressed individuals need to actively "train ourselves to respect our feelings and transpose them into language so they can be shared" (37). This sharing is not just intrinsically important, it is important because it forms the basis for "tangible action" (37).

But Lorde does not think linguistic art is the only way to produce concepts and words that portray the social world accurately and that enable liberation. She thinks that theory and social movements can generate new concepts through developing norms to regulate their shared practices. Lorde's central argument in her essay on the master's tools is not that all of the ideas developed by the dominant are useless. It is instead that widespread understandings of difference conceptualize it as a bad thing to be overcome, or to be kept at arm's length and tolerated. She argues that the women's movement needs to work to conceptualize difference among women as positive and "creative" (111). Instead of seeing differences such as race, class, and sexual orientation as threats to the effectiveness of the movement, the movement needs to develop concepts that would allow the conceptualization of differences among women, and conflicts over those differences, as catalysts for growth. To be able to value difference appropriately, women need to dissociate difference from threat and toleration. Women of color who criticized white-dominated feminist movements were (and are) often met with the criticism that they were either fostering dangerous political division, or that they should simply organize separately. Lorde saw this as the result of a political imaginary that associated political unity and efficacy with sameness. Abandoning the "master's tools" would mean accepting that conflict among those in a shared struggle can be a source of power rather than weakness.

Lorde's argument that the oppressed lack resources for self-understanding and liberatory understandings of social reality should not be taken as an argument that the oppressed do not understand themselves at all, or as an argument that they understand themselves less well than the dominant do. Lorde is careful to maintain that not all understanding is linguistic or conceptual. In her discussion of the importance of poetry for bringing experience into language, Lorde asserts that something can be "nameless and formless" but "already felt" (36). She often suggests that the status of the nameless is one of being submerged but not completely absent; she remarks that there are "no new ideas" (139). Instead, perceptions can precede analysis (105) and survive "beneath language" (83). As she puts it, "some piece of humanness" within oppressed individuals "knows we are not being served by the machine" (139).

Moreover, Lorde is also clear that our existing set of words and concepts impedes the ability of the dominant to understand themselves and the social order. It is not, after all, as though the dominant are not constituted partly by oppression; they are constituted by their status as dominant, and this affects their ability to know themselves and the social order. Lorde's essays about the epistemic vices of domination are often directed at white feminists, who, in spite of sharing a broad political agenda with her, often just "didn't get" the ways they were harming women of color. For example, her essay the

"Uses of Anger" reflects on how white women routinely "misunderstand" allegations of racism. Lorde argues that feminist movements have still done little to make it possible for white women to conceive of themselves as, at once, oppressors and oppressed (130). Lorde's work on the epistemic shortcomings of the dominant shows how it is one thing to claim that we lack the words to accurately describe an oppressive social reality and another to hold that oppressed individuals are particularly ignorant. It may make the oppressed especially *harmed* by our existing language, but this need not translate to being especially ignorant.

Another reason Lorde's description of deficits in language does not commit her to the view that the oppressed do not understand themselves is that Lorde denies that there is a single shared community of users of a language. Lorde, like many other women of color feminist theorists, such as Maria Lugones (1987), insist that the public is variegated—that is, that there is more than one community of shared meanings. The fact of different publics within a single society means that lacking words and concepts that are intelligible to the dominant group is not the same thing as lacking words and concepts altogether. Lorde emphasizes that subcommunities of women have and create languages for mutual understanding that may nonetheless be opaque to more privileged women. For example, she argues that poor women and women of color understand the nuances that differentiate commercial sex work and the domination involved in traditional heterosexual marriage (according to the feminist critique), because "it is our daughters who line 42nd street" (112). Lorde seems to think that the ability to reveal social reality and liberatory possibilities in language admits of degrees, and that there are some circumstances where subcommunities develop conceptual and linguistic resources that are more illuminating than the ones that circulate in society at large. The upshot for attempts to arrive at knowledge about social reality, and how to change it, through discussion (especially cross-group discussion) is that the creation of alternative concepts is often necessary for such discussion to be illuminating. As long as existing words and concepts shed a positive light, or no light at all, on oppression, it will be difficult to understand the workings of power in society.

11.2. Epistemic Labor Flows: Preoccupation with the Concerns of the Dominant

The lack of adequate concepts is, for Lorde, abetted by another epistemic phenomenon, one that is often embodied in calls to engage in rational discussion or debate. This phenomenon is the flow of epistemic labor from the oppressed to the dominant. Lorde argues that one way to keep the oppressed from liberating themselves, including from generating the concepts they need to accurately describe and communicate about social reality, is to keep them "preoccupied with the master's concerns" (113). In other words, the dominant can set the agenda of what is to be discussed and keep demanding that the oppressed turn their attention there. Given that the number of questions we could ask about social reality and liberation is infinite, choosing to focus on some subset of them is always to direct intellectual labor toward certain issues and framings and away from others. This inability to pursue every possible knowledge project is not inherently pernicious, but it can become a tool of oppression when the oppressed are expected to discuss and explore the issues and framings that the dominant prioritize and there is no such reciprocal expectation.

Interestingly, Lorde's discussion of this phenomenon in the famous "Master's Tools" speech, initially given in 1974, predates the vast literature on what is now called "discursive power." Discursive power is the ability to shape society by determining what the parameters and norms governing discussion are. In her speech, Lorde repeatedly returns to what has become a familiar example of the agenda-setting power of the dominant: the expectation that oppressed people explain the vices of domination to, or educate, members of (often well-intentioned) dominant groups. As she puts it:

> Whenever the need for some pretense of communication arises, those who profit from our oppression call upon us to share our knowledge with them. In other words, it is the responsibility of the oppressed to teach the oppressors their mistakes. I am responsible for educating teachers who dismiss my children's culture in school. Black and Third World people are expected to educate white people as to our humanity. Women are expected to educate men. Lesbians

and gay men are expected to educate the heterosexual world. The oppressors maintain their position and evade responsibility for their own actions. There is a constant drain of energy which might be better used in redefining ourselves and devising realistic scenarios for altering the present and constructing the future. (115)

It is difficult for members of oppressed groups to dedicate energy and resources to the knowledge projects they prioritize when such expectations obtain. For example, Lorde notes that white feminists often prefer not to examine their own racism unless a woman of color is there to educate them (125). Yet the issues about racism that white feminists, and white people, most often ask about are already well-documented. In some cases, white people overcoming their racism would also be more effectively accomplished by their examining their own attitudes than by having people of color educate them. Furthermore, finding the "right" way to talk to white women about racism may not be an epistemic priority of women of color. For example, they might wish to develop more nuanced ideas about racism that it is difficult to develop when one is repeatedly trying to prove that racism exists. To do this and things like it, though, members of oppressed groups might need to engage in dialogue primarily with others who share their oppressions.

In fact, members of dominant groups might have epistemic priorities that do not have to do with explicitly describing racism, sexism, or another form of inequality at all. They may, for example, prioritize developing non-oppressive conceptual resources that would allow similarly dominated people to relate to one another, as Lorde argues Black women need to do. Or they may prioritize developing knowledge to solve problems in the communities they live in. Or—and Lorde was especially emphatic about this point—marginalized people have important insights into universal questions. They may not wish to be constantly relegated to reporting on their particular position. Lorde indicts a conference program that relegates Black women to panels on race and lesbians to panels on sexuality by saying that it looks as though "lesbian and Black women have nothing to say about existentialism, the erotic, women's culture, developing feminist theory, or heterosexuality and power" (110). Part of the epistemic task for members of oppressed groups is often to "search for the right questions" (161), rather than to answer the questions that the dominant group has made into epistemic priorities.

It may be objected that the expectation that members of oppressed groups participate in an epistemic agenda set by the dominant is compatible with the oppressed engaging in their own knowledge projects. Of course the options are not mutually exclusive, but the epistemic priorities of the oppressed and those of the dominant often compete with one another. This may be because of intrinsic incompatibilities between the knowledge projects; for example, sometimes the epistemic priorities of the dominant amount to a search for knowledge about how other groups came to be inferior. But another part of the reason is just time. Lorde is quite explicit that producing knowledge is a type of labor, and that the oppressed producing knowledge about oppression is a particularly demanding type of labor.

Simply put, all epistemic work takes time and energy. Oppressed individuals are especially short of these because of the basic demands of survival, because they are expending more time than members of dominant groups engaged in physical labor, the labor of caring for children, and because they are engaged in the emotional labor of preserving themselves and their communities under hostile conditions. Lorde offers the following analysis of why it is difficult for Black women to devote energy to understanding themselves: "we spend so much of our substance having to examine others constantly in the name of self-protection and survival, and we cannot reserve enough energy to scrutinize ourselves" (172) and earlier "black people have always had to attend closely to the continuous work of survival in the most material and immediate planes" (171). Interestingly, this is also why Lorde thinks poetry is particularly likely to be chosen as a site of knowledge production by oppressed people. In her words, poetry was the "most economical" art, because it can be done "between shifts" and "in the hospital pantry, on the subway, on scraps of surplus paper" (116).

Lorde also points to another reason preoccupation with the concerns of the dominant competes with attention with the concerns of the oppressed: the structures of academia institutionalize and reward preoccupation with the concerns of the dominant. Literary and philosophical canons prioritize, focus the attention of teachers and scholars on a canon dominated by elite white men (44). Conferences designed to incorporate marginalized knowledges into academia still treat these as the topic of a panel or two that exist alongside a program focused on more traditional questions (125–126). White women academics perpetuate an oppressive system when they rely on their professional and citational networks to decide who to include and exclude (113). In Lorde's view, this leads not only to a "diversion of energies" (113) to the knowledge projects of the dominant, but also to an asymmetry in expectations of the dominant and the oppressed. In a word, in order to survive in academia—and often in the world at large—oppressed people have to "become familiar with the manners and language of the oppressor" (114) while "white women have not educated themselves about Black women" (113).

Preoccupation with concerns of the dominant can make it difficult for the oppressed to sustain their perceptions, which, in turn, sustains the lacks of linguistic and conceptual resources I mentioned earlier. But there are also other ways it can make self-understanding and understanding of social reality into a struggle. Lorde discusses the ways that focusing on the knowledge projects of the dominant can lead the oppressed to project *partial* analyses of what they know to the social world. Sometimes the only way to funnel what one wants to say into an existing conversation is to leave something out. So, for example, the Black lesbian feminist woman is forced to "pluck out" one identity in explaining oppressions—for example, to focus only on sexual orientation in explaining the fear of lesbianism in Black women (121). Similarly, representations of women of color are only of interest to white women when they offer examples of extreme and ravaging sexism, not when they embody examples of women's power (121), so women of color may end up focusing on elements of their experiences to be heard at all—as for example in cases where trafficked women emphasize their victimhood rather than collaboration with traffickers because they need to evoke pity to gain refugee status (see Meyers 2014).

This tendency to omit information that does not fit the dominant group's frame is closely related to another cause of epistemic labor flows from the oppressed to the dominant. Members of dominant groups often lack the background to understand claims made by members of oppressed ones, and this causes the latter to expend energy, not just explaining, but also just discerning and weighing how much to reveal and conceal. When an oppressed person is contributing to dominant knowledge projects, or, more basically, when they are in a context where dominant group members have a set of shared understanding that is different from their own, that person is likely to truncate or curate what they say to produce maximum intelligibility. Contemporary philosopher Kristie Dotson has given a name to this phenomenon: "testimonial smothering" (2011).

One example Lorde offers is that Black women will resist calling attention to their Blackness because they know that hypervisibility often leads to danger (42). But Lorde also notes that the stakes of honesty about one's perceptions often go beyond being misunderstood; oppressed people often court harm if they describe their perceptions completely and accurately. Black people in the United States are acutely aware that making themselves visible will cause them to be targets for violence, so they may go out of their way not to share the elements of their experiences and views that would mark them or confirm stereotypes. Similarly, Lorde also argues that Black lesbian women may conceal their sexual orientation within the Black community (121). More generally, Lorde's book is full of examples of multiply oppressed individuals hiding elements of their identities to remain intelligible as members of the oppressed group they are circulating within at a given moment.

The inability or unwillingness of the dominant to understand the views and contributions of the oppressed stifles knowledge production at the *collective* level more than at the individual one. The likelihood that they will not be heard impacts what members of oppressed groups *say* more than what they know. But it is also true that a lifetime of curating and truncating one's reporting of one's own perceptions can affect what an individual thinks is worth knowing, or their sense that their perceptions are reliable. I have already mentioned that the energies any person can put into pursuing knowledge are finite, and that spending one's time pursuing the knowledge projects of the dominant has opportunity costs. Another reason, in Lorde's view, is the fact that a lifetime of explaining oneself to others without being understood can instill a lack of self-trust (42).

11.3. The Silencing of Righteous Anger

So far, I have discussed the ways that lacks of words and concepts and the flow of epistemic labor from the oppressed to the dominant impede the construction of accurate, shared knowledge about social reality. Lorde also theorizes a third type of impediment: norms discouraging the experience and display of strong emotion. The idea that knowledge would be negatively impacted by norms *discouraging* emotion flies in the face of the predominant strand in the Western philosophical tradition, one that traces its line through Plato, Descartes, and Kant. This dominant view, which is embodied in traditional descriptions of rationality and science, holds that emotion exerts a potentially corrupting influence on knowledge. In contrast to the dominant view, feminist analyses often portray emotion as epistemically beneficial. However, these tend to focus on positive emotions, such as love and feelings of connectedness.[3] Lorde has a body of work in this positive vein, which I will not say much about here. Her "The Uses of the Erotic" discusses the liberatory potential of desire and nurturance, though even there she emphasizes their chaotic and disruptive potential. I will instead examine Lorde's work on a negative emotion that she emphasizes across many essays and poems, namely anger.

Lorde argues that "anger is loaded with information and energy" (127). She assigns at least three distinct epistemic roles to anger. First, righteous anger is a "clarifying" (124, 145) force. Anger helps the person feeling it assign an appropriate moral valence to injustice against them. It is especially useful for identifying injustice, because to feel anger is to know that one has been treated as lesser, as not at the level of a "peer" (129). In "The Uses of Anger," an essay about the anger women of color feel toward white women, Lorde notes that there is an important feminist history to teaching women to be angry so that they can diagnose their oppression. Consciousness-raising groups encouraged women to feel and express anger against men (130). In spite of this, Lorde argues, feminist white women continue to chastise women of color for expressing anger about racism. Yet Lorde insists that "anger

---

[3] See Jaggar 1988.

is an *appropriate* response to racism" (129, italics mine). She analogizes anger to a spotlight (124) that allows the depth of a wrong to be examined and understood. Indeed, Lorde suggests that there are some phenomena, like racism, that cannot be understood unless one is willing to feel the attendant negative emotions (128–129).

Lorde's view is stronger than simply that anger is a diagnostic tool that facilitates the identification of wrongs; instead she seems to think that, for at least some wrongs, feeling angry about a wrong partly *constitutes* identification of that wrong as a wrong. Throughout the essay, she emphasizes that being denied the ability to feel and express anger about injustice is itself an injustice. She offers a list of interactions with white women where white women, among other things, try to shift the affective tone of discussions of racism; these ask women of color to participate in their "own annihilation." The contemporary philosopher Myisha Cherry (2021) offers an interesting analysis of Lorde's connection between anger and injustice. In Cherry's eyes, Lorde sees righteous anger as including appreciation for justice that is not yet present. In Cherry's view, asking an oppressed person to suppress righteous anger is tantamount to ask them to stop holding open imaginative space for a better future.

In addition to thinking that anger helps us know when we are wronged, Lorde argues that anger can motivate people to know. Anger can give those who are wronged strength to explore realities they may have otherwise turned their attention from. This motivational role of anger is intimately tied up with Lorde's view that epistemic labor flows and conceptual and linguistic schemes work to prevent the oppressed from fully theorizing their experiences and using them to illuminate the social order. If language and institutions inhibit the articulation of the realities of the oppressed, anger that survives these practices of distraction and distortion can call them to explore the knowledge projects that matter to them. Simply put, the gnawing feeling that something is not right can awaken a need to change one's understanding of the world and one's place in it.

But anger not only has the quality of demanding attention, it also has the quality of evoking fear of what it will do, both to others and the self. Anger is "an electric tapestry woven into every emotional tapestry on which I set the essentials of my life" (145). The desire to escape being destroyed by this anger (anger, if lived in and unmetabolized for too long can "lay . . . visions to waste"; 124, see also 152) can motivate a person to examine the source of the anger. This is why Lorde insists that listening to anger is a skill to be cultivated. In her view, harnessing anger's epistemic value means learning to "train that anger with accuracy" (145).

Some think of this fear of anger as well-founded, especially because all of us have experiences with anger that has gone wrong, by choosing the wrong target, or by making us act in the heat of the moment. However, Cherry argues in her defense of Lordean anger that this feature is not unique to anger. It is characteristic of all emotions that they can lead us astray when directed at the wrong target—as happens when we fall in love with, or feel compassion for, the wrong person. Even the most traditionally prosocial of emotions can cause harm when misguided, as in the case of what I have called "empathy excesses" toward Muslim women on the part of Westerners whose empathy turns into narrow vilification of Muslim men (2018) or in what Kate Manne has referred to as "himpathy," wherein we worry about what will happen to the futures of men accused of sexual assault but not their victims (2018). It is consistent with Lorde's desire to assign a positive epistemic value to a wide range of emotions that she refuses to treat the fear of anger as reflecting its intrinsic qualities.

But more importantly, there is an important sense in which Lorde would say that our worries about the harm anger can wreak tell us more about the unjust social relations that try to suppress it than they do about anger itself. For many of the reasons that anger can lead to harm have more to do with the unjust social order than intrinsic features of anger. Recall Lorde's discussion I referenced earlier on how Black women may downplay their race in some contexts because they know their race makes them targets for violence. Recall also Lorde's claim that white women stand to lose the benefits of being seen as "good girls" for keeping their emotions in check. In both of these cases, fear of anger is justified, but it is fear of the negative social repercussions that are *contingently* bundled with anger. That is, nothing inherent in anger makes it the case that it will lead to dire social punishment for the person who expresses it. The contemporary philosopher Amia Srinivasan names this state of affairs, in which oppressed people have to suppress important emotions in order to survive, "affective injustice." Though Srinivasan takes the centerpiece of Lorde's view on anger to be the idea that anger is epistemically useful, I take Lorde's analysis to also valorize anger precisely because it resists this affective injustice. In a social order that tells one not to feel or think certain things, just thinking and feeling them is resistance (see Khader forthcoming). To be clear, Lorde is not claiming that oppressed individuals are obligated give up on their survival to feel and express anger, but central to her view is that anger constitutes expressive resistance to a system that is rigged to incentivize a near-exclusive focus on survival (Srinivasan 2018).

I have focused so far on Lorde's positive evaluation of righteous anger, but it is important to be clear that Lorde neither sees all anger as righteous nor as positive. The idea that anger should not generally be feared must be distinguished from the idea that all forms of anger are good. Anger, for Lorde, is insufficient for the recognition of injustice. Anger, if it remains inarticulate, is harmful "unmetabolized" pain (171–172). Moreover, there are some species of anger that harmfully turn inward, toward the self or toward other members of one's group. For women, who are socially discouraged from feeling and expressing anger, anger is often transformed into some other more socially respectable feeling or is redirected toward the self who has dared to become angry. For Black women who experience not only discouragement from anger, but also a barrage of hate and degradation, anger can turn toward Blackwomanness (146) or cause Black women to mistrust and hate one another. In other words, Lorde thinks letting anger in is always risky, partly because the difference between righteous and useful anger is not always easy to recognize. It is just that the price of closing ourselves off to this risk is refusing to know an unjust world.

So norms that discourage anger distort, or discourage oppressed people from examining, and appropriately diagnosing, injustices that face them. These norms derivatively also prevent members of dominant groups from learning about social reality. Many types of harms, particularly those enacted by social structures, cannot be seen without attention to the testimony of members of oppressed groups. Preventing this testimony from being developed, or refusing to hear it unless it is delivered in the "right" tone, gets in the way of understanding these harms. The need to be open to understanding ourselves as agents of structural harm is present for members of oppressed groups as well as members of dominant ones, given the existence of intersecting oppressions.[4] In both "The Uses of Anger" and "Eye to Eye," her essay on the specific anger of Black women, Lorde argues that processing the anger of others is morally important. Even within oppressed groups, those with more power have to learn to hear and feel anger from those with a variety of positions; "we have to learn to orchestrate those furies so they do not tear us apart" (129).

Though it might be argued that everyone is discouraged from expressing anger, norms that discourage the feeling and expression of anger are particularly effective at preventing dominant audiences from assimilating the testimony of oppressed individuals. Norms discouraging anger simply do not equally apply to everyone in practice. Such norms also interface neatly with the content of specific oppressive norms and stereotypes. Sexist norms push women to tolerate and express dissatisfaction as sadness or disappointment. Much of Lorde's rhetorical strategy in her essay on white women's reactions to women of color is to point out that their aversion to anger is actually the result of internalized sexism. Sexist social structures are kept intact by women's fear of recognizing and speaking out against the injustice of their situation. She characterizes women's fear of anger as a way of remaining "enamored of [their] own oppression" (132). She also suggests that white women mistakenly believe that rejecting anger will preserve the social perception of them as morally good and accuses them of making the "terms of [their] own oppression a precious and necessary ticket into the fold of the righteous" (132; see also 131).

Lorde also points out that norms discouraging anger also interface with stereotypes of people of color, and Black people in particular. Stereotypes of Black people as angry, and angry without justification, circulate widely in Western societies (Jacobs 2018; Jerald et al. 2017). These also buttress other anti-Black stereotypes, including associations

---

[4] Crenshaw coined this term in 1989. See Kimberle Crenshaw, Demarginalizing the Intersection of Race and Sex: A Black Feminist Critique of Antidiscrimination Doctrine, Feminist Theory and Antiracist Politics, *University of Chicago Legal Forum* (1989), Article 8.

between Blackness and danger and violence. The result of norms discouraging anger in societies where Black people are especially susceptible to being perceived as angry is the disproportionate suppression of their speech. Lorde notes that white women go out of their way to preemptively avoid speech by Black women to protect themselves from having to feel like they are the targets of anger. In one of Lorde's examples, a white woman says that she prefers to read work by non-Black women of color so that she can have a rage-free reading experience (160). In Lorde's eyes, the epistemic effect of this is a refusal to encounter Black women's speech at all.

Another, related way that norms discouraging anger get in the way of attending to knowledge claims about oppression is that they provide an excuse for not listening to the content of speech. Lorde explicitly distinguishes the "content" of speech from "the manner of saying" (131) and argues that discomfort with anger allows preoccupation with the latter to get in the way of attending to the former. Lorde does not believe our ability to distinguish tone from content is as reliable as many of us think it is, especially given background social norms and stereotypes. If we believe that worthwhile content can only be expressed coolly, then content that is not expressed coolly, or that is perceived not to be expressed in that way, may not be registered at all. There are at least two ways the norm deflects attention from speech about oppression. First, if, as we have discussed, oppression rightly elicits anger in its victims, norms against expressing anger will have a silencing effect on those who have the correct moral response to oppression. Second, if oppressed individuals are subject to stereotypes and perceptions that code them as angry even when they are not, their speech is less likely to be heard at all.

A final way that norms discouraging anger prevent our arrival at knowledge about social reality has to do with the way fear of anger affects our moral perception. Lorde notes that fear of anger makes us direct our attention to stifling the source of anger, the angry person. This is a problem, for Lorde, because, in cases where anger is righteous, anger should direct our attention to the external cause of anger and to doing something about it. In a world where anger is caused by unjust social structures, the perception of angry *persons* as the cause of negativity can displace our attention from the real, often structural, injustices to which their anger bears witness. Put simply, the desire to stop anger can cause us to locate the source of the anger in an (easy to isolate) person rather than a (more diffuse) set of social conditions. Lorde repeatedly cautions the audiences of her work on anger to remember that Black women's anger is simply not the cause of social ills; it is a justified response to their corrosiveness. In her work on Black women addressed to Black women, she emphasizes the origin of the anger in having to live with years of hatred from a racist society (147–148). She finishes her essay on the anger that women of color feel toward white women by asking why white women fear Black women's anger, when it is clearly not the anger of Black women that is causing sexual violence, militarism, global labor exploitation, and environmental destruction "bent upon the annihilation of us all" (133).

11.4. Conclusion

I opened this chapter by suggesting that Lorde has something to teach us about the norms that should govern our practices of attempting to know social reality. Now that we have seen how she characterizes the actual state of our practices of creating, and sharing, knowledge of social reality, we can see why "public discussion" is likely to fall short in revealing truths about it. Members of oppressed groups need to cultivate epistemic resources for describing their reality, but many of the resources that are available, and most of the resources that are widely *legible*, are selective and distorting. The oppressed are impeded in their quest to fully create (and preserve) such resources because of unjust epistemic labor flows that keep them "preoccupied with the concerns of the dominant," rather than allowing them to ask and explore the questions that they themselves prioritize. Being constantly expected to explain themselves to, and educate, the dominant takes time away from making progress on their own knowledge projects. To make matters worse, when they attempt to communicate to the dominant, norms around anger prevent their speech from getting uptake and the moral wrongs they are diagnosing to be recognized.

To take the project of arriving at collective knowledge about social reality seriously would require abandoning the idea that public discussion can do its job absent changes to our communicative and epistemic norms, including those brought about by social movements (whose work cannot, and should not, reduce to the creation of knowledge or conversation). Lorde recommends that we all accept that righteous anger is going to be a part of speech about injustice. She also notes that there are many situations where members of oppressed groups need to be able to pursue their knowledge projects without constantly having to translate them to the dominant.

One way to do this in society and in the academy is, as Lorde herself was fond of suggesting, to stop making discussions framed in the terms of the dominant be the only ones that get airtime and institutional funding. Lorde also emphasizes the need for all of us to be aware of the lack of transparency in linguistic communication—especially across relations of difference and domination. Sometimes those who are speaking are forced to refract their experiences and claims through concepts that do not do them justice; sometimes they are silent, or conceal the appropriate moral emotions, because this is the price of being heard. In our unequal social world, it is simply not the case that all positions and experiences are equally articulable, or equally capable of achieving shared uptake. We need to create epistemic and communicative norms that acknowledge the background difficulties facing attempts to shed light on the realities of oppression, rather than simply imagine them away. Finding ways to acknowledge the reality of injustice, and to dwell in the epistemic messiness it creates, is for Lorde, the path to a more hopeful future. As she concludes her essay on silence, "The fact that we are here and that I speak these words is an attempt to break . . . silence and bridge some of those differences between us, for it is not difference which immobilizes us, but silence. And there are so many silences to be broken" (44).

Bibliography

Cherkaskey, Catherine (2018). Christine Blasey Ford Is No Poster Child for Women's Rights. *USA Today*. https://www.usatoday.com/story/opinion/voices/2018/10/04/false-accusations-kavanaugh-ford-innocent-column/1488329002/.
Cherry, Myisha. 2021. *The Case for Rage*. New York: Oxford University Press.

Chumley, Cheryl (2018). Michelle Obama: Still Hating after All these Years. *The Washington Times*. https://www.washingtontimes.com/news/2018/nov/13/michelle-obama-still-hating-after-all-these-years/.

De Veaux, Alexis. (2006). *Warrior Poet*. New York: Norton.

Dotson, Kristie (2014). Conceptualizing Epistemic Oppression. *Social Epistemology* 28(2): 115–138.

Gleeson, Jules Joanne (2018). On the Guardian's Transphobic Centrism. *The New Socialist*. https://newsocialist.org.uk/on-the-guardians-transphobic-centrism/.

Jacobs, Tom. 2018. For Black Students, Stereotyping Starts Early. *Pacific Standard*. https://psmag.com/education/for-black-students-stereotyping-starts-early.

Jerald, Morgan C., et al. (2017). Controlling Images: How Awareness of Group Stereotypes Affects Black Women's Well-Being. *Journal of Counseling Psychology* 64(5): 487–499. https://doi.org/10.1037/cou0000233.

Jaggar, Alison, 1988. Love and Knowledge. *Inquiry* 2: 151–176.

Serene J. Khader. (2018). Victims' Stories and the Postcolonial Politics of Empathy. *Metaphilosophy* 49(1–2): 13–26. https://doi.org/10.1111/meta.12289.

Lorde, Audre (1983). *Zami: A New Spelling of My Name*. New York: Kitchen Table Press.

Lorde, Audre (1984). New York: Crossing Press.

Lugones, Maria (1987). Playfulness, World-Traveling and Loving Perception. *Hypatia* 2(2): 2–19.

Manne, Kate (2017). *Down Girl*. New York: Oxford.

Meyers, Diana (2014). Feminism and Sex Trafficking. *Ethical Theory and Moral Practice* 17(3): 427–441.

12

Ethics in Place and Time

Introducing Wub-e-ke-niew's *We Have the Right to Exist: A Translation of Aboriginal Indigenous Thought*

Alexander Guerrero

12.1. Introduction

Much of our day is spent looking at and manipulating various plastic, glass, and metal contraptions that we did not and could not build. We spend most of our time in boxes and enclosed containers of varying sizes. Food appears on shelves in stores. We obtain it from strangers, among strangers. We interact with at most a few different large animals on a regular basis: other human beings, a pet or two, a bird singing on a particularly nice morning. We control the temperature around us with buttons and dials. We take thousands of steps a day, but on concrete, tile, stained wood, more concrete. We live on earth, but not really. We are not connected to land, to places, to other animals. We spend much of our time away from our families, further away still from our extended families. Most of us don't move our bodies very much, but we move regularly from place to place. We live in what we imagine to be a straight line, with our plans and goals and broken progress into and through the future; the past receding, fading, unremembered; and death—an always looming tragedy—ahead. We learn about what has happened before us from books and TV, if we learn about it at all. We don't think of ourselves as having a history. We are basically alone; perhaps we have found another person to connect to, to have children with. We live close to people, but we are not close to them. We stand out on the earth. We leave our mark. We do not live in harmony with the world around us. That world has been killed, contained, sanitized,

Alexander Guerrero, *Ethics in Place and Time* In: *Neglected Classics of Philosophy*. Edited by: Eric Schliesser, Oxford University Press. © Oxford University Press 2022.
DOI: 10.1093/oso/9780190097196.003.0013

paved over, subjugated, dominated to make things easier for us, convenient. This is the modern world.

Most of us have had little direct role in building this world. We were born into it. It is all we know. Without thinking about it, we do our small part to keep it alive—although that is not the right word—day by day. Departures from it strike us as romantic, perhaps even attractive, but also difficult, unfathomable, and not something we could choose. We are deep into these lives. From within them, the world we are in has significant attractions and advantages. I like air conditioning. I hate mosquitoes.

Some philosophers, like poets, take a perfectly ordinary part of our existence and make it seem strange, puzzling, even horrifying. The Ahnishinahbæó'jibway philosopher Wub-e-ke-niew (1928–1997), writing from a life that began in one world and moved into another, does this.

In his epic *We Have the Right to Exist: A Translation of Aboriginal Indigenous Thought* (1995), he presents a distinct philosophical worldview and way of life, that of the Ahnishinahbæó'jibway, and contrasts it with what he calls the Lislakh perspective and way of being in the world. For most of us reading the book, we will recognize the Lislakh perspective as something like our own. Wub-e-ke-niew is like Alexis de Tocqueville writing about America, but in reverse. He's not the visitor here; we are. He is someone who explicitly stands with those who have been here for thousands of years, but who has had to learn the ways of these newcomers, these trespassers. He looks at us with at least part of himself in a different world—able to see us better than we see ourselves.

Like de Tocqueville's classic work, the book is hard to categorize. This is not incidental. As Wub-e-ke-niew puts it, "[t]he Ahnishinahbæó'jibway religious and philosophical tradition, the *Midé*, is holistic—there is no compartmentalization between religion, economics, science, philosophy, and politics" (195). Indeed, he is explicitly critical of the disconnected, fragmented approach to thinking about the world that is embodied in academic and social institutions and disciplinary and professional boundaries. This fragmentation enables a person to go "to Church on Sunday morning, and then [to go] back to destroying the environment again" or to be an "accredited scientist with a Ph.D." but also engage in and justify policies of "irreversible environmental destruction" (94). The holism is evident in the book, as he provides a broadly comprehensive presentation of the Ahnishinahbæó'jibway perspective on a variety of philosophical topics: identity, tradition, language, ethics, space and time, social and political life, and much else. And the book does many other things, too. It is also a partial autobiography; a carefully researched history of centuries of abuse and genocide of the indigenous people of North America at the hands of the United States government, in particular the history and genealogy of Red Lake Reservation and the people he refers to as Ahnishinahbæó'jibway;[1] and a personal and moving account of the way in which forced education and physical abuse by members of the dominant culture attempted to eliminate an entire way of living and thinking about the world. Wub-e-ke-niew is concerned to set the record straight, and he does this as a historian would—with detailed references to records (some even included in the book's appendices), careful footnotes, and a decade of research behind his efforts.

Amidst this recording and documenting, philosophical ideas shine through on almost every page. I will concentrate on two central philosophical themes: (1) the contrast between Lislakh and Ahnishinahbæó'jibway conceptions of time; and (2) the related differences between Lislakh and Ahnishinahbæó'jibway conceptions of ethical life.

It is a remarkable book: blunt, brutal, funny, delightful, meticulous, scholarly, elegant, and engaging. It is hard not to be affected by it. It is also remarkable that it exists at all.

---

[1] This name is important to Wub-e-ke-niew, and he takes "Ojibwe" to be an objectionable, inaccurate alternative. He also refrains from using "Anishinaabe," the standard autonym used by a group of culturally related indigenous peoples resident in what are now Canada and the United States, including the Odawa, Saulteaux, Ojibwe (including Mississaugas), Potawatomi, Oji-Cree, and Algonquin peoples. He argues at length that the "Euro-Americans invented artificial Indian tribes, and gave these tribes names" (3), and that accordingly many of these names and self-identifications are inaccurate and are the result of missionary and Western European influence and efforts to destroy the language and identity of aboriginal indigenous communities. Obviously, this is a controversial position.

12.2. Wub-e-ke-niew and the Ahnishinahbæó'jibway

Wub-e-ke-niew was born in 1928 in his grandfather's log house, "on the shores of Red Lake at Ba-kwa-kwan, where my people of the Bear *Dodem* had lived in birchbark longhouses for many thousands of years" (xxix). His early years were spent with his grandfather, father (his mother died of tuberculosis when he was three), brother, and other extended family living "in *Ahnishinahbæó'jibway* space and time" (xxx). The life he describes there, although not identical to those of his ancestors thousands of years prior, included many deep connections to that life. He references a life full of dark nights of storytelling and elders smoking *kinnikinic*, speaking the Ahnishinahbæó'jibway language, with traditional crops—squash, potatoes, onions, several kinds of beans—being grown and stored underground in long-practiced ways, fishing and hunting, and the basic retention of "our Aboriginal Indigenous self-sufficiency" (xxx–xxxi). And this despite the fact that this life was taking place in what he describes as a "P.O.W. camp"—a large, unmodernized reservation of land that the Ahnishinahbæó'jibway were not allowed to leave.

He was abruptly cast out of this life at the age of seven by three tragedies: the death of his grandfather, his father being placed in a tuberculosis sanitorium, and his being forced into a Catholic boarding school by the US government as part of a compulsory education mandate. As Wub-e-ke-niew describes it, "the U.S. government said that the boarding schools were meant to civilize us, but they intended to destroy us as a people—genocide" (xxxii). He spent nine years in this boarding school, a time of abuse and miseducation, until he eventually ran away, finding work in a number of itinerant jobs until eventually joining the US Army at age eighteen. After leaving the army, he worked as a trucker for almost a decade. During those trucking jobs, he taught himself to read and write in a serious way.

He includes this introductory autobiographical material in the book reluctantly, stating explicitly that it was the product of a compromise with the publisher, rather than something he wanted to include. But it is helpful to understand how he could come to occupy the distinctive philosophical perspective that he does—both as an advocate, expositor, and translator of core Ahnishinahbæóʰjibway ideas, and as a fierce critic of the philosophical worldview of the people he refers to as Lislakh, but which we might refer to simply as white people or white Americans or, really, most Western Europeans and Americans in dominant social positions. "At this point in my life I have the advantage of being able to stand in the context of either culture, and see from both the European and the *Ahnishinahbæóʰjibway* points of view" (xxxi), he writes.

One of the core ideas that emerges from the book is that there is a distinctive perspective, a philosophical worldview, of the dominant group in the United States—a group that he refers to with the neologism *Lislakh*. This is a word which he credits to the linguist Carleton Hodge, used to "refer to the inter-related and historically connected peoples who share societal, cultural, language and/or patrilineal roots within that usually referred to as an abstract entity, Western Civilization" (251). This is a broad category, certainly. The precise breadth isn't as important as the core: these are white people, people with "Western European" ancestry, Euro-Americans, white Americans in particular. Presenting the details of their worldview is a significant part of the book's project. A central part of the identity, as Wub-e-ke-niew describes it, is constituted by absence, ignorance, and self-alienation. He describes them as people who "have been severed from their roots and their own identity" and "who have no name for themselves" (251).

Names and their connection to identity are deeply important to Wub-e-ke-niew. Chapter 1 begins: "We, the *Ahnishinahbæóʰjibway*, are among the Aboriginal Indigenous peoples of this Continent" (1). Throughout the book, he refers to himself and the group of which he is a part as Ahnishinahbæóʰjibway—rejecting (as many do) the terms "Indian," "American Indian," and "Native American" as Lislakh impositions intended to control, erase, and render ignorant Aboriginal Indigenous people. More strikingly, he is equally disdainful of group names like "Chippewa," "Métis," and "Ojibwe," which he also sees as Lislakh creations, often the direct result of agreements with and regulations from the federal government of the United States and the Bureau of Indian Affairs. None of this is innocent, according to Wub-e-ke-niew:

Western European stereotypes and labels are used to create *identities* which prescribe behavior for those who accept these external definitions as a description of themselves, pre-empting their own knowledge of who they are. . . . Labelling is done to maintain the hierarchical class system, so that the Western European elite can continue to live a life of luxury at the expense of everybody else. (97–98)

The politics of this is complicated and personal. Many people embrace the labels "Native American" and "American Indian" as describing their identity, and many embrace "Ojibwe" and similar tribal designations more specifically. Wub-e-ke-niew's unsparing tone on this front might be off-putting or worse to some, and there is a politics of authenticity that is troubling, and might be very troubling, if that were Wub-e-ke-niew's central project. This seems an uncharitable interpretation of his main point, even if he does sometimes veer into a kind of purism ("[o]f the nearly eight thousand people presently defined by the United States Government as members of the Red Lake Band of Chippewa Indians, only about two hundred are *Ahnishinahbæó'jibway* . . . the rest are White and Métis people trapped by the Indian identity" [xxv]). His main point is that understanding and, in some cases, reclaiming and returning to, traditional Aboriginal Indigenous ways of living, thinking, speaking, and self-conceiving is of paramount importance. He is stridently and powerfully against adaptation to the modern Lislakh world and perspective, against thinking of being Native American as just being another kind of minority group. As he puts it, "The *Ahnishinah bæó'jibway* are completely outside of the Lislakh systems. We are not a minority, no matter how few our numbers, and we remain a Nation on our own land" (xliv).

The book is his attempt to offer the first presentation of the actual Ahnishinahbæó'jibway perspective, not something filtered through a Lislakh perspective, ideas of "Native Americans," or new-age wisdom literature that might offer Lislakh people a respite from the Lislakh world they have constructed. The omnipresence and dominance of that perspective, however, means that he knows much of his audience will have that perspective in mind as they read his words. So, the project ends up having two core aims: (1) to articulate and make known the Ahnishinahbæó'jibway perspective; and (2) to make visible the often obscured moral and metaphysical commitments of the Lislakh, the Western, the Euro-American, the white people who do not know who they are, and whose perspective on the world has become the dominant one in many places. The rest of this chapter will detail and explore the contrasts that Wub-e-ke-niew draws between the Ahnishinahbæó'jibway and Lislakh perspectives with respect to two large topics: time and ethics.

12.3. Ahnishinahbæó'jibway Time

Wub-e-ke-niew describes his early years with his extended family living "in *Ahnishinahbæó'jibway* space and time" (xxx). Several sections of the book expand on the differences between Ahnishinahbæó'jibway and Lislakh conceptions of time, and the connection between time and place. You may have noticed the "time" in the above quotation. Wub-e-ke-niew uses "time"—as distinct from "time"—to mark the difference between the Ahnishinahbæó'jibway concept from that of the Lislakh (roughly, Western European) concept of time. Throughout the book, Wub-e-ke-niew is focused more on the phenomenology of time, or the shared social conception of time, rather than the metaphysics of time, although it is an interesting question how these interrelate.

As Wub-e-ke-niew describes it, for the Lislakh, time is linear, precisely measured, characterized by a detached past, a definite if distant beginning (whether the Big Bang or some moment of creation), and an implied end. Individuals experience an "utter lack of hope" (87) at the thought of their inevitable death. They avoid thinking much about the future. In some fairly real sense, "time is money . . . [m]oney and time are a part of the same thing" (89)—an abstract thing that we measure carefully, tracking the orderly, linear, drip, dripping away of these units of value until they are gone and we are gone. Time does not accumulate in us or strengthen us; it ravages us and slips away. Rather than being more valuable with age, then, we live in a society in which we have been "manipulated by corporate advertisers in the media to idolize youth," so that we "become convinced that the young know more than their elders" (86). The past "vanishes into obscurity," with history becoming "what they describe as the dead past, hypothetical and in a sense perennially unknowable, inaccessible in the abstract" (86). For the Lislakh, "time is fragmented, splintered into mechanically defined seconds and minutes and hours, boxed into externally imposed segmented days on a blank calendar, defined without dimension or texture" (87). Time for the Lislakh is not connected to place, it is something that we assume moves along completely independently of us or of the living world. Einsteinian ideas of spacetime, on which the three dimensions of space are fused with the one dimension of time into a single four-dimensional manifold, are now generally accepted as the correct scientific view, but remain deeply foreign to ordinary thinking about time.

This conception of time is, fundamentally, sad, precise, mechanical, indifferent, and terrifying. Wub-e-ke-niew suggests that walking around with it in our heads leads Lislakh people to act without thought for the future (and certainly not the distant future) and without regard to the past; to live "in the moment," stuffing ourselves full of distracting pleasures, or to tell and believe stories in which we have infinite amounts of time. Those of us who do not manage these things, or who briefly let our guard down, are left with a feeling that Philip Larkin aptly characterizes in his "Aubade":

> Waking at four to soundless dark, I stare.
> In time the curtainedges will grow light.
> Till then I see what's really always there:
> Unresting death, a whole day nearer now,
> Making all thought impossible but how
> And where and when I shall myself die.
> . . .
>
> And so it stays just on the edge of vision,
> A small unfocused blur, a standing chill
> That slows each impulse down to indecision.
> Most things may never happen: this one will,
> And realisation of it rages out
> In furnacefear when we are caught without
> People or drink. Courage is no good:
> It means not scaring others. Being brave

> Lets no one off the grave.
> Death is no different whined at than withstood.[2]

If asked, many of us would describe this as the clear-eyed, unblinkered way to understand the world. That is just our situation. This is just what time is like. To Wub-e-ke-niew, this is "a morbid declaration of complete powerlessness and utter lack of hope, a pathological symptom of linear time" (87). That is not because there is some afterlife or heaven further down the line. It is because this is the wrong way to understand time.

Time, or, better, ţime, is not a line; it is a circle. It's hard for those of us who are deeply within the Lislakh perspective to get away from our conception of time. Two things might help.

First, think of seasons. If one concentrates on the seasons that one would experience in a place like Red Lake—hot buggy summer, rich colorful autumn, bone cold winter, melting awakening spring—what one feels is not a line, marching toward death, but a circle. Going around the block, not leaving town. There is no sense of linear progress or advancement or forward motion; the idea of being somehow ahead of those who lived before for us or in a different place than them. And what we measure is not mechanical, detached from us and from life. To the contrary, we notice time moving because of what we feel, what we see, what we touch and smell. Our experience of time is an experience of life and of what even we call life cycles: growing, reproducing, giving birth to new life, dying, decomposing, becoming part of some new thing growing. Imagine how it would feel if we did not number the years, if we did not mechanically count seconds, minutes, and hours.

Second, think of nostalgia, in particular, the feeling one has returning to, say, one's childhood neighborhood, or college town, or the first apartment you had after leaving home. Imagine walking around those places. Being in a place, in *this* place, one is returned—emotionally, mentally—to a time. There is a way in which experiences of a particular time are deeply intertwined with particular places. Now imagine—as is perhaps, but not likely to be, the case—that you have spent your whole life in the same basic places. Walking on the same

[2] Philip Larkin, *Collected Poems* (New York, NY: Farrar, Straus and Giroux, 2001).

paths, through the same woods, noticing the same particular trees. Wading and washing in the same river, running over the same rocks. Looking out at the same hills. And imagine that not only have you spent your whole life there, but so did your parents, and their parents, and their parents, back dozens or even hundreds of generations. This is where your parents met. This is where your uncle fell and broke his leg. This is the place you were told your grandmother saw and named a turtle. This is where your great-great-great-grandfather learned to fish as a boy. But all these markers happened in the same physical places—and they are the places that you see and spend time in, and learn in great detail about, and live in, and come to love. Time, then, or time, would not feel detached from place, would not seem to be some placeless abstract thing. It would not be like: OK, so, it was April 1997, so I was still in Los Angeles—where this requires a kind of complex mental calculation where one matches the measured time with one's own physical location in the world. Time would be more intimately grounded, placed. We might even find it natural to talk about space-time, or, perhaps better: timespace.

I am not sure that these suggestions provide a fully accurate way into understanding the Ahnishinahbæó'jibway conception of time. Something like them is suggested by Wub-e-ke-niew, who writes that in Ahnishinahbæó'jibway time, "the circle always comes around, and the past is never gone," that "time is perennial and unending, harmonized with the cycles of the seasons, flowing as an inseparable part of reality," and that "time is intrinsically life and death, Grandmother Earth, Grandfather *Midé*" (87). Some of these phrases are familiar ("the circle always comes around"), but are also typically understood in some supernatural way having to do with reincarnation, ideas of karma or cosmic justice, and so on. That is clearly not the view. Wub-e-ke-niew suggests a picture that is naturalistic, but also unfamiliar:

> Aboriginal Indigenous time has absolutely nothing to do with hours and minutes. We are on our own land, and our time is ancient and inseparable from our land. The meaning of the *Midé* title of my great-grandfather, Bah-se-nos, is in part in honor of time, the four seasons and the four directions. In European time, he has been dead for more than ninety years, and is therefore gone, forgotten. In *Ahnishinahbæ*

> *ó'jibway* time, Bah-se-nos is present and real, along with the phases
> of the moon, the intricate harmony of the time of the flowering and
> fruiting of each plant, the fleging of birds and the metamorphosis
> of insects, the time of making sugar, the time of dreams, the time of
> harvesting *mahnomen*. (90)

It is hard to imagine a perspective that is further from that of Larkin's.
It is also hard, coming from something like Larkin's perspective, to feel
confident that one has fully understood this alternative perspective, or
that one has not simply reduced it to some other, more mystical or supernatural set of ideas. And Wub-e-ke-niew was concerned that these
ideas might prove deeply elusive to those raised in a Lislakh world with
a Lislakh worldview as I was (and as you probably were, too). I do find
them elusive and puzzling, but also interesting and powerful, particularly when taken together: that the proper spatial metaphor for time
is a circle, not a line; the connection of time to place; the connection
of time to life and life processes, rather than to anything abstract or
artificial; the rejection of the idea that that which has existed before is
gone, dead, causally inert; the acceptance of the idea that our life has
consequences far into the future; the interconnection of time, place,
and life all as part of inseparable reality.

One question that we might consider, when comparing the Lislakh
concept of time and the Ahnishinahbæó'jibway concept of time, is
how we might decide which concept is the one that should be endorsed
or embraced—which concept is *better*. One route to go is to ask which
better captures reality—which is *true* (or something like that). And
there are further questions to ask about how the phenomenology
or social conception of time interacts with what we should believe
about the metaphysics of time. I hope others take those questions up.
Another kind of question, arguably related, is which concept is such
that embracing it, having people adopt it, raising people with it, and so
forth, produces better *results*.[3] (Raising the important further question
of how we should evaluate results.)

---

[3] For useful general discussion of one way of framing these issues, see the introduction and papers in A. Burgess, H. Cappelen and D. Plunkett (eds.), *Conceptual Ethics and
Conceptual Engineering* (Oxford: Oxford University Press, 2019).

There is a powerful case for the Ahnishinahbæó'jibway concept of time on both counts. Wub-e-ke-niew clearly thinks that the Lislakh concept of time is bad both for people on an individual level and for the world on a global scale, not just because it leads them to personal despair like Larkin, but also because of how it leads them to act. What I want to consider next, then, are the implications of this view of time on how we should live, taking up, in particular, the Ahnishinahbæó'jibway ethical view described by Wub-e-ke-niew.

12.4. Ahnishinahbæó'jibway Ethics

On a certain naturalistic, scientific picture of the world (informed by work on ecosystems and complex dynamical systems, for example) some Ahnishinahbæó'jibway ideas about time—the claims about interconnection and far-reaching consequences—should seem familiar and attractive (in theory, if not in our actual practices). A number of philosophers and scholars of Indigenous knowledge and Indigenous environmental movements have demonstrated the importance and usefulness of Indigenous thought regarding what we might in English call "environmental stewardship" or "caretaking" or "sustainability," as well as Indigenous knowledge and science regarding the complex relationships that exist in the natural world.[4] Many have pointed out that this seems to be something that the Lislakh (or the extensionally equivalent groups) have gotten badly wrong, as we now start to open our eyes to the horror of environmental degradation and climate disaster that we have created over the past few hundred years.

Wub-e-ke-niew is highly critical of the Lislakh way of life, informed by widely shared Lislakh ethical views—both of which he takes to be an outgrowth of the Lislakh conception of time. He argues that it is

---

[4] For classic work in this tradition, see the work of the Tewa philosopher Gregory Cajete, *Native Science: Natural Laws of Interdependence* (Santa Fe, NM: Clear Light, 2000). See also the extensive body of work by the Potawatomi philosopher Kyle Whyte, including, for example, Weaving Indigenous Science, Protocols and Sustainability Science, *Sustainability Science* 11(1) (2016): 25–32, coauthored with J. P. Brewer and J. T. Johnson; as well as the work of the Climate and Traditional Knowledges Workgroup, including their 2014 report, Guidelines for Considering Traditional Knowledges in Climate Change Initiatives, available at https://climatetkw.wordpress.com/guidelines/.

because we see ourselves as coming from nowhere and always heading into nonexistence that we are prone to not thinking about the future or about the consequences of what we are doing, except in the most short-term way imaginable. As he puts it,

> The Western Europeans become detached from their continuity in time and thus seemingly insulated from their history, encapsulated in a present reality which has been severed at its roots.... I have spent a time studying the White man, and have heard him use the motto, "Eat, Drink, and Be Merry, for tomorrow we may die." . . . From an *Ahnishinahbæó'jibway* perspective, this is a very strange thing to say . . . their assertion which has endured for a millennium that "The World Will End" . . . enables brutal hierarchy to exist by warping time, and deludes their subject peoples into both a terrible hopelessness and sense of futility. (86–87)

The two basic failings, according to Wub-e-ke-niew, are (1) a failure to realize that we are fundamentally connected both synchronically and diachronically with everything, and (2) a failure to appreciate that we are not different than—not distinct or detached from, nor better or more important than—other living things. The Lislakh are prone both to a short-term, atomistic ethical perspective, and to an exceptionalist, speciesist, hierarchical ethical perspective. These two fundamentally false views have combined to disastrous effect, so that in only a few hundred years (a blink in terms of human history, and not even close to that in terms of geologic time), we may have managed to make earth nearly unlivable for us and for many of the other living things that share the planet with us. And it is no exaggeration to say, as Wub-e-ke-niew does, that this emanates directly from the Lislakh perspective, with its license and encouragement toward control, domination, hierarchy, colonization, exploitation, and the use of violence to subjugate people or creatures who stand in the way of the pursuit of short-term pleasure, power, wealth, and a more and more slothful, inactive, inattentive existence.

What is perhaps most striking is that while all this has been happening over the past four- or five-hundred years, the Lislakh have at the same time convinced themselves (ourselves) of their unrivaled enlightenment, civilization, and ethical progress. As a philosopher, I feel this acutely: How is it that philosophical ethics of the past several hundred years has missed or even intentionally ignored so much that is so obviously troubling about the Lislakh way of life? That's to paint with a broad brush, of course. In the remainder of this section, I want to draw out some of the implications of Wub-e-ke-niew's discussion of the Ahnishinahbæó'jibway and Lislakh ethical perspectives for several issues in theoretical ethics. It is hard to know how much "trickle-down" influence philosophical discussions of ethics are capable of having, but it is possible that seeing some of these issues differently might be significant. This might be part of Wub-e-ke-niew's project in writing the book, combined with his highly tempered optimism that, maybe we, the Lislakh, "will end up adopting some of the Aboriginal Indigenous peoples' culture" so that "[m]aybe [the Lislakh] will become civilized, after all" (72).

The dominant ethical perspectives in Western, Lislakh philosophical ethics include Kantian deontology, various nearby contractualist (or relational) views, Aristotelian or Neo-Aristotelian virtue ethics, and consequentialist views. These first three share a number of components that are in significant tension with the Ahnishinahbæó'jibway perspective as presented and defended by Wub-e-ke-niew. Interestingly, the Ahnishinahbæó'jibway view has significant resonance with consequentialist views and provides improvements and insights that might be brought into useful dialogue with those views. What I say here will of necessity be only suggestive and gestural, but my hope is that it will make evident the value in exploring Wub-e-ke-niew's presentation and defense of the Ahnishinahbæó'jibway perspective.

Let us begin with the differences. First, Kantian deontology, contractualist or relational ethical views,[5] and Aristotelian virtue-focused views all focus in central ways on the beliefs, intentions, reasons, motives, dispositions, maxims, plans, and character of individual agents. They look predominantly at what is going on inside of

---

[5] Here I have in mind, most prominently, Thomas Scanlon, *What We Owe to Each Other* (Cambridge, MA: Harvard University Press, 1998); Stephen Darwall, *The Second-Person Standpoint: Morality, Respect, and Accountability* (Cambridge, MA: Harvard University Press, 2006); and R. Jay Wallace, *The Moral Nexus* (Cambridge, MA: Harvard University Press, 2019).

agents as those agents think and feel and react and act—rather than what is going on outside in the world. Of course, even for those views, what actually happens matters. But it is not at the center. These are *inside-ethics* ethical theories. Second, these views all focus on human beings, or the nearly extensionally equivalent "persons," interacting with other persons. The ethical focus is limited to different ways of treating and interacting with persons: thinking of them this way rather than that, treating them only this way and never that way, thinking about how and whether one could justify one's actions to them, thinking about what we owe to them, making claims of each other, asking how would I feel if a person treated me in those ways, and so on. Non-persons might factor in at various points, in various ways, but in different, almost always categorically less significant, ways.[6] These are *person-first* ethical perspectives. Third, these views suggest that ethical assessment of an agent acting at a time is possible either at the very moment of action, or shortly thereafter—after the action has caused an intended or foreseen or "reasonably" foreseeable set of consequences (where what is "reasonable" is often indexed to the agent's subjective perspective and local community norms). What matters, ethically, are the short-term effects of the agent's action (and, particularly, the effects on other persons), what we might call the *local causal contribution*; or the relatively short-term things that the agent was trying to bring about, which they foresaw might be brought about, or which they "should" have foreseen (allowing for a bit of assessment of certain kinds of negligence and recklessness). These are *causally restricted* ethical perspectives. Drawing these threads together might make it evident how one could see "ethical" people involved in factory farming, massive but (unintended and unforeseen!) environmental degradation through industrialization, and even "well-intentioned" but deeply racist and prejudiced colonization and "civilizing" projects.

---

[6] For recent relevant discussions aimed at defending or modifying these views in various ways on this front, see Martha Nussbaum, *Frontiers of Justice: Disability, Nationality, Species Membership* (Cambridge, MA: Harvard University Press, 2007); Christine Korsgaard, *Fellow Creatures: Our Obligations to the Other Animals* (Oxford: Oxford University Press, 2018); Shelly Kagan, *How to Count Animals, More or Less* (Oxford: Oxford University Press, 2019).

Consequentialist theories—at least in their most common guises—are, by contrast, not inside-ethics, person-first, or causally restricted. Consequentialist ethical theories suggest that we should be concerned, ethically speaking, with the effects of our actions, and all of the effects of our actions—not just those that we might have been intending or even foreseeing when acting. Nor are effects on persons the only relevant effects—although there is typically a limitation to effects on creatures that are sentient, conscious, capable of feeling pain and pleasure.

The Ahnishinahbæó'jibway perspective that Wub-e-ke-niew describes is not any kind of maximizing consequentialist view, as there is no suggestion that right action requires doing what will bring about the best consequences, however defined. But there are powerful connections here with consequentialist views with respect to the rejection of an inside-ethics, person-first, causally restricted ethical perspective. The non-hierarchical, non-speciesist, non-anthropocentric, naturalistic, causally interconnected picture of what matters, morally, is an attractive component of consequentialist thinking—even if many resist the maximizing demands. Those elements appear in an attractive form in Wub-e-ke-niew's description of the Ahnishinahbæó'jibway ethical perspective, where "harmony," rather than maximizing utility, emerges as the proper aim of ethical living. He writes:

> In the ancient religious philosophy of the *Ahnishinahbæó'jibway*, life is based on a circle: a circle of equals rather than a hierarchy, inter-connected spheres of life in harmony with each other. . . . There are no words for war, or peace, in the *Ahnishinahbæó'jibway* language. There is no word for God, no word for Devil. . . . for us all time, all thought and all action, is within the non-violent context of Grandfather *Midé* and Grandmother Earth. Our land and our forests are, and have always been, an integral part of our religion, our philosophy and our very identity as *Ahnishinahbæó'jib way*. (34–35)

One could, with some distortion, recast this view as a kind of constrained consequentialism, with the good to be brought about the good of harmony with all living things, and the constraints being connected to the use of violence.[7] I don't want to put forward that version of the view, but I do want to offer a sketch of the ethical view that emerges from Wub-e-ke-niew's book.

[7] There are questions we might ask about what Wub-e-ke-niew asserts here and elsewhere throughout the book concerning (a) the historical reality regarding Ahnishinahbæó'jibway life and culture, (b) the Ahnishinahbæó'jibway language, and the relation these have with (c) the normative ideals or ethical theory of the Ahnishinahbæó'jibway and (d) Wub-e-ke-niew's own views about normative ideals and ethical theory. Wub-e-ke-niew is clear that he takes the language to be evidence for both the historical reality and the normative ideals. As he puts it:

> Ahnishinahbæó'jibway language is more than words. It is the totality of communication in several dimensions of reality. . . . All languages have embedded in them the ways in which the native speakers of that language understand and interact with the world. Each language contains the history and the values of the people whose language it is. . . . The Ahnishinahbæó'jibway language is balanced, both male and female, non-violent, egalitarian. Our Aboriginal Indigenous language is the compiled wisdom of hundreds of thousands of generations of our people. (215)

He is equally clear that the Ahnishinahbæó'jibway language is not identical to or even close to the "Chippewa" or "Ojibway" (or "Ojibwe") language. He writes, "Chippewa has never been an Aboriginal Indigenous language," and notes that "[t]he book which is mislabeled A Dictionary of the Ojibway Language is really a Chippewa dictionary, and has the tracks of missionaries all over it" (234). It is harder to know what Wub-e-ke-niew would say about The Ojibwe People's Dictionary project (which was started right around the time of his death), or what he would say, for example, about the fact that that dictionary offers "miigaadiwin" as equivalent to the English word "battle" or "war," or that it offers "gizhe-manidoo" as equivalent to the English word "God." See The Ojibwe People's Dictionary at https://ojibwe.lib.umn.edu/. But it is certainly possible to imagine that he would be similarly skeptical of this project as capturing the actual Ahnishinahbæó'jibway language or even a genuine Aboriginal Indigenous language. These questions of linguistic relationship I leave to others with actual knowledge and skill relevant to answering them.

Still, this leaves us with other questions, none of which I am going to attempt to answer here, but which seem like excellent questions for others to take up. One is the question of what we should make of his strong claims about what languages show about history and culture and values. One certainly hears echoes of the Sapir-Whorf hypothesis, much debated (and largely derided) by linguists and psychologists, and which has now been defended in something of a weaker form. See, for example, the introduction and a number of the chapters in Dedre Gentner and Susan Goldin-Meadow's edited volume, Language in Mind: Advances in the Study of Language and Thought (Cambridge, MA: MIT Press, 2003). There are also clear resonances with J. L. Austin's defenses of "ordinary language" philosophy: "our common stock of words embodies all the distinctions men have found worth drawing, and the connexions they have found worth marking, in the lifetimes of many generations: these surely are likely to be more numerous, more sound, since they have stood up to the long test of the survival of the fittest, and more subtle, at least in all ordinary and reasonably practical matters, than any that you or I are likely to think up in our armchairs of an afternoon." J. L. Austin, A Plea for Excuses, Proceedings of the Aristotelian Society, New Series, 57 (1956–1957): 1–30. Of course, Austin also goes on to say that "ordinary language is not the last word," something that seems to concord with Wub-e-ke-niew's own views here. Language might reveal some of the worldview, but it is not a justification or defense of that worldview.

The basic components are something like this:

INTERCONNECTION: all living things in a contained ecosystem (like Earth, and at much smaller scale, too) are causally interrelated and interconnected in complex ways.

HARMONY: when this interrelation and interconnection are sustainably beneficial for living things within the ecosystem, we can describe it as being in a state of harmony.

ETHICAL EVALUATION OF ACTIONS: actions are to be evaluated in large part, if not solely, based on their consequences with respect

A second question concerns what we should think about his specific claims about Ahnishinahbæó'jibway language, culture, and history. Some of what he says is based on claims about the Ahnishinahbæó'jibway language, but much else is based on his own early experiences and in particular on the testimony and education provided to him by his family and extended community. There are some moments when it is clear that he is setting out the Ahnishinahbæó'jibway normative ideals, without making further claims that they were always or consistently lived up to in practice. But in other moments he says stronger things about thousands of years of actual harmonious, nonviolent, warless existence. With very good reason, Wub-e-ke-niew is wary of those academics and other outsiders—historians, anthropologists, archaeologists, social workers—who have brought their Lislakh perspective with them while studying and writing about Aboriginal Indigenous groups like the Ahnishinahbæó'jibway. Much of this work has been terrible—from both an epistemic and moral vantage point. More recent, perhaps better work, done with and by Aboriginal Indigenous people, certainly holds out more promise for helping us to evaluate these claims. Given what we are learning about the historical record and incredibly long time-span during which Aboriginal Indigenous groups lived in particular places through what we now call North America (see note 11 below), I am inclined to view my own Lislakh, skeptical perspective on the possibility of extended nonviolent, warless, non-hierarchical, egalitarian, sustainable social living with suspicion. It's not as if Hobbes presented any evidence for his claims about "human nature." And it does seem that the historical record supports the view that many Aboriginal Indigenous groups did exist in some of these very places for thousands of years prior to the arrival of Western Europeans. But this is an interesting and important question for further inquiry by people better placed to do this work than I am.

A final question concerns whether and how the historical claims matter. Wub-e-ke-niew is clearly articulating an ethical view. It would definitely seem to be a point in favor of that view if wide-scale adoption of that view had in fact been both possible and causally responsible for thousands of years of nonviolent, egalitarian, sustainable, harmonious existence of communities of significant numbers of people. But that is not the only argument in favor of the view. And it could be an attractive ethical view even if no one has ever lived up to its requirements, particularly given that it does not seem to include any components that make it in principle impossible or even unreasonably difficult to live up to its requirements. So, I am inclined to see the historical claims as very powerful if true, but I don't think the interest of the view turns on them. By saying that, I in no way intend to imply that I doubt the historical claims—let me say that explicitly to cancel any possible implicature.

to harmony—do they promote and sustain harmony, or do they threaten and undermine harmony?

NO CAUSAL RESTRICTIONS: whether an action promotes or threatens harmony is a function of its full causal effects.

ALL THINGS MATTER: all living things matter, morally.

These seem to be central parts of the Ahnishinahbæó'jibway view as presented by Wub-e-ke-niew.

With this much of the picture in view, some further questions arise naturally. Do all living things matter *equally*? On one interpretation, the reason all living things matter is *because* of INTERCONNECTION, perhaps in combination with some principle of uncertainty and acknowledgment of our epistemic limitation: we don't know which things will end up having effects on which other things. This would be something of an instrumental version of the view. But that doesn't seem well grounded in the text. Wub-e-ke-niew writes, for example:

> In my great-grandfather's time, old growth forests covered more than half of this Continent, from the Atlantic Ocean to the tallgrass prairies west of the Mississippi. The trees rose to meet the skies, and the sentience of these ancient living beings was a part of our *Ahnishinahbœó 'jibway* community, part of the seamless continuity of time. (91–92)

The view seems to be that all living things matter morally, that there is no hierarchy of importance, and that this is because all living things have intrinsic or final significance.[8] It might even be getting the view wrong to focus overly much on discrete individual living things as having intrinsic or final significance. It might be that even this fails to appreciate the truly seamless continuity that exists as a result of interconnection, so that what matters morally is somehow both the

---

[8] Wub-e-ke-niew attributes "sentience" to the old growth forest trees and suggests that this sentience was a part of the community. Some readers might find this implausible, but in addition to reading the book under discussion here, I would also recommend to them Peter Wohlleben's *The Hidden Life of Trees* (Vancouver, BC: Greystone Books, 2015), which at least makes evident the sheer interest and complexity of forests and the trees that comprise them. They might not satisfy some criteria for "sentience" focused on by philosophers, but they might also suggest the need to rethink that focus when thinking about what matters, morally.

harmony of the whole and the way each individual entity participates in that whole. These are hard issues both at an interpretive and theoretical level, and there is not room to resolve them here.[9]

There is an interesting view—although probably not the Ahnishinahbæó'jibway view—that ends up with non-hierarchical moral egalitarianism but through instrumentalist considerations. On this view, egalitarian commitments arise from the empirical facts about INTERCONNECTION, not a theoretical view about moral status. We all matter equally because we all have an equally important role in the ecosystem—or because we all stand in equal or nearly equal relations of dependence on and vulnerability to other living things. It is precisely the instrumental picture that yields the egalitarianism, rather than some non-instrumental intrinsic/final good view that generates the egalitarianism.

At one point in time, many readers of this—human beings, all of you—might have scoffed at the suggestion of mutual vulnerability and dependence. Surely, we human beings can use and control and dominate as we see fit! Those other creatures might depend on us (and our generosity or goodwill), but the reverse is surely not true! But I assume few readers feel nearly as confidently independent now.

I want to make two other points—both about connections between epistemic concerns and moral ones. It is a common objection to "causally unrestricted" ethical views like consequentialism that they cannot serve as a decision procedure by which we can decide what to do, because, from our limited epistemic vantage point, we do not know what the full long-term (and long-long-long term) consequences of our actions will be.[10] I have always taken this to be a serious objection to consequentialism as an ethical theory. But Wub-e-ke-niew's articulation of the Ahnishinahbæó'jibway view and way of life suggests an

---

[9] For recent work taking up some of these issues from an Indigenous Native American perspective, see Brian Burkhart, *Indigenizing Philosophy through the Land: A Trickster Methodology for Decolonizing Environmental Ethics and Indigenous Futures* (Lansing, MI: Michigan State University Press, 2019), particularly chapters 4 through 6.

[10] A somewhat subtler and perhaps more profound version of the objection suggests that consequentialism can't even be correct as a criterion of the rightness of actions, on the grounds that it would seem to leave open or epistemically uncertain the rightness (or wrongness) of actions for which we are certain of the action's status as right or wrong. For discussion, see James Lenman, Consequentialism and Cluelessness, *Philosophy & Public Affairs* 29(4) (Autumn, 2000): 342–370.

important kind of response on behalf of causally unrestricted views; namely, whether we can know (or at least have justified beliefs) about the long-long-long term consequences of our actions depends on the context in which we take those actions, as well as on the extent to which those actions are in an important sense unprecedented or not. The combination of INTERCONNECTION and NO CAUSAL RESTRICTIONS might seem to suggest an impossible epistemic demand: having to come to know or have reasonable and justified views about all of the consequences of one's actions across a wide range of domains. In the modern context, in reacting to consequentialism, we do often act like this is impossible—and we have created a world in which it might be. But it is worth reflecting on that.

Imagine someone in Wub-e-ke-niew's situation, or perhaps better, that of his great-grandparents. They had been living in a way, and in a particular place, that they knew to be basically the same as those of their parents, and their grandparents, and their great-grandparents— back for thousands of years. Wub-e-ke-niew writes:

> *Ahnishinahbæó'jibway* understanding of space, place, and land is different from that of the Euro-Americans. We have a permanent relationship with specific places, defined partly in terms of our permaculture. My people of the Bear *Dodem* had a certain sugarbush, where we tapped our trees, made our sugar from one year to the next. We harvested and processed our *mahnomen* in the same place, century after century. Our permanent residences—our community of longhouses—had been in the same place for millennia. There were specific places where we fished, where our gardens were, where we hunted, where our fruits and nuts and medicines and everything else that we needed were maintained by our people. . . . *This* land, right here, is where my many-times-great-grandfather of the Bear *Dodem* was born about 27,000 B.C., where he lived and died. . . . This land is the open, living textbook of *Ahnishinahbæó'jibway* history, values, philosophy and religion. . . . (3–4)

The *Midé*, the comprehensive religion/philosophy of the Ahnishinahbæó'jibway, is described by Wub-e-ke-niew as providing a way of acting toward harmony. He says of it:

> The *Midé* is so vast, it's impossible to describe how it makes me feel, but one of the words which comes to mind is humility. The *Midé* is a compilation of the wisdom of my people over the course of about a million years, as well as the tools for understanding reality. (8)

This body of knowledge, combined with the facts of deep connection to particular, specific places,[11] makes the consequences of one's actions—if one learns, and listens, and follows—considerably less uncertain. At least if the overall ethical focus is not dominated by focus on the potentially unpredictable and messy details of human interpersonal interactions, but is concerned in a broader way with HARMONY, taking that to be of central ethical importance in the evaluation of actions or character. It then seems that a causally unrestricted ethical theory might not be implausible—either as a decision procedure or a criterion of rightness—at least given certain background social conditions. But it would also seem to motivate a duty or ethical responsibility to create and preserve social conditions that would make morally good action possible, even acknowledging our non-omniscience and epistemic limitations.

The second point concerning connections between ethical and epistemic concerns is closely related. Once one accepts an ethical view on which all things matter, all things are interconnected, and the effects of one's actions matter in a causally unrestricted way, it makes evident the corresponding need for high epistemic sensitivity and observation of the world around oneself, and the importance of proceeding with

---

[11] There are ongoing archaeological and anthropological debates about how long people have been living in what is now called North America. The Bering Strait Theory, which suggests that people arrived via a land bridge across the Bering Strait, had people migrating for the first time around 13,000 years ago, and now seems clearly false—at least if suggested as the first arrival of human beings on the continent. There is extensive evidence that there have been people in North and South American since at least 15,000 years ago, before the land bridge would have been passable. And there is evidence that suggests people might have been present even as much as 20,000 or 30,000 years ago—although it is harder to be sure given the archaeological traces and limited record. Many Indigenous groups—not just the Ahnishinahbæótjibway—claim historical, generational continuity for tens of thousands of years. For an overview of some of the evidence and debates, see Craig Childs, *Atlas of a Lost World: Travels in Ice Age America* (New York, NY: Pantheon, 2018).

caution when breaking with precedent in dramatic ways. Importantly, what we need to know about isn't just other people, or how what we are doing might affect them. All knowledge—including what we might call scientific knowledge or knowledge of the natural world—becomes essential to acting ethically. Indeed, many Indigenous and Native American philosophers stress that "all knowledge" is properly directed at "finding the proper moral and ethical road upon which human beings should walk."[12] Unfortunately, many of us, as I suggested in the opening, are significantly closed off from the natural world, from the way in which our actions produce and sustain disharmony. There is not an easy route from where we are to anything like the deeply placed existence that Wub-e-ke-niew describes. Although we are all interconnected, we have acted in horribly short-sighted ways, and our survival, along with the survival of many other living things, is connected in complicated ways to whole systems of life and environment that we are coming to understand too late.

Wub-e-ke-niew and other Indigenous philosophers have been making these points long before "climate change" and the "Anthropocene" were a part of our vocabulary. There is a powerful case that if we are assessing which worldview—both in terms of the conception of time and the conception of ethics—is "better," in terms of producing better results, the Ahnishinahbæó'jibway perspective is better. Wub-e-ke-niew makes this point starkly in some of the closing words of the book:

> The abundant permaculture, the magnificent forests, the pristine waters and the multitude of other beings who lived in harmony with *Ahnishinahbæó'jibway* and other Aboriginal Indigenous people, are the embodiment of our language, our culture, our egalitarian values, and our thought and our ways of life. Western European civilization has had five hundred years on this Continent to prove the "superiority" that they asserted when they

---

[12] Vine Deloria in *Spirit and Reason: The Vine Deloria, Jr., Reader*, ed. Kristen Foehner, Sam Scinta, and Barbara Deloira (Golden, CO: Fulcrum, 1999), 43. See also Burkhart (2019), 251–257, for further discussion.

first came here. The ecosystem is shattered, their cities are ripped by violence, and the American Dream has always been an illusion for many. . . . . If there is to be hope for anybody in the future, we have to work together to recreate a network of harmonious societies which provide for all people. (242–243)

12.5. A Neglected Classic

This volume encourages reflection on what it is for something to be a "classic" and what it is for something to be "neglected."

I don't know what makes something a classic. For my taste, it seems as if it should have something to do with how perspective-altering the work is—perhaps for how many people it is perspective-altering also matters, although maybe we all care primarily about a work's effect on us. Perspective alteration is a function of not only how different the ideas are from one's own (how creative, imaginative, and perhaps simply unfamiliar), but also how compelling those ideas are. That will make "classic" status relative to one's own perspective upon encountering the work. For most readers of this essay, who will come to the work from the broad Lislakh perspective, I am confident the book will at least do well on the former score. I hope that what I have said so far suggests that it might also do well on the latter score as well.

Neglect—well, that is easier. I would not know of this book if it had not been mentioned to me by the Native American philosopher Anne Waters (who is one of the first Native Americans to receive a PhD in Philosophy). Thank you, Dr. Waters, for bringing it to my attention, and for your work to bring Native American and Indigenous philosophical ideas to broader attention more generally. Noam Chomsky blurbs the back of it, in part as a result of his personal correspondence with Wub-e-ke-niew. But the book is virtually uncited, and although it is known within the small circle of people who work on Indigenous and Native American Philosophy, it should have a much wider audience than it presently has. I hope you will become part of that audience.

Bibliography

Austin, J. L. (1956–1957). A Plea for Excuses. *Proceedings of the Aristotelian Society, New Series* 57: 1–30.

Burgess, A., Cappelen, H., and Plunkett, D. (eds.). (2019). *Conceptual Engineering and Conceptual Ethics*. Oxford: Oxford University Press.

Burkhart, Brian (2019). *Indigenizing Philosophy through the Land: A Trickster Methodology for Decolonizing Environmental Ethics and Indigenous Futures.* Lansing: Michigan State University Press.

Cajete, Gregory (2000). *Native Science: Natural Laws of Interdependence.* Santa Fe, NM: Clear Light.

Childs, Craig (2018). *Atlas of a Lost World: Travels in Ice Age America.* New York: Pantheon.

Climate and Traditional Knowledges Workgroup (2014). *Guidelines for Considering Traditional Knowledges in Climate Change Initiatives.* https://climatetkw.wordpress.com/guidelines/.

Darwall, Stephen (2006). *The Second-Person Standpoint: Morality, Respect, and Accountability.* Cambridge, MA: Harvard University Press.

Fantl, Jeremy (2016). Mary Shepherd on Causal Necessity. Metaphysica 17(1): 87–108.

Foehner, K., Scinta, S., and Deloria, B. (eds.) (1999). *Spirit and Reason: The Vine Deloria, Jr., Reader.* Golden, CO: Fulcrum.

Gentner, Dedre, and Goldin-Meadow, Susan (ed.). (2003). *Language in Mind: Advances in the Study of Language and Thought.* Cambridge, MA: MIT Press.

Kagan, Shelly (2019). *How to Count Animals, More or Less.* Oxford: Oxford University Press.

Korsgaard, Christine (2018). *Fellow Creatures: Our Obligations to the Other Animals.* Oxford: Oxford University Press.

Larkin, Philip (2001). *Collected Poems.* New York: Farrar, Straus and Giroux.

Lenman, James (2000). Consequentialism and Cluelessness. *Philosophy & Public Affairs* 29(4): 342–370.

Nussbaum, Martha (2007). *Frontiers of Justice: Disability, Nationality, Species Membership.* Cambridge, MA: Harvard University Press.

Scanlon, Thomas (1998). *What We Owe to Each Other.* Cambridge, MA: Harvard University Press.

The Ojibwe People's Dictionary. https://ojibwe.lib.umn.edu/.

Wallace, R. Jay (2019). *The Moral Nexus.* Cambridge, MA: Harvard University Press.

Whyte, K., Brewer J. P., and Johnson, J. T. (2016). Weaving Indigenous Science, Protocols and Sustainability Science. *Sustainability Science* 11(1): 25–32.

Wohlleben, Peter (2015). *The Hidden Life of Trees.* Vancouver, BC: Greystone Books.

Wub-e-ke-niew (1995). *We Have the Right to Exist: A Translation of Aboriginal Indigenous Thought.* New York: Black Thistle Press.

Index

For the benefit of digital users, indexed terms that span two pages (e.g., 52–53) may, on occasion, appear on only one of those pages.

affect(s), 110–11, 112–13
Ahnishinahbæótjibway identity, 282n.11
Ahnishinahbæótjibway perspective, 282n.11
Ahnishinahbæótjibway, philosophy, 282n.11
allegory, 1, 8
ambiguity, 43, 46
Amida, 9, 78–81, 78n.1, 86–89, 90–91, 92, 94–95, 94n.27
Amida's grace, 80–81, 82n.7, 85–87, 90–91, 92–93, 94–95
Amida's Original Vow, 78–79, 78n.1, 82–83, 90–91, 92–93
Amo, Anton Wilhelm, 118–40, 119–20n.4, 123n.11, 125n.20, 125n.23
  On the Right of Moors in Europe, 118
analytic philosophy, 192–214
analytical philosophy canon, 13–14
analyticity, 200
anger, 32n.54, 84, 243, 252–59
Anjin, 87–89
Annihilation of Caste, 216, 216n.6
Apathy. See *Impassivity*
appetite (appetitus), 134
applause/*applausus*, 121–22, 136
Aquinas, Thomas, 125–26
argument, 3, 7, 7n.16, 11, 45–46, 62, 99–107, 111–15, 119, 141, 142–43, 142n.2, 148–51, 151n.10, 152–53, 154–55, 154n.11, 157, 159–61, 172, 173–74, 183, 185, 188, 203, 216, 233n.45, 244–45, 277–78n.7
  as (possibly) constitutive of philosophy, 11, 23, 45–46, 57
Aristotle, 1, 2, 8, 14, 19–20, 23n.15, 25, 26–28, 105n.13, 116, 125–27, 132–33, 169–70

Asaṅga, 59–60
Augustine, 125–26
authorship, 60, 61, 61n.2

Bacon, Francis, 3, 126
barbarism, 5–6, 5n.13
  barbarous society, 1
Benítez, Laura, 98n.2, 100n.6, 101n.7, 116
Berkeley, George, 141–42, 142n.2, 144n.6, 169, 170, 171
bonbu, 83–84, 84–85n.14, 85–87, 88–89, 90–91, 92–95
bonno, 83–84, 90–91, 92–94
Boyvin, Jean Gabriel, 125–26
Brahminism, 222–24, 228–30
Brahmins, 218n.9, 221n.13, 222, 223, 223n.16, 224, 225–27, 228, 229–31, 233–35, 235n.51
Bright, Liam Kofi, 11, 138
Büttner, Christopher Andrea, 122

canon/canons, 13–14, 61n.2, 212–13, 216, 249–50
  Shakespearean canon, 61
  See also philosophical canon
care, 233–34, 243
caste, 12, 215–38, 215n.1, 217n.7, 217n.8, 218n.10, 219n.11, 221n.13, 223n.16, 225n.19, 225n.23, 227n.31, 229n.38, 230n.40, 234n.47, 234n.48
  Jatis, 216–17
causal essentialism, 142–43, 149, 169–70
causation, 11, 25n.27, 57–58, 141–44, 145, 150–51, 158, 160n.13, 161, 164n.16, 165–70, 171, 229–30, 229–30n.39, 236

cause, 27–28, 28n.37, 100, 141–71,
146n.7, 146n.8, 164n.14, 180, 218,
224–25, 228, 229–30n.39, 235n.51,
244, 250–51, 254, 255, 257–58
Chasm, 26, 27–29, 30
Cicero, 125–27
civility, 239–60
civilization, 1, 2–3, 4–6, 5n.13, 7, 175, 191,
222, 273–74
civilized society, 1
great civilization, 3–4, 5
Western civilization, 3–5, 8,
265, 283–84
climate change, 68–69, 68n.6, 75,
272n.4, 283
cluelessness objection to
consequentialism, 280–81, 280n.10
coffee, 62, 63, 64
concepts, conceptual, 131–32, 134–35,
194, 195–96, 197–99, 200, 201–5,
206–8, 209, 243, 244–46, 247,
252, 259
confirmation holism, 196, 198–99, 203,
204–5, 207–8, 209
confusion, 41–42, 52–53, 55–56, 57, 84,
84n.13, 133–34
Creighton, James Edwin, 192–94, 197n.4,
207–8, 209, 210, 211, 212–13, 214
Crespin, François (Franciscus Bonae
Spei), 125–26
critical philosophy, 193, 193n.2, 209,
210, 211–12
criticism, 7, 10, 15, 24n.18, 34n.62, 110–
11, 123–24, 141, 193n.1, 206–7, 208,
209, 210, 216, 230n.40, 234n.46,
239, 244–45
cultural worlds, 70

Darwin, Charles, 202, 211, 213
De Laguna, Grace, 192–214, 193n.1,
197n.4, 198n.5, 200n.6, 202n.7
De Laguna, Theodore, 192–214, 193n.1,
197n.4, 198n.5, 200n.6, 202n.7
death, 28–29, 28n.34, 31–32, 43–44,
44n.6, 53–54, 53n.9, 55, 78n.1,
82n.7, 83, 90–91, 94n.27, 100n.5,
226–27, 228n.35, 233–34, 261–62,
264, 267–68, 269, 270, 277–78n.7

decline, 31–32, 32–33n.56, 33–35
Descartes, René, 103n.11, 105, 106n.15,
112n.29, 113n.30, 115, 115n.31, 119
Meditations on First Philosophy, 103–
4, 112–15
desire for knowledge, 105, 106–7, 110–11,
112, 115
epistemic desire, 11, 99, 111
desire(s), 6, 80–81, 83–84, 92–93,
94n.27, 99, 105, 105n.13, 106–7,
108n.22, 110–11, 112, 115, 174–75,
198–99, 227–28, 241–42, 252, 253–
54, 257–58
Dewey, John, 193–94, 205, 210, 212–13
difference, 28, 34, 34n.61, 50–51, 52,
57–58, 63, 66, 100–1, 132–33, 136,
137–38, 142–43, 144, 159, 160, 161–
62, 163–64, 164n.14, 232, 233n.45,
235n.51, 244–45, 255, 259, 263,
267, 274–75
difference principle, 232, 233n.45,
235n.51, See also Rawls, John
Dilthey, Wilhelm, 19–20, 25, 25n.28
discovery (self-discovery), 94–95
disputation, 45–46, 52–53, 119, 123–
24, 135
diversity, 100, 114–15
Dogen, 78–79, 80–81, 81n.5, 94–95
Genjōkōan, 80–81, 81n.5, 94–95
dogmatism, 12, 192–214
dream, dreams, 28–29, 43, 63–66, 75, 76,
77, 116, 244, 270–71
Du Bois, WEB, 215–16, 216n.4

education, 7, 13–14, 34–35, 34n.64, 47, 125–
26, 234–35, 262–63, 264, 277–78n.7
educating, 247–48
emotion(s), 83–84, 92–93, 94–95, 109–10,
109–10n.25, 110n.28, 111–12, 115,
117, 252–53, 252n.3, 254–55, 259
emotional labor, 249
empirical, 64–65, 176, 202, 203–4, 211–
12, 280
empiricism, empiricist, 12, 163–64,
169, 171, 192–94, 201, 202–3, 209–
13, 214
endogamy, 218–22, 223–24, 228–
30, 231–32

enlightenment, 2–3, 2n.4, 3–4n.9, 5n.13,
     6, 29–30, 34, 74n.12, 78n.1, 83n.11,
     87n.20, 94–95, 273–74
environmental philosophy, 262–63, 272,
     274–75, 280n.9
Epictetus, 126–27
epistemic injustice, 177–81
epistemic labor, 239–60
epistemic objection to consequentialism,
     280–81, 280n.10
epistemic priorities, 248–49
Eros, 26, 27–28, 27n.32, 30
ethics of harmony, 261–62, 276–77, 278–
     80, 281, 282, 283–84
ethics, consequentialist, 274, 276
ethics, deontological, 274–75
ethics, environmental, 272, 274–
     75, 280n.9
evolution, 12, 192–214, 216n.4
     Darwinian evolution, 202, 211
exogamy, 218–19, 219n.11

fallibilism, fallible, 194–97, 201, 203
feminist movement, 240–41, 244–46
     white feminism, 245–46
friendship, 43–44, 44n.6

Gandhi, 216, 217n.7, 227–29, 227n.32,
     227n.33, 227n.34, 228n.35, 228n.36
Gassendi, Pierre, 131–32, 132n.53, 135
Gellius, Aulus, 121–22
genre, 19n.3, 97–99, 99n.4, 110–11, 115,
     124, 137, 138
girl marriage, 12, 221, 222, 223–24, 225,
     228–29, 231–32, 236–37
Guinea (geographical region), 123–
     24, 138
Gundling, Nicolaus Hieronymus, 125–26,
     126n.31

habits, 57–58
     habituation, 67–68, 69
Hallbauer, Andreas Friedrich, 121–22
Halle, 120–21, 122, 123n.11, 129, 137–38
hallucinations, 63–64, 74
happiness, 46–47, 93–94, 105–7, 113–14,
     115, 129
Harras, Samuel Christian, 122, 138

Hart, Stephen M., 108, 108n.23, 116
Hegelian, 192–94, 205–8, 209–10, 213
Heim, Maria, 60
hell beings, 57
Hermann, Johann Christian, 122
hermeneutic injustice, as distortion
     rather than lack 232–33, 244, 253
Hesiod, 6, 7, 18–39, 18n.1, 18n.2, 19n.3,
     19n.4, 19n.5, 21n.9, 22n.13, 22n.14,
     23n.17, 24n.18, 25n.24, 25n.27,
     27n.31, 28n.38, 32–33n.56, 33n.57,
     36n.67, 38n.75
     Theogony, 18–39, 19n.3, 22n.13,
     25n.28, 26–27n.30, 28n.34, 28n.35,
     29n.44, 31–32n.52, 33n.59,
     36n.68, 37n.71
     Works and Days, 18–39, 19n.3, 28n.38,
     35n.65, 36n.67
historiography, 1, 11
history, 1, 4–5, 5n.13, 8–9, 10, 10n.20, 12,
     13–14, 14n.24, 18–20, 22–23, 31–35,
     33n.57, 58–59, 61, 66, 68–69, 78–79,
     176, 192–93, 203–4, 218–19, 262–63,
     267–68, 277–78n.7
history of philosophy, 4–5, 13, 18–19,
     61, 98n.2, 112n.29, 116, 117, 170,
     171, 214
Hōnen, 9, 78–96, 82n.7, 82n.8, 84–
     85n.14, 86n.17, 87n.20
     Senchaku Hongan Nembutsu Shū
     (Senchaku Shū), 9, 78–96, 79n.2,
     80n.3, 86n.17, 87n.19, 87n.20, 88n.21
Hountondji, Paulin, 118n.1, 123, 138,
     138n.64
Huizi, 46, 46n.7, 53–54
human understanding, limits of, 99, 103–
     4, 103n.11
Hume, David, 141, 143n.5, 144, 145, 146,
     147–48, 149–50, 151, 153, 154–55,
     156–57, 158, 163–65, 169
humility, 5, 52–53, 282
hungry ghosts, 57, 66, 67–71

idealism, 72, 75, 77
ignorance, 41–42, 45–46, 61, 62, 66, 67,
     68–69, 68n.7, 70n.8, 73–74, 84,
     84n.13, 84–85n.14, 93–95, 102, 103–
     4, 178, 225–26, 232, 265

Impassivity, 119–20, 123–24, 125–26
indigenous philosophy, 284
initially empty world thought
    experiment, 152–56, 154n.11
intersectionality, 231–32, 231n.41, 236
intuition, 158, 182–83, 192, 201, 203,
    204–6, 209, 236n.52
Islamic philosophy, 8

Jahn, Daniel Friedrich, 125–26
James, William, 96, 193–94, 205, 210
Jena, 13, 118, 119–20n.4, 121–22,
    122n.9, 123–24, 126–27, 129,
    137, 138–39
Jōdo (Pure Land Buddhism), 9, 78–79,
    78n.1, 82–83, 87, 87n.20, 89, 90, 93,
    94n.27, 96
joy, 40–41, 46, 53–54, 55–56, 93–94, 100,
    101, 104, 111–12, 121–22, 223
judgement, suspension of, 101
justice (*Dike*), 24–25, 35n.65, 37–38,
    134–35, 176, 183, 186, 189–90, 236,
    236n.52, 239, 253
    divine, 22, 23, 24, 29n.41, 30–32, 31–
    32n.52, 35–37, 36n.69, 129
    human, 2, 21n.10, 22–23, 26, 30–38,
    31n.50, 31–32n.52, 32n.55, 32–
    33n.56, 34n.62, 34n.63, 35n.65,
    36n.69, 43–44, 45, 48, 53, 55–56, 60,
    61, 66, 67–68, 81–82, 84, 88–89, 99,
    101, 103–4, 103n.11, 106–7, 110–11,
    119, 131–32, 143–44, 207, 218–19,
    221, 261–62, 274–75, 280, 282–83,
    282n.11
    natural, 20, 22, 23, 25, 26, 28–29, 30–
    31, 36n.69, 37–38, 37n.73, 53–54,
    97–98n.1, 103n.12, 104, 105, 106–7,
    108n.21, 111, 112n.29, 131, 134,
    169–70, 176, 211–12, 218, 269–70,
    272, 282–83
Jyotirao Phule, 215–16, 216n.4, 217n.7,
    226n.29, 227n.30

karma, 270
    karmic process, 57
    karmic relations, 93–94, 94n.27
Ketar, S. Venkatesh, 218
Kittler, Johann Gottfried, 122

knowledge, 11–12, 22, 34n.63, 43, 60, 80–
    81, 82–83, 88–89, 102–3, 103n.10,
    103n.11, 104, 105–7, 108, 108n.21,
    111–12, 113, 115, 115n.31, 130, 131–
    32, 136, 147, 158, 160, 163–64, 187,
    188–90, 192, 201, 211–12, 229–30,
    232, 239, 240–41, 242, 246, 247–51,
    252, 253, 257–59, 266, 272, 277–
    78n.7, 282–83

Larkin, Philip, 268, 269n.2, 271, 272
Laws of Manu, 217, 225
Le Clerc, Jean, 126
Leibniz, Gottfried Wilhelm, 126
liberal political theory, 216, 232, 235n.51
Lislakh perspective, 262, 266–67, 269,
    273, 277–78n.7, 284
literary canon, 249–50
Locke, John, 103–4, 105, 153, 157
    *Essay Concerning Human
    Understanding*, 103–4, 117
Lohia, Ram Manohar, 229n.38
Lorde, Audre, Chapter 11 *passim*
    The Master's tools, 243, 244–45, 247

meaning, 48, 79–80, 85–86, 89, 94–95,
    145, 147, 159, 175, 194, 195,
    196, 197, 198, 200, 201, 202–3,
    204–5, 206–8, 216–17, 234n.47,
    246, 270–71
meaning holism, 194, 196, 198–200, 204–
    5, 207–8
Melanchthon, Philipp, 125–26
Mencke, Johann Burkhard, 125–26
meta-philosophy, 1, 15
metaphysics, 1, 8–9, 11, 12, 23n.15, 25,
    25n.27, 57, 60, 71–72, 76, 94–95,
    105n.13, 109–10n.25, 110n.28,
    116, 127–28, 138, 141–43, 145, 153,
    155–56, 158, 161, 165–70, 171, 193,
    211–13, 266–67, 271
Midé, 262–63, 270–71, 276, 281, 282
Mill, John Stuart, 10–11, 160, 161, 167
Mills, Charles W., 216, 232–34,
    233n.43, 236–37
Modern Philosophy, 12, 103–4, 169, 170,
    192–214
Myth of Ages, 31–32

Native American identity, 266
necessary connections, 57–58, 145
Nembutsu, 78–80, 78n.1, 82–83, 82n.6,
    82n.7, 82n.8, 85–95, 86n.17, 87n.20,
    94n.27, 96
    Other-Power method, 86–87
Nietzsche, Friedrich, 8–9, 19–20, 25, 32–
    33n.56, 34–35
normativity, 20, 35–38, 75
nostrification, 121–22

omens, 102, 112
oppression, 11–12, 70–71, 172–73, 178–
    79, 181, 190, 216, 224–25, 226–28,
    232–34, 236–37, 240, 241–42, 245–
    46, 247–49, 250, 252–53, 255–56,
    257, 259
Ovid, 125n.20

patriarchy, 220, 226–27, 227n.31,
    231–32, 233–34, 236–37, 240–
    41, 243
Paz, Octavio, 97–98n.1, 101n.7, 117
Periyar (E. V. Ramaswamy), 225n.23,
    229n.38, 235n.49
Peter the Great, 129–30
Philo of Alexandria, 7
philosophical canon, 14, 73, 97–99, 249–
    50. *See also* canon
    analytical philosophy canon, 13–14
    literary canon, 249–50
    political philosophy canon, 216
    Western philosophy canon, 41–
    42, 240–41
philosophy of history, 18–20
philosophy, academic, 4–5, 10n.19, 11–
    12, 41, 43–44, 73, 137
    philosophy, professional, 11–12,
    13, 41–42
Plato, 1, 2, 5–6, 7–8, 10–11, 14, 18n.2, 19–
    20, 21, 24n.18, 24n.19, 25, 25n.23,
    25n.24, 27n.32, 28n.37, 33n.58,
    34–35, 36n.67, 38, 39, 100n.6, 109–
    10n.25, 128, 252
Platonism, 1, 7–8, 100n.6
play, 41–42, 50, 99–100
poetry, 97–99, 107–8, 108n.23, 109–11,
    109–10n.25, 115, 244, 245, 249

pollution, 217
polyhistory, 130
Port-Royal, 131–32
pragmatism, pragmatist, 12n.22, 14n.24,
    188–89, 192–94, 193n.1, 201, 205–8,
    210, 213
presentations (*vijñapti*), 62, 63, 71
principle of sufficient reason, 27–28,
    142–43, 153
prostitution, 220, 226–28, 233–34
publics, 246

Quine, Willard V., 12, 13–14, 192–
    214, 211n.8

racecraft, 69, 70–71, 75
racial categories, 68–70
Ramabai, Pandita, 225, 225n.19
rationalism, rationalist, 192–94, 201,
    202–4, 213, 229n.38
Rawls, John, 232–33, 233n.45, 234n.46,
    235n.51, 236–37, 236n.52
realization (self-realization), 80–81, 82–
    86, 92–93
reason, 6, 8, 27–29, 29n.41, 32–33, 52,
    80–81, 87–88, 100, 101, 102, 105–6,
    107, 111–13, 114, 115, 119n.3, 122,
    127–28, 135, 136, 142–44, 145, 148–
    49, 157, 159, 163–64, 169, 183–84,
    197, 198–99, 246, 249–50, 279
Rechenberg, Adam, 125–26
representation, 22, 65, 70n.8, 71–72, 107–
    8, 109–11, 109–10n.25, 115, 128,
    135, 211–12, 233–34, 240–41, 250
revelation, 6, 23
Russell, Bertrand, 1, 4, 4n.10, 4n.11, 5–6,
    5n.13, 6n.15, 7–11, 12, 12n.22, 13–
    14, 142n.4, 171
    The History of Western Philosophy, 1,
    4–5, 5n.13, 10, 12
rustic, 7–9
    rustic thought, 1

Said, Edward, 2, 2n.2
Saint-Joseph, Pierre de (Petrus a
    Santo Josepho Fuliensi), 127–28,
    127n.36, 127n.37, 127n.38, 128n.40,
    128n.41, 131–32

Sanjin, 87, 89, 92, 93–94
  jin-shin, 89–90, 92, 93
  shijō-shin, 89–90, 92, 93
Sati, 219–20, 228
Schardius, Friedrich Ludwig, 120–
  21, 120n.8
Scholastic, 3, 3n.7, 13, 125–27, 138–39
science/sciences, 6, 14n.24, 18–19, 38,
  44n.4, 97–98n.1, 108n.21, 129–30,
  156, 160, 182, 193, 194, 198–99,
  198n.5, 210–12, 232, 252, 262–
  63, 272
self, 80–87, 80–81n.4, 93, 94–95, 255
Seneca, 43–44, 45, 130
Sextus Empiricus, 101, 117
Shepherd, Mary, 11, 141–44, 142n.2,
  142n.4, 143n.5, 144n.6, 145, 146–47,
  146n.8, 151, 151n.10, 152, 153,
  154–56, 157, 158, 159, 160, 160n.13,
  161–62, 163–64, 164n.14, 165, 167,
  168, 169–70
silencing, 190, 239, 252–58
Simecek, Karen, 109–10, 110n.26,
  110n.28, 117
skepticism, 11, 42n.2, 43–44, 43–44n.3,
  48–49, 55–56, 55n.10, 75, 99, 101n.7,
  103–4, 111–12, 113–14, 115, 181
social change, 184, 244
social inequality, 216, 229n.37
society, 68–69, 190, 216–17, 223n.16,
  235n.51, 239, 240, 246, 247, 257–58,
  259, 267–68
Socrates, 6, 7–8, 8n.17, 43–44, 50, 52–53,
  98n.2, 100n.6, 104, 116
Sor Juana Inès de la Cruz, 11, 97–99, 97–
  98n.1, 98n.2, 107–8n.18, 108n.23,
  116, 117
  'Let us pretend I am happy', 11, 97–117
  *Response of the Poet to the Very Eminent
    Sor Filotea de la Cruz*, 108
space, 20, 24, 25n.26, 26–31, 27n.31,
  39, 65n.4, 69–70, 109–10, 123,
  143–44, 166–67, 182–83, 262–63,
  264, 267–68
speculation, 1, 239
speculative philosophy, 193, 210, 211–
  13, 214

Spinoza, Baruch, 2, 3, 7, 124
Stahl, Georg Ernst, 120–21
strife (*Eris*), 24–25, 28–29
stupidity, 52–53
Sufi, 1
surplus, 218–22, 219n.12, 221n.13
systematic, 18–20, 22, 22n.13, 26, 79–80,
  123–24, 126, 127, 178, 199
  systematic thinker, 7
systematization, 20, 22, 28, 29–30, 169

theology, 6, 97–98n.1, 125–26, 127, 129–
  30, 131
Thomasius, Christian, 120–21,
  122, 125–27
time, 20, 26–31, 33, 34–35
  cyclical, 30–31, 31n.50
  linear, 30–31, 31n.50, 267–68, 269
time, phenomenology of, 267, 271
transformation (self-transformation),
  80–81, 94–95
truth, 21–26, 25n.21, 41–42, 45, 51, 83,
  89–90, 102–3, 105, 108, 113–14, 122,
  127–28, 131–32, 134–35, 138, 153,
  176, 184–86, 188–90, 197, 198, 200,
  200n.6, 203–4, 206–7, 244, 258
truth, standard of, 102, 105
Tufayl, Ibn, 1, 1n.1, 2–3, 2n.4, 8

uncertainty, 41–42, 43, 52–53, 279
Urbanism & *Urbane* thought, 1, 7, 8–9
uselessness, 46, 49

Varnas, 216–17
Varro, 125–26
Vasubandhu, 57–74
  Treasury of the Abhidharma
    (*Abhidharmakośa*), 58–59
Vierge Marie, Augustin de la (Augustinus
  a Virgine Maria), 126–27
views, 6, 10–11, 42–43, 53–54, 53n.9, 79–
  81, 79n.2, 80–81n.4, 82–83, 84n.12,
  96, 110–11, 126, 141–42, 142n.4,
  143–44, 144n.6, 146, 152, 169–70,
  204–5, 217, 224–29, 229n.37,
  229n.38, 239, 251, 272–73, 274–75,
  275n.6, 276, 277–78n.7, 280–81

Western philosophy, 1, 2, 4, 5–6, 9–10
  non-Western philosophy, 5–6
widowhood, 12, 220, 222, 223–24, 225,
  226–27, 227n.30, 228–29, 231–
  32, 236–37
wisdom, 7–8, 8n.17, 19n.3, 23, 38, 40–41,
  50–51, 52–53, 83–84, 86–87, 88, 96,
  127–28, 266–67, 277–78n.7, 282
Wittenberg, 13, 118, 119, 119–20n.4,
  120n.7, 138–39

Wolff, Christian, 120–21, 123n.11
Wub-e-ke-niew, 8, 261–85, 263n.1, 277–
  78n.7, 279n.8

Yogācāra, 59–60, 62, 65n.4, 67–68, 70–
  71, 75

Zendō, 79–80, 82–83, 85, 86n.17, 90,
  93–94